THE CHINESE LADY

THE CHINESE LADY

AFONG MOY IN EARLY AMERICA

NANCY E. DAVIS

OXFORD
UNIVERSITY PRESS

OXFORD
UNIVERSITY PRESS

Oxford University Press is a department of the University of Oxford. It furthers
the University's objective of excellence in research, scholarship, and education
by publishing worldwide. Oxford is a registered trade mark of Oxford University
Press in the UK and certain other countries.

Published in the United States of America by Oxford University Press
198 Madison Avenue, New York, NY 10016, United States of America.

CIP data is on file at the Library of Congress
ISBN 978–0–19–064523–6 (Hbk.)
ISBN 978–0–19–758198–8 (Pbk.)

3 5 7 9 8 6 4 2

Paperback printed by Marquis, Canada

To Kurt—with gratitude

CONTENTS

ACKNOWLEDGMENTS

———

I CANNOT CLAIM THAT MY desire to present Afong Moy's story arose from a personal or even a rational motivation. I admit that my initial interest lay with the Chinese objects that surrounded her. As I explored them, I recognized their function as "not only . . . the product of history, they are also active agents in history" with "communicative, performative, emotive, and expressive capacities" as argued by historian Leora Auslander.[1] With Afong Moy's presence in the United States, the objects had an affective agency that mediated between American and Chinese cultures. But as her story evolved, so did the concept of what constituted the "object" being displayed. Sadly, Afong Moy became the exotic "thing." The process of that gradual transformation to "object," always there but becoming profoundly more explicit in her life, was to me a compelling aspect of Afong Moy's story. Family, friends, and all who would listen were drawn into my compulsion to uncover the details of her life.

Such history, pulled and tugged from fragmentary bits, required help from many sources and enablers. The traces of Afong Moy's life lay hidden

1. Leora Auslander, "Beyond Words," *The American Historical Review* 110, no. 4 (October 2005): 1017.

in many repositories. My colleague Susan B. Strange willingly gave her precious free time to travel with me to many of these sites. She often saw what I overlooked and served as a second pair of eyes to help sift through the massive quantities of diaries, letters, newspapers, manifests, and records to locate a single bit of information. She read through all the text with a penchant for grammar and enthusiastically supported my work to the very end.

My deep appreciation to those scholars who read all or portions of the manuscript and who provided insightful commentary and many helpful suggestions. LiLi from Salem State University gave helpful clarification on Chinese life. Kate Haulman from American University asked thought-provoking questions regarding gender and race that encouraged a closer look at these aspects of Afong Moy's life. Katie Knowles of Colorado State University good-naturedly read the manuscript numerous times to helpfully consider the way material culture wove through the work and how it could be more effectively highlighted. Early in my work on Afong Moy, Patricia Johnston, College of the Holy Cross, encouraged the global perspective on this topic. Her symposium talks, and the conference she organized at the Peabody Essex Museum in 2010 on Global Trade and the Visual Arts, were instrumental in the development of this work. In addition, she carefully read sections of the manuscript that pertained to Salem, correcting misconceptions and making valuable recommendations. Kathleen Franz, friend and colleague, formerly at American University and now at the Smithsonian Institution, read portions of the manuscript, supplying a meaningful critique and, most importantly, gave me confidence and support when it was most needed. My thanks as well to John Grigg, University of Nebraska, who willingly reviewed sections related to New Jersey poorhouses.

Many thanks to my Smithsonian Institution colleagues who supported my work and encouraged my research efforts: William Yeingst, Bonnie Campbell Lilienfeld, Barbara Clark Smith, Mary Jo Arnoldi, David Allison, Stephen Velasquez, Jennifer Strobel, Tim Winkle, Shari Stout, Madelyn Shaw, Kay Peterson, Debra Hashim, Lauren Safranek, Carlene Stephens, Mallory Warner, John Gray, John Kingsley, Dara Shore, Shagun Raina, and Carrie Beauchamp.

Many librarians, archivists, photographers, researchers, and museum staff helped to uncover the sources that revealed aspects of Afong Moy's life: Marlly Wang Fang, Guangdong Museum; the archives staff at Guangdong Provincial Archives; Anthony Hardy, Hong Kong; Libby Chan and Nina Wan, Hong Kong Maritime Museum; Jacob Fromer, independent researcher; Katrina Brown, Jim Roan, and Alexia MacClain, National Museum of American

History Library—Smithsonian Libraries; Michele L. Hopkins, independent photographer; George Joynson, research assistant, and Gary D. Saretzky, archivist, Monmouth County Archives; Randall Gabrielan, Monmouth County historian; Gail Hunton, Monmouth County historic preservation specialist; John Fabiano, Monmouth County Historical Commission; Laura Wasowicz, Jaclyn Penney, and Marie Lamoureux, American Antiquarian Society; Jessica Pigza, New York Public Library; Christina Bryant, Louisiana Division, New Orleans Library and Archives; Carla Galfano, Peabody Essex Museum; Francis O'Neill, H. Furlong Baldwin Library, Maryland Historical Society; the library staff at the New-York Historical Society; the museum staff at the Barnum Museum, Bridgeport, Connecticut; the librarians at the Library Company of Philadelphia; the librarians at the Massachusetts Historical Society; the librarians at the Historical Medical Library, the College of Physicians of Philadelphia; the staff at Olana New York State Historic Site; staff at the Mortimer Rare Book Room, Special Collections, Smith College; staff at the Hagley Museum and Library; and Gretchen Sullivan Soren and Audrey Wolfe, Cooperstown Graduate Program, SUNY Oneonta.

Over the years many friends and family bolstered my efforts. When I doubted the wisdom of continuing, they pushed me forward. Many thanks to my daughters, Abigail and Kate, who gave me forbearance when I missed events, and heartily cheered when chapters were completed. My sister, Joan, and her family kindly, and often, checked my progress. Friends Anne and Roger Whidden lodged me when I completed research in New York City, and Kym Rice, George Washington University, frequently provided advice and reassurance.

My special thanks to my Oxford University Press editor Nancy Toff who quickly saw the conjunction between the story of Afong Moy and the related aspects of material culture. Her encouragement gave me the impetus to complete the work. Her assistants, Elda Granata and Elizabeth Vaziri, answered my many questions with grace and patience.

This work necessitated my husband Kurt's profound trust that this enormous devotion of time would result in a product. I acknowledge with deep gratitude and love his willingness to give me the gift of time and the patience to ignore my many undone tasks. He also was a skilled and kind editor, evaluating my text with thoroughness and care while spending many hours correcting my wayward spacing and formatting. This book was very much a joint effort—a determination to see this project through despite the many distractions and challenges. I dedicate this book to him in hopes that it partially makes up for the years of missed hours together.

Introduction

IN 1834 AFONG MOY WAS the first recognized Chinese woman to arrive in America. Through the course of her travels across the country, she became the first Chinese person to receive wide public acclaim and national recognition. While her fame was short-lived, she introduced Americans to China through her person and the goods she promoted.

Yet she was not the first Chinese person on American shores. Nearly fifty years before, in August 1785, the ship *Pallas* under Captain John O'Donnell landed in Baltimore, Maryland, with Chinese men aboard. O'Donnell, one of the first to take advantage of America's newly won commercial access to China after the War of Independence, brought to port a valuable cargo of teas, china, silks, and satins. The Baltimore newspapers acknowledged the prized goods—but they also gave significant heed to the crew. One reported approvingly: "It is no unpleasing Sight to see the Crew of this Ship, Chinese, Malays, Japanese, and Moors . . . employed together as Brethren; it is thus Commerce binds and unites all the Nations of the Globe with a golden Chain."[1] The writer implied that the worldwide circulation of goods might link all peoples in mutual commercial benefit. This "golden chain" could enrich nations while promoting unity among those who labored to achieve it.

But how might this global commercial "brethrenship" provide mutual benefit? Though all might be employed as "Brethren," the international crew of the *Pallas* felt the chain tighten as their departure for China became less and less certain. For nearly a year, during the fall of 1785 and into the summer of 1786, they waited on Baltimore streets and docks for a vessel to take them back to their home ports. These men may have been among the first Chinese to experience the new United States and witness the less positive aspects of this commerce.

Over the next fifty years, America's commercial activities with China grew and intensified. Hundreds of American vessels departed from the ports of Baltimore, Philadelphia, New York, and Salem, Massachusetts, to Canton (now Guangzhou), China, to take part in this golden chain of commerce. The sale of imported Chinese goods enriched the coffers of many American merchants. To achieve these gains, some of these merchants lived and worked on a narrow slice of land in Guangzhou, the only location in China where they were allowed to do business.

During this same time period, on the other hand, only one Chinese merchant visited America. Guangzhou trader Punqua Winchong traveled to the United States on the Nantucket-based vessel *Favorite* in 1808 purportedly seeking to resolve a debt due his father. Like the Chinese crewmen in 1785, he found himself trapped in America as a result of President Jefferson's export embargo that year. Punqua, unlike the common seamen in Baltimore, had more clout, and he appealed to the influential merchant John Jacob Astor. After Punqua requested aid, Jefferson permitted Astor's vessel *Beaver* to return him to China. He visited twice more within a decade, most likely exploring and benefiting from numerous trade opportunities. The apparent ease with which he moved between the two countries was highly unusual and his presence was reported in the American press.[2]

Nearly a half-century after the Chinese crew arrived in Baltimore, the golden chain of commerce brought the young Chinese woman, Afong Moy, to the United States. Her coming was likely not of her own volition but rather to promote the commercial success of several American merchants and a ship captain. Situated in an elaborately contrived "oriental" parlor, she presented, through an interpreter, the goods that surrounded her. The eighteenth-century newspaper writer in Baltimore had sanguinely envisioned trade as a way to unite nations, binding them together in a common desire; in so doing, all would be enriched—even the crew who labored as "Brethren." Later, however, this golden chain would bind Afong Moy—a woman without recourse—to a country not her own.

This focused account looks at American merchants and consumers and an emerging public culture tinged with commerce and race consciousness as they confronted Afong Moy's difference at close quarters. Unwittingly, she served as the first cultural bridge in the American public's perception of China. Her presence moved Americans from what had been an abstract, imagined notion of "Chineseness" to a more specific and concrete understanding of the "East" through objects, clothing, images—and herself. Afong Moy's performance as a presenter of Chinese goods, intertwining and overlapping with the commodity trade and show business, shaped and changed the way Americans viewed China and influenced American popular and material culture. That shaping affected hairstyles, foods, clothing, imagery, household goods, decorative objects, and even new ideas.

This inquiry gives an intensive look at Afong Moy's experiences, as well as those who displayed and observed her, in the time period defined as "commercial orientalism." In contrast to the earlier period of "patrician orientalism," when Chinese luxury goods served the elite as markers of status, commercial orientalism was the manifestation of a fully operational market revolution and developing urbanization that allowed middling consumers (people of moderate means) to become aware of new representations of Chinese things.[3]

During the seventeen years of Afong Moy's visible presence in America, her treatment as a Chinese woman varied over time. When she first arrived in 1834, the public generally responded to China in a positive way. On the edge of patrician orientalism, the perceived "Orient" was one of exoticism, beauty, dignity, and revered history. The Carnes merchants, Francis and Nathaniel G., and the ship captain Benjamin Obear, who brought Afong Moy to America, took advantage of this perception, using the sensual stimulus that came from marketing China trade goods with an exotic. They played on, controlled, and mediated the public's consciousness of her visual difference—her bound feet, Chinese clothing, and accessories—all to promote their goods. Unlike the luxury objects of O'Donnell's *Pallas*, these Chinese imports were everyday items accessible to the middling class. Afong Moy's interactions with such audiences allowed them to engage with the goods, associate them with an exceptional place, and imagine them within their homes or on their persons. The objects' presence largely characterized the public's engagement with China, serving as a bridge to the "Orient" with Afong Moy as their explicator. In this effort her Chinese interpreter, Atung, provided public commentary regarding Chinese life and the use of these articles.

In the second phase of her experience in the later 1830s, Afong Moy made a transition from a promoter of goods to that of spectacle. During this time, she experienced the conjoining of two worlds—that of the market and the theater. Afong Moy operated simultaneously as entertainment, edification, and billboard. Her new manager occasionally set her against a panoramic backdrop of an illusionistic oriental scene, thus highlighting her cultural exceptionality through her clothing, objects, and images. Afong Moy's arrival in a period of great upheaval in American cultural and economic life placed her in the crosshairs of slavery, Native American removal, the moral reform movement, and ambivalent attitudes toward women. On her three-year journey from 1834 to 1837 throughout the mid-Atlantic, New England, the South, Cuba, and up the Mississippi River, her race provided an occasion for ridicule, jingoism, religious proselytizing, and paternalistic control.

After a heart-rending, eight-year interregnum out of the public eye, Afong Moy once again took to the stage in the late 1840s and early 1850s. P. T. Barnum, the master marketer of difference, became her manager. He recognized her promotional value as the only Chinese woman in America whose bound feet, clothing, objects, and experience signified an "orientalist" presence that might titillate the American public. Later he paired her with Charles Stratton, known as Tom Thumb, exceptional because of his smallness of stature, and together they served Barnum as markers of difference. Afong Moy's time in America provided an additional benefit to Barnum: she no longer needed an interlocutor. Though occasionally she required an interpreter, her language skills were likely sufficient for most audience interactions. On stage she provided evidences of her dissimilarity from the use of chopsticks to the demonstration and explication of Chinese religious rituals.

Yet with the passage of time, and with new views of China made possible with the opening of four additional Chinese ports in the later 1840s, public sentiment regarding China had become less accepting. Derisive and mocking commentary in the press and on Afong Moy's presentation on the stage became more prevalent. The public began to form stereotypical views of the Chinese as backward, arbitrary, undemocratic, and sometimes cruel. The classification and designation of "types" of peoples by scientists and philosophers lent credence to this view. Promoters and commentators associated negative characterizations of the Chinese with Afong Moy: a woman, an "oriental," and a performer on the stage.

Through her presentations the contrasts and vast differences between the East and the West became obvious and the result often gave rise to an arrogant response from the public. Thus her position was less a bridge to an alien and ancient culture as it was a foil for the new one. Her bound feet and clothing and the customs of her Chinese womanhood called forth contrary definitions of American womanhood. Her religious beliefs, often characterized as heathen, gave rise to responses from moral reformers and other Christians. Her explanation of the Chinese emperor's absolute power and governance compelled a contrast with American republicanism and its emphasis on virtue, self-government, education, and self-control.

A presentation of China's ancient ways reinforced the notion of America's progress. Through these dichotomies, Afong Moy provided her visitors a clarification, as well as a verification, of their national identity. Unlike those early nineteenth-century Americans who traveled the South Seas for fame and fortune, and in the process defined their country's character as they came into contact with peoples unlike themselves, Afong Moy provided that experience of contrast on Americans' native soil.[4]

So little is said, written, or spoken of Afong Moy's life in America that one of the principal ways to reach into her narrative is through sensory expression. Her gestures, movements, posture, and even tears convey the sentiments that lie beneath the few words she spoke. The observations of onlookers provided telling descriptions of Afong Moy's fleeting moments of emotion as she irritably responded to proselytizing, unwelcome contact, and unbinding of her feet. These expressive moments allow us to read her character and at times her alienation.

Afong Moy's disparity lay not just in her "Chineseness" but equally in her womanhood. In the 1830s, only a small handful of male Chinese lived in America, but likely she was the only woman. Her gender placed her in a unique position. As an unmarried woman without family, she was dependent on her managers for her livelihood. With bound feet, she was restricted in locomotion. Her position, first as a merchant's billboard and then as a spectacle, compromised and limited her place as a woman living in American society. Whether Afong Moy's gender gave her greater or lesser acceptance on stage is difficult to ascertain. Her presence was likely less threatening than that of a man, and perhaps encouraged a greater openness and sympathetic response to the lives of those in China. Conversely, her Chinese womanhood was defined as the source of her passivity and timidity. Those viewing Afong Moy on the stage may have perceived her merely as a static artifact, an exhibit, rather than as a woman. In that regard, then, it was acceptable to be a woman on a public stage.

Who was the audience for Afong Moy's messages generated from the stage and presented in the athenaeums, theaters, museums, and lecture halls across America? Of the thousands who saw her, we know the names and particular experiences of only eleven audience members who recorded commentaries in their diaries, poems, letters, or scrapbooks. They include three merchants, a banker, a physician, a teenage girl, an older woman, and four people who had church-affiliated positions. Most were of the middle or upper middle classes, and only one might be considered elite. Though they were a very small number, the distribution corresponds to the typical composition of a mid-nineteenth-century theatergoing audience. They were people who could afford the twenty-five or fifty-cent admission fee, which roughly equated to a day's wages for a female worker in a Lowell, Massachusetts, mill.[5]

Though certain places of public entertainment were considered suspect, unruly, and indecent in the 1830s, select locations had attained a slightly different cast. Americans had an increasing desire for edification; museums, athenaeums, and salons provided those opportunities to learn about a wider world. They also were places to be seen engaging in that activity. In the first, and much of the second, phase of her staging, Afong Moy's events took place in these more respectable sites, where many people had begun to gather.

The Carnes merchants and Captain Obear, Afong Moy's minders, took advantage of this burgeoning desire for public education. In 1834 they cleverly intertwined their sales campaign with the public exhibition of Chinese "curiosities," which would include Afong Moy, in a salon near New York's City Hall. In December 1834 they published a two-page catalog of their exhibition with images of the "Chinese Lady" (Afong Moy) featured on both sides. On one side they listed historic Chinese objects such as six-hundred-year-old mirrors, a 1366 iron cup, a 1486 Chinese bell, and five Chinese musical instruments. On the other side they recounted information on Afong Moy, whom visitors would find "surrounded by various articles of Chinese manufacture, worthy the attention of the curious." This was the first, albeit the smallest, published American catalog presenting Chinese objects to the public. In 1838, China trader Nathan Dunn would publish *Ten Thousand Chinese Things* to accompany the opening of his Chinese Museum in Philadelphia, and in 1845 John R. Peters printed a descriptive catalog for his Boston Chinese Museum. The merchant entrepreneurs, the Carneses and Obear, were in the forefront, the first to capture the public's curiosity and desire for knowledge about China. In their catalog, they conflated the historic Chinese objects with contemporary ones available for purchase and heightened the appeal by including exotic, "oriental" images of Afong Moy. Their small publication promoted sales while promising to inform the public about China. The historic objects, with their ancient histories, validated the ancestry of Afong Moy and the value of the contemporary goods. The golden chain of global commerce bound the historicity of "oriental" China to the Chinese lady and the goods she promoted.

In America, Afong Moy's whole known life was one of performance. We have no other way to evaluate her meaning to others but through her life on the stage. Her presentations were as much the concoction of her managers' presumptions about China as they were her own infusions of Chineseness. Visitors assumed that the objects, clothing, and images affiliated with Afong Moy had historical validity. Yet as Edward Said remarked, Orientalism "is a system of representations framed by a whole set of forces that brought the Orient into Western learning, Western consciousness."[6] The diffuseness of what Orientalism means can therefore be widely interpreted and applied by Western influencers. Afong Moy serves as a bridge, a foil, and then equally as a window, to America's cultural perception of China. She must therefore be evaluated in light of what her American managers permitted her to convey and what objects and images she had available as conveyances.

Despite these hindrances and possible misrepresentations, Afong Moy's presence on the stage provided the most powerful portrayal of China that America had yet experienced. Josephine Lee rightly determined that "The 'liveness' or 'presence' of theatre suggests an immediate, visceral response to the physicality of race; the embodiedness of theater is experienced or felt, as well as seen and heard. The theatre does not let us forget that questions of racial difference concern our most basic gut reactions, experiences, and sensations."[7] Afong Moy experienced the white audience's gaze, but she, in turn, gazed back. The gazing back, confronting passively or actively, was her significant contribution.

PART I

—————◆◆◆◆◆—————

SETTING THE STAGE

I

The Cast

THE ARRIVAL OF AFONG MOY, a young Chinese woman, in Washington, DC, on February 15, 1835, was not auspicious. Several days earlier Richard Lawrence, a disgruntled, unemployed house painter, had attacked Andrew Jackson while he attended a funeral at the United States Capitol. It was the first assassination attempt on an American president.[1] Fortunately, both of Lawrence's guns misfired and caused no harm to the president, but the city's mood remained grim and Jackson's attitude suspicious. A witness to the attempt claimed that Jackson flew into a "tremendous passion" that remained "virulent and protracted" for several weeks, as he assumed the attack was politically motivated.[2]

In this charged atmosphere, a young Chinese woman arrived at the Executive Mansion to meet the American president. It was not her first glimpse of America, nor was she an unknown. Martin Van Buren, Jackson's vice president, had met Afong Moy in New York City soon after she arrived in the fall of 1834. Van Buren chose not to remark on the meeting, but the *Essex Gazette* in Massachusetts thought it significant, headlining: "IMPORTANT The following . . . is one of the most important items furnished by the last mails: The Hon. Martin Van Buren paid his respects to the Chinese Lady yesterday, and expressed himself highly pleased with her cast."[3] What he found pleasing about her person is unclear.

Though she was meeting the highest-ranking men of the country and was the first Chinese person to visit with an American president, the young woman's mission was far from diplomatic. She did not carry greetings from China or represent the country in any official capacity; her task, as assigned by the escorts who accompanied her, was pecuniary. Like the international crew of the *Pallas* in 1785, Afong Moy had been caught in the web of Americans' commercial activities, and now, in 1835, she was part of its valuable cargo.

She spent her time in Washington principally performing her role as an exotic personage from a distant land. Approaching Jackson on bound feet and likely with trepidation, she relied on others to convey her salutation. At the Executive Mansion the president sat beside her, conscious of her unstable footing. Newspapers mentioned that he questioned Afong Moy on the condition of her bound feet. Several days later the Washington, DC, *Globe* provided her translated commentary on the meeting with the president. She questioned "why the Emperor did not sit in the highest seat."[4] Many years earlier a Chinese man had a similar response when he met the Holy See's diplomatic representative in Paris.[5]

In Afong Moy's China, rulers governed by divine decree; their subjects kowtowed and expressed subservience in their presence. Emperors lived and behaved impressively to set themselves apart as acknowledged superior beings. Afong Moy's expectation for Jackson's behavior was based on her knowledge of, though surely not her experience with, Chinese officialdom. To her, Jackson's expression of equality was odd and unbecoming behavior for a man of such position. Almost certainly Afong Moy's understanding of the American electoral system was limited; that he was a man "of the people," elected "by the people," was incomprehensible.

Though the Chinese woman found Jackson's egalitarian behavior puzzling, many Americans were drawn to the great equalizer. New York diarist Philip Hone, though an anti-Jackson Whig, conveyed the prevailing American sentiment when he wrote in 1833 that Andrew Jackson "is certainly the most popular man we have ever known. Washington was not so much so. His acts were popular . . . but he was superior to the homage of the populace, too dignified, too grave for their liking. . . . Talk of him as the second Washington! It won't do now; Washington was only the first Jackson."[6]

Foreign women were equally charmed by Jackson's personal, and often warm, approach. The English reformer Fanny Wright made frequent critical commentary on American life, castigating Americans for their lack of public morality and civic enlightenment. Yet Wright sought Jackson's advice and championed his egalitarian ways. Harriet Martineau, another English writer, who visited Jackson several days before Afong Moy's arrival in the city, found him kindly. She said, "He did the honors of his house with gentleness and politeness to myself, and as far as I saw, to every one else."[7]

Jackson's consideration for women, especially those who might be considered apart and outside the constraints of polite society, may have resulted from the earlier mistreatment of his frontier Kentucky wife at the hands of his political opponents. Deeply offended when they exposed scandalous accounts of her previous marriage, he strenuously defended his beloved wife. Distraught when she died in 1828, shortly before his inauguration, he blamed his political enemies for her death. In a similar manner, he defended Peggy Eaton, the shunned wife of his secretary of war. Jackson's willingness to meet with a Chinese woman during this stressful time may have been a reflexive response to women who were outside society's strictures.

Asher B. Durand, the accomplished American painter, also sought an audience with the president in February 1835. Unlike Afong Moy, Durand had difficulty gaining access for a portrait sitting, waiting ten days to see the president.[8] However, his time was well spent. The visage he painted is considered the most accurate likeness of Jackson. What one sees in the painting is the intimidating man Afong Moy met that day, and it is aptly described by an anonymous visitor to the President's House at that time:

> His face is unlike any other: its prevailing expression is energy. . . . His eye is of a dangerous fixedness, deep set, and overhung by bushy gray eyebrows, his features long, with strong, ridgy lines running through his cheeks; his forehead a good deal seamed; and his white hair, stiff and wiry, brushed obstinately back, and worn quite with an expression of a chevaux de frise of bayonets. In his mouth there is a redeeming suavity as he speaks; but the instant his lips close, a vizor of steel would scarcely look more impenetrable.[9]

Jackson's loyalties were strong, his sense of chivalry southern, his hatreds unconcealed, and his military bearing and discipline rigid. As the seventh US president he saw his role as a restorer of republican virtue. These character traits and ambitions may explain his attitudes toward Native Americans, and those whose points of view he dismissed or disparaged. Cherokee, Seminole, Choctaw, and additional Indian nations suffered indignities and humiliation as a result of Jackson's actions before and during his presidency.[10] Often he bullied them into submission or dismissed them as unworthy of recognition. Despite his strong opinions on issues of egalitarianism and fairness in government, and his kindness toward those he accepted or protected, those he did not have such feelings about did not fare well.

Though these peoples may have been questionably treated at home, Jackson saw great trade potential with those of different races abroad. Trade with Asia so enticed Jackson that in 1831 he commissioned Edmund Roberts, the first envoy to Southeast Asia, to negotiate trade agreements with Cochin China (Vietnam), Siam (Thailand), Muscat (Oman), and Japan. Upon Roberts's return in 1834, his "most favored nation" commercial treaties with Siam and Muscat were ratified by the Senate; they were the first American treaties with Asian and Near Eastern nations. In 1835, a delighted Jackson would send Roberts back to Asia to negotiate a similar treaty with Japan.[11] The coincidental arrival of the first Asian woman to visit Washington the same year may well have kindled Jackson's interest in Afong Moy.

Unfortunately, Jackson kept no record of his visit with Afong Moy or any specific evidence of what they discussed. His only known comment to his Chinese visitor, as recorded in the local newspapers, was his request to her to "use her powers to persuade her countrywomen to abandon the custom of cramping their feet, so totally in opposition to Nature's wiser regulations."[12] Jackson voiced the typical Western response to a practice that non-Chinese found abhorrent yet exotic and even titillating. Jackson's message of republican self-determination and egalitarianism as reported in the newspapers was meant for an American audience, not for Afong Moy, who would have been unable to effect such a change in her home country.

Despite Jackson's rhetoric, Afong Moy served as the first concrete example of China to a sitting American president. It was her decisive performance as both bridge and foil—providing Jackson a connection to an Asian culture while serving as a frame for his explication of an "advanced" nation—that made this such an important moment. Not until 1868 would another Chinese person meet an American president.[13] Not until 1935, one hundred years after Afong Moy's visit with Jackson, would a Chinese ambassador be installed in Washington.[14]

The rest of Afong Moy's Washington visit was uneventful, rating only one mention in the papers and no later comment from Jackson, Martineau (who was still in the city), or others in the area. She edged into Americans' lives from a distant place and a life of incomprehensible separateness. The only foreigner with whom she had more than a brief connection was Augusta Haskell Obear, the woman to whom she had been entrusted upon leaving China and who perhaps accompanied her to the President's House.

Obear, born near Salem, Massachusetts, was acquainted with China, as well as with the business of shipping, from her early life with her ship captain father, Samuel Haskell. In 1807, the year of her birth, Salem was a principal port of overseas trade with China. In the hope of reaping immense profits, Salem merchants took great risks by sending vessels captained by young men, such as Haskell, to the far corners of the world. By the age of twenty he was sailing to Lisbon, Portugal, St. Petersburg, Russia, and the West Indies.[15] After retiring from the sea in midlife he became a merchant, possibly in the lucrative Asian/Indonesian pepper trade. With the import of exotic goods and the wealth that it engendered, Salem became one of America's most prosperous cities. The Haskell family profited from the town's commerce.

Little is known of his daughter's early life; however, it is possible to infer from family documents some aspects of her upbringing. The notice of Samuel Haskell's death in the *Salem Gazette* of September 1829 stated that he was a "warm friend of general education." It also remarked that he had given much of his time to the improvement of common schools near Salem. The inventory of his estate shows that Haskell had a seventy-five-dollar vested interest in a schoolhouse on Washington Street. That investment, coupled with the large quantity of books in his inventory, indicated that education was of value to him. As the second-oldest child of eight, Obear surely benefited from her father's interest in education. One can reasonably assume that she was literate and attended the common school on Washington Street.

The detailed household inventory had an impressive total value of $1,493. It recorded eight bedsteads and their accompanying bedding, bolsters, and curtains, a mahogany desk and bookcase, a pair of mahogany card tables, a mahogany bureau, a clock, three looking glasses, three dozen silver spoons of various sizes, and several sets of "blue" tea service and plates. These possessions, as well as the fine quality of the furniture, suggest a household of means and a life of relative affluence. The quantities of textiles appointing the beds indicate an elite status, for the cost of textiles equated to the time it took to make them. Obear may have taken her tea and dined on Chinese blue-and-white Canton ware, given the numerous notations of "blue" china.

Most Salem citizens, and particularly those with ship captains in the family, knew something of foreign lands. Their livelihoods depended on this knowledge. Many had seen Chinese goods—teas, ceramics, silks—coming into the Salem port, stacked in warehouses and retail shops near the wharves, and enhancing their homes. Community members had the opportunity to join subscription and rental libraries supplied with voyage narratives and travel journals side by side with novels and the classics. Sea captains discussed ports in distant lands at meetings of the East India Marine Society, and they donated exotic souvenirs from their Asian voyages to the society's museum, where townspeople could view them.

Young Augusta Haskell may have imagined Afong Moy's China as did the Salem girl Caroline Howard King in the 1830s, who recorded her musings on a place she probably never expected to see because of her gender. King entered the East India Marine Society and was transported "into that atmosphere redolent with the perfumes from the East, warm and fragrant and silent."[16] She described the presence of China and the "Spice Islands" as so immediate that she conceived them geographically as places lying not far off the New England coast.

The East India Marine Society, filled with the oddities and marvels that earned King's fascination, had been founded in 1799 by Salem's sea captains and traders. Its bylaws encouraged members to bring home "natural and artificial curiosities" from which they could learn the ways of foreign cultures.[17] The Society, composed of captains and traders (supercargoes) who traveled beyond the Cape of Good Hope at the tip of southern Africa or Cape Horn at the tip of South America, continued to add to the collection of Asian artifacts over the years.

Like King, Haskell probably saw these East India Marine Society objects that presented the customs, habits, and dress of the Chinese and other Asian cultures. King reminisced that

> from the moment I set my foot in that beautiful old hall, and . . . was greeted by the solemn group of Orientals, who, draped in Eastern stuffs and camel's hair shawls stood opposite the entrance . . . the hours were full of enchantment. . . . Three of them were life-size likenesses of East Indian (Asian) merchants, in their own dresses, presented to different sea-captains by the originals.[18]

No other place in the Western world provided an everyday citizen similar access to the goods and appearance of China and the rest of Asia. It would later afford some background for Augusta Haskell Obear's understanding of Afong Moy's Chinese experience.

In her youth Augusta Obear probably encountered this lifelike sculpture of the Chinese merchant Yumqua in Salem's East India Marine Society museum. *Yumqua, 1801. Carved by Samuel McIntire, possibly painted by Michele Felice Cornè, body by Jonathan Bright. Photograph by Mark Sexton. Peabody Essex, E7161.1, gift of Captain Benjamin Hodges, Peabody Essex Museum, Salem, MA*

In 1828, a year before her father's death, twenty-one-year-old Augusta Haskell married Benjamin Thorndike Obear, a son of Captain Josiah and Elizabeth Obear. Their marriage in Beverly, Massachusetts, near Salem, provoked little comment. As neighbors, their lives, and that of their families, had been intertwined in this community for generations.

Born in 1801, and six years older than his wife, Benjamin Obear had already traveled to distant ports, serving aboard Beverly and Salem vessels. Soon he would take responsibility as a ship captain. Unlike his forebears, whose seafaring lives centered on colonial Beverly and Salem trade in the Atlantic basin, young Obear would establish his fortune and reputation much farther afield. Salem was no longer the place for an ambitious sea captain.

The Salem port's decline began with Jefferson's 1807 embargo, which forbade the import or export of goods by land or by sea. Intended to compel France and Great Britain to accept American neutrality during the Napoleonic Wars, instead it virtually eliminated American trade with these nations. Most New England merchants heartily opposed this measure and tried to circumvent it, but ultimately, they were unsuccessful. The War of 1812 followed, and now all foreign ports and international trade closed to American vessels. Salem merchants were particularly hard hit, and many were unable to sustain their businesses. The port lost its footing and never regained it. By the late 1820s, Salem had a diminished prominence in the China trade.

In contrast, after the War of 1812, the rival port of New York began to capitalize on its relatively ice-free, sheltered, deep, and secure harbor. The development of the US western market as a result of the construction of the Erie Canal, which opened in 1825, was also a major impetus to the port. Western farmers now had an outlet for their produce through the canal. Money from the cash crops paid for the imported fancy goods from New York that many westerners soon desired. Significantly, it was not the flow of goods from west to east that encouraged the New York port's growth, but rather the movement of goods east to west. Imported goods sent westward from the New York port far exceeded the flour and other goods sent eastward.[19] The small, back-country store was the distribution point for the goods that Captain Obear would later obtain in China and bring back to America.[20]

Augusta Obear was familiar with the vicissitudes of the life of a ship captain's wife. She spent large portions of every year apart from her husband, and they had little opportunity for a normal life together. Their first recorded separation occurred soon after they were married in 1828, when Benjamin Obear served as captain of the *Nile*, a 403-ton vessel built in New Market, New Hampshire, in 1825 by Dike & Company. One of its four owners included a William Haskell, probably one of Augusta's relatives.[21] The *Nile* sailed out of Beverly for Liverpool, England, in late 1828, returned the following year, and then was sold in Salem by its owners in 1830.

Following the sale of the *Nile*, and possibly finding little work in Massachusetts, Captain Obear turned his attention away from Salem and toward New York for his seafaring future. It was there that he and his wife set up residence in the early 1830s. In 1831 Benjamin Obear began his collaboration with two men who would change his life and the lives of Augusta Obear and Afong Moy.

The northeastern American network of merchants, sea captains, and shipping firms was not a large universe. The times were fluid and trade required participants to relocate to take advantage of the speculations at hand. Both Benjamin Obear and his new employers, the F. & N. G. Carnes firm, were transplants from New England to New York City. Though often noted as brothers in contemporary accounts, Francis and Nathaniel G. Carnes were first cousins who had lived near one another in Boston. Their fathers were Boston merchants who imported European goods.[22] Initially the cousins went separate ways. Francis graduated from Harvard in 1805 and practiced law in the city for ten years. Nathaniel took a different path. In 1811, he went to China as a young merchant, a supercargo, on his uncle's vessel.[23] On his return Nathaniel established a Boston firm with Charles D. Rhodes importing goods from France, London, and China.

In 1820 this firm dissolved, and by 1822 Francis and Nathaniel were listed as dry goods brokers in the Boston directory.[24] Though Francis was listed in the directory, his person was elsewhere, for by 1819 he had moved to Paris.[25] It is unclear what prompted the relocation or what contacts Francis had in Paris, but the firm prospered by his presence there. The cousins' 1822 Boston newspaper notices frequently advertised French linen sheeting, laces, and plumes, along with fancy Canton goods. Nathaniel was also on the move. In 1823, he reestablished the firm in New York City. The Carneses' New York firm was first cited in Longworth's *American Almanac–New York City Directory* of 1822–24, which listed them as commission merchants located at 173 Pearl Street, the hub of the New York commercial district. In 1823, they were well enough established to advertise in New York and Boston as merchants who "pay particular attention to the sale of Dry Goods and Drugs."[26]

By 1826, the future direction of their enterprise began to evolve with the importation of much larger quantities of French fancy goods. They advertised in Boston papers: "Receive orders for the importation of every description of Paris fancy goods—perfumery, porcelain, stationery, hardware and drugs on eligible terms having partner residing in France—possess facilities for prompt execution."[27] By the time the Obears met Nathaniel

Carnes, the firm had moved to 73 Pine Street in New York. Walter Barrett, a nineteenth-century chronicler of New York merchants, noted that in addition to their New York firm, by 1833 the Carneses owned a Parisian house as well.[28]

The Carnes firm functioned within the new merchant capitalist world of commodity trading. The cousins sold the goods they imported to larger commercial fancy goods traders such as the well-respected Fletcher and Gardiner firm in Philadelphia.[29] Though Fletcher and Gardiner were principally known as silversmiths, their business world was a great deal more extensive; they sold fancy goods in their own store and, in turn, their excess fancy good stock to retailers as far away as New Orleans.[30] In a letter to a store owner in New Orleans, Thomas Fletcher inquired: "Will Carnelian beads, watch keys etc. sell well (in New Orleans)? We have received a quantity of carnelian from the East Indies & should be glad to dispose of some of them, also some tortoise shell combs."[31] Retail and wholesale power centered in New York, and the Carneses made every effort to dominate their segment of the trade.

A Massachusetts connection probably brought Benjamin Obear, the Carnes firm, and other financial backers together on their first mercantile venture to China, taking part in the profitable global trade. Obear was assigned the position of captain of the Carneses' ship, the *Howard*. Though the ship was not registered with Lloyd's of London, presumably it was the same vessel seen in the watercolor attributed to Michele Felice Cornè. The 200-ton Kittery, Maine-built vessel sailed out of the New York harbor sometime in the early spring of 1831. According to the *Canton Register*, the *Howard* arrived in China on October 12, left on December 27, and returned to New York with its cargo of "teas, silks, etc." as stated in the ship's manifest on May 25, 1832.[32] Obear spent little time in port with his wife. The *Howard*, with Obear again as captain, must have quickly set sail for China in the summer of 1832, for the *Canton Register* notes its arrival at Guangzhou on November 7. Like clockwork, it returned to New York the following May with a similar cargo. Walter Barrett remarked that to facilitate these risky ventures, a knowledgeable clerk in the Carnes firm accompanied Obear on the *Howard*. The clerk's experience paid off and Barrett observed that "The speculation succeeded, and such a cargo was never brought to this country before. The profit was immense."[33]

The ship *Howard* captained by Benjamin Obear sailed twice to China under the Carnes mercantile firm. Ship Howard, *c. 1803, watercolor by Michele Felice Cornè. Photograph by Mark Sexton. Peabody Essex Museum, M2698 © Peabody Essex Museum, Salem, MA*

To extend this commerce and to increase its China trade successes, the Carnes firm engaged additional affluent merchants to invest in the experiment to import a variety of less costly Chinese goods. Barrett described the blue-eyed, brown-haired Nathaniel Carnes as having "a tongue, great energy, and plans sufficient in his head to load and employ ten Chinese ships."[34] Carnes likely used all these skills as he approached two of the more prominent New York mercantile firms: Gracie, Prime & Company and Henry and William Delafield. As general commission businesses they were well connected to many avenues of trade, but not specifically to the China trade. Nor were the Carneses members of the select group of New York China trade merchants, such as the Griswolds, the Goodhues, the Olyphants, and the Howlands, who had already established their stake in this risky market. The Carneses' challenge was to develop a successful business in a bold and nontraditional way in order to compete with the more recognized New York China traders.

The Carneses were business innovators. They were the first American merchants to conduct a type of trade with China that would not occur again until the late twentieth century: bringing in large quantities of Chinese mass-produced goods that were imitative of Western fancy goods and condiments to sell in America at a cheaper unit cost than Western-made goods. Barrett affirms this in several of his commentaries: "In these cargoes every fan ever made in France was re-copied by the Chinese, and hundreds of cases of feather, palm, silk, ivory, mother-of-pearl and peacock fans included. Palm leaf fans were abundant; and one of these ships bought $20,000 worth of these articles alone."[35] He gave further details:

> Carnes also sent out a sample of pure attar of roses, worth $25 an ounce. The Chinese . . . made a capital imitation, costing about six-pence an ounce. . . . About 10,000 ounces came out in one ship, and druggists and perfumers bought it up rapidly at from ten to fifteen dollars an ounce. From Paris and London, the most famous sauces, condiments, preserves, sweetmeats, syrups, etc. were procured. The Chinese imitated them all, even to the facsimiles of the printed London or Paris labels, and $20,000 worth at least of these imitations were imported at prices underselling the London and Paris manufacturers. An immense profit was realized.[36]

Through Francis, the Carneses developed a multinational company. While in Paris, he surveyed the fashionable European styles and tastes. His connections placed him in an elite social network. The Carnes family scrapbook contains numerous letters from the Marquis de Lafayette inviting Francis to his home, La Grange, thanking him for trees, nuts, cocks, and hens, and questioning Francis about raising American birds in France.[37] Carnes both received and sent invitations to those in the uppermost ranks of French society: Madame Dolomieu, lady-in-waiting to Queen Marie-Amélie de Bourbon; Duchess D'Abrantès, widow of Junot and grande dame of the salon elite; and Prince George Comnène, member of the Greek royal family. Their presence at the wedding of Mlle. Natalie de Lafayette (General Lafayette's granddaughter) to Adolphe Perrier in 1828 signified their social standing.[38] Exposure to these fashionable people and their possessions encouraged an appreciation of the types of fancy goods, which, if produced in mass quantities and at lower prices, could sell in America. The Carnes firm developed an effective "V-shaped" trade.[39] Unlike the triangle trade, where goods were purchased, resold, and then reinvested in other goods, the V trade took French goods as models for imitation to China, where they were reproduced for eventual sale in America.

This concept was not completely new. On a lesser scale, European merchants in the mid- to late eighteenth century had sent Western ceramic forms to China for reproduction and resale in Europe. The Carneses were the first American merchants to explore this international commercial transaction. This manner of business anticipated America's future global trading activities with China in the late twentieth and early twenty-first centuries.

In a second innovative approach, the Carneses heavily invested in less expensive, native Chinese goods that they hoped would be of interest to the American market. These were generally small items, were moderately priced, and had exotic appeal—representing the commercial orientalism of the China trade. Some of these objects were familiar to Americans in urban centers, yet even this populace might not have seen the array of Chinese goods Carnes imported. Again, Barrett provides commentary:

> The fireworks that Carnes ordered were tremendous. Every pattern, shade and name appeared. Fire-crackers, rockets, revolving wheels, and all the rest. For the first time, rice paintings were brought out to this country as an article of commerce. They were assorted, large, and small sized silk books, each containing twelve plates of Chinese paintings. The shawls imported by the Carnes concern were never equaled. . . . Very small quantities of Chinese matting had been brought in any one ship up to that time. But the 'Howard' had on board . . . all sizes, patterns and colors—black, white, checker goods, fine, coarse, and so forth. Over 6,000 rolls came in, and the owners doubled their money.[40]

Though small quantities of these goods had often been part of shipments from China in the past, they were generally carried as shipmates' personal investments, as gifts, or as the lesser cargo. The Carneses, however, carried vast quantities of native Chinese goods as their principal cargo.

Most significantly, the Carneses promoted these goods in an extraordinary fashion. In 1834, to acquaint Americans with these unfamiliar Chinese goods and to bring attention to their unusual cargo, the Carneses, with Benjamin Obear's help, employed Afong Moy to hawk their objects in the United States. This was a bold and extreme measure, and a high volume of sales would be necessary to recompense them for the negotiations, logistics, and cost of bringing Afong Moy from China to America.

The Carneses' speculation may have been prompted by the knowledge of an earlier English venture. In late 1831, William C. Hunter, then a member of the American firm of Russell & Co., traveled from Guangzhou to New York as a passenger on the *Howard* captained by Benjamin Obear.[41] On that voyage, Hunter may have recounted to Obear a fascinating story of his earlier encounter with an Englishman. Hunter, traveling from New York to Guangzhou in 1824, was accompanied by a passenger, Doctor Smyth, who was on a mission shrouded in mystery. Hunter noted in his 1882 book that when Doctor Smyth arrived in China he

> took (a) fast boat and went to Macao. Soon after, we heard that he had there engaged two young Chinese small-footed women to accompany him to Calcutta, from whence he took passage with them for England as a "speculation." Subsequently we learnt that he was associated in the enterprise with Captain C———, also of the Honorable East India Company's service on board whose vessel he had filled the office of surgeon. While in England, these "Golden Lilies" had the honour of a presentation to H. M. George IV. The enterprise, however, was not successful. It met with great opposition in certain quarters, and finally it ended by those young daughters of "Han" being returned to their own country.[42]

It is unclear who expressed concern in England, though possibly missionaries found their presence objectionable. It is also unknown whether Hunter conveyed this account to Obear, or whether Obear, in turn, relayed an account of this English venture to the Carneses. Though their intentions were dissimilar, the stories have commonalities. However, the Carneses' hopes for Afong Moy lay more in sales than in spectacle.

Advertising in early nineteenth-century America consisted of small snippets of information placed in newspapers, notations on broadsides or circulars, and the name of the firm printed on trade cards. Word of mouth, carried on the tongues of satisfied customers, had impact. The Carneses, leaping over decades of tradition, initiated one of the first advertising and branding campaigns. Branding by affiliation with a person, a particular design, or a slogan would not become widespread for several decades. Yet the young Asian woman served that purpose; widely advertised across America in large cities and smaller towns as the "Chinese lady" with bound feet, she met the public for several years amid goods from the Carneses' vessels. Her presence provided the American people a cultural bridge to China through her presentation of their Chinese objects.

The story of Afong Moy, the sale of these Chinese goods, and the lives of their merchandisers unwraps a history of early American consumption, attitudes toward the Chinese, and nineteenth-century mercantile practices that foretell the rise of the late twentieth-century US-China trade and the twenty-first-century global marketplace. America's participation in this commerce with China began in the eighteenth century. It would have a profoundly personal effect on Afong Moy in the early nineteenth century. How she became enmeshed in this commercial activity unfolds from an account of Augusta and Benjamin Obear's travels to China in 1834.

2

Behind the Scenes

WITH THE HIGH EXPECTATIONS OF the Carnes merchants, Francis and Nathaniel, and their associated partners, the ship *Washington* left New York harbor in the fall of 1833, bound for Guangzhou. Their intentions included both the purchase of Chinese goods and the procurement of the agent to promote them once they arrived on American shores.

On this third voyage to China, Captain Benjamin Thorndike Obear brought along his wife, Augusta.[1] It is unclear whether she had previously traveled aboard ship, though certainly she had never ventured as far as China. Augusta Obear may well have welcomed the opportunity to see the husband with whom she had spent only several months since their 1828 marriage; however, she also accompanied him to perform a duty. Captain Obear needed a woman's presence to ensure the proper conveyance of a young Chinese woman to America. This agreement, likely made by Captain Obear on a previous trip to China, and in consultation with the Carneses, would have required a female chaperone.[2] His wife was charged with Afong Moy's care. Twenty-seven and childless (and so she remained), Augusta may have functioned as a surrogate mother or accepted the young Afong Moy as a welcome companion. Yet Obear left no record to indicate if she found this duty pleasurable, rewarding, or onerous. Whether she was recruited under duress or completed the job willingly, Obear signed up for a long and rigorous journey on the *Washington*.

The *Washington*'s registration confirmed that the 298-ton, three-masted ship was well built, well fitted out, and only two years old.[3] Obear and her husband shared a small cabin and perhaps a separate stateroom for sleeping in the aft quarters close to the stern. The space was built into the deck and was accessed through a companionway of several steps. Mary Dow described her own accommodations on a similar vessel, the 279-ton bark *Clement*: "It is about eight feet long and twelve wide. One third is occupied by a bedstead, the other two-thirds is filled up with cabin furniture, such for instance as one table, one chair, one sea-chest, two small trunks, one band-box, one box of claret wine, the ship's main topsail, and a variety of small articles."[4] Augusta's quarters were no doubt equally incommodious.

Early nineteenth-century ships were unequipped for female passengers. Women generally were not welcomed by the crew, who found them disruptive, perhaps demanding, and consumers of scarce resources. Captains' wives accompanying their husbands on board ship for a lengthy voyage were not unheard of, but it was rare. Of the 154 diaries, letters, or reminiscences of seafaring wives or captain's daughters, only seven record their voyages before Augusta's.[5]

If sea voyages were treacherous for men, they were doubly so for women. Women's dress made navigating on board precarious. Sea spray on the deck and fires in close quarters below made long skirts soggy or fire hazards. As one seafaring wife recorded, an ankle-length "wash dress," worn on land for Monday's laundry activities, was the most accommodating outfit women could wear.[6] Pattens, wood- or metal-soled overshoes, protected their feet from the splash of seawater on deck.

As a shipmaster's daughter, Obear may have previously experienced the roll of the sea, but even the hardiest seafaring wives found the motion of the open sea challenging. Seasickness was common. In her diary, Harriet Low of Salem, who accompanied her aunt and uncle, merchant William Henry Low, to China on board the *Sumatra*, remarked on her sea voyage: "I awoke this morning, but with no desire to move, speak or look at anything; I was sure I was alive, but I cared very little whether I remained so, or whether any one else did. I defy any one, even the most brilliant colorist, to depict the horrors of seasickness."[7] The pitching, even of the larger ships, made daily chores such as washing clothes an adventure. Hannah Winn poked fun at herself as she rolled across the *St. Paul's* cabin in 1837: "Poor me went one way and the chair another, broke the chair not a little. I can imagine how my Salem friends would have laughed to have seen me in that plight."[8]

Obear was not the first American woman to travel to the southern Chinese city of Guangzhou. Low, arriving four years earlier, kept a diary, and the account of her travels at sea and in China from 1829 to 1834 provide an insight on what Augusta might have experienced. Low's outgoing voyage

was likely equivalent to Obear's, for both vessels intended the Chinese foreign trading port of Guangzhou as their immediate goal. When no interme-
diate trading activity took place, most American vessels followed a similar
sea route to Guangzhou.

Unfortunately, Low left Macao, the Portuguese island near Guangzhou,
several months before Augusta arrived, and there is no record that they knew,
or met, one another. Had their time in China overlapped, our knowledge of
Afong Moy would have been far richer. In her diaries and letters home, Low
recounted the lives and happenings of Americans in Guangzhou. Augusta
Obear's accompaniment of Afong Moy would have been sensational news
to convey home.

Low's descriptions of her outgoing voyage to China recount a harrowing
trip across three oceans. Traveling across the Atlantic Ocean, around the
tip of Africa at the Cape of Good Hope and into the Indian Ocean, vessels
anchored at Anjer on the west coast of Java in present-day Indonesia to
get supplies. Though Low decided not to go ashore, she described the area
surrounding Anjer: "The scenery about here is very beautiful, the land
very high, and covered with verdure. Along the coast grow coconuts and
plantains."[9] Most American vessels in the early nineteenth century made
this first land stop by the fourteenth week.[10] Vessels then entered the narrow
Sunda Straits between Java and Sumatra and into the Java Sea while traveling past the northwest coast of Borneo. Their destination may now have
felt nearer, for the Java Sea flowed into the South China Sea; the terminus
was, at most, two to three weeks hence.

All foreigners followed a typical procedure as they sailed up the Pearl River
to approach Guangzhou, the only Chinese trade port open to outsiders.
Foreign vessels first landed in Macao, sixty miles south of Guangzhou at the
mouth of the Pearl. Landfall would be appealing anywhere, but on arriving
Low found the views from her Macao home in 1829 arresting: "From the
front of the summer-house we have a fine view of the fort on one high hill.
Below we have a view of the town and the beach, the Franciscan Church,
and the green where the ladies walk; . . . On the other side we have a little
view of the sea, . . . in the other direction we have a fine view of the harbor
and the surrounding hills. . . . It is really a delightful spot."[11] For foreign
women, Portuguese Macao was their last stop, and the nearest they would
get to China, because Chinese law restricted foreign women from entering
mainland China.

Sea captains and traders then moved their vessels forty-seven miles farther
up the Pearl River to Whompoa Island, still thirteen miles from Guangzhou.

All foreign ships anchored in Whompoa to meet the Chinese customs agents and hire Chinese linguists who served as personal interpreters.[12] The traders proceeded even further up the river to the foreign factories (warehouses and residences) in Guangzhou where sales were negotiated and suitable transactions made with the Chinese merchants, called the hong. These men were responsible for all foreign activities and transactions. Many foreigners had close relationships with these few men who had the precarious job of serving as the interface with the Chinese government and enforcing its regulations.[13]

Americans and all other foreign traders accepted the Chinese process. Samuel Shaw, the supercargo on board the *Empress of China*, the first American ship to Guangzhou in 1784, indicated his favorable attitude toward the Chinese. He acknowledged with grace the usual Chinese trade practice of accepting a bribe, calling it a "doucent or sweet[e]ner." Shaw respected the Chinese merchants' acumen. He admitted that they were capable bargainers, yet even-tempered and open. In the future, not all American traders would be as complimentary.

The Chinese felt no compunction to smooth the way for European or American merchants. They had not actively sought foreign trade. As an insular nation, China was self-sufficient, with little need for outside goods. By contrast, the English, Portuguese, Dutch, Danes, Swedes, Spanish, and French, and, by 1784, the Americans, saw the potential for great profit in the trafficking of Chinese goods, such as teas, silks, and other fine objects of interest to the West, and later, the illicit sale of opium. The Chinese therefore put heavy strictures on foreign trading activities. Though the process was carefully scripted and purposefully organized by the Chinese, to foreigners it seemed cumbersome, rule-bound, and difficult.

One of the principal rules, meant to discourage long-term foreign settlement, was the prohibition of all foreign women in Guangzhou. Wives of sea captains and traders set up house in Macao, seeing their husbands infrequently. The *Canton Register*, an English-language newspaper in Guangzhou, repeatedly addressed the issue. In 1831 the newspaper reprinted an earlier 1830 proclamation from Taou-Kwang, governor of the province:

If any again dare obstinately to oppose the prohibitions by presuming to bring foreign women up to the provincial city, I the Governor, have commanded the civil and military officers . . . to examine strictly, prohibit and stop them, and if they dare to persist in opposing, immediately to open their guns and fire on them: also to examine what nation's merchant ship, or foreign merchant, has brought up a foreign woman, that I may immediately close the hatches of that foreign merchant ship, drive it back to its country, and never again allow it to come and trade, thereby to chastise their barbarian obstinacy. Decidedly, not the least clemency shall be shown—each ought trembling to obey.[14]

The 1830 proclamation was in response to the infringement of long-established Chinese rules of foreign occupation in Guangzhou by an English merchant's wife who joined her husband in Guangzhou that year. In her diary Harriet Low wrote: "They have threatened to send soldiers to take her away, upon which Mr. B. [Baynes, the English merchant] has had up a hundred armed sailors from the ships, and cannon placed at the gate of the factory. For the last fortnight we have been in a great state of excitement, but it is thought generally that it will blow over, and, though the Chinese will never consent to ladies going to Canton, they will wink at it, and as Mouqua [sic a hong merchant] told Uncle 'they will shutty eye and shutty ear.' I should be very glad to have the English carry out the point if it can be done without bloodshed, but time will show."[15] Mrs. Baynes remained in the English factory several weeks and then returned to Macao. Either her husband was unwilling to push the issue with the Chinese, or he was ready to see her leave.

Nine months later Low and her aunt boldly determined that American women should follow the English woman's example. Under cover of darkness they shipped out from Macao wearing caps and cloaks for disguise. Low's description of approaching Guangzhou by moonlight provides a sense of what Augusta Obear might have seen three years later: "At eleven the moon rose in splendor, so that we had a fine view of the pagodas as we neared Canton, and the endless variety of boats. The tea-boats are immense, and ranged along in such order that they form complete streets upon the water. There are also houses built upon boats and forming streets."[16]

Still in disguise, the two women found their way to the American factory, recognizing it by the description Mr. Low had given them. In her depiction of the site in a letter to her sister, Harriet Low presented it as it is seen in contemporary paintings of the factories: "And now you will perhaps wish to know what a Hong, or factory is. Perhaps you will fancy looms about; but it is nothing more nor less than a range of houses built one back of the other, and entered by arches, with a passage under the house to get to each. We have the advantage of being in front, where we can see everything that goes on. There are four houses in this Hong."[17] The American factory, one of the thirteen, was a large building, three stories high and three to four hundred feet long.

The American flag, flying prominently in the center, identifies the location of the factory where Harriet Low and Augusta Obear briefly resided in Guangzhou. *"View of the foreign factories at Canton," c. 1805. Photograph by Jeffrey R. Dykes. Peabody Essex Museum, gift of the Misses Aimee and Rosamond Lamb, E78680 © 2007 Peabody Essex Museum, Salem, MA*

Several days later their exploit was discovered. The irate Chinese officials reissued the 1830 proclamation that had attempted to discourage foreign women from entering China. Low claimed that Mouqua had earlier tried to cover for the English woman by asserting that her merchant husband was sick and needed attention. But, according to Low, Mouqua had run out of viable excuses for the Americans, saying: "I no can talky sick any more. Now I know not what talky."[18] Here Low quoted the hong merchant using a racist pidgin dialogue often repeated by Westerners to denigrate the language ability of the Chinese; now it implied Mouqua's ineffectualness. There was no appreciation for the difficult position in which she and her aunt had placed him.

The senior Chinese officials, putting pressure on the hong merchants, threatened to cut off all trade with the Americans if the women remained. The Chinese recognized the foreign merchants' vulnerability and used it to enforce the law. Not wishing to destroy the livelihood of other traders, Harriet Low and her aunt left after three weeks. However, the matter did not die down. Subsequent issues of the *Canton Register* addressed the concern. In a letter to the editor a "Canton Batchelor" complained that foreigners had a moral right to dwell with their wives in Guangzhou. He complained that "after a day of harassing toil and controversy what have we to fall back on? The Cegar! Or the bottle! place this in contrast with Home!"[19] He then went on to threaten much higher commission prices because of the hardships of living apart and the cost of maintaining two residences. A March 1832 letter to the editor continued this tirade. This merchant claimed that he never signed up for the Roman Catholic priesthood, and he asked in hyperbole, "With equal reason . . . might the Chinese restrain our eating and drinking."[20]

No foreigners addressed the central Chinese concern of settlement and fraternization. The merchants claimed not to understand why their rights had been denied, nor did they know whether the ban on women was a local or an imperial penalty. Without the larger understanding of the Manchu, they could not have known that this was a consistent policy. After their overthrow of the Ming dynasty (1368–1644) in the seventeenth century, the Manchu, adopting the Chinese dynastic name of Qing, restricted all alien cultures, including the Chinese Han, from their North Manchuria homeland. This designated separation was an attempt to maintain the purity of their racial group and retain their distinct identity. They constructed a willow palisade of several hundred miles along the border to delineate the boundary, past which no ethnic Chinese settlers might enter.[21] The embargo on foreign women in Guangzhou was an extension and application of this policy. The mingling of alien foreigners with any native peoples—Manchu or Han—was anathema to the Manchu government, which therefore restricted foreigners only to the areas near the factories and discouraged the concept of being "at home" in China.

With the American and English women's entry and consequent ejection from Guangzhou a recent memory, it is extraordinary that in February 1834 Augusta Obear was permitted the apparent freedom to enter the same city without a Chinese response.[22] Because Obear's accounts of her experiences in China are unrecorded, we are aware of her foray only from much later American newspaper accounts. In their obituaries for Augusta Obear in 1891, the *Beverly Citizen, Salem Register*, and *New York Times* noted that she was the first American woman to enter a Chinese city. The *Beverly Citizen* later published a retraction upon learning that Harriet Low and her aunt had been there several years before.[23] However, the remembrance of Obear's adventure many years earlier signified its lasting importance, perhaps as evidence of an American woman's defiance of Chinese authority, or her adventuresome spirit.

Obear's undisguised presence in Guangzhou, flouting the stated rules, indicated that the hong merchants and Chinese officials had foreknowledge of her visit, permitted her short-term presence in China, and surprisingly complied with the terms of Afong Moy's voyage to America with Obear as chaperone. Had they objected, they would have posted another edict in the papers, and threatened retaliatory action such as they had done when Low entered Guangzhou in 1831.[24] Unlike that of most American women, Obear's early life in Salem prepared her for the cultural differences she would encounter in China and provided some understanding of the woman she would soon assist.

Afong Moy's lineage remains a mystery. We know her name only from the ship *Washington*'s October 18, 1834, manifest records, which listed her as "Auphmoy." This phonetic appellation was later changed to Afong Moy and may have been assigned by the Americans with little correlation to her true Chinese name.[25] In China, the use of the "A" as the first syllable of a proper name, was (and still is) colloquial and indicated an informal or a diminutive address. According to an English traveler, Charles Toogood Downing, many of the Chinese women who serviced foreign vessels as washerwomen had names that began with "an A, so that it would not be at all strange if you were to find Ally, As-sou, As-say, and A-moy all in the same boat together."[26]

The October 18, 1834, ship manifest for the vessel *Washington* listed Auphmoy, female, Canton, several lines beneath Mrs. Obear's name; an unnamed Chinese female servant from Canton was recorded as well. *National Archives and Records Administration, Passenger Lists of Vessels Arriving at New York 1820–97, M237, roll #25, October, 13, 1834–March 25, 1835*

On her arrival in New York, several newspapers worked out other versions of her name that were more muddled. They used appellations that sounded vaguely "oriental," implying an exotic person, while combining this with an English forename and honorific titles as well: Miss Julia Foochee-ching-chang-king, Madame Ching Chang Foo, or Miss Keo-O-Kwang King.[27] They presented her as the daughter of a "distinguished" Chinese citizen who lived in the "suburbs" of "Canton" by the name of Hang-wag-tzangtzeking—another fictionalized name that sounded appropriately Asian to an American audience.[28] With so little to ascertain from her name, one primary aspect distinguished her: Afong Moy's bound feet.

The practice of Chinese foot binding likely originated in the mid-tenth century. Its early intentions remain obscure. Whether done for fashionable style or as a means of restricting the actions of the female population, it affected a sector of the Han Chinese female population until the early twentieth century. From the outside looking in, foreigners found it a perverse oddity and a method of control that demeaned women. From an insider's perspective, it was normal and acceptable.

By the time of the Ming dynasty, the incapacitation of a woman by binding her feet indicated a family's economic viability and hence its social standing.[29] The elite foot-bound woman remained outside the workforce and needed to be supported in her incapacity. Servants attended to her needs and completed the work she was unable to accomplish. By the early nineteenth century, nonelite Chinese families also participated in foot-binding traditions. The sacrifice of their daughter's labor could be significant. The bound-footed woman's chances of an upwardly mobile marriage, or position of greater status as a concubine, depended in some measure on the size of her feet rather than the look of her face or the shape of her body. The successful effects of foot binding, resulting in tiny feet, could provide a Han Chinese family access, through marriage or association, to greater economic opportunity and status.[30]

Afong Moy's visual appearance was typical of Han women in China. The Han, the indigenous and principal ethnic group in China, were invaded and overthrown by the outlying Manchus of the northeast in 1644. The Manchu adopted enough of the Han traditions to maintain stability. Otherwise, they preserved a strikingly separate culture that discouraged miscegenation. The Han men were required to distinguish themselves from the Manchu by keeping their hair in a queue (a long braid). And though the Manchu outlawed the practice of foot binding for its own women, social pressure kept the practice alive for Han women like Afong Moy.

Zhao Yi, a Chinese historian of the late eighteenth century, claimed that foot binding occurred throughout the Chinese empire; however, he specified that in Guangdong, the province where Guangzhou is located, women in the cities more often had bound feet than those in the countryside.[31] In 1835, the *Chinese Repository*, a Guangzhou English-language newspaper for foreigners, noted that "it prevails more or less throughout the country, but only among the [Han] Chinese. In the largest towns and cities, and generally in the most fashionable parts of the country, a majority of the females have their feet compressed."[32]

Though foreigners were unable to travel outside Guangzhou to document the practice in the early nineteenth century, the tradition likely varied by locale and by class. Zhao seemed to confirm this, noting that foot-binding customs differed greatly from place to place.[33] Many rural families, sustained by their work in the fields, could ill afford to exempt their women from farm toil by binding feet. In contrast, women of rural families involved in the cotton or silk industries in the eighteenth century could perform their work of silk weaving in the home with bound feet. Similarly, a proportion of urban families relied on female members to labor in workshops, and these women too might have engaged in the custom. Women with bound feet therefore could be found in middling to upper-middling Han Chinese families depending on their circumstances and ambition.

Foot binding required knowledge and skill, and only other women knew the special ways of wrapping and unwrapping the binding cloths that constricted the foot. Women selected for foot binding began the procedure at a young age, generally by the age of five to seven. Mothers usually attended to this excruciatingly painful process. The foot was mutilated by breaking the four lesser toes and bending them under the sole. The sole and heel were then pushed close together to create a tiny compact mass. Because the broken physical mass reacted like a wound, it had to be cleansed and re-bandaged frequently. This process took place through adolescence and into young adulthood and could not be reversed without severe discomfort. Special cleansing and caring for bound feet was a lifetime preoccupation and commitment. In the 1990s, oral histories of elderly Chinese women whose feet had been bound provided an insight into the tradition and procedures.[34] Most recounted the severe pain. Some resisted their families' decision, but many accepted the procedure because it set them apart. They recognized the status it conferred and willingly endured the torture for the outcome: tiny feet and an elevated position in their society.

Several Americans visiting or working in China in the early to mid-nineteenth century found the tradition abhorrent, yet morbidly fascinating. Early in her Macao stay, Harriet Low chanced on women with bound feet: "On our way . . . we saw two of their women with small feet. I was perfectly astonished, although I had heard so much of them; but I never believed it, and always supposed I must be deceived. These women's feet were about the size of our little Charley's (boy of three). Only think of a full-grown and rather fat person having such feet!"[35] Two years later after adjusting to life in Macao, Low continued to reflect on the topic: "what a state they (Chinese women) are in now, poor degraded beings! Mere toys for the idle hours of their masters, crippled and tortured merely to please them. As I was walking this morning, I saw a poor creature toddling along on her little feet. I am told that the agony they have to endure is beyond conception; they commence swathing the feet at the age of two, and for years they suffer excessively, all to gratify the mother's pride."[36]

Robert Bennet Forbes, an American merchant in Guangzhou, recounted his brief observation of bound-footed women. Attending the funeral of Tinqua, a hong merchant, in 1838, Forbes was titillated by the view despite the solemn nature of the occasion: "at the other end was a sort of altar having a picture of Tinqua before it, on either side were curtains drawn hiding the female members of the family assembled to mourn, they looked out shyly to see foreigners probably a great curiosity to them & I got sight of several very decent faces & sundry very small feet."[37]

Though Low and many other Americans decried the tradition as "barbaric" and inhumane, they were not above returning home with a souvenir of this cultural practice. William Wood, in his 1830 book *Sketches of China*, complained that it was the fashion of American visitors to China to have "shoes for bound feet as decorative items in their homes."[38] Low's brother Abbot, who joined the family firm in Guangzhou while Low was still in Macao, provided a pair of slippers for their niece: "Abbot sent me a pair of Chinawoman's shoes, which I shall bring home for your first girl. They will fit her when she is about a week old. It seems incredible that they can wear such things, but I have seen them as small upon the Campo."[39] Americans' focus on the bound foot, a condition indicative to them of Chinese backwardness and female oppression, would continually resurface in Afong Moy's American experience.

Like Abbot Low, American Frank G. Carpenter much later purchased shoes for bound feet in China for his collection of international footwear. *National Museum of American History, Division of Work and Industry, Smithsonian Institution, A2937, gift of Mrs. William Chapin Huntington*

Knowledge of her physical condition places us no closer to Afong Moy's specific identity. Without recourse to her full name, and absent the Obears' accounts of the event, we can only speculate about Afong Moy's Chinese life. It is probable that she resided in an area of Guangzhou, in Guangdong Province, to which Americans had access. In some manner they came into contact with her, or her family. There were some possible moments when a foreigner might engage with a Chinese woman or a local family, and these provide several hypotheses on who Afong Moy might have been.

Harriet Low's diary recorded her encounter with bound-footed women on her walks in Macao. These Chinese women were referred to in an 1835 article in the *Chinese Repository*: "there are frequent cases, among the poorer classes, where the unhappy victims of this barbarous custom are compelled to walk on their little feet."[40] If William C. Hunter's story about Dr. Smyth is to be believed, he recruited bound-footed Chinese women from Macao for his English venture. However, if Afong Moy had been one of these Macao women, Augusta Obear would have had no reason to enter the city of Guangzhou.

Low also met female Chinese servants working for foreign families in Macao, but they did not have bound feet and usually assisted as wet nurses. A rare image of a Chinese female servant appears in a family group portrait by George Chinnery, an English artist working in Macao. The Chinese woman, situated behind the family of Charles Marjoribanks, leans into the picture toward the youngest child. Her hand moves to solicitously still the wriggling girl. Only her upper body is depicted, yet the dress of her hair and a portion of her Chinese tunic define her as the outsider.[41]

Another form of servitude was characteristic of southern Chinese culture. When impoverished families were unable to care for their young daughters they might sell or give them to other Chinese families as servants. Called *mui tsai*, which translates as "little sister," these young girls were accepted as charity cases, but not infrequently they ended up in a lifetime of indenture, slavery, or prostitution. Afong Moy's experience partially fit this description; however, her bound feet and her more public life in America are inconsistent with the typical life of a *mui tsai*.[42] The *mui tsai* are more generally associated with later nineteenth-century Chinese women's experience in California. After coming to the United States as servants, they sometimes ended up as prostitutes in American Chinatowns.

It is equally unlikely that Afong Moy was one of the Chinese women Americans encountered in the harbors of Macao and Guangzhou and on the Pearl River Delta. Upon reaching Macao harbor in 1837 Caroline Hyde Butler, who traveled to China with her supercargo husband Edward, needed their assistance to reach the shore: "No boat of any size can approach near the shore. But there are hundreds of little boats, no bigger than egg shells, guided entirely by women, which are ever ready to take passengers. Two of them were soon by our side screaming with all their might. 'My boat, my boat.' "[43] These were the Tanka, or boat women, whom William Wood described in some detail in the 1830s: "On them and their children principally, devolves the task of navigating the multitudes of small boats which cover the Chinese rivers. The women, from the continual exposure to sun and wind, become very dark, lose all that soft listlessness of expression, and delicacy of form, for which the higher class are distinguished."[44] The Chinese considered the Tanka an inferior ethnic group. Because they were not permitted to own land, they spent much of their lives on the water. Tanka women did not participate in the traditions of bound feet, and their weathered faces and less-than-delicate appearance would not suit Captain Obear's objective.

"Sampans" or "wash boats" manned by three or four Chinese women would pull alongside a newly arrived vessel at Whompoa to provide washing, cleaning, and mending services to the sailors and petty officers. According to the English traveler Charles Toogood Downing, these women were good-natured, hard-working, and honest in their dealings. Dressed in blue nankeen tunic and trousers, and always without shoes, they robustly plied their trade, and with Downing's report, they would sing out to an approaching ship: "Ah you missee chiefee mate, how you dooa?"[45] Some chief mates allowed the washerwomen on board, perhaps not always for their assigned cleaning tasks. Downing implied that one might not want to examine their moral character too carefully.[46] John Kearsley Mitchell, an American physician on board the US vessel *George and Albert* from Philadelphia in 1817, also commented on the washerwomen. They approached his ship thirty miles from Whompoa. "The first who came alongside was a fine lively girl with an agreeable countenance, lively sparkling eyes black glossy hair neatly braided and very white regular teeth—. She seems to be instinctively a co-quet. . . . with petitions for employment . . . some cry 'I want your washee give me your washee.' "[47] Afong Moy, with her bound feet, did not fit this character type.

Chinese ladies of pleasure resided in ornamented "flower boats" on the Pearl River. Though the women lingered in full view on the boats' balconies and decks, they were off limits to foreigners. These women often had flowers in their hair, were festooned with abundant jewelry, and had bound feet, yet their clients were only Chinese. Downing noted that several foreign sailors tried to gain access to the boats by force; one was assailed and beaten, the other never heard of again.[48] William Wood recounted in his *Sketches of China* that these women were regularly licensed and monitored and therefore were not anonymous or unaccounted-for women.[49] As a foreigner, Captain Obear had no access to these women.

At the other end of the spectrum of class status, American newspapers speculated, without any foundation, that Afong Moy's father was a

The unknown artist of this painting eliminated the side panels of the flower boat so the viewer could see the activity within: female musicians entertaining on the left; wealthy Chinese men feasting in the center. Dinner aboard a "flower boat," *c. 1780.* *A. J. Hardy, Hong Kong*

"distinguished" Chinese citizen. They claimed that her father's appellation "Hang," or perhaps the misunderstood transliteration "Hong," implied that Afong Moy was the daughter of a hong merchant. Robert Bennet Forbes had only a fleeting opportunity to see elite, bound-footed women while in the company of hong merchants' families in Guangzhou. It would be unlikely that a hong merchant would agree to release one of his female relatives into the Obears' care. Such an exchange would provide little benefit to either, and could have imperiled future trading relationships. Their wealth, power, and position placed them above such an arrangement.

Neither one of high birth, nor a servant, nor a washerwoman, but rather, a woman of middle-class status, might better fit Captain Obear's criteria. In Guangzhou, the streets near the hong factories were open to foreigners such as the Obears. Thirteen Factory Street behind the hongs faced a square bounded by three streets: Hog Lane, New China Street, and Old China Street. There, Chinese merchants in small shops unaffiliated with the official hong traders sold handicraft goods, teas, ivory, bird cages, matting, and fireworks to foreigners. Here American traders might have the opportunity to converse with a middle-class Chinese merchant whose family lived above the shop.

On a later trip to China, the ship physician John Kearsley Mitchell commented on his accessibility to the Chinese shop men and their dwellings. He remarked that as foreigners walked the streets, "the term Fan qui or strange devil was shouted along and the whole female population ran to peep at us through the blinds over the doorways. Some of them, more daring than the rest, ventured to peep out—showing us their faces with flour, after the manner of our southern ladies. Their hair was completely covered with flowers and tinseled ornaments."[50]

Afong Moy's status as the daughter of a local merchant or a comprador, a middleman who assisted foreign merchants in their households or in their businesses, is the most likely explanation of her background. Conceivably these men had some means to support a daughter with bound feet. An opportunity for a liberal payment might persuade such a merchant or comprador to release his daughter to Americans for such a voyage, even though transport on a foreign ship was illegal in China. Although Chinese law provided some protection from the "sale" of female commoners within China, in actuality relatives did, and could, effect this transaction.[51] Although the Obears would not have considered her enslaved, likely Afong Moy had little say in this financial exchange. Augusta's presence gave respectability and credibility to such a contract and possibly reassured the Chinese of the Obears' good intentions.

Extenuating circumstances within southern China in 1833 and 1834 may also have precipitated Afong Moy's voyage. In the spring and summer of 1833 and the winter of 1834, the weather was erratic and severe. Possibly due to volcanic eruptions from Mount Kaba in Sumatra, the climate in Guangzhou was unseasonably wet and cool.[52] In August 1833, thirty-six inches of rain fell in Macao.[53] In her diary Harriet Low commented on the deluge and the impact it had on shipping. The heavy rains and high tides caused a total cessation of shipping, and no goods could be shipped out, or brought in, due to the inundation of the hong factories.

More significantly, the rains caused unprecedented inland flooding. Cool temperatures and wet weather resulted in a meager rice harvest. The scarcity of rice, and its high cost, brought mass starvation in the fall and winter of 1833–34. The *Chinese Repository* recorded the great suffering, stating that it was common to see parents selling their children in the streets of Guangzhou for as little as twenty-five dollars to anyone who would promise to feed and house them.[54] Articles in the July 1834 *Canton Register* proposed a subscription for the relief of the distressed Chinese whose suffering the foreign merchants saw all around them.[55] Following through, they did provide monies to the Chinese treasury for flood relief to the poor that year.[56] Though this may not be the explanation for Afong Moy's departure, it does indicate that times were hard and many Chinese needed money to offset the high cost of food.

That money changed hands for Afong Moy's transmission is hinted at in two American newspapers. One article published soon after her arrival in the United States in October 1834 remarked that "perhaps it was her filial love that induced her for valuable pecuniary consideration to her parents, to violate a fundamental law of the empire, and to consent to be smuggled out of her father's pagoda on board an American ship."[57] Here the reference to "filial love" possibly was an allusion to—and a critique of—"filial piety," which was the fundamental Confucian value. It was the duty of children to support and obey their parents, no matter the obstacle. However, this devotion was not quite what would have been expected of an American child.

Another article, printed a year after her arrival, in an Albany, New York, newspaper remarked that Afong Moy had a guarantee to return to her parents "who are handsomely remunerated for her temporary absence."[58] Neither article speculates on the amount her parents might have been paid. In 1836, the New York Herald noted that the Chinese lady had "cleared $23,000."[59] Possibly this was the amount that her parents expected to receive. Even today, this seems like a large sum. It could be compared, however, with one American merchant's earnings in Guangzhou at the time. Forbes conveyed to his wife in a private letter of February 1840 that his share of a two-month company profit was thirty thousand dollars.[60] This possible remuneration for Afong Moy's several-year commitment seems more reasonable in that context.

Whatever the actual background of Afong Moy, her life changed quickly and dramatically. To reach America by October 1834, the Washington needed to leave Guangzhou by spring of that year. In the several months before departure, Captain Obear had to complete financial arrangements to secure Afong Moy, locate a servant to accompany her, and outfit a separate cabin on the vessel to accommodate them. Though the servant is unnamed, the Washington manifest records a female servant, resident of Canton, listed below Afong Moy's name—possibly the first such Chinese female servant in America.

Male Chinese servants occasionally accompanied their employers to America. Though Chinese law prohibited Chinese sailors and workers from leaving the country, there were ways to circumvent these restrictions. Bribery of customs officials at the mouth of the Pearl River and boarding vessels in out-of-the-way places enabled them to join foreign ships.[61] Andreas Everardus van Braam Houckgeest was the first American to include a retinue of Chinese attendants on his return trip. Houckgeest, a Dutch American merchant returning from Guangzhou in 1795 after long years in China, made an unusual effort to refashion himself as a Chinese Mandarin on American soil. His infatuation with China extended to his re-creation of a Chinese-style home outside Philadelphia attended by five Chinese male servants.[62] The servants also guided select visitors through his temporary Chinese exhibition installed in Philadelphia. Houckgueest's lifestyle quickly got him into financial trouble, and in debt, he left for London soon after. Presumably his Chinese servants went with him. No record exists of their experiences.

Much later, in 1834, Ayok, the Lows' Chinese manservant, who had attended to the family while in Macao, traveled to America with them. According to Harriet Low, it took little encouragement, for a number of their Chinese servants were willing to make the voyage. Ayok, listed as thirty years old in the 1834 passenger manifest of the *Montreal* arriving in New York, was an appropriate candidate. The Lows knew his father, Afun, who assisted their friend Dr. Thomas Richard Colledge in his work as a surgeon for the East India Company and at the Macao Ophthalmic Hospital.[63] George Chinnery, an English painter in Guangzhou, depicted Colledge and Afun as they worked at the hospital.

On the trip to America, Ayok's solicitude comforted Low when her uncle died while on the return home: "Indeed, I have never met a Chinaman who has manifested such good feeling as he has ever since he has been with us. We have become quite attached to him, he has been so faithful. If he only continues so, we must consider ourselves very fortunate."[64] In London, Ayok attracted attention with his queue and dress: "Poor Ayok excites so much attention that I believe . . . he will be very willing to doff his Chinese costume. Being rainy to-day, he had on his great umbrella hat, and cut a curious figure, to be sure, to those who are not in the habit of seeing them."[65] On their arrival in New York, Low disregarded Ayok's presence. Either she was too absorbed in the return to her homeland, or New Yorkers were less inclined to gawk. Later accounts of Low's life gave no indication of Ayok's experience in America or what became of him.

Four years later, when Forbes set out from Salem to Guangzhou, he was accompanied by two Chinese men: one returning to China after serving the Cushing family in America, and the other a steward. While Forbes was in China, a "Mr. Copley" in New England requested him to send a "chinaman" (likely a servant), but Forbes seemed doubtful of finding an appropriate person.[66]

Though male Chinese servants apparently spent time in America in the late eighteenth and early nineteenth centuries, their presence was considered inconsequential. Once they arrived, they were absorbed into the household, their lives deemed undeserving of mention by those who could keep a record. Possibly they spent several years in the United States and, like Cushing's servant, later returned to China.

Up to this point, however, no female Chinese servants were known to accompany their employers to America. Chinese servants for foreigners in Guangzhou and Macao were principally male, with Chinese wet nurses the exception. Captain Obear's situation was different. Afong Moy required a knowledgeable Chinese woman to care for her bound feet (cleaning and rebinding them) and practical support to assist her in everyday tasks. Augusta Obear's role was that of chaperone, not servant. Perhaps Afong Moy already had an attendant in China who was required to accompany her, or Captain Obear quickly needed to locate one. No mention has been found of this Chinese female servant's name or her fate . in America.

Upon securing his Chinese passengers and receiving appropriate Chinese permissions, Captain Obear negotiated for his return cargo and supplied the vessel with foodstuffs for the voyage. Forbes recounted in detail the sorts of foods they brought on board for his 1840 trip home. They included salt beef, pork, ham, tongue, salmon, preserves, anchovies, navy bread, pilot bread, boat crackers, "china sweet Cakes good," Indian meal, arrow root, rice, sweet potatoes, vermicelli, buffalo humps, sugar candy, tea, coffee, pickles, sweet herbs in bottles, eggs, brandy, gin, and cigars.[67] If one compared this food with the fare the Americans consumed when attending an occasional dinner at the home of a hong merchant, the contrast was quite extreme. There they had rice, duck, shark fin, fried frog, carrots, fish, many fruits in syrup, almonds, watermelon seeds, bird's nest soup, and other dishes not recognizable by the Western guests.[68] Afong Moy may not have enjoyed such a daily fare, but surely she and her female Chinese servant found the food on board the ship strange and unappealing.

Because of prevailing winds, the return trip to America followed a slightly different course than the one taken to China. Forbes's and Low's trips were both at the same time of year as the return of Captain Obear on the *Washington*, and probably all three followed a similar path. Cutting across the South China Sea, passing along the coast of Mindanao, the second largest island in the Philippines, they moved across the Celebes Sea, through the narrow Makassar Strait, into the Java Sea, and on to Anjer. After four or five weeks at sea, New York newspapers noted that the *Washington* stopped at Anjer for supplies. This was Afong Moy's first landfall since her departure from Guangzhou. One might imagine her trepidation on the first part of this voyage as she contended with a strange language, foreign ways, and unusual foods, compounded by the difficulties of navigating on a rolling ship with bound feet.

The vessel then moved across the Indian Ocean, past the small island of Mauritius off the coast of Madagascar and sailed around Africa at the Cape of Good Hope. There, on June 29, they stopped at Mowbray, near Cape Town, South Africa.[69] News of American vessels in the *Baltimore Patriot* noted that here the *Washington* took on wood and water. Harriet Low's ship had also stopped in Cape Town several months before. She remarked: "The town itself looks pretty, and more like civilization than anything I have seen for a long time."[70] The Lows delighted in their first carriage ride in five years and in the numbers of Caucasian women strolling in the streets. All that Low enjoyed in Cape Town as reminders of home would have impressed Afong Moy as strange and foreign.

Another five or six weeks brought them to the island of Saint Helena in the South Atlantic, where they again likely disembarked for supplies. William Carrol, a merchant on St. Helena, advertised the stopover port in the *Canton Register*, informing American ship captains that he could provide all they needed on "shortest order, and on the most moderate terms."[71] There, too, they could get the current European fashions and "drawings of the Tomb." At that time, Napoleon's remains were on St. Helena, not yet having been transferred to Les Invalides in Paris, and many visitors on the island traveled to view his grave. Possibly Augusta and her two female charges made this tourist pilgrimage as well, although the tomb's occupant would have meant little to the Chinese.

The final leg of the trip took the vessel across the Atlantic, up the New Jersey coast, and into the port of New York. The English writer Harriet Martineau arrived in New York City from England for the first time on September 19, 1834, only a month before Afong Moy's arrival. Her account on entering the port gives an indication of what Afong Moy would have seen: "I saw the dim shore; a long line of the New Jersey coast, with distinguishable trees and white houses. . . . We were in sight of a score of ships crossing the bar at Sandy Hook; the last company of porpoises was sporting alongside, and shoals of glittering white fish rippled the water."[72]

Unlike later nineteenth-century immigrants and foreigners, those who arrived in the early nineteenth century received little official attention from the national government. Each locality enforced its own restrictions. However, an outbreak of cholera in 1832 modified New York City's approach to incoming vessels with foreigners aboard. Thereafter, ship captains were responsible for identifying possible carriers of the disease. To ensure a "clean" ship, many foreign passengers were required to enter quarantine on Staten Island. The passengers on Martineau's vessel were detained for three hours waiting for the doctor's clearance in order to enter New York. It is unclear whether Afong Moy and the five other passengers aboard the *Washington* suffered through the quarantine process on Staten Island. If so, it would have been another uncomfortable hurdle for the young Chinese woman.

Martineau said on arriving in New York: "The moment of first landing in a foreign city is commonly spoken of as a perfect realization of forlornness."[73] Even Martineau, who spoke English and had lived a Western life, could feel despair. Afong Moy and the accompanying female servant must have felt similarly as they gazed on this utterly strange city and new world.

PART II

THE SHOW

3

The Curtain Rises

ON NOVEMBER 12, 1834, AFTER a brief description of a recent opera performance, New Yorker Philip Hone set down in his diary his impressions of the Chinese woman, Afong Moy, he had seen exhibited that afternoon in New York City. Afong Moy's American world was, from the very first, framed by a stage. Here, objects, images, clothing, and Afong Moy herself provided the setting for a narrative that others scripted. The composition changed, dependent on manager, viewer, year, and inclination. Yet several aspects rarely varied: she was the exotic, the Oriental, and the "other," whose presence was assessed through the lens of Americans who sought to define themselves in this new republic. Hone's written account of her first staging considered her person; the first pictorial account of her staging addressed the objects that surrounded her.

The visitor, Hone, was a man of refinement, though his discernment came by way of experience rather than formal education. His life began in humble circumstances near the end of the American Revolution. He valued the ideological and moral virtues of republicanism, but unlike the earlier republicans of a purer strain who eschewed luxury, he enjoyed aspects of enterprise that the market revolution afforded. His social circles were extensive. After making large sums of money in New York as a young merchant he was able to retire early, travel to Europe, and serve as the city's mayor, and he now acted as New York's cultural custodian. In

Eng'd by J. Rogers.

Philip Hone

The fifty-four-year-old merchant Philip Hone met Afong Moy with the same serious and discerning visage as seen here, about 1830. *Engraving by J. Rogers. New York Public Library, B13476046-EM11381*

that unofficial capacity, Hone provided social commentary on the events in the city.

The November 12 entry, headlined "Chinese Lady," is longer than many in his diary, taking up slightly more than a full page. He began by explaining where he, his wife, Catherine, and his children met the "Lady," noting: "Capt. Obear has brought out from Canton a young Chinese woman 19 years old whom he is exhibiting at ½ dollar a visitor at his house on Park Place."[1] Hone lived nearby at 235 Broadway, just below the corner of Park Place. Though this location was considered desirable, it was just beginning to experience a change. Business and trade began to encroach, and the commercial activity that Captain Benjamin Obear arranged at his home on Park Place indicated the shift away from a strictly residential area. Eventually responding to the change, Hone sold his house in 1837 and moved uptown to Broadway and Great Jones Street.

The newspapers accounts of the event note nearly the same information that Hone included in his diary: the age of the woman, her place of origin, the cost of admission, and the location of her salon. The newspapers omitted what Hone knew: the residence was that of the Obears. There is no listing for the Obears in the city directories, or in any of the usual documents of the period. Possibly the transitory nature of his profession as a ship captain precluded the permanent listing. More significant is the presumed close association the young Chinese woman, whom we know as Afong Moy, had with the ship captain and his wife Augusta. She was not only on exhibit there but lived there as well.

In 1834, Afong Moy lived with the Obears in the fourth house from the far-right corner on Park Place in New York City. It was situated very near city hall and its associated park. After the home was demolished in 1913, the Woolworth Building was erected in its place. Park Place, New-York, *1831, engraving by George Hayward. Collection of the New-York Historical Society*

In his diary, Hone continued his evaluation of the visit: "Her appearance is exactly the same as the figures on tea chests a large Head, small features and a countenance devoid of expression."[2] The association of Afong Moy's visage with a flat and static image on a tea chest is unsurprising. Most Americans envisioned the Chinese from the only illustrations they knew: those found on tea chests, china ware, fans, lacquer, or wallpaper.[3] Hone brought that conceived image with him to Park Place, and Afong Moy mirrored it. Retaining these idealized views of the Chinese based on trade objects hampered Americans' engagement with the actual person. Hone probably found her countenance "devoid of expression" because no interaction between them had occurred.

The most extensive remarks in Hone's diary account focus on Afong Moy's feet: "her foot is a great curiosity it is not four inches in length."[4] Hone repeated nearly verbatim the same prate regarding her feet as that found in the New York papers. He explained the process of cramping the foot and then confining it in an iron shoe. Many contemporary American newspaper articles reported, inaccurately, that the Chinese woman's bound foot was encased in an iron shoe. In November 1834 the *New-York Commercial Advertiser* remarked: "There is something painful in the reminiscence of the tortures she [Afong Moy] must have endured in infancy, by the iron shoes, worn for ten years from her birth, by which this unusual deformity was acquired."[5] Hone, knowing no more than what was provided in the press, assumed this was true.

The fabricated story of the iron shoes possibly originated with missionary accounts. Not knowing the process of foot binding, missionaries may have developed this story as a way of eliciting sympathy for the Chinese, encouraging donations to the cause that would improve and uplift them, and bring them to Christianity. Even Elizabeth Cady Stanton in an 1895 speech referred to the "perversion of the religious element in woman that has held her for ages the patient victim . . . on the funeral pyre, in iron shoes, in the Turkish harem."[6] As late as 1935 an Ohio *Community Church News* article mentioned that "women in China were compelled to wear iron shoes."[7]

In his diary entry Hone associates Afong Moy's cramped feet with a cramped mind: "This confinement occasions an unnatural expansion of the whole and the poor little animal is deformed and decrepid [*sic*] in person as from her want of Education. She is deficient in Ideas."[8] Hone again presents the argument that the newspapers offered: that the condition of bound feet equated to a woman "trained up without any kind of education, literary or religious; and even unable to read or write in her own language. She is but a single representation of the millions of her sex who are thus tortured and deformed in their bodies while their minds are kept in a state of ignorance and vassalage to the lords of the other sex."[9] The "state of ignorance" of particular concern was that of Christian ignorance. Several articles expressed the hope that the "blessings of the gospel into China" would dispel this degrading custom and promote the education of women.[10]

Americans had just begun their religious work in China with the departure in 1830 of two missionaries to Guangzhou, Rev. Elijah C. Bridgman and Rev. David Abeel. However, many Americans knew the earlier missionary work of Rev. Robert Morrison, an Englishman, who in 1807 spent a month in America before departing for China. Because the British East India Company's policy forbade missionary support, Morrison sought, and won, protection from the American consul in Guangzhou. There he translated the Bible into Chinese, compiled a dictionary of the Chinese language, and then he founded the Anglo-Chinese College in Malacca. American newspapers frequently addressed and praised his missionary work in China, calling him the "great and good Morrison."[11] It was his effort that the newspapers referenced as contributing to the elevation of Chinese thought, and it was this missionary work that would "uncramp" the minds of women such as Afong Moy.

Hone also wrote about the general dress and ornamentation of Chinese women, likely reacting to what he had just seen at Afong Moy's salon: "their only occupation a little occasional Embroidery. Their only pride in the tinsel ornamenting of their persons."[12] One might assume that Hone spent little time investigating the lives of Chinese women, and therefore his evaluation likely came from general information in the press. The *New-Hampshire Gazette* (repeating reports from other press sources) reported that "Miss Afong Moy had not yet completed her toilette [when they visited] which we understand consumes about four hours (think of that, ye fashionable dames of Gotham!)"[13] Completing the article, the press declared that "She passes her life at her toilette or at her tambour; sleeps much, and eats as we do."[14] And Hone's diary concludes: "They [Chinese women] sit or lie day and night and perhaps hobble from one side of their prison to another and the most important object of life, indulgence in eating, drinking and sleeping. It may well be said that the most arresting [*sic*] evidence of a nation's prosperity is the improvement of the condition of the female sex."[15]

Hone's uniformed assumptions about another culture appear chauvinistic and severe, but his comments are predictable and typical in the context of the period. Reflecting the moralistic republican outlook, Hone found her idleness—if one might consider regularly meeting the public eight hours a day in Captain Obear's salon indolent—an expression of licentiousness.[16] The intonation of Thomas Jefferson's admonition ("Determine never to be idle. Of all the cankers of human happiness, none corrodes it with so silent, yet so baneful a tooth, as indolence") might be heard in the background refrain.[17] In his diary, Hone provided a personal, and presumably private, narrative on his family's New York City encounter with the Chinese lady. On November 18, several days after Hone's meeting with Afong Moy, the press went to visit her. They remarked that she stood smiling at the company and then walked to a cushioned chair which was situated on a platform. She remained there for some time while an interpreter provided comments. On their return trip on November 22, Afong Moy seemed more animated and engaged.

> This time she gave us, from her cushioned throne, a gracious nod, *a la mandarin*, and a smile and a speech in Chinese, *four words in length*, to all of which we made due homage. . . . At the same moment . . . she thrust forward her pretty little foot. . . . This scene drew, as might have been expected, all the company in the room to the place where we were standing in front of the balustrade, expecting no doubt to see us fall prostrate and bump our heads three times on the floor; . . . While her private secretary receives the guests, [Miss Moy sic] sits gracefully, with all becoming dignity upon the fauteuil assigned to her.[18]

On the second visit the press got the message that Francis and Nathaniel Carnes and Obear intended to convey—Afong Moy was royalty. They found her seated on a "throne" separated from her audience by a balustrade. Though likely in jest, the reporters recognized an expectation of obeisance in the form of kowtowing performed in front of Chinese emperors.

In early 1835, slightly more than a month after Hone's diary account and the press report, lithographers Charles Risso and William Browne offered the larger public, those who might not have an opportunity to view her, a visual commentary, a stage setting, for Afong Moy. The lithograph presents a diminutive Afong Moy in a salon environment, presumably that of Captain Obear on Park Place. Chinese goods are scattered about the room, several types of which the Carneses' business imported. It was a comprehensive picture of commercial orientalism.

Visitors viewed Afong Moy in the salon of the Obears' Park Place home. The "oriental" environment conveyed the exotic nature of the goods and the person. *Afong Moy, the Chinese Lady, 1835, lithograph, Charles Risso and William R. Browne, Print Collection, Miriam and Ira D. Wallach Division of Art, Prints and Photographs, The New York Public Library, Astor, Lenox, and Tilden Foundation*

Dwarfed by the objects, only the elaborate curtained canopy situated above her and her central position on the dais highlight her presence. It is likely that the Carnes firm or Captain Obear commissioned the lithograph to promote their goods, placing Afong Moy among them. The service of this "low" art was to advertise the goods, and to depict and popularize the exotic "Chinese Lady." Not long after its completion, a version of this image circulated in newspapers throughout the country. Through this, and one other illustration, the American public came to know Afong Moy and the objects and attire associated with her.

The view of Afong Moy's salon provided by Risso and Browne may have omissions and distortions, yet it offers the only detailed visual depiction of Afong Moy, her dress, and the goods surrounding her. The newspapers speculated that her costume "is that of ladies of her rank," or "the rich costume of a Chinese lady."[19] However, Afong Moy wore the typical dress of an unmarried Chinese woman: a knee-length upper garment or tunic [*ao*] over trousers [*ku*].[20] As with all such Chinese women's clothing, the neck was high, the sleeves long, and the fit loose. By the 1830s the Chinese woman's sleeves had become wider than previously and her tunic was cut much larger, extending to the calf. Even in the 1820s the physician John Kearsley Mitchell wrote to his fiancée Matilda from China that the "sleeve of their outer robe is wide enough to make a gown for you."[21] Ample amounts of fabric indicated wealth and dignity, for silk of this quantity took much time to produce.[22] Though the lithographers represented the fullness of Afong Moy's garments, they erred in their representation of the tunic, for in China the curved front overlap always fastened on the right side; it is reversed in their image. The detail meant little to the illustrators, but it would have been glaringly apparent to the Chinese.

Because Chinese female dress was so different from their own, American travelers in China made many comments about it. Several described the dress of Chinese boat women or female servants they encountered in Macao. Rebecca Kinsman recorded the clothing of her child's Chinese nurse in some detail: a "dress of dark blue cotton edged with black, with an undergarment of white cotton, the sleeves of which show below the blue ones at the elbow—black cotton trousers & embroidered sandals. The sleeves of these Chinese women's dresses are very handsome."[23] Afong Moy's sleeves had similar detailing.

American newspaper accounts gave a vivid and colorful account of Afong Moy's attire: "an outward mantle of blue silk, sumptuously embroidered, and yellow silk pantalettes from beneath the ample folds of which peeped her tiny little feet."[24] Color had symbolic meaning to the Chinese. The choice signified elements of the earth, a state of being, as well as rank and social position. Therefore, Afong Moy's color selections may not have been as random as her visitors supposed. The Chinese lady's bold employment of the color yellow—even for her "pantalettes"—indicated an assumption of high rank.[25] As Charles Toogood Downing, wrote in 1836: "Yellow habiliments are distinctly prohibited, as this colour is expressly reserved for the members of the Imperial family; and even the mandarins and others in the employ of the government have each their dresses assigned to them according to their dignity."[26] The Qing dynasty (1644–1912) published the rules regarding the use of color for both clothing and utensils in 1652 as a method of control and proper governance. Colors worn by the emperor varied depending on the particular ceremony, but yellow designated the Qing dynasty and was available only to the emperor.[27] Even a foreigner's export of yellow silk was prohibited, and in the 1760s an English ship was inspected and fined for its noncompliance in this regard.[28] Since Afong Moy's sponsors cast her as royalty by placing her on a dais above the visitors and treating the event as an audience with a head of state—and the newspapers likened her to Napoleon's Empress Maria Louise—she had cause to dress imperially with rich colors and ample embroidery on the borders of her sleeves and the hem of her tunic.[29]

Afong Moy's hairstyle also aroused comment. Fashionable American women's styles of the early 1830s emphasized abundant hair with elaborate ringlets of curls and looped and knotted braids. Afong Moy's coif, by contrast, was severe: "jet black hair, combed upward from her fine forehead and brunette temples," into a tight bun at the top of her head.[30] In China, hair, and the dressing of it, signified important life-course markers for Chinese women. As a young girl, her hair was "tied up" in tufts; at puberty it was gathered up in a knot held with a pin at a special hair-pinning ceremony; and at marriage the hairs on her forehead were removed to "open the face."[31] Because she was an unmarried woman, Afong Moy's hair was dressed in the second phase, pinned in a knot at the top of her head.

Osmond Tiffany, a Baltimore merchant who visited Guangzhou in the 1840s, had an opportunity to meet affluent Chinese women in a hong merchant's household. He recorded that "their heads were uncovered and their style of coiffure is singular . . . and becoming. The front hair of unmarried females is combed straight back. . . . When married or shortly before, the whole hair is combed up, and a false piece set on the back of the head fastened by clasps and pins of gold. . . . A beautiful ornament is sometimes worn by rich women, representing a bird with extended wings."[32] The women of the imperial court and Chinese women of wealth wore hair jewelry made of kingfisher feathers inlaid in precious metals—perhaps this relates to Tiffany's "bird with extended wings." The turquoise-colored feathers of the birds were held in high esteem.[33] Afong Moy, however, had a limit to her aspirational reach. These ornaments were beyond her, or her sponsors', financial capacity. Her hair ornaments were "large gold pins."[34] Rebecca Kinsman euphemistically described her Chinese nurse's hairpins as "two silver bodkins, which stick out like horns in front of the hair."[35] Afong Moy's style was probably similar.

Risso and Browne's lithograph is unlike their other work of the same period. The setting of "Afong Moy the Chinese Lady" was delineated in much detail, with a clutter of objects set at disjunctive and odd perspectives in a room with a highly patterned carpet. This is in contrast to their typical work portraying intimate and sentimental views of fashionable, but unnamed, women in various poses with little background detail. The artists' rendering is valuable because contemporary accounts give few details of the salon's layout. In the Afong Moy lithograph, the artists used a wide lens, moving the viewer through the space as though in attendance at the New York salon. The viewer proceeds up the platform to face what one newspaper described as a "porcelain vase(s) filled with exquisitely beautiful flowers."[36]

Osmond Tiffany commented on such porcelain while in Guangzhou, where he visited various shops, evaluating and commenting on the wares. In Cumchong's porcelain shop he rated the china vases by size, price, and quality. The smallest, at two feet high, cost $16 to $20; the second largest, at three and a half feet, $50; and the five-foot, $250. He averred that the "vast numbers of vases #1 [the smallest] come to America and are of ordinary workmanship."[37] Given the foreground perspective (and a comparison to the dimension of the chair on the same level) this is the size and type defined as vase #1. The shape and pattern, possibly rose medallion, are typical of the cheaper Chinese export wares of this period, which the Carneses likely imported in large enough quantities to receive a discounted price much below Tiffany's estimates.[38]

On the same level the artists depicted a bamboo chair. Though intricate in design, and therefore appearing costly, it was exceedingly cheap in China. Above, on the dais, Afong Moy sat among a warehouse of furniture forms: a dressing mirror on a pier table, a lacquer tea chest or workbox, a small octagonal occasional table, a center table, and a settee. The small octagon table and the settee are almost identical to the ones in a Guangzhou bamboo furniture shop seen in an 1830 watercolor.[39] Nearly all of these relatively inexpensive furniture items had earlier crammed the holds of the Carneses' vessels.

The artists heightened the picture's drama with wall settings that surrounded and encompassed Afong Moy. Close to the ceiling, an elaborately festooned curtain and bulbous, orientalized winged pediment held the center of the composition while the swagged draperies partitioned the stage's space. The extensive use of fabrics in the parlor may seem excessive, but this swathing became typical for such a space, providing a cocooned sense of gentility.

Afong Moy was flanked by large images of Chinese figures that emphasized the two sides of the stage. The standing woman on the panel to the right mirrored Afong Moy in costume and hairstyle. The male figure on the left held a scroll. The Carnes firm, which the staging benefited, imported large quantities of pith paper (paper made of wood bark) watercolors. Many were small images bound into books or sold individually, but others could have been the larger views on rolled paper scrolls seen in the print. Tiffany stated that merchants could order sets that included views of chief mandarins and court ladies "in the most magnificent attire," for eight dollars.[40] The implication was clear: Afong Moy sat in the company of the Chinese elite.

At the rear of the set, above another vase, hung a large lantern. Both Downing and Tiffany commented extensively on the use and look of the Chinese lantern. Downing wrote, "The Chinaman and his lantern seem wedded together, and you will hardly find one without the other, even among the most miserable of natives. They are placed in the streets, in the temples, in the boats, and are always found in the hands of the pedestrians who are out after dark."[41] He described their bright colors, the range of their designs, and the way they folded conveniently: "the smaller kinds are of the form of a lengthened drum, and shut up by pressing the top and bottom together."[42] Tiffany noted the variety of materials—oiled paper, silk, glass, or horn—and their cost—the least expensive one or two dollars and the most magnificent, hundreds of dollars. He particularly elaborated on the glass lanterns that seem to be the type on this stage and one of the sorts the Carneses imported. Tiffany expressed surprise that more of these had not been introduced to America as hall lamps, but he may not have realized that the Carneses were actively addressing this void with their imports. He described them as "square or hexagonal, the glass plain or painted, set into rich rosewood frames. At each angle are placed crimson silk tassels, fringe of high quality."[43] Surely of appeal to the Carnes firm was the convenience of shipping, for as Tiffany remarked, the lanterns were purchased disassembled, with every component clearly marked and easy to assemble.[44]

The message of the staging was apparent. By situating Afong Moy as an elite woman with objects familiar to her life, visitors were encouraged to envision a similar experience for themselves. Those who viewed the display could purchase useful and attractive items comparable to those that, supposedly, the wealthiest people in China enjoyed. In the salon, the Obears presented objects for the merchants' pecuniary purpose, but the objects also served the public as a cultural bridge, which Afong Moy and her interpreter explicated.

Despite the multiplicity of these exotic, as well as practical, objects and the grandeur of Afong Moy's setting, the stage presented in the lithograph was static. It was set for something to happen. The light from the window shining across the tablecloth, and the gleam from the lantern, would soon illumine a show. Though unlike any theatrical presentation in China, the event contained some elements of Chinese dramaturgical form and construction.

Foreigners in early nineteenth-century Guangzhou commented on open-air Chinese stage productions and theatrical exhibitions that took place in areas to which they had access or to which they were invited. The American trader Nathan Dunn described a theatrical production during a banquet at the home of hong merchant Chinqua in 1824.

> The party met at 4 o'clock in the afternoon in a portico in front of his dwelling . . . a stage was erected for theatrical exhibitions. . . . As the evening advanced the play became more interesting. There were two exhibitions between the scenes. The first representing the principal flowers of spring and the second the fruits of the different seasons. The rich dresses of the actors and the decoration of the stage could not I think be excelled in any country . . . the amusements of the evening ended with about 200 lads of approximately 10-14 years performing feats of tumbling.[45]

Chinese open-air presentations were a bit more baffling to foreigners. Generally, these took place with no scenery. The all-male cast spoke in loud and piercing tones and gestured wildly to the accompaniment of gongs and drums. It was not surprising that foreigners were unimpressed with these productions. One complained that "a striking peculiarity in the Chinese plays is the repeated introduction of singing into the most serious and affecting scenes."[46] According to the author, in the middle of an intense dialogue the actors would begin to sing as an expression of emotion. Another viewer remarked on the exceptional costuming of the actors in silk robes.[47] What they saw was an element of Kunqu which, by the early nineteenth century, had been a Chinese theater form for more than two hundred years. It was widely performed across China by professional male actors who developed a strong rapport with their audiences, both commoners and elite. Dressed in elaborate costumes, but without props, these artists created the scenes and the dramatic action with gestures, words, songs, and accompanying instrumental music. Several decades later the Kunqu form would evolve into Jingxi, or the Beijing Opera, which is more familiar today.

Kunqu was the only form of stage performance Afong Moy would have known about. However, it is possible that she had never seen it. Rarely did women attend such performances in China, and never did they perform in them. But accompanying Afong Moy on stage was someone who surely had familiarity with this dramatic tradition. After her initial introduction in New York, another Chinese person joined the staged production. Atung, also known as Acung, soon made appearances with Afong Moy as her translator, emcee, and personal assistant. The newspapers effused about the courtesies of "that very interesting and polished youth, A'tung, whose handsome face, graceful manners, and Chinese dress, and well-spoken English, are of themselves a principal attraction. In fact, A'tung moves about . . . with all the grace of a gentleman and is at the same time an excellent cicerone to explain the different curiosities. His hair is shaven in front, and behind ends in a long plaited queue of jet black color, and his animated and elegant features and voice are quite fascinating."[48] Though there is evidence that Afong Moy sang and spoke on stage in the latter days of her tour, it was Atung, in the male tradition of the Kunqu, who carried the stage action here.

With no visual representation of his person, and few accounts of his activities on the salon stage, we can only imagine his role. In English, he probably provided information about Afong Moy's life in China, discussed her bound feet as she moved across the dais, described the costume she wore, and gave an account of the objects on stage. Reporters observed that in the salon he wrote in Chinese characters and later personally connected with the audience by offering to inscribe their names in Chinese characters on "porcelain cards" for twelve and a half cents. This may have given him an opportunity to present a brief history of China and the Chinese people. We have no evidence that he sang or gave a dramatic presentation in the Kunqu style, and there were no gongs or drums to accompany him, as in the traditional Kunqu, but his familiarity with the form may have influenced his actions, his gestures, and the way he presented himself on stage.

There is no record of Atung's arrival in New York and no ship manifest has been found containing his name. The *Washington Globe* averred that he "was a youth of 17 lately arrived from Canton."[49] However, Atung's facility with the English language and his capacity to write in Chinese may offer a partial explanation. Atung's language skills placed him in a very small minority. In early nineteenth-century China the study of the English language was forbidden, as was the teaching of the Chinese language to foreigners. Pidgin English, the patois that facilitated trade across the Pacific Basin, was not what Atung spoke on the salon stage. Few Americans would have understood this tongue, and the newspaper accounts of his language facility belie this as well. Though Atung calligraphed only individual names in Chinese, he had, at least, this proficiency. Few Chinese males of commoner status in the early nineteenth century had such literacy skills.[50] Atung's presence in New York likely resulted from one of two situations: he was either a knowledgeable China trader's servant who decided to remain in America, or a missionary protégé of some stature. Either position would have given him the opportunity to learn English and perhaps to possess a fairly sophisticated knowledge of Chinese writing.

China traders often returned to America with their Chinese male servants who had assisted them in the factories in Guangzhou. Chutang Ahoo, a clerk for China trader John Cushing, came to America with him in the 1830s.[51] He may have been a servant in the United States, but when he returned to China in 1835 he participated in the American trade as a merchant. In 1846, the American Rebecca Kinsman welcomed him into her home in China: "Several Chinese gentlemen called today. Among others Ahoe, formerly Mr. Cushing's servant, who went twice with him to America, but now a tea merchant. He speaks perfectly good English and is a fine looking Man—He was splendidly dressed in Mandarin Satin."[52] The Kinsman family themselves had a Malay (perhaps a Chinese Malay) servant named John Alley who lived with them in both China and America for sixty-seven years. Alley attended school, had his own bank account, and even owned railroad stock.[53] It is likely that he too spoke English fluently. Therefore, an American merchant trader may have permitted his young servant to serve as Afong Moy's translator and emcee.

Very possibly America's Second Great Awakening provided Atung his language fluency. By 1800 religious self-determinism began to sweep through the United States. Revivalists condemned Calvinist predestination and proclaimed that anyone could be saved, or "reawakened." They preached of a benevolent God whom one could know and celebrate through self-disciplined industry and personal improvement. Several young, college-educated American evangelicals yearned to spread this gospel of salvation to "Heathen" nations. In 1810 these young men convinced their elders to establish a missionary society to extend Christianity and the gospel of Jesus Christ to American Indians and people in foreign lands. The American

Board of Commissioners for Foreign Missions was formed in Massachusetts under the Congregationalist faith but later became interdenominational.[54]

In 1812, just as the United States declared war on England, five American missionaries set sail for India supported by the American board. Four years later the board of commissioners embarked on an equally ambitious undertaking. With hopes of spreading the gospel to other nations by educating "heathen" young men, they established the Foreign Mission School at Cornwall, Connecticut. In 1818 twenty-four students from China, Malaysia, Bengal, India, Hawai'i, and the Marquesas Islands, as well as those from the Cherokee, Choctaw, and Abenaki tribes, converged on this remote, small New England village. There they learned English and studied astronomy, calculus, surveying, geography, navigating, theology, and the useful arts of coopering and blacksmithing. The school managed to survive for nearly ten years, educating more than one hundred students, but dissolved when Mission School students began intermarrying with local Cornwall girls. Racist attitudes then emerged within the Cornwall community, and the school was forced to disband.[55]

The histories of two Chinese students who attended the Mission School are recorded, though it is thought that at least five Chinese males were enrolled. Wu Lan (known in the United States as Henry Martyn Alan) left behind his Chinese Friendship Album full of his engaging watercolors, including views of Chinese flowers, fruits, vegetation, and Chinese goldfish, as well as labeled drawings noting "These Chinese Lady," a "Chinese King" (wearing a yellow robe), and a self-portrait.[56] It is unclear how long Wu Lan remained in the United States, but it is likely that he returned to China to work with Western merchants. American missionaries asserted in 1834 that they met a young Chinese man named Henry Martyn Alan who had studied at the Foreign Mission School in Cornwall, now teaching English to Chinese servants. John Joseph Loy also returned to China, though no documentation exists of his later occupation. Possibly Atung, too, was one of those unrecorded Chinese Cornwall Foreign Mission School students who remained after the school closed and whose languages skills and abilities would have been remarkable to an American audience.[57]

The Chinese could acquire English-language skills in only two other ways: through the work of the missionaries sent to China by the same board that established the Foreign Mission School in Cornwall, or by the London Missionary Society. The society supported the work of missionary Robert Morrison, on whose foundation all subsequent missionaries built. In 1818 he established the school for Chinese and Malay students in Malacca since

this was not permissible in Guangzhou.[58] Here, with a sizable population of Chinese, Morrison could bring both the scriptures and knowledge of English to an otherwise inaccessible populace.[59] Morrison also established a much smaller mission school in Macao where several Chinese students learned English.

In 1830, two separate missionary societies sent Bridgman and Abeel to China as the first American missionaries. Bridgman learned Chinese from Morrison, taught some Chinese students on the island of Macao, and founded the *Chinese Repository*. Another American missionary, Rev. Samuel Robbins Brown, came to Macao in 1838, four years after Atung's presence

唐朝天子李世民

Chinese .... King

In his album, Wu Lan provided his interpretations of a Chinese king and a Chinese lady. The woman's layered robes resembled female court dress rather than everyday wear. This explains Wu's omission of the traditional female trousers which, if included, might have provoked discussion in the Cornwall, Connecticut community. *Chinese Friendship Album, Foreign Mission School Collection, MS 038, box 8, Folder 16, Cornwall Historical Society*

in New York, to run the Morrison Education Society, the first Protestant school established in China. Though we have no record of Atung's attendance at Morrison, Bridgman, or Brown's schools, we do have record of what a twelve-year-old Chinese boy, Achik, experienced attending Brown's school in 1840. His letter to Dr. William Lockhart, an English medical missionary, stated: "I am very glad to live in Mr. Brown's house and learn the English language and other things such as Geography and Arithmetic. The Englishman and American have very good heart to come to China teache Chinese boys and teache them to learn about God and to be wise men. . . .

I have lived in Mr. Brown's house a whole year and learned about God. Mr. Brown give me food to eat, and teaches me to read the Bible . . . and teaches me to pray to God and sing."[60]

The Second Great Awakening's primary purpose of extending the gospel to all mankind had the secondary consequence of foreign-language instruction that would put distant cultures into contact. Neither the Carneses nor the Obears had a particular interest in spreading the gospel. They wished to sell goods. However, the stage on which Afong Moy and Atung operated, and the audience they engaged, did consider the broader issues of cultural difference. As with Hone's diary account and newspaper reports of Afong Moy and Atung's presence on the stage, the audience brought to the encounter their imperatives and religious constructs. But the merchants were not interested in saving souls. It was the goods that mattered to the impresarios, and it was the goods that needed to be sold.

4

Afong Moy Presents Chinese Objects
for Personal Use

IN THEATRICAL PARLANCE, PROPS REFER to objects used by an actor on stage to develop a narrative or storyline. A "prop" must to be essential to the story and meaningful to the development of the plot, not merely a set decoration. The term originated in the Renaissance when actors supplied their own costumes, but other devices needed on stage to relay the message were company property, simplified to the word "prop." Most props are ordinary objects that are expendable, easily replaced by a substitute.

The objects on Afong Moy's first stage qualified as props. As company property, likely owned by Francis and Nathaniel Carnes, these Chinese objects of little monetary value provided the meaningful tableau Afong Moy and Atung presented to the public. With Atung's explanations, Afong Moy's demonstrations, and translated commentaries and asides, the objects relayed a life in China and provided a direct connection and appeal to the audience. The goods, manifesting a commercial orientalism, served as a bridge to an unfamiliar culture. They effectively functioned as extensions of Afong Moy's exotic persona. These were everyday objects that the visitor could later purchase and own—perhaps associating with them the cultural messages Afong Moy and Atung had earlier imparted. Yet taking these props from Afong Moy's stage to a willing consumer required some engineering. Without that capacity, the staging was a futile effort for the American merchants who brought her to the United States.

Business transactions moved the goods from the Carneses' vessels to the retail market, providing accessibility to the everyday buyer. Unlike most eighteenth- and earlier nineteenth-century merchants, the Carneses were specialized commission merchants—wholesale marketers—rather than general, all-purpose businessmen as their fathers had been. They concentrated their interests in the high-volume trade of imported dry goods, notions, and sundries. This specialization was more efficient, but it also left them more susceptible to swings in the market.

Alongside the transformation of the merchant's position, the market revolution brought other business changes to New York.[1] With the Erie Canal completed in 1825, New Yorkers quickly secured another advantage through the modification of their auction laws. By 1825 the state legislature passed a new bill reducing the state duties on imported articles—East India goods paid a low 1 percent.[2] The law also required that duties on all goods be paid by the auctioneer. Because this policy, as well as others advantageous to merchants, was not in effect in Boston or Philadelphia, importers and buyers of goods gravitated to New York, where their business was encouraged and goods sold swiftly. In the 1820s, auctioneers sold 44 percent of New York City imports. Though that percentage slipped to 21 percent in the 1830s as a result of widely fluctuating prices at auction, the import market was safeguarded for New York.[3] The Carneses' China trade business could have existed only in a market such as the New York port provided in the 1830s. The Erie Canal gave them access to a middle-class clientele, and the auction houses served as their principal means of distribution.

Newspaper advertisements indicate that the Carneses principally used the Mills, Brothers & Co. auction house located at the corner of Wall and Pearl Streets. According to the loquacious Walter Barrett, who provided contemporary information on nineteenth-century New York merchants, Mills, Brothers & Co. consisted of three partners: Philo L. Mills, his brother Levi, and Thomas M. Hooker.[4] The auction house sold its goods to local merchants or to jobbers who bought in large quantities to sell to other, perhaps nonlocal, businesses. In early June 1832 Mills, Brothers & Co. issued a five-page catalogue of the goods from the Carneses' first ship, the *Howard*, to sell at auction. The printer, Snowden, at 58 Wall Street, gave the piece some flair with an attractively bordered cover and a variety of typefaces.

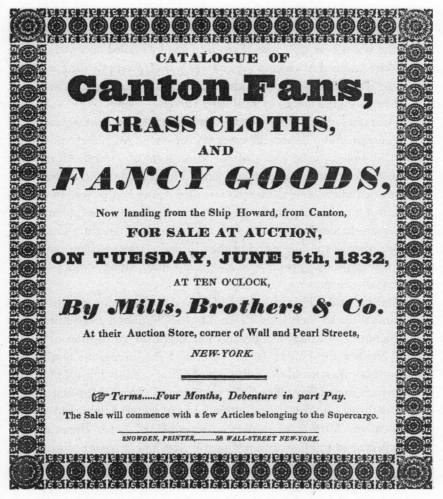

CATALOGUE OF

Canton Fans,

GRASS CLOTHS,

AND

FANCY GOODS,

Now landing from the Ship Howard, from Canton,

FOR SALE AT AUCTION,

ON TUESDAY, JUNE 5th, 1832,

AT TEN O'CLOCK,

By Mills, Brothers & Co.

At their Auction Store, corner of Wall and Pearl Streets,

NEW-YORK.

☞ *Terms.....Four Months, Debenture in part Pay.*

The Sale will commence with a few Articles belonging to the Supercargo.

SNOWDEN, PRINTER,..........58 WALL-STREET NEW-YORK.

Using hierarchical typefaces on the catalogue cover, the auctioneers indicate which Chinese goods would be principal at the June 5, 1832, sale: fans of all types, listed on the pages within, numbered in the thousands. *Mills, Brothers & Co. Catalogue reprinted from the original for the Child's Gallery, Inc., Boston, Massachusetts, 1968*

The terms were clear and stated on the front: "Terms . . . Four Months, Debenture in part Pay," indicating that the buyer put down some cash along with a fixed four-month loan.[5] One New York merchant who purchased goods from the *Howard* auction, William Pike, reneged on the $521.63

promissory note he provided to the auction house. According to court proceedings Pike took delivery of the Chinese goods on that day in June, but when the notes were called in, Pike's business had failed and many of his goods were assigned to another merchant. He then promptly died in July of that year.[6] The Mills Brothers lost the case, and the Chinese goods were long gone, likely into the homes of local New Yorkers.

The Carneses' 1834 *Washington* cargo provides a look at the Chinese goods sold at auction and indicates the types of clients who might have purchased them. The objects were many of the same sorts of "props" Afong Moy presented at her salon. The clients, such as Philip Hone, with his wife and adolescent children, were those who attended Afong Moy's New York salon in the fall of 1834. Though the Hone family (Philip Sr., his wife Catharine, his sixteen-year-old son Philip Jr., and his fifteen-year-old daughter Catharine) was positioned at the upper end of the Carneses' targeted client range, the Hones were typical of people who had experienced Afong Moy's salon and saw the Carneses' goods.

Catharine and Philip Jr. typified the young clients to whom the merchants directed their sales appeal. During childhood and adolescence, this generation of Americans began to embrace the cultivation of refinement.[7] Neither the Hones' father, born into an immigrant family, nor their mother experienced the full effect of parlor- and sitting-room behavior in which their offspring so fully participated. Afong Moy and Atung, too, were thrust into this curious moment of America's heightened interest in refinement. All four of these young people, of nearly the same age, were expected to fulfill aspects of the etiquette and behavior of gentility's credos: card giving and receiving, letter writing, conversation, and pleasing parlor behavior. The objects that the Carneses imported, that Afong Moy hawked, and all hoped that the Hone siblings would buy—card cases, parlor games, fans, paper folders, handkerchiefs, and shawls—assisted in this operation of gentility. Their parents and older adults provided the opportunities, the settings, and the props. Entrepreneurs like the Carneses responded to society's demands and ingeniously offered these objects at affordable prices.

In 1834 Philip S. Hone Jr. and his sister Catharine, the youngest of the six Hone siblings, still lived with their parents, and were most likely the "children" Hone mentions in his diary who visited Afong Moy's salon in Captain Obear's home on Park Place. We know little of Philip Jr.'s aptitude or interests, though he later attended Columbia University; there is no record of Catharine's education. Their father's inclinations possibly encouraged his son and daughter to investigate other cultures and explore new ideas.

Parental attitudes toward childrearing differed from the generation who had raised their children prior to the American Revolution. There was an increasing emphasis on a nurturing environment with opportunities for education and a recognition that children could profit from entertaining activities in the home.[8] A general rise in middle- and upper-middle-class incomes coupled with a greater amount of leisure time encouraged a proliferation of new consumer goods for a younger age group. Toys and games flooded the marketplace. The Hone children surely benefited from this new view of child-rearing and a rise in consumer spending on the young.

Afong Moy experienced a very different upbringing in Guangzhou. As a young child, she likely had a certain amount of freedom, but by early adolescence with bound feet, her life changed. As the daughter of a comprador (one who acted as a foreigner's middleman) or a shop merchant, she was confined to the home or immediate vicinity of her village. Young Chinese women were not educated outside the home, and most received little education, other than domestic instruction, inside the home. The concepts of a nurturing household environment with specialized games or goods, or activities to encourage wider thought, were not part of a typical life for young Chinese women.

The Carneses imported a range of items that might have appealed to Philip Jr. and Catharine, such as the intricate Chinese games and puzzles that challenged the mind. Though one of the Carnes-affiliated vessel manifests lists "toys," this heading encompassed a wide range of games. There were many different types of these Chinese skill-oriented strategy "toys" available for the Western market. The puzzle most often noted was the "puzzling angle" or tangram made up of a square, a rhombus, and five isosceles right triangles of wood, ivory, or mother-of-pearl that fit together in a flat box. Conceived by the Chinese in the late eighteenth century, later than most Chinese puzzles, it became a global fad after the Chinese sage Sang-hsia-k'o provided a book of tangram puzzles along with their solutions in 1813.[9] Such puzzles were particularly popular in the foreign quarters of Guangzhou, and American merchants who played the game in China returned home with it. In 1817, American publisher A. T. Goodrich took Sang-hsia-k'o's tangram problems and solutions and repackaged them in the book *The New and Fashionable Chinese Puzzle*.[10]

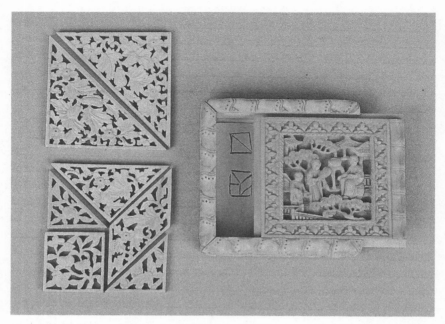

An ivory tangram puzzle (*c.* 1840) offered a surface to display decorative Chinese carving and provided intellectual stimulation. *Photograph by Michele L. Hopkins. National Museum of Natural History, Department of Anthropology, Smithsonian Institution, E380635, gift of Cornelia and Alfred Pell*

The publication explained how the player could arrange and rearrange the shapes to form specific outlines.

The Chinese considered the ring puzzle, with its circular metal, ivory, or bone pieces sliding along a center rod, their greatest puzzle. Its origin dates back seven thousand years, but by 1821 Zhu Xiang Zhuren, writer of the Chinese activity books *Bits of Wisdom*, had provided a chart that enumerated the puzzle's secrets.[11] Baltimorean Osmond Tiffany, who often recounted stories related to Chinese goods on his Guangzhou jaunts, noted its popularity in America in the 1840s: "[It is] in extensive use in the United States; it consists of a number of rings, which are attached to each other by wires, and slip on and off the other part of the puzzle by an ingenious though at first sight an apparently impossible method."[12] The Carneses and fellow merchants counted on its popularity, for in one 1835 shipment they brought in eight hundred rings and assorted ivory whistles.[13]

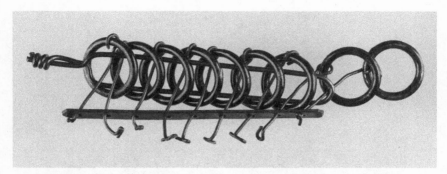

This Chinese rings puzzle (*c.* 1880) challenged players to remove all nine rings from the handle. The process took 341 moves. *National Museum of American History, Smithsonian Institution, Division of Medicine and Science, 2015.0027.01, gift of Hermitage of St. Joseph*

Concentric puzzle balls of perforated ivory, one ball within another, were marvels of Chinese craftsmanship which were designed as much to contemplate for their intricacy as for play. Tiffany noted that he found one with seventeen balls, one encircling the other, with each of its seventeen surfaces wholly carved.[14] Several American travelers remarked that these works were completed by young boys who had the small fingers and the dexterity necessary to complete such a laborious craft. In the mid-nineteenth century, American sinologist Samuel Wells Williams demystified the process:

A piece of ivory or wood is first made perfectly globular, and then several conical holes are bored into it in such a manner that their apices all meet at the centre, which becomes hollow as the holes are bored into it. The sides of each having been marked with lines to indicate the number of globes to be cut out, the workman inserts a chisel . . . with a semicircular blade, bent so that the edge cuts the ivory, as the shaft is worked on the pivot, at the same depth in each hole. By successively cutting a little on the inside of each conical hole, the incisures meet, and a spherical is at last detached, which is now turned over and it faces one after another brought opposite the largest hole, and firmly secured by wedges in the other apertures, while its surfaces are smoothed and carved. . . . It takes three or four months to complete a ball with fifteen inner globes.[15]

The Chinese designed puzzle balls principally for the marvel of their intricacy, rather than for entertainment as a game to align the enclosed balls.
This puzzle (*c.* 1835) contains fifteen ivory concentric balls. *Photograph
by Michele L. Hopkins. National Museum of Natural History, Department
of Anthropology, Smithsonian Institution, E396141, Aaron and Lillie Straus
Foundation*

By the 1830s Chinese toys and games became ubiquitous aspects of a
middle-class, white American child's experience. Many of the packaged
Chinese games were called Sunday boxes, so named because they were
mind-engaging puzzles acceptable for children's play on Sundays, when
more boisterous activities were frowned on. On other days of the week, children might play with Chinese automaton figures whose heads bobbled, or
with Chinese pasteboard figures. In Nathaniel Hawthorne's children's story
"Little Annie's Ramble," published in 1834, Annie and her adult companion
stroll the streets of a small American town. On their walk to the circus they
encounter an organ grinder, a bakery, a bookstore, and finally a toy store
where they see a Chinese toy: "suddenly we pause at the most wondrous
shop in all the town. . . . Is this a toy shop, or is it a fairy land? Here stands

a turbaned Turk. . . . And next a Chinese mandarine, who nods his head at Annie and myself."[16] But with the exception of the ring puzzle, which she may have used as a child and could therefore demonstrate, it is unlikely that Afong Moy saw, knew, or owned these Chinese games and puzzles as a girl in China.

In addition to the numerous lots of toys or puzzles shipped to America, the Carneses imported substantial numbers of board games. Unlike the toys and games whose origins were principally Chinese, many of the board games such as chess and backgammon were not indigenous to the country. Yet as early as the Han dynasty (202 BCE–220 CE) the playing of board games was a popular pastime in China. Records of such activity are found in stone relief carvings and pottery models located in tombs. The game liu-bo, possibly the antecedent of chess [xiangqi], had, as its objective, the capturing of the opponent's men. Such adult games of strategy and skill were an important element of the upper-class Chinese male's intellectual life.[17] There is no evidence that Chinese women of any class played the game of chess. In her salon, Afong Moy could relay information about its use in China only from hearsay.

Newspaper advertisements provided helpful information regarding the sale of Chinese-made board games in America prior to their importation by the Carnes firm. Stationers, those merchants who most often sold these board games, described their products in detail. In 1832, Bostonian A. Willard's "elegant assortment of ivory chessmen—carved in very superior manner" went for four to sixteen dollars each, which, he asserted, were unusually low prices.[18] The emphasis on reasonable costs for board games in the Boston, New York, and Philadelphia newspapers indicated the stationers' desire to reach a broad audience. Even Thomas Handasyd Perkins, the well-known Boston China trader, suggested to his supercargo in 1828 that expensive sets were not profitable "but something might be made I expect on the less expensive sort, and I think one or two sets would do well."[19]

Though the Carneses were of course unaware of Perkins's recommendation to his supercargo, they sensed the potential for a profitable investment. On just two vessels in the 1830s they imported more than 415 chess sets. The board games came at different price points. In 1835 the Carnes firm purchased the greater proportion of its ivory chess sets in China for fifty-five cents each; the most expensive, fewer of which were imported, for eight dollars and fifty cents each.[20] Though all of their chess sets are listed as ivory, the most expensive would have been more fully embellished. Even with a generous markup, chess sets became more readily available to a middle-class market.

Benjamin Franklin furthered the interest in chess in America. He played frequently, averring that the activity enhanced his mental skills. His 1750 essay "Morals of Chess" encouraged Americans, men and women, to play chess in order to gain foresight, circumspection, and caution and learn perseverance. Increased attention to the game came in the late 1820s and early 1830s, when Johann Maelzel, a German inventor and showman, toured his automaton chess player across America to the delight of large crowds. The chess player would later be paired with Afong Moy's program on her salon circuit. Nathaniel Carnes's awareness of the game's popularity in America may well have encouraged him to more heavily invest in large numbers of cheaper sets. If Philip Hone Jr. played chess, he likely did so on a Chinese-made board.

The Carneses also imported a large number of lacquered backgammon sets: about eight hundred in two shipments during the 1830s.[21] The purchase price in China for each was forty cents.[22] Backgammon sets, unlike the chess sets whose players could be less or more highly carved, all looked nearly the same. However, to play backgammon one needed dice. The 1832 Mills Brothers auction catalogue alone listed forty thousand sets of ivory dice. Quite possibly the dice were used for other games and for gambling, yet many of them would have accompanied backgammon games. Play pieces are moved according to the roll of the dice. Though not considered a serious gambling game, backgammon relied more heavily on chance than chess, and often it was played for money. Several of the founding fathers stated the moral improprieties of gambling games. Washington forbade his soldiers to engage in such activities, and Jefferson said: "Any person who shall bet or play for money, or other goods, or who shall bet on the hands or sides of those who play at any game in a tavern, racefield, or other place of public resort, shall be deemed an infamous gambler, and shall not be eligible to any office of trust or honor within this state."[23] Yet in 1770 and 1771 Jefferson recorded in his Memorandum book that he wagered on four backgammon games, winning twice and losing twice.[24]

In addition to games, other American leisure activities involved goods from China. Setting off fireworks was a popular one. The Chinese developed fireworks from their extensive experimentation with gunpowder as early as the year 1000 and therefore incorporated them into their many rituals and religious celebrations. While Americans primarily enjoyed fireworks to celebrate public events such as the Fourth of July, the Chinese used them to chase away evil spirits, to appease the immortals they worshipped, or to celebrate momentous events such as the dedication of a new building. It is likely that Afong Moy frequently saw fireworks from her home or viewed them at a distance.

There are several Western accounts of the sort of Chinese firework displays Afong Moy might have witnessed. Though obviously unable to set them off in the salon, she could describe their effect. Osmond Tiffany, the Baltimorean visiting Guangzhou in the 1840s, spoke of "fountains that would spout jets of fire, and rockets to emulate those of Vauxhall Gardens" to celebrate the birthday of an eighty-year-old mother.[25] Other descriptions of events note statues whose eyes, nose, and mouth discharged fireworks, and another festival presented a shower of firework lanterns with the eruption of an artificial volcano as the finale. These ingenious and imaginative presentations evidently lost some of their dramatic effect, according to Western accounts, because many were shown in daylight.

Philip Hone Jr. might well have desired fireworks—one of the Carneses' more prolifically imported goods. His father may not have been so enthusiastic. On several occasions in his diary Hone Sr. mentions the disturbance of fireworks on the Fourth of July. He noted, "it seemed as if the whole population has been seized with pyrotechnic mania . . . the reports more or less loud in every direction would have led to fancy that the city was undergoing vigorous siege."[26] On another Fourth of July he complained that the juvenile "lazzaroni" of the city had set off " 'Independence file firing' (as we used to call it in the artillery) . . . of (crackers) . . . to the bitter annoyance of all persons of quiet habits and sensitive nerves."[27] Hone likely read the squib in the *Niles Register* of 1834 which tallied the:

> damages sustained in the City of New York by the firing of Chinese crackers, by children is estimated at 50,000 dollars a year and many persons are injured by the running away of horses, etc. There ought to be a power, <u>and it should be exerted,</u> to relieve the people of this pest. The little urchens (sic) are hard to manage—but those who supply

them with the means of annoyance may be reached. The evil has been cured in Boston![28]

Though Philip Jr. might not have fired off crackers at his home at 235 Broadway, he could have done so when visiting his brother-in-law's family at their country house at Hell Gate, then on the outskirts of New York City. There Hone Sr. noted that on the occasion of the Fourth the "boys gave us a grand display of fireworks."[29] Like the merchant John Sword's son, who received a box of fireworks from his father (who was working in China) and anxiously anticipated setting them off in the summer, so Philip Jr. could well have looked forward to the joys of detonating the crackers.[30]

There were many types of fireworks, but all seem to have been composed of varying amounts of sulphur, saltpeter, and charcoal. The most common fireworks, called simple, included crackers, squib, rockets, serpents, maroons, pinwheels, leaders, gerbes, and Roman candles.[31] Firecrackers, the largest category imported within the simple fireworks, usually were made of rolled cartridge papers, 15" x 3½", placed on strings. There were many varieties but the most common were called "gold chop dragons," "Chinese babies," extra gold papered dragons," and "Chinese festivals."[32] According to an 1824 manual on pyrotechnics, crackers were harmless, though loud.[33] No one could compete with the "bang" of the Chinese cracker until Marsten and Wells patented the American Cannon Cracker in 1885. They claimed that "the explosion far exceeds in noise any imported Chinese cannon cracker ever manufactured, and are in effect like a cannon salute."[34]

The United States imported the greatest quantity of fireworks of any Western nation.[35] A review of the Philadelphia ship cargo manifests, the only complete run of China trade cargo manifests, indicated the numbers coming into this port. From 1796 to 1840, nearly a million packs of firecrackers arrived there. At various times between 1832 and 1837 the Carneses brought in boxes of fireworks and cases of firecrackers. The most detailed accounting, the Carnes *Mary Ballard* cargo manifest of late 1835, notes 2,500 cases of firecrackers, each case holding forty packs, at sixty-three cents per case. Shooting off firecrackers was an inexpensive entertainment in the 1830s.

The Carneses also imported Chinese goods intended for young women, a clientele whom Afong Moy would have been more comfortable

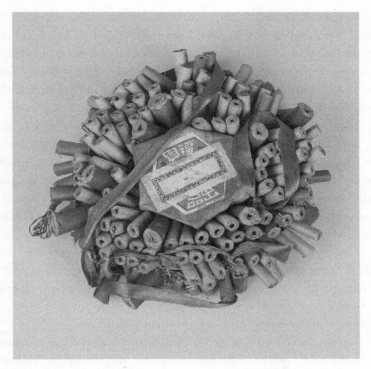

Setting off this coil of 161 firecrackers (*c.* 1840) would have produced a significantly noisy disruption in Philip Hone's New York. *Photograph by Michele L. Hopkins. National Museum of Natural History, Department of Anthropology, Smithsonian Institution, E 400379, donated by the Taipei Museum*

addressing. Catharine, fifteen years old in 1834, was the youngest of Philip Hone's six children. Hone reveals little of his family life in his diary, but several comments help us understand the possible interests of a young girl as a potential client for the Carneses' goods. Unlike her mother and namesake who was more reclusive, the young Catharine enjoyed outings and social occasions. She accompanied her father to the theater and a masked ball in New York and to one of the presidential inaugural events in Washington, DC. With the rest of the family, she occasionally spent several weeks in the summer at Saratoga Springs, a resort town in northern New York State. Hone describes Catharine as "happy as the day is long, and enjoys the gayety of a first season in society with a light heart and excellent disposition."[36]

Catharine's place in society prescribed certain social activities. These included the ritual of making afternoon calls, attending teas and evening levees, and participating in dancing schools or other activities of refinement. Not all young women in America had these advantages—surely not the urban or rural poor, or the enslaved—yet many in middle-class households participated in these genteel activities.

In China, Afong Moy's days differed greatly from those of Catharine's. There were few social activities—no dancing lessons, no outings to distant places. Young men did not mingle socially with young women. The fact that Catharine accompanied her father to balls and political events indicated a very different parental relationship from that which Afong Moy would have experienced. In China, parents were not companions. Following Confucian norms, they were to be revered, honored, and obeyed, but not enjoyed.

Certain objects complemented Catharine's pursuit of gentility and the Carnes firm imported a number of them. Some of these goods would have been familiar to Afong Moy; others, though made in China, were foreign. How would the objects from China affect the life of this young American girl and how might Afong Moy present them in her salon?

As the youngest of three sisters, Catharine had sufficient advice on dressing the part. *Godey's Lady's Book* magazine, established in Philadelphia in 1830, offered the information that young ladies needed in order to dress appropriately for social occasions. With the increased availability of Chinese goods, fashion began to appropriate and absorb some aspects of what was considered Eastern dress. Wearing these textiles and Asian accessories indicated a worldly familiarity. In July 1830 the suitable attire for a tea or evening event in the "Chinese fashion" required a shawl over the shoulders and hair held with a tortoiseshell comb.[37] In June 1831 the *Godey's* cover plate illustrated a woman wearing a white shawl and carrying a carved fan. Henry Sargent's early nineteenth-century painting *The Tea Party* provides an excellent visual account of the shawl's use. Of the twenty-five young women in the room only five are without shawls, and one of the five has draped hers over a stool.

Though American women may have considered themselves dressed in the height of "Chinese fashion," neither Afong Moy nor any Chinese woman had ever worn a shawl. The shape, rectangular or square to be arranged about the shoulder, is unknown in traditional Chinese dress.[38] The English term, derived from the Persian word "shal," was made of fine wool or animal fleece, and was adapted by East Indian men who wore it draped across the shoulder, a style Western women would later emulate. Like some other export items, the Chinese silk shawl, fringed and embroidered, was made explicitly for the Western market. Had Afong Moy presented this clothing at her salon, it may have occasioned an awkward moment. She might have turned to Augusta Obear to determine how it was worn. Though in America the shawl had a romantic affiliation with the exotic and mysterious East, it would have been entirely unfamiliar to Afong Moy.

However, it was the accepted fashion in the United States, and the Carneses and other China trade merchants obliged by importing vast quantities of Chinese silk shawls and other accessories. Of all the apparel items recorded in the Philadelphia manifests and in the Carneses' surviving cargo documents from the 1830s, shawls arrived in the greatest numbers. At the time, the term "shawl" was expansive, encompassing rectangular scarves as well as square and semicircular shapes.[39] Nearly all were silk. Beginning in 1818 and throughout the 1830s silk shawls were most often described as "crape" or "crepe." John Blake in his 1835 *Parlor Book* described crepe as "a light, transparent stuff in the manner of gauze, made of raw silk, gummed and twisted on the mill."[40] The twisted threads of silk gave the fabric a textured and pebbled appearance. Manifests, advertisements, and Walter Barrett's account in his book *The Old Merchants of New York* provide descriptive information about the color and measurements of the shawls. Shawls were described as white, crimson, scarlet, cream colored, pink, colored, black, high and grave colored—and some were embroidered and fringed. The sizes varied: they were available in 4-4, 6-4, 7-4, and 8-4; the width was a standard 4 dimension, while the length differed. These dimensions (possibly in feet) represent the rectangular form of the shawl, with some amazingly long, to be looped about the neck and draped down both sides of the body nearly to the floor.

Osmond Tiffany had the unique opportunity to tour a Chinese worksite where silk shawls were made. Traveling four hundred miles inland, he recorded the working of the loom which he said was "strikingly rude and clumsy . . . two men work at it, one shifting the woof, and the other throwing the shuttle."[41] He also noted that the embroidery work on the shawls was done entirely by hand. Tiffany may not have known what the New Yorker Walter Barrett averred, that earlier in the 1830s the Carneses had sent samples of Italian, French, and English silks to be imitated by the Chinese. He said: "the Chinese imitated them not only to perfection, but actually improved on the patterns sent . . . and the shawls imported by the Carnes concern were never equaled."[42]

Once the shawls were shipped to Guangzhou, Americans purchased them from Chinese silk merchants and shopkeepers who also dealt in other silk piece goods. A letter from John Sword in 1835 identified one such businessman: "Kingwa, a silk merchant, has sent my Mother a Levantine (silk) Shawl—I have been dealing with him largely for Silks, and I shall tell him by way of a hint that I have a Wife at home."[43] His letters never indicated whether Kingwa took the hint.

In 1835, Philadelphia merchant Henry Pratt McKean, writing to trader Benjamin Etting in Guangzhou, sent a detailed two-page letter of complaint about the shawls he received from China: "Some of the shawls that were ordered in twisted silk truly are in Floss Silk, a very great mistake . . . it frays out, also the colors are not as ordered . . . some of the Emb'd Shawls that were ordered to be damasks in the centre are plain, a very great error, and the few shawls . . . have come Embr'd in white and the fringe torn, the greatest mistake of all."[44] McKean further reprimands his buyer, Mr. Rawle, for purchasing "old" patterns rather than checking on the newest ones. He recommends that he look over "Cooshings" patterns and "pick out as many patterns as you want . . . and contract for those patterns, and there cannot be a mistake."[45] Worried that the buyer still had not gotten the message, McKean describes exactly where the "sprigs of Emby" needed to be on the shawl's surface.

Great numbers of these shawls were shipped to the United States. According to William Wood's import records in his book *Sketches of China*, 888,000 shawls found their way onto American women's shoulders from 1822 to 1826. The less-than-complete accountings for the goods the Carnes firm imported in the 1830s note the purchase in Guangzhou of forty-six canton silk shawls and other crepe shawls of various sizes and prices ranging from $4.00 apiece to $15.00. Shawls, like other apparel, were relatively expensive items and their prices remained stable in the early nineteenth century. The first record of their value found in William Bell's early nineteenth-century record book noted that one box of fifty crepe shawls cost $4.56 each.[46] In January 1815 Captain John Suter's accounts for clothing purchased in Guangzhou listed shawls at $3.50 apiece. These values correspond to those paid by the Carneses in the 1830s.

The fan was another genteel accoutrement for young women such as Catharine Hone. Afong Moy had little difficulty presenting the Chinese fan to American audiences. It was an article she would frequently have used in Guangzhou to cool herself in the steamy and moist climate. One of the first images of Afong Moy in America portrayed her with fan in hand. As a mnemonic, it was one of those objects that immediately established her Chinese, oriental identity. Her fan appears to be made of paper and figured with an overall design. The illustrator's choice was understandable; the paper fan was fashionable, and it was one of the Carneses' largest, and least expensive, imports in the fan category.

Originating in China, possibly before the second century BCE, the fan was an ingenious and useful tool to stir the air and an object of great beauty. In China both men and women carried the fan as an accessory. Women at court used small hand fans as part of an intricate etiquette, while the poor farmers in the southern provinces carried palm leaf fans to cool themselves. Osmond Tiffany explained its use in southern China: "The fan is indispensable for in summer the caps of respectable portions of the community are doffed, and the bare heads would be unsheltered from the sun, were it not for the use of this graceful article which is held in the right hand over the head."[47]

Surely Catharine and her sisters owned fans in America. Presumably they subscribed to *Godey's Lady's Book* magazine or to the *World of Fashion*, the most popular and widely read women's magazines in America at the time; their illustrated plates portrayed the genteel lady with fan in hand. In the 1833–35 issues of the *World of Fashion*, fans were depicted in thirty-eight of the fifty-nine fashion plates. The Carneses and other American China traders probably perused the periodical to ascertain which objects would sell well. Either magazine was likely to be conveniently at hand in Francis Carnes's home, for his daughter Emmeline was the same age as Catharine Hone. The fan was one of the recurrent import articles on the Carneses' manifests. Available in numerous materials and mounts, it was one of China's most appealing and artistic contributions to the Western woman's costume.

The fan came early to the Western world through India and Egypt. In the mid-sixteenth century it became popular throughout Europe as an object used exclusively by noble ladies. By the eighteenth century, it was common for both upper-class noblewomen and middle- and lower-class women to hold fans.[48] In Europe the fan was most often associated with the coquettish activities of the woman. This behavior took place in America as well; however, in the South the fan was a particularly important weapon against flies and the heat. Harriet Martineau, who visited the United States in the 1830s, commented in her travel accounts of the South: "A slave makes a gentle war against the flies with the enormous bunch of peacock feathers, and the agitation of the air is pleasant while the ladies are engaged in eating; so that they cannot use their own fans, which are hung by loops on the piazza, where the coffee is served. There the ladies sit whisking their feather fans."[49]

Between 1784, when the American China trade began, until 1845, with the demise of the old Canton trade, the Chinese fan in America went through two peaks of fashion. Portraiture and advertisements reveal that most women carried brise fans, those made of folding ivory, bamboo, lacquered wood, or bone ribs with paper or silk between. The escalating numbers of advertisements starting around 1820 show that the vogue for this accessory returned, and by the later 1820s a record number of Chinese fans were imported. This time different types of fans were fashionable. The most popular were palm leaf, feather, and paper, in that order, although rice, lacquer, bamboo, isinglass "transparent," camphor wood, pearl, and ivory were also advertised. Real tortoiseshell and sandalwood were too dear for the general market; therefore, the Chinese made imitations of these materials. The Carneses imported both the real and the imitation.

The palm leaf fan was apparently the most popular because a far greater number of these were advertised than other types. The 1832 Mills Brothers auction catalog enumerating articles from the Carneses' ship *Howard* listed seven thousand palm leaf fans. Their embellishment and decoration are not described as often as that of the more expensive fans, though the Mills Brothers catalog lists some with ivory handles. The feather fan appears to be the second most fashionable on the open market.

The best visual record of these fans comes through folk and popular art. Erastus Salisbury Field's 1845 painting of Margaret Gilmore shows her holding a feather fan. In this period, fans also frequently appear in Shaker inspirational drawings, and in each case they are made of feathers. As symbols of the "world's people" and "vain adornment," fans gain new meaning when interpreted by the Shakers as "blowing away buffetings."[50] Such representations show how common the fans were to the American middle class. That they were understood to be Chinese in origin is clear from the 1835 *Parlor Book*: "Fans: The custom that now prevails among the ladies, of wearing fans was borrowed from the East, where the hot climate renders the use of fans and umbrellas almost indispensable. In the East they use chiefly large fans made of feathers to keep off sun and flies."[51]

The making of paper fans in China was an assembly-line process that enabled the Chinese to make large quantities and sell them very inexpensively. The procedure involved cutting the paper to the correct size, shaping it to make the folds, painting the design, carving the stick, attaching the paper to the stick and guards, adding a tassel, and packaging it in boxes.[52] Osmond Tiffany also observed the making of the cheapest of paper fans—blackened oil paper—attached to a bit of bamboo and cut where the paper joins the handle. He reported that "packed in boxes containing five hundred, they were sent away much thicker than the leaves of Valombrosa."[53] In the *Mary Ballard* shipment the Carneses brought in twelve thousand paper fans— some figured on both sides and some plain. Whether embellished or not, each was valued at one cent apiece. They might have purchased them from one of several Chinese merchants in Guangzhou who dealt in fans: Tyshing, who sold fans and combs of ivory; merchant Linching on 121 Old China Street, and Luechun, who sold fans in his No. 6 New China Street shop.[54]

In America, Catharine's preparations for an afternoon call with fan and shawl in hand required the inclusion of a handkerchief. In the lithograph by Charles Risso and William Browne, Afong Moy holds a handkerchief, "shoujuan" or "shoujin" in Chinese. This item serves as one of China's most exploited props. They were widely used in dramatic presentations such as the Han Chinese Handkerchief Dance to accentuate the theatrical action of the dancers. In Chinese shadow puppet shows they were dropped by heroines, to be retrieved by their lovers. The term "handkerchief sisters," meaning those who were dear friends, was employed in the early Qing Dynasty kunqu historical drama *Peach Blossom Fan*. Afong Moy also used her handkerchief as a prop—but for the very different purposes of explication and sales. One wonders, as she held the handkerchief in the salon, whether she might have silently repeated the lines from "The Bride of Jiao Zhongquin," the most famous of folk songs: "A silent girl uses her handkerchief to cover her mouth to cry."

Tucked within her reticule, the nineteenth-century term for a drawstring purse, Catharine would have carried a handkerchief. In the latter part of the eighteenth century women might have worn it about the neck as a kerchief, and men used it as a general cloth, serviceable as a napkin and a cleaning rag for their utensils. Mid-nineteenth century genteel behavior prescribed a more refined application of the handkerchief as an article of display and an object of status for both men and women.

Handkerchiefs were generally sold by the piece in a variety of fabrics. The merchants brought back more than five hundred on the *Mary Ballard* in late 1835. Though pongee, or silk, was listed, those of grass cloth came in greater numbers. In his *Chinese Commercial Guide* John Morrison says of grass cloth: "This beautiful fabric is the linen of China woven from the fibers of the Sida. It is woven into narrow pieces and into handkerchiefs—export chiefly to India and the United States—many handkerchiefs to the latter country."[55] John Sword sent grass cloth handkerchiefs and parceled them out to his relatives in 1835: "Under cover to Jim Musgione six pieces of grass Cloth Handkerchiefs—Please give one piece to my Mother—one to Sophia, one to Sarah and one to Kate and keep the other 2 pieces yourself—they are not as fine as can sometimes be procured here but to get them finer they must be ordered and requires time."[56] Probably Sword is referring to the grade of grass cloth; the finer quality fabric approached that of linen, whereas the less fine was more coarsely woven.

American merchants purchased handkerchiefs from various Chinese sources. They bought small quantities of these goods from peddlers on the streets of Guangzhou. Larger quantities, such as those acquired by the Carneses, came from shopkeepers near the hong factories. Who Yune's grasscloth shop specialized in such objects. Tiffany noted: "If you buy of him (Who Yune) freely, he sends his cooley round to the hong and begs your acceptance of a dozen pocket handkerchiefs."[57] If they purchased from Who Yune, the Carneses' agent must have been well rewarded.

Neither earlier nineteenth-century manifests nor advertisements provide information on the cost of handkerchiefs in the retail market. An early nineteenth-century invoice for 150 silk handkerchiefs consigned to New York merchant William Bell shows a high cost of nine dollars each.[58] A bit later handkerchiefs shipped on board the vessel *Pearl* on Captain John Suter's account cost ten dollars apiece.[59] As with their use in China, silk handkerchiefs were enjoyed by the wealthy, while the cotton and grass cloth were for middling folk. Though we are unable to know how well the Carneses' importations of these goods sold at auction in the 1830s, the price they paid in Guangzhou was significantly lower at fifty-three cents apiece for grass cloth handkerchiefs.[60] Even with a higher retail cost in the US market, most middle-class American women and men could afford to carry a Chinese handkerchief in their pocket in the 1830s.

In addition to a handkerchief, signifying gentility, other affordable beauty products were available to American women of all social classes.[61] However, imported fragrances had been generally too expensive for most. Francis Carnes's location in France for much of the 1830s gave him an advantage in ameliorating this problem. His cultured circle of friends acquainted him with the tasteful and current styles, as well as appropriate scents. Walter Barrett alludes to this in his review of the Carnes goods arriving in New York. He notes that "Carnes (Francis) also sent out a sample of pure attar of roses, worth $25 an ounce. The Chinese Samski made a capital imitation, costing about sixpence an ounce, for imitation attar of roses. About 10,000 ounces came out in one ship, and druggists and perfumers bought it up rapidly from ten to fifteen dollars an ounce."[62] Francis successfully engaged in the "V" trade, sending expensive French perfume to China, imitating it there, and importing that same fragrance to America at a lower price.

The French claimed their premier place as perfumers in the early nineteenth century, and the town of Grasse in Provence was its center. There, perfumers extracted oils from thousands of rose petals into a concentrated essence called attar of roses. A small portion of this essence, infused in waters and oils, created eau de cologne. Used regularly by many in France, perfumes such as Florida water, a mixture of cologne and spices, gained acceptance in America. But the costliness of the French essence, or attar, inhibited American perfume production and its use. The importation of the "imitation" from China by the Carnes firm paved the way for a more affordable perfume that Catharine Hone might well have enjoyed.

Though Barrett called the attar an imitation, the Chinese well knew the art of perfumery. For thousands of years the Chinese had applied aromatic gums and scents to their bodies, clothing, furniture, and even paper and inks. Fragrances came from ginger, nutmeg, sesame oil, and roses. As early as 221 BCE, during the reign of the first emperor of China, Qin Shi Huang, young men wore perfume satchels attached to their girdles to show respect for their parents and in-laws. By the Qing dynasty (1644–1912), the Manchus carried perfume pouches on their bodies year-round. The convention extended to all classes, ages, and genders— nearly everyone carried a "hebao." These pouches, made of cloth, colorful strings, and an aromatic, were often given as gifts. Though appreciated for their fragrance, they also may have been considered a preventative against diseases. Afong Moy may well have worn and displayed a perfume pouch scented with spices or roses, as it was considered a nourishment for both the body and the spirit.

When French peasants plucked the petals from the roses of Grasse for their perfumes, they took them from the hybrid stock of Chinese roses. The genus China Rose, from which the descendants in Grasse and throughout Europe and England developed, came from specimens collected by avid amateur botanists living in Guangzhou. Peter Osbeck, a student of Linnaeus, located the "R Chinensis" in the gardens of the Canton Custom House in 1751; Sir George Staunton collected "The Parson's Pink China" in 1793; and Sir A. Hume introduced "R Indica Fragrans" to England in 1810. By the early nineteenth century the Chinese rose became the rose whose hybrid descendants we know today.[63] The traits of these Chinese roses surpassed those known in eighteenth-century Europe: they were repeat bloomers, their color remained true without fading, and they had a highly fruity and tea-scented aroma. With the most highly developed rose culture in the world, the Chinese surely were capable of making "rose absolute" or the perfume concentrate made from rose petals. With cheaper labor, larger quantities of stock, and a greater variety, Chinese attar could undersell the French market.

Though home recipes in America were still used to freshen the face or provide a scent, pharmacies, druggists, and general stores carried domestic products such as the highly touted bear's oil or the expensive imported essences from France. Yet women's literature cautioned its readers about the application of scents. Too free a use of sachets, scent bags, or dousing oneself with "any foreign essence" might turn away admirers who could find the air around them "insupportable."[64] In New York City, Catharine Hone or her sisters might have purchased their carefully applied perfume from Cutter & Hurd at 72 Dey Street. In 1836 the firm advertised in its catalogue "a large and general assortment of French, English and American perfumery."[65] It also sold drugs, medicines, paints, dye stuffs, glass ware, surgeons' instruments, and "fancy articles." The American perfume they offered may well have contained the Chinese attar of roses that the Carneses brought into New York in such quantities.

Genteel, appropriately scented women required the use of cards and card cases for their afternoon visits. When Afong Moy arrived in New York in 1834 her sponsors prepared a card with her name in Chinese characters.[66] Though no one could read her Chinese name, it was expected that refined persons moving within American and most Western nineteenth-century societies would carry a small copperplate-engraved card with one's name. *Cassell's Domestic Dictionary* noted that "everyone above the lower ranks of society is supposed to have his name and address in his pocket for visiting and other purposes."[67] It was recommended that the card be plain and the engraving relatively simple. These cards were exchanged on morning and afternoon visits with set hours and behaviors.[68] Presumably Afong Moy would present her card to those she wished to visit or to those who visited her.

The custom of visiting and exchanging cards prevailed in China as well. Williams described the convention in detail: "Visiting cards are made of vermilioned paper cut into slips about eight inches long and three wide, and are single or folded four, six, eight or more times, according to the position of the visitor. The simple name is stamped on the upper right corner, or if written on the lower corner."[69] Who participated in the formal visiting procedures was the principal difference between the two countries: Chinese women and young ladies never took part in, nor were present during, this activity. Yet Afong Moy accommodated the American card-carrying custom. In the United States, both men and women visited, and Catharine, her mother, and her sisters engaged in the morning or afternoon calling ritual.

Small cases or boxes protected the cards to keep them unblemished. Presumably, Afong Moy displayed her card within a Chinese case in the salon. Though the case could be tucked into a pocket, it would be seen when the visitor retrieved a card. Ivory, pearl, tortoiseshell, sandalwood, or silver provided an elegant surface to carry a carved or engraved design. However, in 1828 China trader T. H. Perkins expressed skepticism that they would sell, deeming their highly embellished form disproportionate to their use. He said in a letter to his onsite Guangzhou representative: "Card cases bring a good price here but they are difficult to sell and but a few would be sold—I am ignorant of the cost but I should hardly recommend them."[70] Receiving a good price in China, the Carnes firm took advantage of Perkins's disinterest, and the card case's escalating fashion, and imported vast quantities of the form. By 1839 Carroll and Hutchinson, New York City retailers, advertised sixty different card case patterns.[71]

The costlier ivory cases often had carved scenes of Chinese men and women in gardens with encircling flowers and birds. The ivory from elephant tusks could be carved as finely as lace and then stained or painted to highlight areas of the scene. The sandalwood cases were carved as carefully as the ivory, with the additional appeal of being fragrant. The Carneses imported not only ivory cases but sandalwood as well, for three hundred tons of the wood came into Guangzhou in 1834 and that availability lowered the price.[72] Much of the sandalwood came from Malabar, Hawai'i, and the Fiji Islands on American vessels. The amount of carving on both the ivory and sandalwood cases determined the price. The Carnes examples, coming on the *Mary Ballard*, ranged from three to six dollars as purchased in Guangzhou. Advertisements record a range of prices in America from

Many card cases such as this (*c.* 1840) showed scenes of Chinese life not unlike the images on imported Chinese ceramics. Views depicted on these wares helped form American perceptions of China. *National Museum of American History, Division of Home and Community Life, Smithsonian Institution, bequest of Mrs. Julian James*

fifty cents to fifteen dollars, with the more expensive ones billed as "carved in the most elegant manner."[73]

Keeping track of one's afternoon visits required another object that often was as equally embellished: writing tablets. Though they were not used in their country, the Chinese manufactured these items for export. The small writing tablets of ivory, hinged together with one for each day, were encased in a tortoiseshell cover. A contemporary dictionary notes the writing tablet as a "kind of memorandum book to be carried in the pocket. The leaves or tablets are prepared for writing upon with a lead pencil, and the writing can be rubbed or washed out."[74] One example has the day of the week engraved at the top of each ivory tablet with a simple ivory cover. Faintly visible on one of tablets are the erased names of those on a previous owner's calling schedule. Writing tablets were not costly items; the Carneses' agent purchased tortoise shell-covered ones for sixty-five cents each.

Colored paper applied to objects or paper crafted into shapes was a popular, genteel afternoon pastime for many young nineteenth-century American women. However, it required quantities of such goods. Though a small percentage of the Chinese papers were printing press and engravers' papers, and a still smaller amount was wallpaper, the largest category of papers advertised was "fancy paper." In Philadelphia alone, 116 boxes and 26 cases of Chinese paper entered that port from the early nineteenth century to the late 1830s.

Paper is an age-old Chinese product that was early exported to India and the West. In China, paper was used for many purposes: for the covering of windows, walls, and ceilings and, of course, for writing. Afong Moy would have been familiar with paper as a covering in her home rather than as a writing surface or for fancy work.

Chinese paper was of varying quality depending on the substance of which it was made. Most cheap papers were made of bamboo. Yet even as a cheap paper, it was—as Jean Breton de la Martinère (De la Breton), a diplomat in China with the French East India Company, described it—of "almost impalpable fineness."[75] Other extraordinary features of Chinese paper were its whiteness, softness, smoothness, and enormous length. John Blake's 1835 *Family Encyclopedia* notes that it was not difficult to obtain sheets of Chinese paper in lengths of thirty to forty feet.[76] For all its positive characteristics the cheaper bamboo paper was liable to decay quickly, prone to mildew, and susceptible to insect damage. Unfortunately, many early nineteenth-century American ledgers and account books were on Chinese bamboo paper and are now unreadable.

Finer paper was made of cotton, reeds, and the bark, as well as the soft inner portion, of the mulberry tree.[77] Much of the finer paper for fancy work and letters was made from the last, which was commonly known as "rice paper" though it is more accurately termed "pith paper." One of the major attractions of this paper was the assorted colors in which it was available. The Mills, Brothers & Co. catalogue selling from the Carnes vessels lists 1,600 sheets of rose, light blue, orange, pea green, yellow, and buff papers.[78] Later in 1835, on the *Mary Ballard*, the Carneses brought in 200 packs of white rice paper.

Catharine Hone likely spent some of her leisure hours engaging in fancy work. *Godey's Lady's Book* magazine provided instructions and procedures for this activity, and in April 1831 it published a "Chinese painting exercise." Using workboxes and baskets, tables and screens as a base, women ornamented them in the "Chinese style" by applying Chinese patterned paper to the surface. The very term "Chinese" gave the activity an exotic and titillating "oriental" aura. Afong Moy probably found this exercise curious, and completely outside her experience.

To obtain the paper and utensils, American women were encouraged to shop at the local stationer's store. In July 1831, *Godey's* suggested modeling with rice paper: "Make a group of flowers either on cardboard, or affixed to small vases, baskets, etc. in festoons and clusters. Rice paper can be provided in various colours."[79] Advertisements for the paper also explained that the colored paper was used to make paper toys or for "fancy work." These advertisements do not specify the colors; rather, they note the paper is "white," "straw," "colored," "fancy," or just "colored." It is apparent that some papers—perhaps a variant of the wallpapers—were patterned. Notices featured "figured" and "plain" papers, which may have been what the "China painters" used in their fancy work.

Working with paper required tools. Catharine Hone used a paper folder with her fancy work. This tool looked like a thick Popsicle stick with a rounded or pointed end, usually with a decorative handle. Though a simple form, it had many uses, but none that the Chinese might need. Like the shawl and paper folders, which were outside her experience in China, Afong Moy would need assistance from the Obears to explain their use to the public. Catharine Hone probably used hers to burnish, score, fold, or crease decorative papers. Others in the family might have applied the tool to cut the leaves of a book. *Cassell's Domestic Dictionary* suggested that there should be one in every sitting room, for "if one is not at hand persons are apt to use a penknife or scissors, and then the edges of the books are usually torn or made ragged."[80]

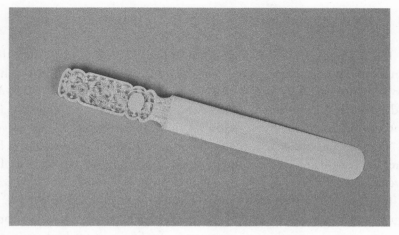

The Chinese likely copied the paper folder form (*c.* 1850) that the Carnes firm provided. The simple tool had many uses; the import garnered ample money for the firm. *Photograph by Michele L. Hopkins. National Museum of Natural History, Department of Anthropology, Smithsonian Institution*

An image from *La Belle Assemblée* (1830) fashion magazine shows the paper folder in use. *National Museum of American History, Division of Home and Community Life, Smithsonian Institution*

The Carneses would have agreed with Cassell as they made sure that American sitting rooms were well equipped. In two shipments, they brought in more than four thousand paper folders made of horn, bone, and ivory. The Carneses undoubtedly commissioned their design and manufacture in China. Their cost depended on whether the handle was carved or "figured." In Guangzhou, the Carneses purchased the least expensive for three and-one-half cents and the most expensive, with carved handles, for seventeen cents.

The Carneses also supplied the India ink that Catharine might use to pen her visiting notes of thanks or regrets. Letter writing—its style, composition, and penmanship—was a matter of refinement for both men and women in the eighteenth and early nineteenth centuries. A nice turn of phrase was considered an art as well as a genteel performance on paper. In the late eighteenth century, Lord Chesterfield, the purveyor of manners and principles of politeness, wrote to his son regarding his letters: "that if your style is homely, course or vulgar, they will appear to as much disadvantage, and be as ill received as your person, though ever so well proportioned, would, if dressed in rags, dirt and tatters." Catharine and her siblings would have been held to similar standards.

Atung, Afong Moy's attendant and translator, was judged by Chesterfield's deportment guidelines. The American press described him as a "polished youth" who moved about the salon with "the grace of a gentleman." One of his gentlemanly acts was writing. At many of the salons he penned in Chinese characters the name of the "Lady or Gentleman" visitors on "handsome Embossed Cards, or in their Albums," no doubt using the India ink that the Carneses imported. The Chinese, too, regarded writing as one of the most highly developed arts. The Chinese scholar spent his life perfecting the characters that indicated his level of accomplishment. However, few Chinese women were provided the opportunity to learn characters, or to write. Unlike Catharine, Afong Moy could not read or write in her own language, or in English.

Four articles used in Chinese writing were precious: ink, paper, the inkstone, and the brush. The Chinese missionary and printer S. Wells Williams noted that the ink "usually known as India ink, is made from the soot of burning oil, pine, fir, and other substances, mixed with glue or isinglass, and scented. It is formed into oblong cakes or cylinders, inscribed with the maker's name. . . . When used, the ink is rubbed with water upon argillite, marble, or other stones."[81] As a printer, Williams was alert to the properties of the Chinese inks. Those he used for printing his *Chinese Repository* were of lesser quality, made of lampblack mixed with vegetable oil that the printers ground themselves. It is likely that the Carneses imported the less expensive variety; one case containing twenty-five catties cost forty-five cents apiece in China.

Like many other early nineteenth-century parents, Philip Hone Sr. and his wife Catharine provided the expectations, the settings, and the props for their children's application of gentility. In their own dress, accoutrements, and household appointments, they too needed to fulfill the credos of refinement. Merchants like the Carneses, and the retailers who purchased their goods, assisted in this effort. Afong Moy presented the objects and afforded the "oriental" bridge that gave heightened value to these objects.

5

Afong Moy Presents Chinese Objects
for the Home

IN 1834, AS AFONG MOY adjusted to her new environment at 8 Park Place
in New York City, a few blocks away Philip Hone and his wife, Catharine,
were preparing for a move. The area where they had resided for a number
of years was changing. In the early 1830s, the fabulously wealthy John Jacob
Astor, the renowned owner of the American Fur Company and a China
trader, began buying up his neighbors' homes near Broadway. By April 1834,
Hone wrote in his diary, "the pulling down of the block of houses next
to that on which I live—the whole front Barclay [Street] to Vesey Street
on Broadway—where he is going to erect a New York *palais royal*, which
will cost him five or six hundred thousand dollars."[1] The demolition went
quickly. In mid-May Hone reported, "Mr. Astor's buildings are nearly all
removed; the dust from the immense mass of rubbish has been almost in-
tolerable for the last fortnight."[2] The construction of Astor's lavish and well-
appointed five-story Greek Revival hotel was well under way by the time
Afong Moy arrived in the vicinity of Broadway that October.

The dust, the noise, and the disruption hastened Hone's search for a
new home. Soon the family would move further north, to the corner of
Broadway and Great Jones Street. This was the time to purchase goods
for a new house. In November 1834, Philip Sr. and Catharine saw some
of the objects Francis and Nathaniel Carnes had imported at Afong Moy's
New York salon. Whether this viewing influenced their choices or whether
they purchased goods we do not know.

New York newspapers directed their readers' attention to some of the noteworthy objects presented in Afong Moy's salon. They remarked on the "engravings" that Charles Risso and William Browne's lithograph had depicted on the walls of her chamber. The *New-York Commercial Advertiser* observed: "In addition to the furniture of the apartments, all of which is of the Chinese character, there are a number of curiosities which look most inviting to the antiquarian as well as some splendid engravings well worthy of inspection."[3] Philip Hone might have taken note of them. In his diary he admitted that he had only "a sort of smattering" of a background in the fine arts, but he acknowledged that he had a facility for recognizing artistic merit.[4] In actuality Hone had more than a passing interest in the arts. He had been a member of the American Academy of the Fine Arts since 1818 and had served four times as one of its directors. In addition, the National Academy of Design made him an honorary member. His personal collection included American paintings by Samuel F. B. Morse, Thomas Cole, Thomas Vanderlyn, and Rembrandt Peale. With this attentiveness to the arts, Hone likely found the "engravings" "worthy of inspection." However, Hone would have immediately recognized that the artworks hanging behind Afong Moy's dais were watercolors, not engravings.

Walter Barrett, the narrator of the Carneses' mercantile exploits, informed his readers of these Chinese artworks. As a merchant, but not an art connoisseur, Barrett, too, was a bit confused as to what they were. He recognized that the Carneses had hit on a fruitful commercial venture but misidentified the medium and incorrectly called them "rice paintings." In fact, the surface was pith, a cheap paper made from the boughs of small trees.[5] With Western encouragement, the Chinese mass-produced vast quantities of these inexpensive watercolors and bound them into silk-covered albums. As Barrett correctly asserted, they comprised views of Chinese life, including the larger watercolors of Mandarins and their wives that the Hones saw in Afong Moy's salon, as well as smaller views of Chinese birds, fish, flowers, fruit, and people in everyday life. Recognizing that Americans had few reasonably priced sources for images they might hang in their drawing rooms, the Carneses imported thousands of these watercolors. Barrett commented on their imports: "For the first time, rice paintings were brought out to this country as an article of commerce. The supercargo of the 'Thomas Dickinson' [one of the Carnes-supported vessels] gave Mr. Levy [Aaron Levy, an auctioneer] a thousand of them, assorted, large, and small sized silk books, each containing twelve plates of Chinese paintings. . . . Well, they took amazingly. They cost . . . twelve dollars per hundred in China; but old Levy ran off every book at over a dollar each on the average."[6]

With the two images of Chinese people behind her, Afong Moy might have felt she was sitting in front of an ancestral altar. This would have been nearly the only place in the Chinese home, or ancestral hall, where such imposing portraiture would have been placed. Yet because the subjects stood, rather than sat, they were not the typical ancestral portraits.[7] By the eighteenth century, commoners were permitted to build ancestral halls or worship ancestors at domestic altars where full-length portraits of their deceased relatives were honored. Perhaps Afong Moy's family had such an altar. Nearly all Chinese portraiture was meant for private rather than public viewing, and participants often performed rituals in front of them. Such a performance would be unthinkable in this public place in front of strangers. Possibly Atung might have explained the significance of the large portraits that hung so prominently on the stage.[8] Conveying this information would be the bridge between cultures that Atung and Afong Moy could so importantly provide to the American public.

In addition to the "engravings," the newspapers also reported that the Chinese furniture in Afong Moy's salon set the ambiance of the moment; its presence served as more than a showy, "oriental" backdrop. The Carneses hoped that such a viewing might lead to sales. One of their returning vessels contained 108 lacquered writing desks as well as center and card tables, and the 1835 inventory of the *Mary Ballard* listed 475 lacquered tea caddies, a case of lacquered teapoys, and lacquered work boxes. Barrett stated in his account of the Carneses' merchandise that "every species of lacquer ware . . . ever made in London or Paris, was imitated closely by the Chinese; and New York was flooded."[9]

The drawing room that Captain Obear arranged for Afong Moy in his home at 8 Park Place contained some of these articles. If we accept Risso and Browne's lithograph as a fairly accurate depiction of the New York City room, Afong Moy sat wedged among a great deal of imported merchandise. The elaborate salon with lacquerware goods highlighted Afong Moy's exotic uniqueness. Though some lacquer objects may have been part of her household in China, surely Western-style card and center tables or writing desks were not familiar pieces in her domestic environment.

Because it was a salon, and not a furniture showroom, not all the lacquer objects that the Carneses imported were on view. In the lithograph only the center table and the tea chest or work table are visible. With the covering of the lace tablecloth, the lacquer base of the center table is barely discernible. The artists delineated the tea chest (possibly a work table) in greater detail. Here the viewers could get a sense of the craftsmanship and glossiness of the lacquer.

Many Westerners in Guangzhou recorded their impressions of Chinese lacquer because the goods looked so foreign and the process entailed such care. In 1838, Charles Toogood Downing remarked: "As we walk down the street (China Street), our eyes are particularly dazzled by the shining glitter of the lackerware, ranged along each side of the passages. . . . Upon stopping to look at these splendid ornaments, we cannot but be struck with the vast superiority of their workmanship . . . fresh from the hands of their makers."[10] The Baltimorean Osmond Tiffany found the lacquer process so intriguing that he gave a detailed description of the activity that occurred in Hipqua's "lac-ware" workshop. Forty people, young boys and old men, crafted objects from the light fir wood that had been floated down the rivers on vast numbers of rafts from the interior Chinese forests. After fashioning the rough shape of the piece, it was then "smoothed" carefully and a layer of lac (the sap of a sumac-like tree) applied. He took note that after each application, the "artist puts on a pair of magnifying glasses and . . . picks out with a sharp instrument the most minute grain that may have found its way into the gum. . . . [It] was left to dry. Rubbed a long time with a smooth stone, repeated again and again until the several coats of lac are polished. [It] is now ready for ornamentation."[11] The application of multiple layers of lacquer, the drying, and the surface ornamentation was time-consuming, exacting work, and the materials were toxic.

A Chinese watercolor view of a lacquerware shop in Guangzhou made about 1840 illustrated these wares and some of the objects the Carneses imported. What appears to be a closed writing desk sits on a shelf nearest the shop's entrance, while a center table, standing outside the shop, functions like a signpost to beckon the buyer into the shop. A similar watercolor of a Western-style Guangzhou cabinetry shop around 1825 shows nearly the same forms seen in the Risso and Browne lithograph: center tables, portable writing desks sitting on top of a tall chest, chairs, and settees.

Furniture made in this cabinetry shop was for Western consumption, yet the materials were Chinese and aspects of the objects' detailing (such as fretting) carried Chinese motifs. *"Making European cabinetry,"* c. 1820–30. *Photograph by Jeffrey R. Dykes.* © *Peabody Essex Museum, Salem, MA*

Americans like Hone would appreciate, as Downing did, the lustrous and glossy finish of the lacquerware pieces. They refracted candlelight or gaslight as few other material goods could. With the importation of such quantities of lacquerware, and in forms that were more diminutive, middle-class Americans might afford such exotic objects. With the outfitting of a new home, Hone might be inclined to consider a portable lacquer writing desk for his library. Hone's diary indicated a great appreciation for this library retreat on the second floor of his home: "Would to Heaven I could pass all my days in my library without the necessity of going downstairs to engage in vexations and troublesome pursuits which seem to be entailed upon me for the rest of my life."[12] In that period, portable desks were often placed in a library space. A watercolor image of US diplomat Richard Rush's library in Philadelphia, for example, shows a closed portable writing desk on a table near the window.[13] Because learning and erudition were highly valued as evidence of gentility, libraries came into greater use in the mid-nineteenth-century home, and with them adaptable forms such as the writing desk.

The Carneses imported large numbers of this sort of desk. The 110 writing desks that appear on just three of the Carneses' shipping accounts provide some indication of their cost and properties. In the 1832 Mills Brothers auction catalogue from the Carneses' ship *Howard*, the writing desks are listed as "black," "maroon," "light," "dark," and "extra quality" and all of lacquer. The "extra quality" may have indicated a more highly worked design. Edward Butler in the *Mary Ballard* manifests listed both desks at three dollars, which is a cost comparable to the smaller lacquerware tea caddies.

The tea caddy, as one of the smallest lacquerware forms, held loose tea. Its name derived from the Malay word "kati," defining a measure of one and one-third pounds that fit the prescribed wooden box of packed tea. Though the outside container was made of wood, the interior holding the tea was lead or pewter. The specialized form indicated the respect and reverence for the leaf, which was housed in a decorated strongbox, often opened with a key at the escutcheon, and designed to hold a treasure. Though the tea caddy had a practical purpose, the elegance of its form was meant for show in the parlor as a marker of refinement. Surely the Hone family owned a tea caddy; it was part of the tea equipage used by most middle- and upper-middle-class households.

By the 1830s tea was affordable at nearly all levels of society. Yet the visual display of the tea caddy preserves the preciousness and status accorded tea. Herman Melville's use of the tea caddy in *Moby-Dick* indicated its ubiquity in the early nineteenth century. In the book, whose action took place in the late 1830s or early 1840s, Aunt Charity helped her brother, Captain Bildad, the co-owner of the *Pequod*, outfit his vessel in Nantucket. Her desire to provide some sense of comfort and hominess, as well as her intention to discourage the use of alcohol, encouraged her to stock ginger, tea, and a tea caddy on board. Its application lay dormant until the harpooner Queequeg needed reviving after a close encounter with a whale. Then, Dough-boy, the steward, provided him a concoction of ginger, water, and tea from the caddy. The response was vehement: liquor was what Queequeg wanted. Aunt Charity's tea caddy was "freely given to the waves."[14]

If Aunt Charity's gift was similar to the least expensive lacquered tea caddy from China, its cost was not insignificant. On the incoming manifest for the *Mary Ballard*, the supercargo Edward Butler listed the price paid for the 475 lacquer tea caddies in China from one dollar to three dollars each. Assuming that the Carneses' resale price was double that, likely the least expensive sold at two dollars in the New York market. Comparative period values are difficult to quantify since costs varied regionally. However, in

When new, the glossy black lacquer tea caddy (*c.* 1780), with its application of gold powdered detailing, shimmered in the candlelight. Even the lid's interior carried a decorative motif. *Gift of Mr. Benjamin L. Huntington, II.* © *Peabody Essex Museum, Salem, MA*

1836 the Illinois county commissioner's court regulated the prices charged for tavern services. In that year lodgings cost on average twelve and a half cents a night, meals between twenty-five and thirty-seven and a half cents, and horses were boarded and fed at fifty to seventy-five cents a day.[15] Aunt Charity's gift, then, would have been comparable to twelve nights at an Illinois tavern.

Though the lithograph by Risso and Browne illustrated only a teacup and teapot on the table beside Afong Moy, probably other small Chinese goods for adult use were presented at the salon as well. The Carneses imported significant numbers of these smaller items, which fit snugly into the holds of their vessels, such as the 208 dozen horn snuffboxes listed in the Mills Brothers auction catalogue. Though this was an extraordinarily large order, Chinese snuffboxes were frequently advertised for sale. In 1792, a private merchant in Philadelphia gave notice that he sold "China snuff boxes on reasonable terms for cash or good Indian corn."[16] Snuffboxes were still in fashion in the 1820s, as T. H. Perkins sent a letter to Robert Forbes in 1822 describing and illustrating snuffbox shapes that would be most salable in America. He suggested that the snuffboxes should be round with a diameter of two to three inches or kidney-shaped, noting the size with a diagram of the type he wanted.[17] Small, airtight containers such as the ones Perkins and the Carneses imported held a day's worth of snuff. This was optimum, for the powdered snuff was prone to dryness and therefore less potent with age.

This kidney-shaped snuffbox (*c.* 1870) fit the style requested by the merchant T. H. Perkins. Made of horn with a lacquered surface, it has a well-fitted telescoping stopper to keep the snuff fresh for each application. *Photograph by Michele L. Hopkins. National Museum of Natural History, Department of Anthropology, Smithsonian Institution, gift of R. H. Sargent*

Snuff, as a powder form of tobacco, could be consumed in a more re-fined fashion than the rolled leaf. Though discreetly taken, it was recognized as habit forming and addictive. In his diary under the heading "Snuff sacking," Jacob Engelbrecht of Frederick, Maryland, recorded his attempt to quit: "We the undersigned have been in the habit of taking snuff for the last two years and we have this afternoon emptied our snuff boxes in the street of their contents and have resolved to 'sack' the same if we can. Witness our hands, this 4th day of June 1824."[18] However, Engelbrecht's dependency continued, for he briefly annotated his 1824 entry with an 1867 note: "I still continue the bad habit."[19] Though women did consume snuff, men like Engelbrecht, his friends, and no doubt Philip Hone and his male colleagues were the principal users.

Curiously, it is Afong Moy who may have been more familiar with snuff than the American public. Tobacco came to China as a New World crop in the 1500s and spread throughout the country.[20] The Chinese combined herbs, spices, and the powdered tobacco leaf into a snuff mixture. Initially only the upper class inhaled it, for its properties supposedly had medicinal powers to cure migraines and some diseases and promote good eyesight. As with many other consumables, the Chinese developed an exquisite con-tainer to hold the snuff. Rather than a prosaic box, the Chinese held their snuff in a bottle most often made of glass. Specially made bottles had scenes painted on the interior. By the beginning of the nineteenth century, snuff consumption spread to all social classes in China—taking a pinch served as a greeting to friends. S. Wells Williams, who lived in China in the 1830s and 1840s as the publisher of the *Chinese Repository*, observed in his two-volume book on the history of the Chinese Empire, *Middle Kingdom*, that "tobacco was one of the widely cultivated plants in China for men, women, and chil-dren smoke."[21] It is likely that Williams meant inhaling the tobacco as snuff, for the Chinese disdained smoking it. Once the snuff was more readily ac-cessible and affordable, the snuff bottle form proliferated throughout all so-cial classes. Though the snuffboxes that the Carneses imported were Chinese made, their box-like form was Western and its decorative nature inferior to those the Chinese used for a similar purpose. Perhaps Afong Moy used snuff and carried her own elegant glass Chinese container to America but presented to the public the Western snuffboxes the Carneses had imported.

The Carneses had their pulse on the market. They understood the middle class's eagerness for proper appearance in the 1830s. Nathaniel Hawthorne also perceived this desire. In June 1835 he jotted down his thoughts while traveling to Boston on a Sunday afternoon. Near the city, Hawthorne stopped at an inn for refreshment. There he observed the company sitting near the bar and sketched a verbal tableau of the gathering: "mostly young fellows—clerks in dry-good stores being the aristocracy among them. Most of the gentlemen had smart canes, bosom-pins &c. One gentleman, very fashionable in appearance, with a handsome cane, happened to stop by me and lift up his foot—and I noticed that the sole of his boot (which was exquisitely polished) was all worn out. I apprehend that some such minor deficiencies might have been detected in the general showiness of most of them."[22] Though the men came from the middle class, Hawthorne recognized that they were desirous of maintaining a sense of gentility, a goal expressed in their personal possessions, even at the expense of other needs. The ownership of a cane, for example, related very little to the need of it as a staff or support but rather was a sign of status and distinction. By the 1830s, young men, as well as old, carried canes as part of their Sunday best attire. Paintings of this period often portray gentlemen leaning on or holding this fashionable item. From his diary account, we know that Philip Hone, too, was conscious of appearances. He wrote, "men are apt to be careless and slovenly in their dress—that is wrong. Great men, . . . divines, physicians . . . should dress well. It gives them consideration and raises their several professions in the eyes of their fellow men."[23] Carrying a cane was part of this proper dress, and likely Hone carried a walking stick when moving through New York City.

The cane was one of the fancy-good articles that did not originate in China. As a Western item, possibly a derivation from the sword, it took many forms which the Chinese then embellished. Several terms were used for the canes depending on the material they were made of. Whangee sticks were canes made of bamboo. Since bamboo was a durable, hardy, pliable substance it was a likely choice for a walking stick. The Englishman William Milburn, who wrote a trader's guide to commerce in China and India, specified that the whangee should be "tough, round, and taper, the knots at a regular distance from each other, and the nearer the knots are to each other the more they are esteemed. Those with crooked heads, if straight and regularly tapered, are always in request. Such as are dark coloured, badly glazed, and light, should be rejected."[24]

The term "malacca cane," used during the same period, referred to a walking stick made of rattan. In contrast to the whangee, malacca canes were preferred when the joints between the wood were more distant.[25] Elisha Tibbits, in writing to the China trader John Latimer, stipulated that Malacca canes should have "long joints, say about 2 feet 8 inches, clear of joints."[26] Canes were also described by the embellishment of their head or mount. Canes were readily available with mounts of ivory, tortoiseshell, bone, or even silver. Occasionally they were carved, though generally this elaboration was done only for special commissions.

The Carneses brought vast quantities of canes into the New York market; thirteen thousand whangee sticks and canes sat in the holds of the *Howard* and the *Mary Ballard*. The most expensive were the white and black bamboo canes acquired at four and a half cents each in China.[27] Surprisingly, the least expensive purchase in China was bamboo canes with bone, horn, and figured heads at 1 4/10 cents each. The markup was considerable, as Captain John Suter noted in his account book; most canes in this period were sold for two to three dollars apiece.[28]

Afong Moy, the person who would benefit the most from a cane to support her bound feet while on her extensive American travels, may have availed herself of one. In her diary, Harriet Low observed: "Went out walking in Macao and on our way we saw two of their women with small feet. Both women carried little canes."[29] Though American men fully participated in the mid-nineteenth-century fashion of carrying walking sticks or canes, American women took it up later in the century. Fashionable or not, Afong Moy's use of a cane may have been, for her, a necessity.

The purchasing of goods in early nineteenth-century American households continued to follow the protocols developed in the previous century. Generally, the male head of household determined the style and the form of costly household items such as furniture and artworks. Less expensive goods, personal items, and foodstuffs were more likely the choices of the wife. Though Philip Hone may not have been engaged in the minutiae of daily purchases, he was well aware of the costs. In 1835, he complained: "Living in New York is exorbitantly dear, and it falls pretty hard upon persons like me, who live upon their income. . . . Marketing of all kinds, with the exception of apples and potatoes, is higher than I ever knew it. I paid . . . for my winter butter, 400 to 500 pounds, two shillings four pence per pound. In the long course of thirty-four years housekeeping, I never buttered my bread at so extravagant a rate."[30] Because Hone carefully calculated household costs, it is possible that both he and his wife found the Carneses' less expensive imported Chinese comestibles an attractive alternative.

Most Americans considered tea a quintessentially Chinese drink even though it originated outside China's borders in Burma or India. With heightened popularity in the eighth century after the publication of Lu Yu's

Book of Tea, by the time of the Ming dynasty the beverage held a significance in Chinese life comparable to the one it holds today.[31] When Afong Moy arrived in America in 1834, tea was as prevalent in American households as it was in China; however, the variety and the quality of the tea she drank in America differed from that in Guangzhou. Cheaper teas for Western consumption were often augmented in China with extraneous stems and sweepings from the tea floor to add bulk and thereby increase revenue.[32] Fewer types of tea were available in America, and the public's discriminating palate was not as heightened as that of the Chinese. We might assume that the tea brewing in Afong Moy's teapot was imported in the Carneses' vessels. Two types referenced in the *Mary Ballard* manifest were pouchong and hyson. Hyson, a medium-grade green tea, was produced in a number of Chinese provinces; pouchong, a lightly fermented oolong tea of a fruity nature, was more specifically a South China tea. The Carneses paid nine dollars a case for the pouchong and slightly more (eleven dollars a case) for the hyson. Afong Moy probably found the pouchong, a tea produced nearer her homeland in southern China, more to her liking.

The activity of taking tea in America varied depending on the region, whether rural or urban, and the numbers of those involved in the activity. Typically, teatime occurred in the evening hours, often beginning at 7:00 p.m. In his diary accounts of 1837 and 1838 the Philadelphia author and lawyer Sidney George Fisher frequently recorded his presence at 7:00 p.m. teas, which he shared with family, friends, and acquaintances in the city.[33] It is during these hours, from 5:00 to 9:00 p.m., that Afong Moy was presented to the public in her New York City salon; thus Risso and Browne set their lithographic view of Afong Moy at teatime.[34] Demurely holding a handkerchief/napkin, as was polite for the American tea-taking activity, Afong Moy sat before a public who might have joined her for the repast.[35] Mrs. Hone likely followed the urban practice of holding teas for mixed company at this same hour.

Mrs. Hone would have owned all the equipage that most upper-middle-class households needed to hold a proper tea, including a tea table (or teapoy), a tray, a teapot, creamer, sugar bowl with tongs, cups, saucers, tea caddy, teaspoons, and likely a tea urn, slop bowl, strainer, and spoon tray. While availing herself of the Carneses' tea and one of their tea caddies, she might also have purchased and utilized one of their teapoys. The teapoy, derived from the Hindi/Persian phrase denoting a three-footed table, supported a tea set or tea-related objects. Not all teapoys were tripod-like tables or sold singly. The Carneses imported lacquer teapoys in sets. These sets could be easily stacked in a corner of the drawing room and brought out at teatime to hold a teacup, a set, or a caddy. The Carneses purchased lacquered teapoys sets for four dollars in China and probably sold them for twice that amount in America.

Afong Moy's tea accessories, as seen in the lithograph, were much simpler than those used by Mrs. Hone. The center table held her teapot, cup, and tray. On the tray sat a handle-less ceramic cup without a saucer. The Chinese drank their tea without sugar or cream at a warm, not hot, temperature. They therefore easily held the cup in their hands without fear of burning their fingers. With the omission of sugar, no saucer was needed to cradle the teaspoon. Mrs. Hone likely poured her tea from a silver teapot, but Afong Moy was content with a ceramic pot, the form the Chinese had used to brew tea for a thousand years.[36] Here, Afong Moy was allowed her difference in tea objects and likely the difference was elucidated and described by her translator, Atung. This domestically acceptable activity of tea taking in America served as a bridge to a Chinese world of goods. Presuming that most Americans appreciated tea and the tea-taking activity, the merchants hoped that Afong Moy would lead the public to other Chinese forms that would provide similar enjoyment in the home.

To accompany teas and suppers, hostesses offered an assemblage of refreshments. In a residence such as the Hones, provisions included jellies, sweetmeats, preserves, cakes, ice cream, and biscuits. Imported Chinese spices and seasonings such as cassia, ginger, nutmeg, curry, anise, and soy flavored and preserved these American foods. As trade with China expanded, recipes relied more heavily on these imported spices and foods in the early to mid-nineteenth century and were more seasoned than they had been at any previous time.[37]

Cassia was the principal spice that flavored many American cakes, cookies, puddings, and warm drinks. The cinnamon cassia tree in the southern provinces of Kwangsi and Hunan yielded the fragrant bark, while the blue berries and distilled bark of the tree provided oil of cassia. The cinnamon from the Chinese tree was sharper than that cultivated in Ceylon, and the latter, less pungent variety was much preferred in China and Europe. Yet Americans were willing to take the less expensive and less refined cassia. Not all found it as disagreeable as Walter Barrett, who claimed that the "nasty stuff from China called cinnamon, impregnated with bilge water, is ground up and sold as cinnamon by all the grocers in the United States."[38]

William Milburn, the English commentator on the China trade, differed. He claimed: "[the] best is manufactured in China, and the finer kind differs but little in its properties from that cinnamon, for which it is generally substituted."[39] Apparently, Americans found it quite agreeable because they imported vast amounts of this spice. The Carneses brought in cases of cassia oil, while other merchants imported cassia in the bark form with 324,101 mats, 62,545 bundles, 27,024 packages, and 20,015 boxes coming into the Philadelphia port alone from 1801 to 1840.[40]

Perhaps Barrett did taste bilge water in his cinnamon, because cassia was considered an excellent filler for dead space in the ship. Hezekiah Pierrepont suggested that Americans pack the mats under the beams of the ship, because the packages were light and flexible.[41] The value of the spice made the packing effort worthwhile; several merchants noted the healthy profit made on this seasoning.

Ginger was often used by American cooks in conjunction with cassia. Spice breads, gingerbread, and Christmas pudding were some of the favorites that called for these spices in combination. As a native seasoning of China, the ginger root served as both a condiment and a medicinal agent. If eaten raw and whole, it settled the effects of a meal; if finely chopped, the warm, sharp taste was an additive to the food. The Chinese used the root with respect, as they were aware that as a medicine its effects on the body were often unpredictable.[42]

Americans imported fresh, ground, and preserved ginger, as well as a ginger substitute called galangal. Many of the China traders mentioned merchant Chyloong's Guangzhou shop as the place to purchase sugared or preserved ginger. His ginger factory, facing the Pearl River in Outer Ngo Chau Street, began production in 1804, and a century later the family business was still in operation. There, ginger shoots were submerged in vats of water, dried, cut, boiled, dipped in rice flour, passed through a water and lime solution, reboiled in sugar, and finally the cold stems of ginger packed in porcelain jars for shipment.[43] Chyloong's shop was the most likely source for the large quantities of ginger that the Carneses imported. On one vessel one hundred cases (each case containing six jars) of preserved young ginger came into New York. In China, they paid four hundred fifty dollars for the lot, with each jar costing seventy-five cents. The cost to consumers would have been at least twice that amount. Preserved ginger was therefore a special treat. Lucy Larcum, in the mill workers' magazine *The Lowell Offering*, noted in the 1840s that she enjoyed "preserved tropical fruit, . . . ginger root and other spicy appetizers . . . for use on election day"—an important and special occasion in the North.[44]

Not all the comestible goods that the Carneses imported were Chinese in origin. In his comments on the Carneses' China trade Walter Barrett remarked that "from Paris and London the most famous sauces, condiments, preserves, sweetmeats, syrups, etc. were procured. The Chinese imitated them all, even to the facsimiles of the printed London or Paris labels, and $20,000 worth at least of these imitations were imported at prices underselling the London and Paris manufacturers. An immense profit was realized."[45] Francis Carnes's hand is evident in this endeavor. From his perch in Paris, Francis scouted out the most appealing and bestselling condiments in Europe which he then sent to China for replication.

In addition to tea, and tastes of cassia and ginger, there were several other aspects of American home life that Afong Moy may have found comfortable and familiar. In China, Afong Moy slept, sat on, and divided her living space with bamboo matting. In the warm climate of southern China, bamboo matting was cool to the touch. Functional and durable, it was also used for packing and protective coverings for fragile objects. This could have been a relatively uncomplicated object for her to present and explain to an American public, yet it was a commodity that had a much greater presence in Chinese domestic life than it did in America.

In America, matting had more defined and specific uses. Its application as a floor covering dated to the middle of the eighteenth century, when inventories in New England and account books in the South confirm their use. In 1788, the French writer on American life, J. P. Brissot de Warville, detailed Philadelphians' application of matting in the summer: "A carpet in summer is an absurdity, yet is kept on the floor out of vanity. Sensible people, however, are beginning to take up their carpets during the summer and leave the floors bare or covered with mats."[46] By the turn of the nineteenth century, straw or bamboo matting was becoming more acceptable. Thomas Jefferson's secretary, Thomas Claxton, reported in 1802 that even the "genteelest people" in Philadelphia employ the material as a floor covering and recommended it for use in the President's House in Washington.[47] Jefferson's reply clarified it as Chinese in origin; however, though the president found it an attractive material, it did not answer his particular need for the dining room floor.

Matting was most frequently used in the parlor. Elizabeth Latimer relayed to her cousin in Guangzhou: "We are much obliged to you for the trouble you took in selecting the matting for us, it is very handsome . . . our parlors look very pretty with our new matting on."[48] Catharine Hone may have condoned Elizabeth's practice for her own parlor, for its acceptability by the mid-1830s was quite universal. Even Osmond Tiffany in the 1840s mentioned its use in an oblique way when he described matting shops in Guangzhou: "this looks more like home than any that we have seen, for the long rolls put us in mind of darkened parlors in summer time."[49]

Newspaper advertisements provided extensive information on its variety. Matting came in many sizes, colors, and lengths but most often in set widths. The standards were 3-4, 4-4, 5-4, 6-4, and 7-4, with 6-4 the most common. The Carneses imported all these various standard sizes. However, unusual sizes—4-7, 3-4, 4-1, 4-8, and 3-8—were also available on the market.[50] The range of colors and patterns was even more extensive, with at least fifteen different variations.[51] Many were checked or checked and striped, while the most extravagant had a complex pattern to simulate a woven Brussels carpet. Two of the three Carneses' extant import records document 6,718 rolls of matting; each roll contained 40 yards for a total of 268,720 yards of matting. The three choices—white, red- checked, and checked—varied in cost: white was the cheapest at eight and a half cents a yard and the most expensive, the red checked, at fourteen cents a yard. Similar quantities of Chinese matting also came into the Philadelphia port. From 1790 to 1840, 34,243 rolls and 2,813 bundles of matting moved through this port, making it one of the larger commodities of material culture goods imported from China. Surely many middle-class households on the Eastern Seaboard made use of matting at some point during this period.

It is likely that many supercargoes filled their orders at Manhing's Guangzhou shop. Tiffany noted that Manhing's warehouse contained 100,000 rolls of matting. The supercargoes and ship captains had careful instructions for packing this light and flexible article in compact places onboard. Yet the precaution to choose dry matting, free from mold, indicated that a certain amount of loss occurred when matting got wet on board ship.

Since the Carneses imported such extensive quantities of Chinese matting, they highlighted their offerings in Afong Moy's New York salon. Risso and Browne's depiction of Afong Moy in the New York salon included a floor covering presented with unusual detail. At least four noticeable floor designs appear in the engraving: zigzag, striped, circular, and diamond patterns. Although we have no existing Carnes manifest record of the more extravagant straw matting patterns, we do know that the Chinese copied Brussels carpet designs such as these in their matting. Possibly Risso and Browne provided us with a view of the Carneses' straw matting patterns.

Along with matting, American traders imported blinds from China in large numbers. The high point of the trade occurred in the 1830s.[52] In 1832, the vessel *Howard* returned with more than two thousand Chinese window blinds. Mills, Brothers & Co. auction advertisements for the ship's goods noted some as "silk, painted," some as "nankin," but the majority were identified merely as "green." It is at this point, with more Americans becoming city dwellers, that citizens expressed a greater concern for privacy. Blinds and other window treatments shielded the householder from the prying eyes of strangers walking the streets. The 1830s trade card for Ball and Price's Plain and Fancy Blind Factory in New York City indicated the variety of blind sizes as well as the ornate cornices to mount them that were available to the urban consumer.[53] In the city, Mrs. Hone surely would have secured her home's privacy with window blinds.

The blinds' use in China was similar to their application in America, providing both privacy and protection from the sun. Osmond Tiffany recorded his trip from Whampoa to Guangzhou on a small boat where he sat in a small cabin with "glass sashes to shield off the wind and green blinds to hide the sun."[54] Similarly, Harriet Martineau recalled the blinds in America used as a protection from the sun in both the North and the South. In *Retrospect of Western Travel*, she recorded her pleasure at the Washington Hotel in New Orleans "with its galleries and green blinds, built for coolness."[55] In New England, too, she found the bedrooms "all shaded with green blinds" to protect from the summer sun. Since Afong Moy's travels nearly mirrored Martineau's itinerary at the same date, it is probable that she too enjoyed the green blinds' shelter from the sun in the same locations.

The use of the term applied to applications on both the interior and exterior of the house. However, several descriptions in newspaper advertisements suggest that Chinese blinds were meant for interior use. Whether of silk or bamboo, they probably rolled up to be tied to a window hook. Frances Trollope, the English recorder of American foibles, noted in *Domestic Manners of the Americans* that blinds were "rolled up and then fastened with string awkwardly attached to the window frames."[56] Numerous period images recorded this haphazard arrangement. Nearly any area of the home might have had blinds on the windows. Inventories and accounts from the 1830s document blinds in the parlor, bedroom, dining-room and even in the "backroom downstairs."

In American newspapers, Chinese blinds were advertised in assorted sizes and noted as "small and large," and most often in specific dimensions of 4' x 6' or 3½' x 6', although the Carneses provided their painted silk blinds in a greater variety of sizes.[57] The color choices available for Chinese blinds were not as extensive as those for floor matting; one could buy them in yellow, white, cream, bamboo (unpainted), or green. The Carneses rightly anticipated that the green blinds were most salable, for green was widely considered "soothing" and "friendly to the eyes." Prices are not included in the Mills, Brothers & Co. auction catalogue, so it is difficult to assess their cost. An 1811 letter from a trader in Guangzhou recorded six Canton window blinds at one dollar and fifty cents; with greater numbers imported in the 1830s, they were likely to be much more affordable to the middle-class consumer.[58]

The Carneses imported other household goods from China that, surprisingly, were cheaper to bring from afar than to obtain locally. These included washbasins, feather dusters, fly whisks, and baskets. The Mills Brothers catalogue listed thousands of brown and black feather dusters and a case of five hundred chowries, or fly whisks.

Unlike feather dusters and fly whisks, Chinese baskets and wash "basons," as they were recorded in the 1830s, received notice in newspaper advertisements and letters. The basins were lacquered and according to a letter book account were red on the interior. As a light, durable, and waterproof material this was an obvious choice for such a function. The Mills, Brothers catalogue says little regarding the basins; they sold more than one hundred in their 1832 auction. Baskets received more notice. Advertisements noted that they were used for storing clothes and toilet articles, as "work baskets," for "traveling," and as "fancy" baskets for marketing or for show. In 1848 Mary Sword explained how her nephew employed the baskets his father sent him from Guangzhou: "The little baskets are very useful. John carries one of them on his arm with a pocket handf [handkerchief] in sometimes. He takes it to the market."[59] All baskets advertised in the papers were of bamboo or rattan. George Mason, in his book *Costumes of China*, noted that the Chinese basket weavers worked these materials so adeptly, and the bamboo was woven so tightly, that the baskets could hold water.[60]

More than 2,280 baskets imported by the Carneses were labeled "chin chu" or "chinchew," a word frequently used to describe baskets, sweetmeats, and fans. These were small, miscellaneous, and generally less expensive items imported from China. Baskets brought back on the *Mary Ballard* cost 2.4 cents each in China. Rattan clothes baskets and other baskets for unspecified

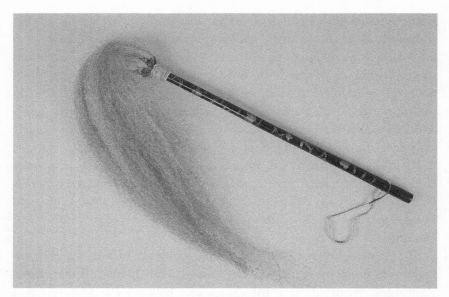

The Carneses found that even commonplace and everyday goods such as fly whisks with lacquer handles and horsehair (*c.* 1850) could provide a profit despite the cost of transport from China. *Photograph by Michele L. Hopkins. National Museum of Natural History, Department of Anthropology, Smithsonian Institution*

A simple duster of Chinese chicken feathers (*c.* 1850) found buyers in America. *Photograph by Michele L. Hopkins. National Museum of Natural History, Department of Anthropology, Smithsonian Institution*

uses that were imported by the Carneses cost significantly more: as much as fifty cents apiece in Guangzhou. Barrett claimed that the Carneses also had fashionable Parisian and London baskets copied in huge quantities by the Chinese, which later flooded the New York market, but no manifest record or image of these fancy baskets has been found.

Paintings and drawings of the period record rattan and bamboo baskets in the corners of American kitchens, hanging on nails in storerooms, filled with corncobs ready to be shelled or clothing items to be mended. Robert E. Lee used a rattan basket to hold wastepaper in his study at Washington College. It is impossible to know whether these baskets were Chinese, though most look very similar to those used by Chinese shoemakers depicted in Mason's book and by Chinese craftsmen in De la Breton's *China: Its Costume, Arts and Manufacture* of 1813.

The Chinese were also known for their cloth, particularly silk. Though Barrett recorded that the Carneses imported silk goods imitating Italian, French, and English patterns, it is grass cloth yardage that is listed in their accounts. The Carneses imported handkerchiefs made of this linen-like fabric, yet Americans were less familiar with this material. China trader John Sword's sister Sarah received several ready-made Chinese dresses from her brother. In a letter of gratitude, she wrote: "My silk dress I admire very much—I shall find it very useful—the grasscloth dress is quite a curiosity—it will make a delightful summer dress."[61] Grass cloth, or ramie, was made from a plant in the hemp family. Because it was silkier and took dye easily, it was the most expensive of these linen-like cloths.[62] The southern Chinese found it particularly comfortable because it was cool against the skin in the summer. As Osmond Tiffany found the matting shop a comforting remembrance of his Baltimore home in the summer, so too did he find Yune's grass cloth shop, where he hung "fondly over the long dress patterns which are so fine and soft as linen cambric."[63] Though he noted that the light, cool material of grass cloth was used in the warm months for dresses, he probably meant the summer robes traditionally worn by wealthy, southern Chinese men.[64] The use of grass cloth for men's clothing carried over into foreign practice as well. The Carneses' vessel *Howard* returned with brown grass cloth roundabouts, a short, close-fitting coat or jacket worn by men or boys. These were listed in the June 1832 Mills Brothers auction catalog—an appropriately lighter jacket for the upcoming summer.

Though Sarah Sword was puzzled by receiving the light grass cloth dress from her brother, she may have been more willing to wear grass cloth on her head. The catalog listed thirty-three pieces of yardage, each thirty yards long, of unbleached grass cloth for ladies' bonnets and thirty pieces of fine white grass cloth without a specified use. Several years later the Carneses imported quantities of fine brown and white grass cloth on the *Mary Ballard*.

American seamstresses found the silk or thread winder, another small Chinese product, of great assistance in their handwork and work on cloth. It was a small thin disc with perforated edges that caught the thread in its ridges for winding onto spools or bobbins. Most were made of mother-of-pearl with delicately incised decorative patterns of exotic Chinese architecture, landscapes, and figures. Often one side held a cartouche that could be inscribed with the initials of the owner. The task of winding thread for embroidery or other handwork became less onerous when using this simple, elegant tool. Purchased for the Carneses at five cents each in Guangzhou, and sold for less than twenty-five cents in America, these small items provided middle-class women with a sense of beauty they could afford, and views of an exotic, faraway place as they labored on their handwork.

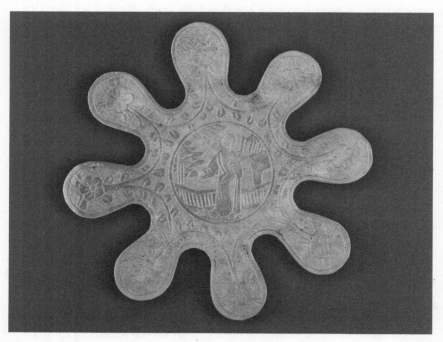

Even on the small surface of a thread winder (c. 1840), the Chinese incised images of life in China. The useful and inexpensive tool found its way into thousands of American women's sewing baskets. *National Museum of American History, Division of Home and Community Life, Smithsonian Institution, gift of Hope Anthony Levy*

The first accounts of Afong Moy when she arrived in New York in 1834 record that she, too, did handwork.[65] As one newspaper observed, "She passes her life at her toilette or at her tambour."[66] The tambour was a wooden frame on which fabric was stretched taut, enabling the embroiderer to move the needle above and below the worked piece.[67]

Philip Hone remarked in his November 1834 diary entry on Afong Moy that Chinese women's "only occupation [is] a little occasional embroidery." Hone was partly correct. According to historian Susan Mann, late eighteenth- and early nineteenth-century Qing men and women differed in their perception of manual labor and the status it conferred. Men eschewed manual labor as a mark of low status. Conversely, women's productive work such as weaving, spinning, and embroidery, in any class, was seen as virtuous. To be idle was to be dissolute.[68] Women of low status—courtesans and prostitutes—were lowly because they did not apply themselves to handwork. Hone would not have known the central place of handwork in a Chinese woman's life. It was a value promoted by the state, by folk tales, and by great Chinese philosophers such as Mencius, whose mother supported her son's studies by weaving.

It is unclear whether Afong Moy actually embroidered. Chinese handwork had a hierarchy. The poorest women wove mats and hats with rough and unfinished materials. Those in the level above were cotton spinners. Next in the hierarchy were those who wove silk, and at the zenith were the silk embroiderers.[69] Embroiderers had the resources to complete elegant work, plus they had access to light and a spacious room for the tambour, and they had uncalloused hands to work the delicate threads through the fabric. Embroidery, associated with refinement and cultivation, would be aspirational for Afong Moy. She knew the markers that it signified, whether or not her handlers recognized it. Assuming Afong Moy did embroider, she would have used a thread winder to organize her embroidery thread to prevent tangling. Handling the smooth, delicate Chinese embroidery tool may have brought home closer.

American women, too, participated in handwork, and for reasons not dissimilar to those of their Chinese sisters—it was a "republican" virtue shared by both cultures. A common sampler verse stated:

This needlework of mine can tell
When I was young I learned well
And by my elders I was taught
Not to spend my time in naught.[70]

The activity of embroidery and needlework provided young American women a corrective to any slothful inclination.[71] However, unlike a young girl's experience in China, a fairly large number of young American women attended seminaries where they learned embroidery skills along with the more substantive studies of arithmetic, geography, music, and languages, such as French.[72] Both Catharine Hones, mother and daughter, were embroiderers who learned this skill to express diligence, orderliness, and competence with the needle. A Chinese thread winder probably lay in their sewing basket.

Quite apart from those goods for the person and home, the Carneses also imported a significant quantity of Chinese pharmaceuticals that Americans purchased from their apothecary. Walter Barrett, in his book *The Old Merchants of New York,* noted that the Carneses, using the "V"-trade concept, had imitated in China every drug known in Europe as well as importing indigenous Chinese medicinal articles.[73] Though their final destination was the American home, initially the products were purchased by druggists such as Cutter & Hurd of New York.

Americans may not have been aware that Chinese medicine was one of the oldest and most developed systems in the world. The sixteenth-century physician and scientist Li Shizhen spent much of his life writing the authoritative pharmacological compendium of herbs, medicinal minerals, and animal parts, which is still consulted today. All Chinese understood and practiced the conception of qi (chi), life energy, as balanced by the yin (female) and yang (male), and correcting deficiencies by ingesting the appropriate natural materials. Afong Moy certainly applied this understanding of the medicinal qualities of herbs and plants in her daily life in America. A knowledge of their efficacies and uses was an important bridge between the cultures that Afong Moy could share with Americans as she, and probably Atung, presented the medicinal goods that the Carneses imported.

Catharine Hone not only instructed her daughters in handwork and genteel activities but also attended to the health issues of her family. She superintended a large household consisting of her husband, three sons, three daughters, and an ailing brother, as well as several servants including a coachman, cook, errand boy, and maids. Women were expected to know the remedies for everyday maladies. In all likelihood, Catharine consulted Lydia Maria Child's *The American Frugal Housewife* for the simple remedies Child cited such as: "for a sudden attack of quincy or croup, bathe the neck with bear's grease, and pour it down the throat" or "Black or green tea, steeped in boiling milk, seasoned with nutmeg . . . is excellent for the dysentery," while "a poultice made of ginger . . . has given great relief to a tooth-ache."[74] Though the bear grease was locally sourced, a number of the ingredients in these recipes came from China. Catharine Hone purchased them from druggists who were also the Carneses' clients.

Rhubarb root was the primary digestive aid in America. *Cassell's Domestic Dictionary* classified rhubarb as one of the most beneficial of all the pharmacopoeia.[75] The dictionary recommended it for stomach problems, indigestion, and biliousness, and as an efficient aperient. Cassell provided a lengthy paragraph describing its appearance and speculating on its Chinese origins, noting that "the exact species of the plant which yields the officinal rhubarb is still a mystery, so jealously do the Chinese authorities . . . guard the secret."[76] In China, the root was prepared in four-, five-, and six-inch pieces and then carefully dried. Though the *India Trader Directory* could not speculate on its genus, it did describe the process of refining it: "They take up the root only in winter—cut it up and lay in shady place with strings of pieces on a cord and hang where dries."[77]

Walter Barrett, too, gave much ink to his description of Chinese rhubarb. Casting aspersions on the Carneses' imported rhubarb, he claimed that the merchants passed off a yellowish Chinese wood resembling the medicinal for the real thing and made a huge profit. He asserted that the "yellow dog-wood, or China rhubarb, is harmless, and so is sawdust; but if as large a quantity of sawdust were to be poked down children as there is of this mock rhubarb, deaths would be [as they are] fearfully large for this cause alone."[78] The *India Trader's Directory* gave directions on checking for the quality, suggesting that the purchaser chew it. If it was "bright nutmeg color," had a "deep saffron tinge," without being "slimy or mucilaginous in the mouth," and tasted "acrid and bitterish," it was of good quality.[79]

Barrett may have exaggerated the poor quality of the Carneses' rhubarb, but he was correct in his assessment of the value they placed on its importation. Rhubarb was the fourth costliest article on the *Mary Ballard*'s manifest. Other traders participated in this market. In his papers, New York China trader Hezekiah Pierrepont pointed out the importance of the root and noted that its sales would show great profit.[80] Judging from the quantity imported into Philadelphia from the late eighteenth to the early nineteenth centuries—1,268 boxes, 242 chests, and 365 cases—as well as the number of advertisements for rhubarb in the New York, Boston, and Philadelphia papers—it was a significant article of trade.[81]

Druggists sold the distilled essence of Chinese rhubarb, taken from the dried plant stalk (left) shown at the 1876 Philadelphia Centennial Chinese exhibition, as a tonic for digestive and constipation ailments (right). *Dried rhubarb, c. 1870. National Museum of American History, Division of Science and Medicine, Smithsonian Institution, gift of the Chinese Imperial Maritime Customs Collection, from the Philadelphia Centennial; Ess Rhabarb, c. 1850. National Museum of American History, Division of Science and Medicine, Smithsonian Institution, gift of Bristol-Myers Squibb Company*

Barrett also commented that the Carneses imported Chinese chamomile flowers. Though similar in appearance to the daisy when fresh, its dried florets contain a powerful oil. Early nineteenth-century medical treatises claimed that a variety of cures could be effected by taking dried chamomile. "They have been found useful in hysterical affections, flatulent or spasmatic cholics and dysentery."[82] By mid-century it served as an aid for insomnia and as an antiseptic, a mouthwash, and a restorative of one's original hair color once it had turned gray.

The travel writer Charles Toogood Downing was a medical doctor in England. Understandably, he found apothecary shops in Guangzhou particularly fascinating and spent many hours chatting with the owners. His accounts of Chinese medical practice and medicines provide a unique insight. Jars, bottles, and boxes, labeled and numbered, sat on the shelves as they did in Cutter & Hurd's establishment in New York City.[83] In contrast to those used in the West, however, Downing found that a greater number of Chinese medicines were derived from nature. He observed, "There is scarcely a plant to be found in the empire, some part or other of which is not used by the physicians; . . . the root of one vegetable, the stalk of another, the fruit of the next, and the flowers of the fourth, are each carefully collected and dried for the service of the invalid."[84] He knew the full range of the typical stock, for when one of the owners became ill, he requested Downing treat him. The owner gave him full access to his shelves hoping that he might concoct a remedy from the materials he found there. Downing found little that he knew or could rely on. He commented that most Chinese ignored the imported Western drugs, which they found ineffectual, and esteemed those which the West would "throw out upon the dunghill."[85] Clearly Westerners had found some of these Chinese remedies effective, rescuing them from the dunghill, and profitably importing them to America, where they were well appreciated.

The New York apothecary shop of Cutter & Hurd at 72 Dey Street presumably carried rhubarb root, chamomile flowers, and other Chinese remedies and European drugs that the Carneses imported. The firm was owned by Marcus Hurd, a medical doctor who received his degree from the University of the City of New-York, now New York University, and Cutter Smith, a druggist.[86] Their shop carried drugs, medicines, perfume, paints, and fancy articles for the general public, as well as surgeon's instruments for the practitioner. Their store contained a more expansive inventory than the apothecary shop that Charles Toogood Downing visited in Guangzhou. One element that surely appeared in both was an article that the Carneses imported. Barrett mentioned in his book that just one Carnes invoice recorded the importation of 100,000 horn scoops "to be used in the drawers of grocers and druggists to ladle out sugar, salt, or any powdered stuff. There is hardly a druggist in this city to-day who does not possess some samples of the Chinese horn scoops."[87]

Many of the first newspaper reports record Afong Moy as "a healthy, bouncing girl . . . with a skin slightly tinged with copper, but sufficiently transparent to exhibit that 'roses are blooming' beneath it."[88] Others commented on her "robust stature" and her apparent well-being. Afong Moy's tenacity while on the voyage to America was attested to by a fellow traveler who called her "a perfect little vixen."[89] If these were accurate reports of her constitution, she was fortunate. Though she seemed healthy to observers, travel may have taken a toll, and if so her physical care in America would differ from that in China. Some of the imported Chinese remedies such as rhubarb and chamomile flowers were available from druggists like Cutter & Hurd. Other Chinese folk medicines that she may have relied on at home, such as rhinoceros and deer horn powders, would have been impossible to obtain in the West.

Americans gained information regarding Chinese medical practice from several sources. The most significant intelligence on the topic came from a young medical student and missionary whose path nearly crossed Afong Moy's. New Englander Peter Parker had an early calling to foreign missionary work. In 1831 he wrote: "I have often felt my soul go forth in longing desires for the conversion of the *whole world*. What a *privilege* will it be . . . that I may light up the way to glory to many a heathen who shall survive me."[90] Though a farmer's son without resources, he worked his way through Yale University, received medical and theological degrees from Yale by early 1834, and the same year became an ordained minister. The American Board of Commissioners for Foreign Missions willingly accepted his application and appointed him to work in China. Provided free passage on a China trader's vessel, and accompanied by Ah Leang, a seventeen-year-old returning Chinese servant who taught him Chinese, Parker arrived in Guangzhou in October 1834, just a few months after Afong Moy left for America. He quickly ascertained that his skills as a doctor might be coupled with his missionary activities. He chose to focus on eye treatment, for it was an area of great need. Giving free treatment initially caused suspicions, yet soon lines of Chinese patients waited to be helped. Though Chinese women were forbidden in the area of the foreign factories, Parker yet treated 270 women of a total of 925 patients in his first quarter.[91] News of his medical work, and the success he was achieving, soon reached America. On a brief return to the United States in 1840, Parker lectured widely on his work and the state of medicine in China.

S. Wells Williams, one of the four Americans who greeted Peter Parker when he arrived in Guangzhou in 1834, also relayed medical information he gleaned from English doctors who worked with the Chinese. They dubbed one of these Chinese medical practitioners, Ta Wang Siensang, "Mr. Rhubarb," for the frequent prescription of this remedy.[92] Like Downing, the English doctors analyzed the contents of the dispensatories and found that of 442 medicinal agents, 314 were vegetable, 50 mineral, and 78 animal.[93]

What surprised them were the number of apothecary shops and the wide-spread consumption of medicines in China.

When she first arrived in America, Afong Moy's care would have been assured; her handlers would have avoided the bad publicity of insensitive care. Yet for Afong Moy, medical attention in China was vastly different from that for the Hones in America. Though Mrs. Hone might utilize traditional remedies, and even some of Chinese origin, family members almost surely consulted a doctor for more challenging illnesses. If Afong Moy ever met a medical practitioner in China, it was from behind a bamboo screen.[94] In the later nineteenth century when more Chinese entered the United States, Chinese doctors would come as well, bringing the plants and medicines that they relied on for their health. But as an early Chinese sojourner in America, Afong Moy did not have that option. Her only recourse might have been the medicinals she carried with her or a Chinese self-help manual such as the *Golden Mirror of Medicine*, which provided diagrams and basic information on bodily care.[95]

Many of the articles that Afong Moy may have used herself and presented to the public illustrate the differences between the imported Chinese objects defined for the middle class—those less expensive goods identified as part of a later commercial orientalism—and those more expensive objects imported for the elite, categorized as the earlier patrician orientalism. This can be seen in their scale and purpose. It was often necessary to modify a Chinese object's design to suit the taste of the upper class.[96] The elite Western client more often adapted, rather than accepted, Chinese objects. In contrast, many articles that the Carneses imported for the general market were often indigenous Chinese objects. Palm leaf fans, fireworks, baskets, toys, matting, blinds, some drugs, and foodstuffs were equally salable in China as in America. Because their Chinese design was often unchanged, they were much less expensive commodities. Most objects advertised and sold by the Carneses on the open market were small in scale. Large porcelain pagodas, punchbowls, casework secretaries, and large chests on chests were rarely available to the general public. Rather it was the compact and portable forms that the Carneses imported, and Afong Moy presented, for this middle-class clientele. Canes, lanterns, snuffboxes, tea caddies, and thread winders were easily packaged for shipment. Most of these objects were produced in an assembly-line fashion by low-cost Chinese labor. Few received specialized handwork or individualized design. Such objects were affordable because the Carneses purchased them in large quantities.

The middle-class American of the 1830s participated in the rewards of trading with China. The numbers of objects imported in these categories were far too large to be enjoyed solely by the few. The variety, cost, and amount of goods the Carneses imported—from fireworks to rhubarb— indicate that middle-class households had access to a substantial quantity of Chinese trade goods. Better roads, new canals, and railroads lowered transportation costs and extended the areas into which such goods could reach. The American public actively participated in the trade as consumers, and a culture they had previously viewed only through objects now shaped their lives and tastes. With Afong Moy's arrival in 1834, and her extensive travel through much of the country for several years thereafter, the middling public for the first time associated these Chinese objects they purchased and used with a human being from this exotic and faraway land. Whether she was promoting goods or performing as her exotic self, Afong Moy's journey would present a China that the American public had never before experienced.

PART III

ON TOUR

6

New York to Charleston

PHILIP HONE'S DIARY RECORDED AFONG Moy's arrival in New York in October 1834. His entry considered the particularities of her person, her bound feet, and, according to him, the issues of her Chinese womanhood, a want of education, and a deficiency of ideas. Hone's intimate diary description introduced us to the woman who would soon have a very public life traveling extensively throughout America advertising Chinese goods and presenting the ways of China to the nation.

In New York, Afong Moy's managers carefully crafted her public persona. They promoted her exotic orientalism with a focused attention on her visual difference—her bound feet, Chinese clothing, and accessories. They established her pedigree—a lady of rank, the daughter of a distinguished Chinese citizen. And, through an accompanying display of historical Chinese objects, Nathaniel Carnes and Captain Benjamin Obear shrewdly exceptionalized China as a distant place of revered history and mystery, of which Afong Moy was a part. They selected New York City, the principal link in America's global commercial efforts, to establish and define her presence in America.

Afong Moy, like most travelers in the 1830s, whether foreign or domestic, found New York City an overwhelmingly busy and commercial city. Between 1820 and 1830 the population of the city nearly doubled to 202,589, and of that increase, 78,883 were immigrants.[1] Americans, like one Princeton University student who visited the city in 1836, noticed that "the many foreigners you meet, gives to the appearance of the street

127

a certain air and style."[2] Another American in 1835 found it "a most astonishing place—it greatly exceeds my expectations in size, bustle, beauty & variety—It is a perfect bee hive—even the boys, dogs and cats seem to borrow the spirit of the place—they move faster than with us."[3] Most people experienced this frenetic activity in a city where buyers and sellers flocked to do business in the warehouses, wharves, banks, auction houses, and mercantile stores.

Foreigners found the pace frightening. Englishwoman Harriet Martineau complained: "In the streets I was in danger of being run down by the fire-engines."[4] A German businessman compared New Yorkers to ants whose "feverish industry seemed to devour these inhabitants."[5] As the most populous city in the nation, it attracted those who had grand ideas and those with nefarious intents. It was into this motley assembly that the Carneses and the Obears plunged the young Afong Moy. It was not the numbers of people that would have disturbed her; Guangzhou boasted a much larger population than New York City. Nor would the foreign faces have unsettled her; her city had 200,000 foreign residents in the seventh century and many more in the nineteenth.[6] Most disconcerting may have been the attention paid to her by strange men in close proximity to her person. For this she would have been completely unprepared. Women in China remained behind closed doors and generally were not seen in public.

The newspapers announced her entrance into the city with lofty fanfare as the "Extraordinary Arrival—The Young Chinese Lady . . . the beautiful and accomplished, the long looked for and anxiously expected *Miss Julia Foochee-ching-chang-king*."[7] As they noted, her presentation to the public was initially somewhat restrained in recognition that meeting groups of people in a new land fatigued her. Soon, however, Afong Moy's handlers were encouraging visitors to purchase fifty-cent tickets well in advance, for crowds wished to see her. Captain Obear, or another agent, sold the tickets in a basement room at 8 Park Place.

On November 7, the *New-York Daily Advertiser* noted that one might see the Chinese lady at 8 Park Place, and "at the same place are also to be seen various objects of Chinese curiosity, themselves well worthy the attention of the curious."[8] Another press article stated that Afong Moy was surrounded with "articles of Chinese manufacture."[9] Starting on November 14, ten notices in the papers announced auctions for specific products from the vessel *Washington*. On November 17, an auction sold pearl buttons, rattans, and china paper; another auction on the eighteenth advertised nankin floor matting; on the nineteenth, curry powder and preserves; on the twenty-sixth, ginger sugar candy and marmalades; on December 5, Canton drugs, Canton fancy goods, toys, firecrackers, and bamboo toilet baskets.

The conjoining of Afong Moy's salon, where some of these goods were shown, and the timing and frequency of the auctions where they were sold were no coincidence. This kind of product placement was an ingenious idea. The Obears, and presumably the Carneses, made money on the entrance fees while Afong Moy promoted their goods in the salon for the upcoming auctions. It was Atung, Afong Moy's attendant and translator, who assisted by highlighting the articles of note, providing background on their use and value, and adroitly helping to market them.

To highlight the exceptional nature of Chinese objects, China as a nation, and Afong Moy as its embodiment, the Carneses and Captain Obear organized a supplemental exhibition at Park Place. Here, in a room separate from Afong Moy's salon, the American public saw, for the first time, an exhibition of "ancient" Chinese artifacts.[10] The two-page "Catalogue of Chinese Curiosities" enumerated the objects on one side; on the other, a history of Afong Moy.[11] It was the catalogue's visual presentation that might first have captured the public's interest. Both sides carried the same image of the Chinese lady, but one most dissimilar from the seated view of Afong Moy in Charles Risso and William Browne's lithograph.

Here, Afong Moy stood—boldly staged to establish an exotic contrast. One clearly visible bound foot pirouettes toward the viewer, an elbow rests casually on a Chinese side table, similar to the one in Risso and Browne's lithographic view in her salon. Afong Moy's trousers and surcoat announce the gulf between Western dress and that worn in China. Fan, hair accessories, and jewelry are carefully delineated to mark the divergence of oriental fashion from that in America.

Unlike the Risso and Browne lithograph, which was probably a fairly accurate depiction of Afong Moy, the managers probably selected this image from one of the generic Chinese "rice" paintings like those promoted in the salon and sold by the Carneses. As one of the earliest public images of Afong Moy, it was hastily printed for publication. The catalogue view closely resembled the watercolor rice painting depictions

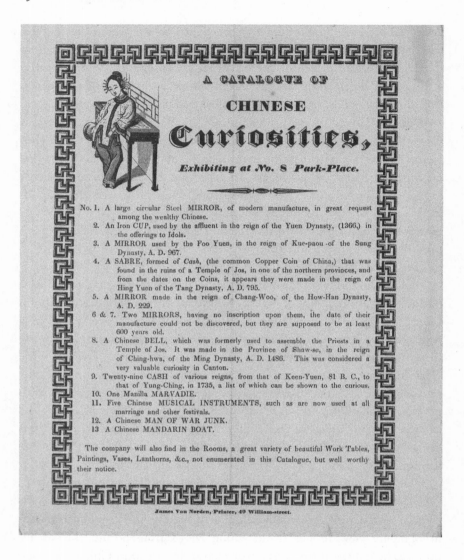

A CATALOGUE OF

CHINESE

Curiosities,

Exhibiting at No. 8 Park-Place.

No. 1. A large circular Steel MIRROR, of modern manufacture, in great request among the wealthy Chinese.
2. An Iron CUP, used by the affluent in the reign of the Yuen Dynasty, (1366,) in the offerings to Idols.
3. A MIRROR used by the Foo Yuen, in the reign of Kue-paou of the Sung Dynasty, A. D. 967.
4. A SABRE, formed of *Cash*, (the common Copper Coin of China,) that was found in the ruins of a Temple of Jos, in one of the northern provinces, and from the dates on the Coins, it appears they were made in the reign of Hing Yuen of the Tang Dynasty, A. D. 795.
5. A MIRROR made in the reign of Chang-Woo, of the How-Han Dynasty, A. D. 229.
6 & 7. Two MIRRORS, having no inscription upon them, the date of their manufacture could not be discovered, but they are supposed to be at least 600 years old.
8. A Chinese BELL, which was formerly used to assemble the Priests in a Temple of Jos. It was made in the Province of Shaw-se, in the reign of Ching-hwa, of the Ming Dynasty, A. D. 1486. This was considered a very valuable curiosity in Canton.
9. Twenty-nine CASH of various reigns, from that of Keen-Yuen, 81 B. C., to that of Yung-Ching, in 1735, a list of which can be shown to the curious.
10. One Manilla MARVADIE.
11. Five Chinese MUSICAL INSTRUMENTS, such as are now used at all marriage and other festivals.
12. A Chinese MAN OF WAR JUNK.
13 A Chinese MANDARIN BOAT.

The company will also find in the Rooms, a great variety of beautiful Work Tables, Paintings, Vases, Lanthorns, &c., not enumerated in this Catalogue, but well worthy their notice.

James Van Norden, Printer, 49 William-street.

of women employed in the everyday occupation of silk making. A mid-nineteenth-century Chinese watercolor album in the Winterthur Library's collection includes ten views of Chinese women weaving, spinning, and winding silk.[12] All the women wore trousers and a surcoat similar to Afong Moy's clothing in the catalogue. One of the watercolors analogous to the catalogue image depicted a seated woman. Both show an abbreviated view of their bound feet with legs crossed in a similar fashion; both dressed their hair in a comparable style with a silk flower tucked into their tresses. Behind the silk worker stood a foreshortened image of the

CHINESE LADY.

THE *Chinese Lady*, AFONG MOY, lately arrived from Canton in the ship *Washington*, will receive visiters at No. 8 *Park Place*, between the hours of 10 A. M and 2 P. M., and 5 and 9 P. M. She possesses a pleasing countenance, is 19 years of age, four feet ten inches in height, and her feet, including her shoes, are but four inches in length, having worn *Iron Shoes* for the first ten years of her life, according to the custom of the country. She will be dressed in the costume of her own country, and be surrounded by various articles of Chinese manufacture, worthy the attention of the curious. Large sums of money have been expended, and great difficulties experienced, in overcoming the extreme jealousy of the Chinese in allowing their females to be carried out of their country, or even to be seen by foreigners; and no pains or expense have been spared, in rendering the exhibition in every way worthy of the attention of the public. Several articles in the furniture of the room are of great value, and in themselves well worthy of the attention of the curious.

ATUNG, the attendant of the Chinese Lady, is a lad of great intelligence, and speaks English with considerable fluency, and will interpret for the company.

Price of admission, 50 cents; Children, 12½ cents.

New-York, December, 1834.

The small text at the bottom of the catalogue spread for *A Catalogue of Chinese Curiosities* (December 1834) makes reference to the additional objects available for viewing in Afong Moy's salon: paintings, work tables, and lanterns. However, these items were not enumerated in the catalogue itself. *Rare Books Division, New York Public Library, Astor, Lenox, and Tilden Foundations*

side table like the one Afong Moy leaned on in the catalogue view. Since the silk-weaver watercolor albums were popular and prevalent in America and perhaps brought by the Carneses, one of them may have been the source for Afong Moy's image in the catalogue.

A silk production album depicts a young woman with a similar stance, dress, and surroundings to Afong Moy in the *Catalogue of Chinese Curiosities*. Other albums illustrated the cultivation of tea and the making of porcelain. *Album of silk production, China, 1849. Courtesy Winterthur Library, Joseph Downs Collection of Manuscripts and Printed Ephemera*

James Van Norden, 49 William Street, printed the first American catalogue of Chinese objects. His place of business was conveniently on the same street as the Carneses' New York City establishment. Van Norden could easily procure the text about Afong Moy directly from newspapers' accounts; his office was over the *Evening Post*, which had circulated this same information well before the December printing of the catalogue. The text related to the artifacts required considerably more attention. Though both Nathaniel Carnes and Benjamin Obear had been to China, neither had sufficient knowledge of Chinese history, or the personal Chinese connections, to locate artifacts or compile the historical background that the catalogue provided. Someone in China had collected this grouping of objects and provided the text.

In early 1834, when Captain Obear had last visited China, and when the objects would have been assembled, few Americans had the capacity or the expertise to locate such artifacts. Samuel Wells Williams, who would later become a noted sinologist, had just arrived in Guangzhou in October 1833, several months before Captain Obear. He therefore had little time to become acquainted with the sources necessary to collect these objects. However, John Shillaber, though the American consul in Batavia (today, Jakarta), spent a good portion of his time in the 1830s in Guangzhou and considered himself a knowledgeable authority on China.[13] His sister, Caroline, lived in nearby Macao and was married to Thomas R. Colledge, an English doctor well loved by the Chinese, whom he had treated since 1827.[14] In 1834, Shillaber hoped to impress Andrew Jackson and Secretary of State Edward Livingston with his expertise on China to secure the Guangzhou consular post. With his brother-in-law's skill, knowledge, and close Chinese contacts, Shillaber could have amassed such a grouping of historic objects with hopes that their display might encourage the American China trade, impress the Jackson administration, and win him a job.[15]

The nomenclature and description of the historic Chinese objects in the catalogue conveyed several messages. If accurately assessed by the collector, most artifacts were of significant historicity, ranging from the Han (206 BCE–220 CE) to the Ming (1368–1644 CE) dynasties.[16] They represented the long history of the Chinese civilization, and displayed the culture's advanced technical capabilities in an early period. By association, this indicated that Afong Moy came from an ancient and esteemed culture, and that Chinese objects seen in her salon also held considerable import. Many of the words used to describe the objects or their past history suggested privilege and rarity: the "MIRROR . . . in great request among the wealthy Chinese," "An Iron CUP, used by the affluent," "A MIRROR used by Foo Yuen . . . of the Sung Dynasty," or the "Chinese BELL a very valuable curiosity." The objects projected prosperity and exclusivity, impressing visitors with the rarity of the goods seen here and, by extension, Afong Moy as an equally rare and important "asset." Other artifacts conveyed Chinese culture including musical instruments, mirrors, vessels, and a bell—exotic anomalies, perhaps explicated on stage by Afong Moy and Atung. Finally, Chinese coins and currencies presented the long history of exchange, the current monetary manifestation of which would fuel the China trade.[17]

Many New Yorkers, including Philip Hone and his family, flocked to see the "curiosities" noted in the catalogue, as well as Afong Moy, the principal curiosity. The press remarked that the rooms were "crowded . . . with fashionables. Among the visitors have been a large number of distinguished individuals."[18] Though he was not mentioned in this account, one of the "distinguished individuals" included New Yorker Martin Van Buren, the vice president of the United States. The numbers may have been exaggerated, but newspaper reports stated that nearly two thousand visitors a week came to see Afong Moy and the objects that surrounded her.[19]

Only obliquely can we gauge her response to such a crowd. Some reporters observed that she seemed composed, yet a few caught her uneasy moments: "for the gentlemen she seems to have no very particular fancy, and indeed, when some of them significantly ogled her through their quizzing glasses, we thought we saw on her brow, a frown of indignant rebuke."[20] Though she uttered no words of displeasure, the audience read her discomfort in her face and posture. This fleeting moment of nonverbal response, or affect, provided audiences then, and—with the newspaper description— readers today, an insight into Afong Moy's character and her sense of alienation. She found mingling with unfamiliar men uncomfortable. Numerous Western accounts of Guangzhou specifically address the absence of women in the shops, in the markets, and on the streets. This may also explain complaints that she was taciturn even when communicating through an interpreter. One reporter enjoined: "Those exquisites who hope to make an impression on this young lady, must be particularly cautious and delicate in their approaches."[21]

Some New Yorkers were perceptive regarding the Obears' and Carneses' strategy. The editor of the *New-York Mirror* asserted: "We have not been to see Miss Afong Moy, the Chinese lady nor do we intend to perform that ceremony to convert a lady into an exhibition. [It is], by no means to our taste."[22] Others recognized that this staged production was a business venture that could yield profitable results.[23] After a month of salon engagements, the papers realized that Afong Moy was not soon returning home to China. Most then knew that this was not a pleasant get-to-know-you visit on her part, but a commercial activity that would be moving on to another venue.

In New York, snow lay on the ground on New Year's Day, 1835. In his diary Philip Hone recorded that it was a "bright and snappy" day. He whirred around the city in his sleigh, paying visits, enjoying the activity of New York, and delighting in the sound of sleigh bells on Broadway. Down the street from Hone, Afong Moy had her first encounter with snow. According to the papers, she found it so unappealing that she wanted to return to "the Celestial Empire" because the climate was too cold.[24] Soon after, the New York *Journal of Commerce* observed that Afong Moy would be leaving the city for the South.[25]

Her southern journey would illumine different facets of her experience in the United States, including both attractive and unattractive aspects of American life. The temperate climate may have suited her, but the observation of slavery was surely chilling. Though her voice was muted by translators and newspaper reportage, Afong Moy's opinions occasionally came through the veil. Because the historical record regarding her is so slim and so few personal accounts remain, the contextual environment helps to shed light on her encounters.

Though Philadelphia was south of New York, it was not too far south. Afong Moy may have been disappointed that her journey to this city in mid-January provided little change in the weather. Philadelphia diarist Samuel Breck noted the early February weather as "extremely severe" and unusually cold, with all the water in rivers frozen.[26] It must have been particularly unpleasant, because one of the notices for her salon stated that, because of the "very inclement state of the weather" which inhibited ladies from attending, Afong Moy would remain some time longer.[27] With an average low temperature in January of 54 degrees Fahrenheit, Guangzhou would have seemed a faraway paradise.

Afong Moy's Philadelphia sojourn was entirely different than her stay in New York. There her salon took place in the somewhat familiar confines of Captain Obear's home on Park Place, in which she resided. During her three months in New York, it is likely that she rarely strayed beyond the environs of his house—and so was shielded from the vagaries of the weather and sequestered from much of the New York rabble. She met visitors in a semblance of her own Chinese milieu and in a space designed for her. In Philadelphia, she received visitors at Washington Hall on South Third Street. Designed for the Washington Benevolent Society in 1816 by the well-known American architect Robert Mills, the hall accommodated a six-thousand-person auditorium.[28] The hall had to be expansive, for in 1834 Washington Hall audiences viewed dioramas. Visitors entered a darkened auditorium. Once their eyes adjusted to the gloom, they saw a scene before them that appeared dimensional and in motion with light manipulated by lamps, windows, and screens playing across a painted, semi-transparent canvas, often as long as twenty-four feet. These presentations required such space to engage the public in their legerdemain. Afong Moy's managers needed a similar room, for their ambitions were much larger than the salon presentation on Park Place.

Afong Moy entered the city with the accolade of the "Unprecedented Novelty!"[29] That novelty would be herself, as well as the novelties associated with Chinese goods. Washington Hall was outfitted as a "complete Chinese Museum" and a "Chinese Saloon." Forty years earlier some privileged Philadelphians had seen a similar exhibition when the Dutch American merchant Andreas van Braam Houckgeest furnished a temporary Chinese exhibition with imported Chinese goods. These were briefly displayed for select visitors with some fanfare and then dismantled when Houckgeest hurriedly left the city for England. In 1832, Philadelphian Nathan Dunn returned home from China after spending twelve years as a merchant in Guangzhou. Soon after, he built a "Chinese cottage," his residence in Mount Holly, New Jersey. Here, too, friends might see some of the Chinese objects he had collected. But not until 1838 would he formally open his Chinese museum to the Philadelphia public. Therefore, the "Chinese Museum" that Afong Moy presented, probably accompanied by the exhibition catalogue printed in New York, was the first of its type available to a broad Philadelphia audience.

This was not Philadelphia's first museum. Charles Willson Peale had established his for-profit public museum in 1784. Though it was initially intended as a picture gallery, its contents soon included the anomalies of nature: dried paddlefish from the Allegheny River, a preserved Angora cat, fossils, and by 1831, 1,310 birds, 4,000 insects, 8,000 minerals, 1,044 shells, and 200 snake, lizard, tortoise, and turtle specimens.[30] Significantly, the proceeds from the museum were sufficient to provide for Peale's large family. By 1810, his annual receipts averaged a substantial sum of $8,000.[31] Entrepreneurs of this period realized that, if they were clever, they could make money running museums. Afong Moy's managers may well have expected similar returns.

The notices of Afong Moy's appearances in Philadelphia cryptically mention the contents of her handler's museum with the phrase "various curiosities of her native country," which probably included the Chinese mirrors, bell, coinage, and various other historic artifacts. The sale of goods by her managers in separate auction announcements in the newspapers clarify some specific objects the public saw in Afong Moy's Chinese "museum." On display—and then for sale at auction—were Chinese lacquered work tables, writing desks, dressing tables with looking glasses, tea tables, china vases, chairs, Chinese stools, a gong, and a number of objects listed under the term "etcetera's."[32] Some of the goods listed in the auction notices corresponded to those depicted in the Risso and Browne lithograph of the New York salon.

In Philadelphia, Afong Moy's visage, with some of the Chinese goods, appeared in newspapers for the first time. The Risso and Browne lithograph had just gone into production. Philadelphia newspapers used an artistically less accomplished and truncated woodblock print based on Risso and Browne's lithograph. The viewer saw Afong Moy seated below the elaborate canopy, but the large Chinese watercolors figures, many of the furniture pieces, and the objects were excised. This image accentuated her tiny feet as they peeked from beneath her robe, as well as her elaborate costume. The artist-engraver highlighted the tunic's border, widened its girth, and gave emphasis to the sleeve by raising her hand to the side of her face—a typical female pose of the period that Risso and Browne used in their 1835 lithograph *Belle of Ohio*.

With heightened visibility through her image in the newspapers, her presentation in a public venue, and the establishment of a "museum," questions as to Afong Moy's background and the veracity of her tiny feet were sure to surface. Audiences were familiar with the arts of visual deception as practiced by a number of traveling shows, and such cultural deceits caused suspicion.

The positioning of Afong Moy on a raised dais, seated in a prominent chair, and under a large canopy, indicated a person of royalty and prestige. This visual messaging encouraged visitors to attend the "Chinese Museum" to view such a notable figure. *American Sentinel, Philadelphia, February 17, 1835*

Show managers attracted audiences with consistent patterns of illusion and deception. They lured visitors in with the action of automatons, seemingly self-operating machines that functioned with human-like capabilities, and they applied magic to make real what was monstrous or fake. Visitors to her salon felt justified in asking questions: Are these her real feet? Are they indeed small? What do her feet look like without shoes?

On January 27, 1835, with the permission of the exhibition's manager, eight physicians privately examined her feet. The newspaper called it a "novel examination" and explained: "The foot of the Chinese Lady was yesterday morning examined, divested of its covering by several eminent Physicians of this city . . . by invitation of the conductors of the exhibition. They expressed themselves highly gratified, and, for the satisfaction of the public, as to the real size of the foot, without being shortened or tightened by bandages, were polite enough to leave the following document with their signatures."[33] The document, published in newspapers, stated: "We, the undersigned, having inspected the foot of the Chinese lady, Afong Moy, divested of its covering, find the dimensions to be as follows—Length of foot from the heel to the end of great toe, 4¾ inches; from the heel to the end of small toe, 2½ inches; . . . and also certify that the model exhibited to us by the proprietor is a good representation of the general appearance of the real foot."[34] Facetiously, *Atkinson's Saturday Evening Post* expressed gratitude to the "respectable" physicians, since their certification eliminated disputes and established that her foot was indeed one-eighth of an inch shorter than previously thought.[35] They also drolly recommended that these important dimensions be written into the Philosophical Society's transactions for posterity.[36]

The eight Philadelphia physicians who signed the document were Governor Emerson, John Bell, Richard Harlan, William Edmonds Horner, Joseph Peace, Jacob Randolph, William Samuel Waithman Ruschenberger, and an "M. Morgan" (likely Mordecai Morgan). All were chosen because of their current or previous work in the medical field. The majority of them— Morgan, Ruschenberger, Randolph, Emerson, and Harlan—had previously served as navy fleet or ship surgeons. Several had traveled to China, and Peace traveled extensively in Europe. Horner served as a professor of anatomy at the University of Pennsylvania, and Harlan was professor of anatomy at Peale's Museum. A number of them also treated the poor at the Philadelphia almshouse or the City Hospital, where they might encounter unusual medical cases. They were all interested in the larger world, fascinated with the uncommon, and curious about the body.

The document also stated that the proprietor of the exhibition mounted a model of Afong Moy's naked foot, which visitors viewed in the museum. Probably it was similar to the image illustrated in the January 1835 issue of *Parley's Magazine*, a children's publication printed in Boston. The article began with the assumption that children had heard of "Miss Afong Moy" since the newspapers were full of notices about her. Along with an explanation of the manners and customs of the East regarding female feet in China, the article also included large drawings of the "undressed" and "dressed" Chinese foot. The writer noted, however, that visitors could see Afong Moy's real "stinted" feet "for very little. Miss Afong Moy would charge you twenty-five or fifty cents, I suppose, for a view of hers."[37]

Foot of a Chinese lady, undressed.

Here is the picture of one of these stinted Chinese feet; which you may see for very little. Miss Afong Moy would charge you twenty-five or fifty cents, I suppose, for a view of her's.

The covering of tne foot and leg is rather odd. First, it consists of a kind of boot, made of plaited straw or cane; as you see by the engraving, which is a very fine one.

An article in *Parley's Magazine* encouraged American children to use their brains and limbs so they might become "large and strong." The piece presents Afong Moy's bound feet, graphically depicted as curiosities, in contrast to this. *"Manners and Customs in the East,"* Parley's Magazine, *January 1835. Courtesy American Antiquarian Society*

Foot of a Chinese lady, dressed

It is not hard to imagine how Afong Moy and her interpreter Atung (called Acung in Philadelphia) responded to the indignities of this intrusive process. Unwrapping, "undressing" her foot, in the company of strange Chinese men would have been unthinkable, and even more so to those of another race. The bound foot was the most private and erotic part of a Chinese woman's body and as such it was kept hidden even to those most intimate.[38]

An earlier incident in Guangzhou illustrated how abhorrent such an "undressing" might be to a Chinese woman. In 1821, Philadelphian John Kearsley Mitchell, the young American ship surgeon, boldly tried to persuade a Chinese woman in Guangzhou to unwrap her bound feet. His letter home recorded the results: "Of their small feet you have often heard. I had much curiosity to see one uncovered, but the beggar girl to whom I applied said she would not take the bandages away and show me her naked foot for one hundred dollars."[39] This was an enormous amount of money in 1821, and even for that fortune, she would not relent and unbind. In 1835, Afong Moy's unwrapping process in the company of American men was a serious infringement of Chinese cultural norms that neither the proprietor, Captain Obear, nor the doctors could understand. Neither Afong Moy nor her interpreter Atung had the power, or the language and negotiating skills, to object.

At the same time as her presentation in Philadelphia with the model of her naked foot on public display, numerous illustrations of the same circulated in magazines. These images, considered pornographic in China, were not available in that country until the development of photography and Western printing techniques. Only in the 1860s did several Shanghai photographers persuade poor women to reveal their bare bound feet. These mid-nineteenth-century images were not for internal consumption but rather for Western tourists.[40] During the same period, American missionary doctors circulated similar illustrations in medical journals and reports. Like the erotica photographs for tourists, these were disseminated only in the West. Yet even though these images were meant for Western consumption, the exposure of women's bound feet in illustrations, and later photographs, humiliated the Chinese. Much later in 1898, the scholar Kang Youwei wrote: "foreigners have long taken photographs of (our vices) and laughed at us, calling us barbaric. And the most laughable matter that brings us the most humiliation is foot binding. Your humble servant is deeply ashamed of it."[41] It is difficult to ascertain whether Kang was shamed by the images or shamed by the process of foot binding. In either interpretation, inspecting a Chinese woman's naked bound feet by any race was reprehensible.

An unusual perspective on the unbinding and revealing of Afong Moy's foot came in *Atkinson's Saturday Evening Post*. The *Post* reporter praised Afong Moy as a "lady of true republican principles" who willingly met all who visited her whether they were rich, poor, aristocratic, or plebeian.[42] The *Post* mockingly toyed with the term "republican." To readers, the term "republican" meant the virtuous and generous accessibility of rights for all. Afong Moy (or the handlers) charged equally for the honor of a visit. All those who wished to see her feet paid the same amount, with the implication that her republican magnanimity was less than virtuous, and instead quite commercial. Such republicanism, they averred, was unexpected from someone who followed Confucian ideals. Most Americans knew very little about "Confucian ideals," which did honor the virtuous, and therefore they applied this analysis in error.

While some Philadelphia doctors examined Afong Moy's feet, Samuel Morton, another prominent Philadelphia physician, gave attention to her head. It is probable that Morton gained access to Afong Moy through his mentor Richard Harlan, one of the Philadelphia physicians who examined Afong Moy's feet. For several years Morton had collected and studied skulls from around the world to determine differences between races.[43] Basing his work on the earlier skull collecting of Harlan, as well as the work of Scottish phrenologists and European naturalists, Morton concluded that human characteristics and intellectual capacity might be determined by the size of the head. The larger the brain, the greater the intelligence; a smaller skull indicated a lesser intelligence. Morton's study supported the theory of polygenesis, which determined that there was a multiplicity of races, and therefore different species. The opposing theory, monogenesis, stated that all humans originated from one species, an interpretation congruent with the biblical account of Adam and Eve.

Morton's comparison of skulls found the Caucasian race to have the largest cranial capacity, the Chinese the second largest, and in descending order South East Asians, American Indians, and finally Africans. In his widely read book *Crania Americana* Morton furthered his consideration of racial diversity by defining the characteristics of such races. He quoted the missionary Robert Morrison's observations on the positive Chinese traits of "mildness and urbanity; docility, industry . . . respect for the aged and for parents" countered by the less attractive qualities of speciousness, insincerity, jealousy, and finally their "generally selfish, cold-blooded and inhumane" nature.[44] However, there is no record of Morton's assessment of Afong Moy's head or her character.

If such theories had remained locked away in books consulted only by medical doctors and naturalists, there would be little reason to address the topic. This was not the case. Morton's concepts, and those of some phrenologists supporting multiple creations, were disseminated widely in newspapers and popular magazines. Morton's work provided ammunition to slaveholders who saw Africans as an inferior race, offered an excuse to those who wished to remove Native Americans from their land because of their supposed "revengeful, and restless behavior," and provided an opportunity to dismiss Asians as an "inhumane" race apart. This polygenic view of race, originating at this time principally in Philadelphia, and the earlier monogenist perspective, would later influence the way the public viewed Afong Moy as she traveled America.

Unlike New Yorkers, Philadelphians expressed their fascination with Afong Moy in artistic and literary ways as well. Not only was Philadelphia the nation's most advanced medical center with well-established hospitals and medical schools whose practitioners would find Afong Moy's physical traits of interest, but it also had a rich artistic and literary heritage. A New York City visitor in 1830 remarked: "Such is the countless wealth . . . of the city . . . such the acknowledged superiority of her artists [engineers and mechanics]—of almost every description . . . she has so much literature, science, and professional talents in her own bosom—that Philadelphia makes a world in itself."[45]

Near the time of her arrival, Richard Charles and Noble & Sylvester tea dealers introduced Philadelphians to the novel merchandising concept of the specialty tea and coffee store. Taking advantage of Afong Moy's presence in the city, they heavily advertised the sale of their Chinese teas, tea caddies, and other tea wares in the newspapers adjacent to the notices of her salon. Going a step further, they published an open letter in the newspapers welcoming Afong Moy and her interpreter and attendant Atung to their new store, Canton House. They asserted that in this city of brotherly love and, most specifically, in their establishment she would receive a "universal greeting." In their shop she could find comfort since they had "recently received from Canton, a splendid panoramic view of the interior of China, exhibiting in highly coloured drawings, the progress of the Chinese in the arts of War, the Drama, and Music; also a Fair with its Gymnastic and Festive Games, public processions, at their feasts, with the interior of their dwellings, exhibiting the domestic industry of the families in their several vocations and employments with which C.&S. have embellished the walls." In addition, they remarked, she would find inspiration from the views of the harbor of Canton from which she had sailed.[46] The watercolors noted in their letter were the same that the Carneses imported. Atung accepted the invitation, and through him Afong Moy conveyed a "polite message from the lady to the proprietors, declining their invitation."[47] According to newspaper accounts, Atung delighted in the views of China, and obligingly sipped the Canton House tea.

The literary response to Afong Moy came from an unlikely source. John Kearsley Mitchell, who attempted to bribe a young woman in Guangzhou to reveal her bound feet, resided in Philadelphia as a medical doctor. Apart from his early travel as a ship's surgeon, he was also a botanist, a chemist, an educator, a prolific writer, and a poet. Some, though not all, of his poetry emerged from his responses to well-known personages. His largest compilation of poetry, *Indecision: A Tale of the Far West and Other Poems*, published in 1837, included a thirty-six-verse poem "To Afong Moy."

Mitchell probably wrote the poem soon after he saw Afong Moy at her Philadelphia museum in 1835. His experience as a ship's surgeon on three voyages to China almost certainly heightened his interest in her arrival. His diaries and letters written in China reveal his opinions and perspectives on the country and its people, and provide insight on a foreigner's isolation in a distant place. The latter sentiment becomes evident in his poem on Afong Moy. Some of his less complimentary commentaries in the letters emanate from the loneliness of a young man far from home. Missing his betrothed, he complained in a letter to her that he is "so sick of this place that I should do anything short of impropriety to escape from it. Not that the place itself is so disagreeable. Any place where you are not is hateful to me and this worse than others only because it is farther from you."[48]

Though the poem's tone is occasionally jocular, Mitchell expressed sympathy for Afong Moy's difficult position. He knew the feelings of loneliness in an utterly strange and distant place. The first thirteen verses of the poem are in Mitchell's voice as he imagined what Afong Moy had come up against as she left behind all that was familiar. He speculated on her moments aboard ship when well-known landmarks slipped from view and then when she was left alone with strangers.

To see thine own Pagoda fade,
And Quang-tong's hills turn blue,
And tall Linton, in flickering shade
Escaping from the view;

To hear the gong's last, sweetest note,
The fife's expiring scream—To see the dragon-standard float
On Ta's receding stream.[49]

Mitchell lauded Afong Moy's bravery but questioned why she left the protection of home. He wondered whether she would have departed had she
supposed "thy tiny feet by day-light could be shown."[50] Mitchell well knew
the indiscretion that had occurred in Philadelphia and, from his previous
experience in Guangzhou, recognized how objectionable this unbinding
would be to a Chinese woman.

Mitchell composed the greater portion of the poem—twenty-three
verses—in Afong Moy's voice, using the conceit of a letter home, which
he purported to translate. In the second section Mitchell's intent became
clear. The first line, "So you're an *antipode,* they say," is the leitmotif of
these verses. Mitchell revealed Afong Moy as a woman of another race, an
"antipode," or an opposite, in her views and behaviors from those living in
America. Here Mitchell presents Morton's polygenic perspective—that of a
separate Asian race with Asian characteristics.[51]

Written to a fictitious Tseen Ngun Qua, presumably Afong Moy's female
relative, Mitchell began her letter with personal observations of American
women and home life. The Afong Moy in Mitchell's imagination criticized
the loose nature of American women who had a direct gaze, met a man's
eye, and circulated through the town like men. Mitchell relayed the ways
of a Chinese woman's life through Afong Moy's critical evaluation of an
American wife's role. Tongue in cheek, Mitchell presented her dismay that
all household duties fell to just one woman:

One wife the married man condemns
To all his household duties;
No female colleague sews or hems,
No flock has he of beauties.
How lonely for the single wife!
No friend for play or toil,
No beauty for exciting strife,
No ugly one for foil.[52]

Through Mitchell's personal letters to his fiancé in 1821 it is clear how he
felt about Chinese polygamy: "I never think of this custom without feeling

how wretched my lot would have been had I been thus forced to unite my-self to an unknown being . . . to know the misery of hopeless love.—But the poor women are still more to be commiserated. They never have a choice, they are not consulted either when they are to enjoy the honourable station of a first wife or when they are sold to their husband to fall into the ranks of his subordinate helpmate."[53] Mitchell reiterated in his letters the demeaned position of women, punctuated with a sad tale of the only child of hong merchant Packqua. The Chinese merchant felt himself unlucky, treated the girl poorly (according to Mitchell), and frequently repeated to strangers how much he and his wife disliked her. In another case, his vessel's seventy-one-year old comprador, whom he described as a "piece of dried apple, yellow and wrinkled," purchased an additional attractive twenty-year-old wife for "the enormous sum of eighty dollars."[54] To his credit, Mitchell objectively admitted in his letter that in America, parents, too, sold their children for money, though not quite so blatantly.

Another portion of the poem spoke to the differences between America and China that Mitchell observed, and to which he assumed Afong Moy would react: writing right to left rather than left to right; the use of a quill pen instead of a brush; using the right hand to shake hands in America rather than the left as in China; and the use of a fork rather than chopsticks. Whether Afong Moy ever seriously considered the cultural and political differences between the two countries is questionable; however, Mitchell used her as a mouthpiece to express them in the poem. Mitchell employed Afong Moy's voice to point out the wrongs he saw in China that she would see as oddities in America: the rights and equality of democracy with its lack of a permanent and constant leader; and the free passage of people through the streets without giving way to the elite. "You see no whips to drive away the idle, gaping crowd; No heads-man cries out, 'Yung-a-lay,' (Get out of the way) As he precedes the proud."[55] The aspect that Mitchell reiterated often, and most pointedly, through Afong Moy's persona was that there was less corruption, selfishness, cold-bloodedness, and exploitation in America. Had Afong Moy truly written the poem, this might not have been *her* perspective. Curiously, the poem ends as she readies herself for sleep, contemplating the only thing that she finds truly delightful in America—a feather bed.

The poem on Afong Moy is set within the larger volume of Mitchell's work. The most prominent piece, "Indecision: A Tale of the Far West," provided the title of the book. The central figure of this work was fictional.

Norman, also a sojourner to America, was from Scotland. His name indicated that he was a stereotypical European American and therefore was an accepted immigrant to the new nation. Rather than leaving all family behind, he emigrated with a wife and child, yet lost both on the voyage to the new country. Like Afong Moy he arrived as a foreigner with no familial support system, and like Afong Moy, he moved from "east" to "west," and then to the "far west" to find his fortune and escape an unpleasant "eastern" life—possibly Mitchell considered Afong Moy's removal to the West a blessing. Unlike Afong Moy, Norman had agency, but as the story unfolded, his past life was uncovered—just as Afong Moy's bodily attributes were uncovered. Although both faced issues of confusion in a new world, because Norman was male, European American, and fictional, Mitchell could provide for him a happier and more conclusive ending. Comparing these poems about immigrants of different races permits the reader a larger context in which to situate Mitchell's piece on Afong Moy.

Neither the public nor the critics responded specifically to the poem on Afong Moy; however, there was discussion on the entire volume when it appeared in print. Edgar Allan Poe, who reviewed the book in *Graham's Magazine*, wrote of Mitchell, "He has . . . given to the world a volume of poems, of which the longest was remarkable for an old-fashioned polish and vigor of versification. His MS is rather graceful than picturesque or forcible—and these words apply equally well to his poetry in general."[56] Poe's response was less critical than it might have been. While he lived in Philadelphia, Mitchell was Poe's family physician as well as a friend. Poe recorded a dinner spent together, and Mitchell's son noted that he met Poe in his father's office.[57] Another reviewer, James Silk Buckingham, writing in the *Athenaeum,* reacted half-heartedly: "The Doctor has, notwithstanding, a touch of the poetic spirit, and gets every now and then on to the very border of the haunted land."[58] Perhaps the haunted land Mitchell located in his poetry was a place where those from afar felt neither at home nor at rest.

Mitchell was not the only Philadelphian who commented on Afong Moy as she traveled through the city. Samuel Breck, a prosperous merchant and respected politician, noted her arrival in his diary on February 15, 1835. He cut out and pasted into the pages a view of Afong Moy and separately, but on the same page, the commentary from the local paper regarding the doctors' examination of her feet. The image of Afong Moy is not the woodblock print that the Philadelphia papers ran at the time but rather the standing image from the New York catalog. This indicates that the catalog was also available to patrons at her Philadelphia museum, perhaps with the 8 Park

Place address excised. After attending the event, Breck cut out the catalog image to accompany his diary account. Below her image he wrote: "A few days ago, I went to see a Chinese lady, now exhibiting, named <u>Afong Moy</u>. She has been brought to America as a curiosity. She appeared modest and cheerful; 20 yr old."[59]

Like many others, Breck focused on the aspect of her feet and her appearance as an exotic curiosity, rather than on the Chinese objects in her museum, or the information she and Atung imparted in the salon. In 1829, he similarly wrote in his diary on Chang and Eng, the Siamese twins, when they visited Philadelphia. The small feet of Afong Moy and the connected tissue of Chang and Eng were only part of Breck's interest—their foreignness, too, likely gave him pause. His oblique remarks on Fanny Kemble, the English-born actress of great popularity in America at this time, were on the same page as those about Afong Moy. Here he wrote: "**<u>Fanny Kemble</u>**. She married a young fellow of some fortune and Expectations name Butler; and resides in Philad'a where, instead of being drummed out of society our un-american, <u>heartless</u>, <u>spirit-less fashionables</u> court and carress her."[60] Afong Moy's presence was less a threat to Breck, and to Americans generally, because it was assumed she would return to China. Her status as visitor, traveler, and stage presence provided some protection from such hostile responses.[61]

This concern regarding outsiders and their intrusions into American society resurfaced several months later in Breck's diary when he traveled by railroad from Boston to Providence. Seated "cheek by jowl" with thirty strangers, he complained: "There is certainly a growing neglect of manners and insubordination to the laws, a democratic familiarity and a tendency to level all distinctions. The rich and the poor, the educated and the ignorant, the polite and the vulgur, all herd together in this modern improvement in travelling."[62] Though he does not specifically mention the foreigner as such, it is implied. However modest and cheerful, Afong Moy, like Fanny Kemble and Chang and Eng, would not be welcomed by Breck as a permanent resident in Philadelphia or America.

From Philadelphia Afong Moy traveled further south, and Baltimore might logically have been her next venue. However, the Philadelphia papers state, and the records confirm, that Afong Moy's managers' destination was Washington, DC. By moving rapidly to the capital, the entourage would arrive before the 23rd Congress recessed on March 4. This would ensure that Afong Moy had audiences with congressmen, senators, and the president. Social activity in Washington flourished during the congressional session but was less lively afterward. Her salon in the city without the presence of Congress would not be as financially remunerative for Afong Moy's handlers.

Men dominated Washington more than they did any other American city. Though some congressmen brought their wives or families with them while they were in session, many more lived in boardinghouses. There they took their meals and socialized. For congressmen from rural areas, the city could have been impressive, but for those familiar with the urban environments of Boston, New York, Philadelphia, Baltimore, or Charleston, the Federal City had a small-town appearance. By the 1830s, the scattered settlement of houses had become something more of a commercial center. Year-round residents, including workmen, government employees, foreign diplomats, shopkeepers, free blacks, and several wealthy families, numbered about thirty thousand.

An 1835 article by "an Old Citizen" in one Washington, DC, paper, the *Daily National Intelligencer*, rebutted a negative review of the Federal City printed in the *New England Magazine*, thus providing an insight into the city, the site, the sensitivities of the residents, and Afong Moy as an outsider. The New England visitor derided the environs of the US Capitol: "It stands by itself in its majestic solitude, scorning connexion or comparison with the rabble rout of rickety old boardinghouses and vile groceries which adorn the avenue on either side for half a mile or more, reminding one for all the world of an abortive attempt of your weak-kneed warriors, on a muster field, to form a line after dinner in dog days!"[63]

The "Old Citizen," a Washington resident, rebuked the visitor's perception and defended the town, noting that the old boardinghouses were actually "new edifices, three stories high, erected, in some cases, not longer than five years ago, and built of good brick, with the front and back walls 14 inches in thickness."[64] The New Englander in the newspaper dialogue continued to disparage both the streets, which were "great, vacant, staring highways" without lamps, trees, or flowers, as well as its citizens, who had no public or private spirit. The latter claim greatly annoyed the "Old Citizen," who then noted that such a remark might be tolerated if it were spoken by Afong Moy, who as a noncitizen would not be expected to know better, "but that a native of this country should manifest it . . . is indeed pitable."[65] Afong Moy, as a foreigner, and perhaps particularly as Chinese, could not have been expected to perceive the spirit or heart of the capital, but, according to the "Old Citizen," one of the country's own should have recognized it.

In the week of Afong Moy's arrival in the Federal City, the House of Representatives debated an issue that illumined how Americans would consider the arrival, and then acceptance, of the Chinese as citizens in the latter part of the nineteenth century. The discussion, as recorded in the *Congressional Record*, provided insights into how men of this time (there were no women in Congress) viewed race. The concern centered on the rights and privileges of American Indians. Congressman Horace Everett of Vermont introduced a bill that would admit an Indian delegate to Congress, claiming it would civilize the Indian. Benjamin Hardin of Kentucky agreed. He "alluded to the indirect and inefficient attempts that had been made to civilize the Indians by sending missionaries among them etc. but he would say give them government, give them property, give them laws and literature and everything would follow. They would then become Christians like ourselves."[66]

John Quincy Adams of Massachusetts strongly objected. He averred that the land was guaranteed to the Indians by treaty and "what right had we to take it upon ourselves to form the Indians into an integral part of the United States."[67] He found the bill "unrepublican" and "despotic." Though Adams had previously voted to admit the territory of Louisiana into the Union, he noted that he did so because he was accepting white men into the Republic. Should he vote for the upcoming bill he would be admitting "another race of beings."[68] Adams's remark reflected Samuel Morton's view of Native Americans as a separate race. Ultimately the bill failed. In dealing with outsiders, the primary goal of the congressmen, and probably other Americans, was to bring civilization and Christianity to those considered heathen but not to admit them as equals.

Arriving in Washington, Afong Moy and her handlers had numerous possible choices of lodging. If they wished to announce their presence they might have stayed at the prestigious National Hotel run by John Gadsby located at Pennsylvania Avenue and Sixth Street, Northwest. The hotel, established in 1827, housed well-known statesmen who kept their rooms as permanent domiciles while they were in Congress. Room 116 was occupied that February by Henry Clay. If they stayed at the same hotel, Clay and Afong Moy might have met. If the National Hotel was too costly, boardinghouses were another option, and there were many of them.[69] Earlier in the century, lodgers shared rooms, but by the 1830s private rooms, and even bedrooms with parlors, were available. Most were furnished with washstands, bowls, looking glasses, carpets, and chamber pots.[70] Meals came with the room and boarders took them together "mess style," seated at a long table; typically meals consisted of soup, lamb, salmon pie, mutton, ham soup, and chicken.[71] By this time Afong Moy presumably had adjusted to, but probably not enjoyed, American food. What would have been more uncomfortable was eating in the supper room under the gaze of mostly men, quite possibly many of them her salon patrons.

As noted in the papers, the Washington Athenaeum was the site of the "SPLENDID CHINESE SALOON" where Afong Moy was presented. The Greeks lay claim to the earliest use of the term "Athenaion," to describe the temple of Athena, the goddess of wisdom. The Romans extended the use of the athenaeum as a school for the study of the arts. Americans readily accepted the athenaeum concept in the early nineteenth century as a center for learning as well as a place to gather and share their edification. The athenaeum distinguished itself from the social library—that institution formed by a membership group with a collection of books—by the contemporary nature of the athenaeum's reading material.[72] Though the latter institution might have a collection of books, its principal service focused on providing its members access to current newspapers, journals, and periodicals.

The Washington Athenaeum followed the lead of others established earlier, such as the Redwood Library and Athenaeum in Newport, Rhode Island (1747), the Providence Athenaeum (1753), Boston (1807), Salem (1810), and Rochester, New York (1829). While athenaeums offered their members access to current periodicals and books, they also provided the community access to art and culture. Because their collections tended to focus on current reading material, many athenaeum bylaws encouraged meetings and events for the purpose of considering issues of the day and the improvement of society. Some, like the Boston Athenaeum in 1827, added art galleries with exhibitions.

The choice of the Washington Athenaeum for Afong Moy's presentation indicated the managers' attempt to position it as an educational asset rather than as a sales event or theatrical show. Though none of the newspaper advertisements specifically state edification, it is implied by the description of what visitors might expect to see: objects from China, Chinese costume, Chinese language and writing, and, of course, the custom of foot binding. Here members and the public could encounter the most current information about a country on the other side of the globe. In the notification of her presentation in the respectable classified section of the *Washington Globe*, below the announcement of William Dunlap's just published *History of Design in the United States*, Afong Moy's promoters stated, "neither pains nor expense have been spared to produce an interesting exhibition,"[73] As an exhibition for instruction, her presentation was clearly differentiated from the offerings in the city's two theaters: shows entitled "Venice Preserved; A Plot Discovered," and the "Farce of Gretna Green."[74]

By portraying Afong Moy as a representative of China's culture and heritage, the managers provided the opportunity for her admittance to the most esteemed Washington address—the President's House. Jackson had reasons for his expression of interest. In 1833, he employed Edmund Roberts, a New England merchant, as his special envoy to initiate diplomatic relations with Siam (now Thailand), Cochin China (now South Vietnam), and Muscat (now Oman). Though unsuccessful in Cochin China, Roberts continued to Bangkok, where in 1833 he negotiated the Treaty of Amity and Commerce with Siam. This first treaty with a Far Eastern nation was ratified by the US Senate in 1834, successfully opening trading opportunities for American merchants. The fruitful mission so pleased Jackson that, in April 1835, he authorized Roberts to return to the Far East to begin treaty negotiations with Japan and renew his diplomatic efforts with Cochin China.[75] Though it was not the most critical issue on Jackson's agenda at the time of his meeting with Afong Moy, it may have precipitated a curiosity about this part of the world. Vice President Van Buren, who had called on Afong Moy in New York on her arrival, could also have encouraged the visit.

From the first inaugural event in 1828, when the President's House was overrun by unruly well-wishers, to 1837, when the general public was welcomed to nibble on the gift of a 1,400-pound piece of cheese in the front entrance hall, Jackson ran a common man's White House. Such an open environment could not have been more foreign to a person from China, where the emperor was divine, inaccessible, and remote. Reporters contended that "the expectations of the Lady [Afong Moy] had been raised to a high pitch as to the magnificence of the *Fonti* (Emperor) as she terms the President."[76] Finding Jackson's abode and attire less than magnificent, she allegedly noted that "his kind and courteous manner appeared amply to compensate . . . for the deficiency of outward grandeur"[77]—the commentator providing a republican gloss on the whole occasion.

Little of their conversation found its way into the press and presumably little was said. What surfaced through translated accounts echoed the concern that many had expressed: that "she persuade her countrywomen to abandon the custom of cramping their feet"[78] This indicated that Jackson saw her as an envoy with both power to effect change in her country and the ability to return home on her own terms. Neither was true, yet his expectation was revealing. Possibly his most recent encounter with Harriet Martineau, a forceful English woman, had conditioned him to perceive foreign women arriving in America as spokespersons and representatives of their countrymen.

In addition to Andrew Jackson, surely many others viewed Afong Moy in Washington. The first American woman to remark on her visit probably saw her here. Eliza Lambert, visiting the Washington area from Richmond, Virginia, discussed her experience with Richmond relatives on her return. Her remarks on the event were passed along by letter to another relative. According to the letter writer, Sally Lambert, who may have been Eliza's sister, Eliza recognized that others found Afong Moy's small feet a curiosity, but she regarded them as a deformity. Most likely she adopted this view in response to Jackson's widely printed description of the custom of "cramping their feet." It is possible that she responded as a woman who objected to the Chinese practice as one of female humiliation and pain. Perhaps she objected to exhibiting a "deformity" as an element of amusement. This interpretation is supported by her additional comment that, though others may have found Afong Moy engaging, Eliza "was most pleased with the curiosities about the room than the lady she saw."[79] The "curiosities" that Eliza found in her visit with Afong Moy were those of objects, not of person; a different interpretation than that recorded by the Philadelphian Samuel Breck. He posted the physicians' remarks on her feet in his diary, called Afong Moy the "curiosity," and never mentioned the Chinese objects that he had seen. Conversely, Eliza Lambert's focus quickly moved from the female body to the goods as something that she might have use for and learn from.

Eliza Lambert not only observed the goods but also wondered about Afong Moy and women's lives in China. Thus, she engaged with the presenters at the event. According to the letter writer, she queried the interpreter (whom she described as a "remarkably well educated boy of about 18") on how Chinese women passed their time, since they never read. Atung provided what seemed to be the rehearsed answer to Eliza's question: that it took Chinese women some hours to dress and comb their hair.[80] His response provoked a negative reaction from Sally Lambert, and by inference Eliza, who found this a wasteful activity, observing: "now suppose Dear Cousin you were to devote as much to your ringlets what would you think of yourself."[81] As though to confirm her difference, as well as her appropriate use of time, Sally Lambert filled much of the rest of her letter with book reports on tomes she had recently read: Fanny Kemble's *Journal of a*

Residence in America, Washington Irving's *A Tour of the Prairie*, and the *Lady Superior's Reply to Six Months in a Convent*.

Here, in their own words, several American women stated their dissimilarity from their counterparts in China. They infer a superiority as knowledgeable American women who, through reading and other worthwhile activities, considered the issues of their time. Afong Moy served as a foil to highlight their presumption of a retrograde Chinese culture whose women had nothing better to do than coif their hair, compared with that of a "progressive" American culture. Philip Hone's personal diary contains the same commentary on Chinese women's activities and American women's superiority. Apart from their dialogue, Afong Moy's life was just a curiosity, ripe for letter-writing chitchat.

The otherwise sparse commentary about Afong Moy's visit to the US capital reveals the transient nature of Washington, especially in the spring. Like Afong Moy, the Englishman Charles Augustus Murray visited Washington in the early spring of 1835. As Congress neared the end of its session, Murray noticed a change in the city: "The Congress had broken up on the 4th [of March] and with it the bustle and gaiety of Washington Society. Every day announced new departures; and the scattered village, denominated a city, began to assume the silent and melancholy appearance which is natural to its construction, and which is only partially cheered by the stirring season of Congress."[82] Afong Moy was one of those departing. On the morning of March 13, she left for what Murray identified as the "wealthy and flourishing" town of Baltimore.[83]

If Afong Moy's journey from Washington to Baltimore had occurred after August 25, 1835, she could have ridden the thirty-seven miles on the newly installed Baltimore and Ohio train in two and a half hours. Without this convenience, Afong Moy and her company traveled the Washington–Baltimore turnpike by stagecoach. Earlier that year Tyrone Power, the well-known English actor, took the reverse trip from Baltimore to Washington. He described the nine-hour trip taken on an "extra," or exclusive carriage, which provided material for six diary pages: "This the only turnpike leading from one of the chief sea-board cities to the capital of the Union" and could be compared with "a Cumberland fell, ploughed up at the end of a very wet November. I looked along the river of mud with despair. Some of the holes we scrambled safely by would, I seriously think, have swallowed coach and all up; the wheels were frequently buried up to the center."[84] Power's carriage passed two others whose passengers had all disembarked, had unloaded their luggage, and were helping to extricate their vehicles from the mud. Though this may not have been what happened to her on this trip, Afong Moy surely encountered such an occurrence at some point on her journey, and one can only imagine negotiating this event on bound feet. Afong Moy's route, like Power's, paralleled the soon to be opened railroad line, ending at the corner of Pratt and Eutaw Streets in Baltimore.[85]

Six months into her stay in the United States, newspapers had so well publicized Afong Moy's presence that the Baltimore public needed little introduction to the "Chinese Lady." Unlike the discreet press notices in Washington, DC, her arrival here was accompanied by the woodblock print image that further promoted and identified her as an eminent attraction. Other activities were now added to the presentation to maintain public interest and earn money.

In Baltimore, Atung, identified in the papers as her companion and interpreter, played a more prominent role than previously. The press stated Atung "will write the names of the company in Chinese Characters on handsome embossed porcelain cards for 12½ cents each."[86] The receipt and collecting of cards well suited the current fashion of the period. Small albums to record and assemble signatures dated back to the sixteenth century, when European university students collected each other's autographs. The practice later extended to the United States, where signatures and sayings were collected in books specifically designed for this purpose.[87] In the *Ladies Repository*, Augusta (no last name provided) remarked that day albums were "kept by the young as a sort of biographical history of their own times."[88]

Album seekers harassed Harriet Martineau when she visited Washington in March 1835. "When I was at Washington albums were the fashion and the plague of the day. I scarcely ever came home but I found an album on my table or requests for autographs." She reported that the ladies in Washington were so persistent that they stood with their album at the door of the Senate chamber, imposing on the doorkeeper to hand them to Daniel Webster. Or, they placed themselves at the entrance to the Supreme Court, requesting Chief Justice Marshall to make an entry on his way to hear pleadings. She noted that President Jackson was the most persecuted by these women, and sadly he had few poetical resources to employ for the entries except the words from "Watt's hymns." Jackson was not a literary man. Martineau refused to provide more than her name and a date, but the rest of the notables felt compelled to include verses and "gallant nonsense."[89]

Afong Moy's manager was particularly astute to initiate this salon activity in Baltimore, for here the album tradition was in high form. Atung's
contributions to the ladies' albums provided little more than a name in
Chinese characters, yet this would have been a treasured and unusual addition to their "biographical history" as a recording of contact with people
of the "Celestial Empire." In Baltimore the album fad transformed from
merely a notation on paper to a textile art. With newly invented indelible
ink, women in Baltimore wrote verses, names, and dates on highly decorated quilt squares. These were then pieced together, quilted, and given as
gifts for special occasions such as weddings or leave-takings. We will never
know whether Catherine Whitridge purchased a twelve-and-a-half-cent
album card with her Chinese name penned by Atung, but there is record of
her unusual bedcover made at this time. Though not specifically an album
quilt, the Baltimorean created an appliquéd bedcover with an image of a
large Chinese vase as the focal point of the piece. An Asian-inspired design
twice encircled the vase. These motifs could have been influenced by the
objects she saw at Afong Moy's Baltimore salon.

The center design on
Catherine Whitridge's
bedcover (c. 1835) was
derivative of ancient
Chinese ding-shaped
bronze vessels. She may
have seen it replicated
in a vase or lantern at
Afong Moy's Chinese
salon. *Courtesy of the
Maryland Historical
Society, 1972.81.18*

During the time Afong Moy visited Baltimore, the press announced the imminent release of a publication she authored. Despite her language difficulty, it was presumed that she, like other foreign women touring the country, would produce a commentary on American manners. The *Baltimore Gazette and Daily Advertiser* noted: "We understand from a literary friend, that Miss Afong Moy! is expected shortly to publish her travels in the United States, accompanied with a description of manners in America . . . we may expect that the forthcoming work will equal in popularity either the productions of Miss Fanny Kemble or Mrs. Trollope."[90]

Though foreign men published numerous accounts of their travels in America in the 1830s, it was foreign women's narratives that captured the public's attention. Their reporting tended to be more engaging, often providing specific and interesting details, and because fewer women traveled extensively, their commentaries were a bit more unusual. They afforded colorful descriptions of places and monuments as well as portrayals of people's dress to a public curious about foreign places before photography was available. Though they were written primarily for American consumption, another newspaper noted that Afong Moy's account would be published in the Celestial Empire as well as in the United States. Americans were attentive to foreign travelers' observations.[91]

Often they were not complimentary. The two foreign women writers mentioned in the *Baltimore Gazette and Daily Advertiser* were English. The actress Fanny Kemble published her *Journal of a Residence in America* in 1835. *Domestic Manners of the Americans* by Frances Trollope came out in 1832. Both authors produced largely critical and negative accounts of American behavior, ways of life, and localities. Baltimore was nearly the only city whose inhabitants and their environs came through unscathed in both publications. Each of them made particularly positive references regarding the women of the city, which might be the reason that the Baltimore papers singled them out. Mrs. Trollope noted: "Excepting on a very brilliant Sunday in the Tuileries I never saw so showy a display of morning costume. I think I never saw anywhere so many beautiful women at one glance. They all appeared to be in full dress, and were really all beautiful."[92] Trollope continued her accolades on the next page with astonishment at "the beauty and splendid appearance of the ladies" who attended mass at the Catholic Basilica of the National Shrine of the Assumption. In her 1835 *Journal*, Kemble recounted an evening with several Baltimore ladies: "They are most agreeable pleasant people . . . their conversation appeared to me totally divested of the disagreeable accent which seems almost universal in this country."[93] Because they had been well received by Kemble and Trollope, possibly Baltimoreans hoped for a similar appreciative response from Afong Moy should she have the temerity to pen one.

That Afong Moy would be coupled with Kemble and Trollope bears remark, since historians have typed her principally as a spectacle.[94] In 1835, there was some public expectation that Afong Moy would function within the larger context of those foreign women who published travel literature and commented on American life, with her place established as a notable similar to Kemble and Trollope. At this point in her tour, Afong Moy's presentation and experiences were akin to both. Like Kemble, she performed before large audiences and similarly had sufficient public recognition to meet the president and other American dignitaries. Trollope's merchandising effort in Cincinnati was not unlike the mercantile aspirations conceived by Afong Moy's managers. In Cincinnati, Trollope built, according to a contemporary account, a "Graeco-Moresco-Gothic-Chinese" bazaar to sell imported fancy goods. The foreign architecture of this onion-domed and castellated building served as a public attraction, just as Afong Moy's exotic costume and bound feet were meant to draw buyers to the purchase of Chinese fancy goods.[95]

Afong Moy never published an account of her travels or observations on American manners as did other female travelers. Unlike her foreign female contemporaries, Afong Moy was unschooled and without English-language capabilities. Dependent on others, she was unable to hire a ghostwriter or a translator. No doubt the papers that announced a forthcoming publication made assumptions based on little more than the actions of previous foreign female travelers. It was left to John Kearsley Mitchell to provide Afong Moy's imagined response to American life in his poem. Like some of the Kemble and Trollope narratives on American women, Mitchell envisioned Afong Moy's response to the ladies she had met:

> What horrid girls they have, and then
> They stare about them so;
> They look, for all the world, as men.[96]

In contrast to Philadelphia, where Afong Moy's manager, likely Captain Obear, arranged his own museum in Washington Hall showcasing objects and simulating a Chinese salon, in Baltimore they took advantage of an already established museum. In 1814, Rembrandt Peale, following the example of his father in Philadelphia, built a museum on Holliday Street that would serve as "an elegant Rendezvous for taste, curiosity, and leisure." The museum focused less on natural history and more on the arts and sciences, including a picture gallery and a section devoted to "products of manufacture." It struggled financially and finally closed in 1830; its collections moved to a building on Calvert Street, where Afong Moy and the Chinese objects were presented to the Baltimore public. This site housed both a theater and Peale's collections, including the famous skeleton of a prehistoric mastodon that Charles Willson Peale had unearthed in Newburgh, New York in 1801, and the only one on view in the world. The museum served as a center of both high and popular culture. The Peales, and later the museum managers, struggled to balance the two. Supplementing the attractions of the permanent collection by bringing in autonomous programs such as Afong Moy's supplied additional revenue, while, in turn, it legitimated the outside productions. Afong Moy's Chinese Saloon within the museum setting fit Rembrandt Peale's earlier museum purpose as an elegant rendezvous for taste, as well as curiosity, and it would set the stage for similar events at museums across the country. Though the association between museums and performance was nascent at this point, the practice would escalate during this decade. By the late 1830s Scudder's American Museum in New York City on Broadway and Ann Streets held magic lantern shows alongside its collection of stuffed birds.

On the afternoon of March 21, John Gordon; his wife, Susan; and four relatives and friends visited Afong Moy's salon in downtown Baltimore.[97] Gordon recorded his impression in his diary. For him the "taste" aspect of the presentation clearly outweighed the "curiosity" since, Gordon scribbled, "I was not much pleased as we did not see her foote, the only thing worth seeing."[98] Possibly Gordon had heard about Afong Moy's feet from his father-in-law, Nathaniel Chapman, a respected Philadelphia physician.[99] This remark indicated that, although her small feet were a draw, they were not the only focus of the museum presentation.

Later that week, seventeen-year-old Margaret Gibson also visited Afong Moy, accompanied by her mother and other friends and relatives. She recounted the event in a letter to her older brother John, who resided in New York City. Perhaps the account was more detailed than most contemporary descriptions, because it was an experience she and her brother shared. By inference, he too had seen Afong Moy, but in New York.[100] Perhaps his description, as well as published accounts, had prepared her for an unpleasant viewing of Afong Moy's feet. During Gibson's museum visit in Baltimore, her feet did make an appearance: "We all visited the

Chinese Lady and were really delighted. I had heard so much of her feet being disgusting, that when I did see her, I was much surprised—Could I divest [*sic*]) myself of the idea of its being to contrary to nature, I should think them <u>beautiful,</u> she placed them very prettily on the ground, and although she totters, and seems pained by walking, I cannot think the appearance disgusting." The perceptive Gibson observed that the Chinese women pictured in the watercolors on the wall looked quite different from Afong Moy: they had delicate skin and wore clothing "with much more taste." This led Gibson to speculate that Afong Moy was "of low birth, for I do not think any real lady would have visited us, and that may account for her being so ugly, and complexion so dark." She remarked that Afong Moy's hands were red and looked as though they needed soap and water! Gibson's evaluation diverged from the lofty newspaper descriptions of the elegantly appointed and highborn Chinese lady.

Near in age to Afong Moy, Gibson interpreted the young Chinese woman's feelings, the unspoken effect of the encounter, more astutely than others did: "Poor thing she is much to be pitied, she seemed very timid, and confused." She also took a measure of Atung, noting that he found pleasure in his surroundings and likely would be pleased to remain in the country. According to Gibson, Afong Moy professed to like Baltimore more than any city she had yet visited. Apparently people were attentive and kind, and additionally, while she was in the city she witnessed a balloon ascension.[101] According to Gibson (probably recounted by Atung), the event initially rattled Afong Moy, for she thought the man was "compelled to mount the sky" against his wishes, and would die. As she presumably had been forced to mount the waves and travel to a distant place, so she assumed this man had been banished to the sky. Her reaction indicated the fears that could overwhelm her as she faced new experiences in an alien place.

It is likely that many in Afong Moy's audience at this time were often of the middle to upper middle classes. Thus they were sophisticated and knowledgeable patrons who, despite Gordon's comment, might find the life of a Chinese person of interest. They also had the ability to purchase goods, and for the managers this probably was the more important objective. John Gordon and his friends and family had the financial capacity to buy what they saw presented on Afong Moy's stage. Gordon, though living in Maryland, was a Virginian. His family resided at Kenmore, the estate previously owned by Betty Washington, George Washington's sister, in Fredericksburg. John, a graduate of Yale, served as the director of the Union Bank of Maryland, a position most likely achieved with assistance from a family friend, Nicholas Biddle, president of the Bank of the United States. Margaret Gibson, too, was from a well-known and established family. Her grandfather, George Grundy, founded a prosperous mercantile business in Baltimore and built Bolton, one of the finest residences in the city. Margaret's mother, Elizabeth, Grundy's daughter, attended Afong Moy's presentation in the museum with Margaret. Elizabeth's response to Afong Moy was more effusive than Margaret's. Surely the managers hoped this enthusiasm might translate into the purchase of Chinese goods shown at the museum and sold by their local business agents.

Even people living in the farther reaches of Maryland, beyond Baltimore city, were aware of Afong Moy. In his more than twenty diaries, Jacob Engelbrecht of Frederick provided a careful record of life in Maryland from 1818 to 1878. Engelbrecht was an inquisitive and meticulous man with strong antislavery opinions and republican sentiments. His curiosity and ecumenical nature were so refined that, despite his affiliation as a Lutheran, he regularly attended all the other churches in the town, including the services of his rabbi neighbor. It would not be surprising, then, that Afong Moy earned an entry in his diary. He remarked on her New York exhibit and mentioned that her costume and the furniture in her parlor "are all from China in real, Canton style . . . and her feet only four inches long."[102] It is unclear whether Engelbrecht viewed Afong Moy in Baltimore, fifty miles from Frederick. When he mentioned the Siamese twins in his diary in 1832 he noted tersely: "I saw them."

Though he may not have seen Afong Moy, years later he had a more direct encounter with a Chinese person. In 1850, Frederick Schley, a clerk who had served with Commodore David Geisinger's East India Squadron, returned home with a fifteen-year-old Chinese boy from Guangzhou.[103] Engelbrecht wrote five entries concerning the boy, Mock Allou Schley, in his diaries, though he never explained why Frederick Schley brought him to America. Engelbrecht recorded that "Allou" attended school at the Academy and "he learns well considering his being a Chinese. He walks our streets every day, dressed in real Chinese style, thick white soled shoes (nearly an inch thick). . . . His hair is about 4 feet long plaited and twisted around his head outside of a blue cloth cap . . . which fits close to his head. Nearly all the boys in town know him . . . and is quite a smart boy."[104] Engelbrecht, as a tolerant and enlightened man, commended Allou on his abilities and his adjustment to the small town. However, rural Frederick in the mid-nineteenth century might never be comfortable for a Chinese man, and in 1852 the diarist noted he left town to return to Guangzhou via a US government vessel. Eight years later Engelbrecht updated his diary account of Allou's departure, as was typical of the author's method. Then the diarist revised the entry with a statement that Mock Allou (Alloo) never left America. Instead he remained in New York working in a "sea store."

Engelbrecht's characterization of Allou was similar to the way he described Afong Moy. He noted that Afong Moy's costume and her parlor furniture were "all from China, in *real* [my emphasis] Canton style." The description reflected a sense of wonder and credulity that such objects might come from a place so far from his reality. Since he could not know what "real" Chinese clothes or furniture might look like, he trusted that the reporters were accurate in their assertions and knowledge of Chinese style. Fifteen years later, when Allou arrived in Frederick, Engelbrecht remarked that he "dressed in real Chinese style." Here he might judge for himself Allou's "realness," for the young man spent time in Frederick, and presumably Engelbrecht knew his sponsor. Because Chinese people were seen so infrequently in the United States, the exotic allure of the actual, the "real," was powerful. Engelbrecht expressed in his diary what most Americans contemplated when they viewed Afong Moy: here is a "real" Chinese person who is not an image on a teacup or a tea chest.

Though admittedly Engelbrecht had little or no contact with Afong Moy, his characterization of her was, as many other accounts of her had been, focused entirely on her Chineseness, her physical attributes, and the Chinese objects associated with her. Her bound feet and Chinese dress set her apart in America. Allou and Afong Moy's interpreter, Atung, though surely perceived as foreign, moved with considerably less difficulty into American life. Engelbrecht's description of Allou as "quite a smart boy" who "learns well considering his being a Chinese" compared to the equally credulous newspaper commentary on Atung. In the Baltimore *Lutheran Observer* of 1835, the reporter presented Atung favorably, noting: "Acung [Atung], who accompanies her [Afong Moy], is a very prepossessing youth—He speaks the English language . . . quite intelligibly, and the attention which he pays to visitors, deserves to be particularly noticed."[105] In each case the writer expressed incredulity at the intelligence of the young Chinese men despite their foreign dress and vastly different ways. As with the description of Atung in newspaper accounts, Engelbrecht presented Allou as well adjusted, moving freely about the town, and though retaining his Chinese dress, fitting in with his peers. The diarist indicated that Frederick Schley brought Allou to America to be educated, and apparently he found success in his studies. Atung, according to the *Lutheran Observer*, came to America, from one of the factories (the foreign enclaves in Guangzhou) and was similarly schooled.[106]

As the Baltimore presentations came to a close, Afong Moy's managers considered the desirability of the climate as they arranged her next appearance. Charleston in the spring was more suitable than Charleston in the summer. Harriet Martineau, on her tour of America in 1835, covered the same route just a few weeks before Afong Moy. Her choice of travel from Baltimore to Charleston was by stagecoach. She stopped in Richmond and from there bumped her way along rough roads for nine days with only three nights of rest. Stage schedules did not accommodate normal patterns of eating or sleeping; therefore, it was not unusual to set off at two or three in the morning. She wrote, "it was my wont to lie down and doze, in spite of hunger; if I could find a bed or sofa, it was well; if not I could wrap myself in my cloak, and make a pillow on the floor of my carpet-bag."[107] Though she admitted that one could take more time on such a journey, she yet advised that a traveler needed to be "patient of fatigue" to move through the South. Afong Moy's managers heeded Martineau's advice. To mitigate the strain such a stagecoach trip might have on Afong Moy, they took passage on a sailing vessel from Baltimore in mid-April. According to the Charleston *Courier* the line brig *Gen. Marion* carried "Miss Afong Moy, The Chinese Lady, of the city of Canton, China and Acung, the Chinese Interpreter, of Macou, [*sic*] China," as well as five other passengers, from Baltimore to Charleston.[108]

In Charleston, Afong Moy found a very different environment than that of the upper South. The majority of the population in the sixth largest city in the Union was black.[109] The enslaved did much of the work, since aristocratic Charlestonians believed that manual labor killed the intellect. The social order crystallized under a class hierarchy that honored family heritage and landed wealth rather than upward mobility and hard work. Family association provided the only route to political or social power.[110] In Charleston, Afong Moy would encounter this sense of privilege and lack of consideration.

Despite Harriet Martineau's staunch antislavery position, she found Charleston a fascinating place of contradictions. She encountered great hospitality, culture, and beauty amidst the heaviness of slavery. Her description of the place gives us an idea of what Afong Moy saw and experienced: "The view from the church steeple was very fine; and the whole, steeped in spring sunshine, had an oriental air which took me by surprise. The heat and moisture of the climate give to the buildings the hue of age . . . the yucca bristling in the gardens below us, and the hot haze through which we saw the blue main and its islands, all looked so oriental as to strike us with wonder."[111] To heighten the comparison Martineau noted the prevalence of the fragrant

Cherokee rose, which also grew profusely in its native habitat of southern China.[112] One can only speculate that such a similar physical environment to southern China may have elicited in Afong Moy a longing for the home that she had left a year before.

Afong Moy arrived in America as its citizens became increasingly receptive to many forms of public entertainment. The middle class had some money in its pockets and was open to new encounters. Entrepreneurs and managers experimented with locations that might draw the public, and Afong Moy presented in a variety of entertainment sites whose variability differed by region. In New York, her staging took place in a private home, in Philadelphia a public hall, in Washington at an athenaeum, and in Baltimore at a museum. Charleston's public congregated for entertainment in "Long Rooms." Though not all Long Rooms were alike, probably they were similar to McCrady's Long Room, a two-story building measuring seventy-five feet by twenty-five feet with an elongated arcade on the first floor and a banquet room of a similar size on the second floor. Originally the second floor, with sixteen-foot ceilings, included a stage, an anteroom, and a dressing room for performers. Such a narrow, but long, building allowed for cross ventilation in the sultry South. The Long Room as an entertainment site may have originated with the French culture of the Saint-Domingue refugees who fled to Charleston after the West Indian island's slave revolt in the early nineteenth century.[113] In 1805 citizens planned a concert to support distressed refugees from St. Domingo in Mr. Sollee's Long-Room; in 1819, in Fayolle's Long Room, the first French benevolent society in America was formed; and in 1831 the Charleston State's Rights and Free Trade Association held its first meeting in Lege's Long Room.

It was in here in Lege's Long Room that Afong Moy presented her Chinese salon on April 20, 1835. The smell of fire might have been still prevalent, because a mid-February conflagration burned sixty-three houses and the historic St. Philip's Episcopal Church. The roof of Lege's Long Room caught fire and the building would have burned to the ground if it had not been for the strenuous efforts of an employee of John Maelzel, the owner of the famous Automaton Chess Player that was on exhibit there.

Afong Moy and Atung followed a similar presentational pattern as they had in the previous cities, but with several variations. Advertisements stated that Afong Moy would speak a few words of English; here more paintings, curiosities, and objects were listed and not only Atung, but the "conductor" of the exhibition as well, would "explain the names and uses of the various curiosities brought from Canton."[114] The presence of the "conductor" indicated the inclusion of another person who was becoming more central to the presentation. Showing some audacity, the manager communicated with the Medical Society of South Carolina in advance of Afong Moy's arrival in Charleston, inviting its officers and members the opportunity to examine her feet. He was identified in the society's minutes as "Mr. H. Hannington, the conductor of the Exhibition of the famous Chinese Lady."[115] Future Afong Moy presentations would reveal his background.

On May 2, after commending Afong Moy for her affability and good humor in presenting the Chinese objects in the exhibition, the newspaper added a late-breaking bit of news: "Since writing the above, we perceived by another advertisement that AFONG MOY will exhibit her feet divested of covering, at 4 o'clock this afternoon."[116] Afong Moy's feet in "all its native nakedness" went on public view that same day.[117] Another article noted "this will indeed be worth seeing, particularly, as we understand, the Lady has been compelled to sacrifice her sense of delicacy in consenting to the exposure."[118] Though we have none of Afong Moy's remarks, the words suggested coercion. Her shame was "sacrificed" to the public's curiosity. As though to

[COMMUNICATED.]

Those who have not yet seen the CHINESE LADY, will do well by embracing the opportunity which is afforded them to-morrow, being the last of her appearance here. It is needless to speak of this Exhibition—all who have seen it, confess that it is well worth public attention ; and it will be rendered doubly interesting from the fact, that the Lady's foot, divested of its bandages, will on this occasion be exposed to the inspection of the curious. It is with great reluctance, we understand, that she has consented to this, believing as she does, that it is compromising her sense of delicacy. The proceeds of that day's exhibition are to be exclusively appropriated to her own use ; therefore do we hope, she will not be disappointed in her expectations.   G.

The Charleston newspapers hawked the unveiling of Afong Moy's naked feet. As noted, she benefited from the proceeds; on this occasion the entrance fee was raised to one dollar. *Charleston Courier, May 1, 1835* ameliorate the action, the advertisements stated that the exhibition charge would solely benefit the "Lady."

Two days later, at Hannington's invitation and following the model of their counterparts in Philadelphia, Charleston physicians examined her naked feet to verify their size, and published their conclusions in the newspapers. According to the particularities of their findings, between February and May the length of her foot had shrunk from 4¾ inches to 4⅛ inches. Perhaps Charleston's climate was to blame. As in Philadelphia, it required eight doctors to confirm these measurements. They included Edward Washington North, Moses Holbrook, William Michel, St. John Phillips, Philip G. Priloeau, Samuel Henry Dickson, J. W. Schmidt, and J. Manning.

In comparison to several of the Philadelphia doctors who had traveled to China and knew something of the ways of the Chinese people, the Charleston doctors' practices and lives suggested a different mindset. None had been to China, few had traveled outside the United States, none practiced medicine in almshouses or assisted the poor in city hospitals, and, significantly, most were slave owners. In Philadelphia, it is possible that the physicians, aware of the affront, objected to a public display of Afong Moy's feet, while in Charleston the medical men ignored her plight as a woman, as someone of a different ethnicity, and her helpless situation. Their backgrounds illumine the differences between Northern and Southern sensibilities to racial difference.

Philip G. Priloeau, of French ancestry, was a general practitioner who moved in elite circles and must have done well; his estate records indicated that at his death he owned 360 slaves. He mentored his fellow physician Samuel Henry Dickson, whose professional life was the most distinguished and the most conflicted of the eight. A graduate of Yale and the University of Pennsylvania and one of the founders of the Medical College of South Carolina, he was also a staunch defender of slavery. His book, *Remarks on Certain Topics Connected with the General Subject of Slavery*, provided a rebuttal to an English antislavery advocate.[119] His argument was typical for an elite Southerner: the enslaved person was incapable of attaining equality with his master and therefore he was unfit for freedom. As "the minor is denied all political and many civil rights because he is thought to be unfit to enjoy or exercise them" and "for the same reason, . . . they are withheld from women. I hold that they can never be accorded to the negro, precisely on that ground. Politically, then he can never cease to be a slave, and his inferiority being stamped upon him by the hand of God himself. He is . . . in no worse condition than a woman or a child."[120] Not surprisingly, Dickson strongly supported the Philadelphian skull collector Samuel Morton and publicly encouraged Morton's view of separate races.[121]

From Dickson's perspective, and probably those of the other Charleston doctors, Afong Moy's status was little different than that of the enslaved. Though she was not black, Afong Moy was also not white. As a woman dependent on her manager for her sustenance, she had little agency. She was considered little more than a child, and her male manager determined her fate and directed her affairs. Dickson would not object, as perhaps the Philadelphia physicians did, to unwrapping her feet to the Charleston public since, as a nonwhite woman and of a separate race, her sensitivities were immaterial. Dickson's close friend, the poet William Cullen Bryant, provided the doctor's revealing epitaph: "an eminent teacher of the Medical Art; able, learned and eloquent; . . . of frank and engaging manners . . . nobly disinterested, and inflexibly just."[122] Dickson's noble disinterest, pro-slavery stance, and polygenistic viewpoint would provide little advocacy for Afong Moy in her Charleston humiliation.

Dr. J. W. Schmidt, a slaveholder, presumably had little sympathy for a nonwhite, non-English-speaking woman. In May 1835, he was preoccupied: the transfer of a Charleston enslaved man named Neptune, given to Schmidt by a patient to liquidate a debt, had gone awry. The pulling and tugging between the patient's heirs and Schmidt rattled Neptune and he ran away. Once located, he was jailed until the case could be heard. In May the case came before the Court of Appeals.[123] Though the outcome of the case is unclear, Schmidt's attention in early May was not on Afong Moy.

That several of the doctors actively participated in the slave trade and defended the institution of slavery was not surprising. Several blocks from Afong Moy's salon at Lege's Long Room stood the Exchange Building, where most of the city's slave auctions took place. She had probably seen such slave markets in Baltimore and Washington, but Charleston's was unusually active. The city served as a nexus where slave owners and traders from the upper South brought the enslaved, often for transport to New Orleans. Because Georgia officially banned traders from importing slaves, many Georgians came across the state line to purchase the enslaved at auctions in Charleston.

Slave trading became such a spectacle that the Charleston City Council worried about the city's reputation and public order. In 1856, long after Afong Moy's time in the city, the council addressed the problem, but it reaffirmed its position on slavery in its public statement: "The committee apprehended that this community entertains no morbid or fanatical sentiment on the subject of slavery. The discussions over the past twenty years have led it to clear and decided opinions as to its complete consistency with moral principle and with the highest order of civilization." But the council also expressed consternation that "it was thought a common spectacle to see troops of slaves, of all ages, and both sexes, uniformly dressed, paraded for air, exercise and exhibition, through the streets and thoroughfares. This spectacle of a large number of negroes, . . . brought together from all quarters . . . for purposes purely of speculation and cupidity, entailed on this community by strangers, citizens of other states, was repugnant to the moral tone and sense of our people."[124]

Afong Moy surely saw this "spectacle" of the enslaved paraded in the streets, for it was a routine occurrence. Though this was the slower time of year for slave trading, as it was past planting time, slaves were always marketed in Charleston. To be sure, there was slavery in China and, in fact, Afong Moy's departure to America may have been the result of it; however, selling was done singly and between individuals and surely not in a way that drew the sort of public attention to the transaction that she saw in Charleston. There is no way to know what she thought, but it is easy to imagine that she was aware of and disturbed by it.

Unable to read English, Afong Moy could not understand the broadsides posted in the marketplaces announcing upcoming slave auctions. Had she been able to read, they would have been frightening, since some descriptions closely fit the description of her person. One posted near Potters Mart in March 1833 advertised "A likely yellow girl about 17 or 18 years old has been accustomed to all kinds of house and garden work. She is sold for no fault. Sound as a dollar."[125] The description of the mulatto "yellow" girl was the skin color later attributed to Afong Moy. Crude newspaper announcements of Afong Moy's performances describing her body and the unwrapping of her feet were not unlike the detailed accounts of the slave's physical attributes. The newspaper notices relaying information on Afong Moy's naked, "undressed" feet were in preparation for her public humiliation, in a slave mart of a different sort.

The Charleston aristocracy's unusually heavy dependence on slave labor, family hierarchy, and class tradition made for an uneasy and fearful response to change, which would erupt in violence not long after Afong Moy visited. She left Charleston just weeks before the city underwent great turmoil. Targeting Charleston as the most egregious of the slave trading cities, abolitionists mailed bags of newspapers and journals published by the American Anti-Slavery Society to the Charleston post office. Citizens who received the unrequested mailings were incensed. Word spread, and the postmaster was confronted by a vigilante committee demanding the rest of the tracts. Citing the need to protect federal mail, he resisted. That evening a mob ransacked the post office and located the offending bags, and the next evening a crowd of nearly two thousand burned them in a raucous public bonfire. Afong Moy and her party had already slipped away on the brig *Laura* for Baltimore.

7

Return to the North

CONCLUDING THEIR SIX-MONTH SOUTHERN TOUR in Charleston, Afong Moy and company returned to New York City in June 1835. Publicity generated from her presentations in the South now preceded her. Newspaper articles, commentaries, and even satirical epigrams, such as this little witticism, created popular impressions and attitudes about her before she stepped onto a stage.[1]

Dear Miss Afong Moy—if you have joy
Because your feet are small;
How happy she must surely be,
Who has no feet at all.

The second phase of her experience—the transition from a promoter of goods to that of spectacle herself—had begun, and the blurring of market and theater commenced.

Though she was back in New York, her previous host, Captain Benjamin Obear, was not. At some point in the spring of that year, Captain Obear, with the Carnes family's financial support, left again for Guangzhou as master of the vessel *Mary Ballard*.[2] An auction notice in the *Evening Post* in early April 1835 informed New Yorkers that the "fashionable furniture . . . of the Chinese Lady" at 8 Park Place was up for sale.[3] The listing included the objects in Afong Moy's salon as delineated in Charles Risso and William Browne's lithograph. The notice also enumerated everyday household items, indicating that Benjamin Obear and his wife, Augusta, had moved on.

Who now took charge of Afong Moy's affairs? Initially Benjamin and Augusta Obear served as guardians when Afong Moy traveled from Guangzhou to America. When she arrived in New York City in October 1834 she lived with the couple on Park Place; however, it is unlikely that they traveled with her beyond Washington, DC, in the early spring of 1835.[4] One can surmise that the Obears and Carneses still had a financial interest in the enterprise of her salons and the sale of Chinese goods but were no longer engaged in her daily affairs after her southern tour.

Though Afong Moy's interpreter Atung accompanied her, and possibly the unnamed female servant who arrived with her from China as well, a manager was necessary to arrange the presentation sites, encourage the sale of objects, and organize events. This person provided a sense of respectability and authority that Afong Moy needed as she traveled from city to city. We know something of a manager's position from the diary of Henri Herz, a French pianist whose concert tours in the 1840s took him to many American cities. Herz spoke some English, but he needed assistance in an unfamiliar country. He turned to Bernard Ullmann, a young and rather untried hustler, who immediately took charge, telling Herz: "I will take care of the concert posters, I will have your programs printed, I will see that everything is in order in the hall where you hold your concert, I will present you favorably to the newspaper editors . . . I will act in your interest, which will become mine."[5] As a Chinese woman with little knowledge of English and limited in locomotion by her bound feet, Afong Moy needed far greater assistance on the event circuit and someone to serve as her advocate. Few women in the 1830s traveled alone, and surely not someone who knew so little of the country and its ways.

The identity of Afong Moy's manager surfaced in the Medical Society of South Carolina minutes of May 1835. With his petition to present her unbound feet to their members, it was revealed that Mr. H. (Henry) Hannington was Afong Moy's manager. Henry, with his brother William, had a business producing dioramas in New York City.[6] With skills as glassblowers and commercial decorative painters, the brothers expanded their talents into this new arena of public spectacle. Based on the 1822 invention of Louis Daguerre and Charles-Marie Bouton, the diorama debuted in Paris in 1823 to great acclaim. Soon the phenomenon spread across the ocean. Originating from the Greek *dia* (through) and *horama* (view), dioramas provided visitors with a theatrical experience through the use of paintings on transparencies which were viewed with lighting, mechanical, and sound effects.[7] The Hanningtons became showmen in the 1830s, producing elaborate dioramic programs at their City Saloon on Broadway and on tour in other American venues. Their familiarity with theatrical productions and the sites across the country to stage them may have commended them to the Carneses and Captain Obear, who had little expertise in this arena. Though William Hannington may have had some contact with Afong Moy, it was his brother Henry, and Henry's wife, Catherine, who accompanied her.

How effectively or diligently Henry hawked the sale of the Carneses' Chinese goods through Afong Moy's later presentations is hard to esti-mate. There are no records that enumerate an arranged fee or a commis-sion agreement between the merchants and manager regarding object sales. Though many of the less costly, and more portable, objects were present on her stage, how these were then made available to those in attendance is un-clear. Possibly the Carneses sold them in advance to local merchants at each location, a typical procedure for a commercial wholesaler. However, with the sales of Chinese objects lessening, and a change in manager, Afong Moy became the principal commodity on stage. She was the focus of fascination, as well as apprehension, about all things oriental.

Hannington arranged for Afong Moy to present her Chinese salon at the American Museum in New York City from June 19–24, 1835. Like all museums of the period, this one was privately run. The museum initially had some pretext in its appellation as an "American" museum. It was founded by the Tammany Society in 1791, and its members collected whatever related to the history of the young country, but they went farther afield and also in-cluded objects from China and other foreign countries. First established in a back parlor at New York's city hall, the society later sold the collection to John Scudder in 1802. His museum moved several times, but Afong Moy must have presented at Scudder's Chambers Street and Broadway site, the old City Almshouse.

Scudder loved things and was an avid collector. Typical of most museums then, the American Museum was an oddment of natural curiosities, such as stuffed animals and fossils, as well as foreign objects and antiquities. Though it may have been an exaggeration, it was said that Scudder had accumulated 150,000 objects.[8] Early in the life of the American Museum, Scudder found that things alone did not attract a crowd. Soon he was presenting "moral lectures" pertaining to the collection and allowing outside performers the use of the lecture hall.[9] Since her salon presentation related to portions of Scudder's collection, it was an appropriate venue for Afong Moy.

It was at the American Museum that moral reformers found the Chinese woman. After engaging with slavery and issues of race in the South, Afong Moy now experienced the full effect of moral reform in the North. Though opposite in intention, both conveyed powerful emotional messages that she could not ignore. Both spoke to her condition—in slavery to her race—and in religious culture to her supposed heathenism. As she moved across the American continent, these attitudes would continue to haunt her.

During one of her museum presentations in June 1835, the audience included Margaret Prior, and Phebe and John Robert McDowall, the principal moral reformers in the city, if not the nation. Prior had served as a member of the first board of managers for the New York Female Moral Reform Society, as well as the society's first woman missionary. The McDowalls had devoted their life to moral reform in New York. According to Phebe McDowall's subsequent reminiscences, Prior had requested McDowall and her husband go with her to the museum to see a Chinese lady who was drawing significant notice in the city.[10] Mrs. Prior approached Afong Moy while she was on stage. Phebe McDowall later recalled: "Mrs. Prior was led to address her on the subject of her eternal salvation. So affecting was her appeal to Afong, that many who were present could not refrain from weeping. The tears flowed profusely from the eyes of the interesting girl while Mrs. P conversed with her, saying, she hoped her visit to this country would prove an invaluable blessing to her soul."[11]

Afong Moy's arrival in America came at a time of great transformation. The forces of the market revolution upended many of the social institutions that had been in place for centuries. The developing industrial-commercial economy disrupted traditional family relationships, and the country experienced a wave of immigration. These changes led to many social ills: unemployment, poverty, inadequate housing, disease, and prostitution. Not surprisingly, it was also a time of great religious fervor. Moral reformers, many of whom were spiritually minded women, found their calling in combating these ills, as well as the perceived moral disintegration of society. They assumed the responsibility of saving souls, not only for the lost souls' sake but for themselves as well. Culpability for unrepentant neighbors both near and far rested on their shoulders and could equally determine their salvation. There may have been multiple reasons for the reformers' presence at Afong Moy's salon that day. At this time Margaret Prior was near the end of a long life devoted to missionizing among the poor. She visited locations where few middle-class women of respectable reputations might go— destitute New York City households, poor neighborhoods, and brothels. With Bibles, religious tracts, and firm resolve she attempted to change the lives of those she considered immoral, spiritually dead, or needing redemption.[12] To moral reformers like Prior, Afong Moy was one of those heathens who required spiritual awakening and salvation from the forces of hell.

Phebe's husband, John Robert McDowall, was a controversial figure in the religious life of New York City. A convert of Charles Grandison Finney, the Second Great Awakening revivalist, young McDowall plunged into the reformist movement by attacking the issue of New York City prostitution. Leaving his theological study at Princeton University unfinished, McDowall devoted all of his time to converting prostitutes in New York's Five Points neighborhood. Supported by female evangelists, he established the New York Magdalen Society, which operated the House of Refuge for repentant prostitutes. A firestorm occurred when he published a paper supported by the society claiming that there were ten thousand prostitutes in New York City, and that many men of prominent families were their clients. Philip Hone, who had visited Afong Moy's salon the previous fall, found McDowall's paper "a disgraceful document."[13] The disgrace was not the prostitution but rather, to him, the overblown numbers, and the irate censuring of New York City and its male population.

John McDowall did not consider Afong Moy a prostitute. Probably his concern and apprehension regarding her staging were the moral attitudes he presumed she brought with her from China. One of the other planks in his moral reform platform was anti-licentiousness. McDowall reasoned that the availability of pornographic literature encouraged young men to seek prostitutes and caused a degenerate society. Only by virtue of her race did this issue relate to Afong Moy.

McDowall had recently returned from several steamboat trips up the Hudson River. On one of the trips he conversed with a young man who showed him obscene images. When he queried him as to the literature's source, the young man responded that sailors provided it from China.[14] On another occasion, in a discussion with a young man from Maine, the same story was repeated. McDowall inferred thus that the Chinese condoned licentious behavior through the publication and dissemination of tawdry pictures that infiltrated the United States. Afong Moy's presence as a young, unmarried woman exhibiting, as well as selling, images from China and displaying her naked feet in public was enough to raise his suspicions. Though apparently he found no evidence of salacious material in her presentation, her situation inferred a potential illicitness.

The public's sensitivity to the life of a lone woman in the 1830s was sensitized by press accounts of single women going astray. Though the April 1836 murder and later sensationalized and well-publicized trial of New York City prostitute Helen Jewett had not yet occurred, earlier press reports of prostitutes' activities enlivened daily news. Nearly all of them emphasized the conditions that promoted a woman's wayward behavior: a foreign background, abandonment by her parents, lack of funds, no set address, lack of community support, and the absence of a man to provide for them.[15] Afong Moy fit all those criteria.

Phebe McDowall, the third member of the moral reformers' group who visited Afong Moy at the museum presentation, well knew the life of destitute single women. As a young woman, she accompanied her first husband, Solomon Carpenter, on his revivalist missions in western New York. At his death, she married the much younger John McDowall, and their marriage centered on their devotion to the cause of wayward women. Supported by the New York Female Benevolent Society, they managed and lived in an asylum for such fallen women. In her role as counselor and spiritual advisor, Phebe McDowall recognized the hazards of being single and defenseless.

She also shared in the development of new roles the Presbyterian Church was claiming for women. Extending their interests in female charitable societies, several Presbyterian women attempted to form their own interdenominational female missionary organization.[16] Their cause was encouraged by David Abeel, a missionary recently returned from China, who preached in New York on the plight of Chinese women. In New York City, he was supported by Joanna Graham Bethune, the philanthropic Presbyterian reformer. Undoubtedly Phebe McDowall and Bethune were compatriots and together heard Abeel's plea to develop a female missionary society in China. Since Chinese women were unable to congregate with men or appear in public, they had little contact with missionaries and their teachings. According to Abeel, the Chinese women asked: "Are there any female men among you to come and teach us?"[17] Communicating with Afong Moy at the museum may have been Phebe McDowall's answer to that call.

One might question how Prior drew such an emotional response, what one might term "affect," from both the audience and Afong Moy, who apparently was overcome with tears. What might she have said that elicited such a reaction from the Chinese woman who knew little English and even less about Christian religions? Since Prior's words on this occasion went unrecorded, we can only rely on previous testimonies from her missionary reports to the American Female Moral Reform Society for insight. These notes indicated that she was skilled in addressing an indifferent audience. In one year alone she visited between four and five thousand families.[18] In one household she met a group of fashionable young women working around a quilt frame. As she talked of God she warned them "of the coming wrath, and pressed upon them the duty of repentance." The women ridiculed her at the time, but according to Prior's later account, one young woman was so overcome "with the remarks then made sent by the Spirit directly to her heart" that she later converted.[19] To another recalcitrant she said, "It is my duty to say to you that if you do not repent, and love the Lord Jesus Christ you will be lost forever." Apparently, the irreligious man replied that he did not believe in Christ. Her retort: "it is useless to talk to you, for you are now a lost man."[20] Her conviction was so strong that when she returned to him several days later, he was a changed and contrite man. Prior used these sorts of words, in her insistent and determined manner, as well as her tears, to communicate with Afong Moy in New York. There is no way to know whether the moral reformers' confrontation had a lingering effect on Afong Moy's thought or changed her in any way. Neither Prior nor the McDowalls approached Afong Moy again.

From July to October 1835, Afong Moy and her conductors traveled the roads of New England. Many of the populace had some familiarity with China. From the earliest days of the republic, seafaring vessels along the entire New England coast quite regularly went to China and returned with objects and images of its people. These were displayed not only in the homes of ship captains but also in sailors' dwellings and others' engaged in aspects of the China trade. Though the presence of a Chinese person in New England was not ordinary, it also was not unusual. In the early nineteenth century, Chinese men such as "Boston Jack" and Punqua Winchong frequented the region. "Boston Jack," also known as Bohsan Jack, worked as a ship's comprador for American vessels in Whampoa. He made a visit to Boston, possibly by invitation from the China trader Thomas Handasyd Perkins, with whom he stayed for a short period of time.[21] Punqua Winchong came to New England as a shopkeeper and merchant. They both stayed briefly and then returned home to China.[22]

Afong Moy met Bostonians at Washington Hall on 221 Washington Street, near the Marlboro Chapel where John R. Peters would establish his Chinese Museum in 1845. According to Abel Bowen's 1829 *Guide to Boston*, the establishment, like the nearby Pantheon Hall, was "a neat and convenient hall for holding various assemblies."[23] It was here that the Southern, abolitionist Grimké sisters, Sarah and Angelina, held their public meetings affiliated with the Boston Female Anti-Slavery Society.[24] More than four hundred women attended, which gave some indication of the hall's capacity.

When Afong Moy presented in New York, Philadelphia, Washington, DC, Baltimore, and Charleston, the term "saloon" described her offerings. In Boston, it was called an "exhibition." Yet, unlike the extensive descriptions of goods on view in other cities, the Boston papers provided no information on the objects in this exhibition. However, one salient element of the notice set the presentation in Boston apart from all others. Here Afong Moy's manager targeted schools as an audience. The newspaper notice read: "A Day Exhibition for schools or parties, if notice is given the preceding day. An allowance to schools."[25]

Few locations in the country had a higher literacy rate than Boston. A large percentage of middle-class boys and girls attended primary schools in the city. By 1839, Boston had ninety-one primary schools educating 2,612 girls and 2,790 boys.[26] The large number of young girls in school was unusual in the early years of the nineteenth century in other American cities, but not in Boston. Parents took to heart the republican ideology that educated mothers would raise virtuous citizens. Benjamin Rush, Noah Webster, and Benjamin Franklin maintained that, in order for this democratic experiment to succeed, education would perform an important role. It would give men the knowledge to vote intelligently and women the insight to prepare their sons for such a duty. In Rush's *Thoughts upon Female Education,* which he presented at the Young Ladies' Academy of Philadelphia in 1787, female education should consist of reading history, travels, poetry, and moral essays along with the practical studies of bookkeeping and even chemistry. What it should not encourage was the reading of British novels, which, he noted, "are as foreign to our manners as the refinements of Asiatic vice."[27] Parents, and many of those in Boston, recognized that educating daughters was their duty in a democracy.[28]

What might students, and particularly young girls, learn from attending Afong Moy's exhibition and why would teachers find this an educable experience? The *Boston Traveler* noted: "The Chinese Lady has arrived in this city, accompanied by her Interpreter, Acong, a Chinese Youth, who will explain the curious customs of their country, while each being dressed in their exact costumes, and the apartment being hung with Canton satin damask, will present a fair specimen of that singular race and their peculiar style."[29] The emphasis on the authenticity, the "realness," of their dress, habits, manners, and style indicated the unusual opportunity to view Asian culture—though not the "refinements of Asiatic vice"—close at hand.

Two diaries of Boston schoolgirls attending Bronson Alcott's Temple School in 1836 reveal that the study of world geography, including Asian nations, was occurring in some Boston classrooms at the time. Alcott's teaching methods at his coeducational school were not traditional; he encouraged independent thinking and expressive forms of writing. The diaries of Martha Anne Kuhn and Emma Savage recorded their classwork in geography, literature, and biology; Martha drew an image of a house in Siam and both read *Arabian Nights*.[30] While Rush might be concerned about the influence of "Asiatic vice," Alcott alternatively encouraged his students to explore the lives of those in Asia. Since school sessions in Boston continued into July, it is possible that Martha and Emma's classes visited Afong Moy and Atung at Washington Hall.

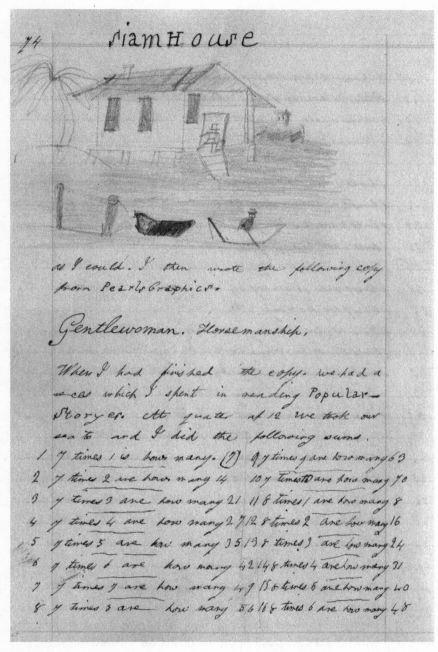

74 ſiamHoUſe

as I could. I then wrote the following copy
from Pearl & Graphic.

Gentlewoman. Horsemanship.

When I had finished the copy. we had a
recas which I spent in reading Popular—
Stories. At quater of 12 we took our
seats and I did the following sums.

1 7 times 1 is how many. (7)   9 7 times 9 are how many 63
2 7 times 2 are how many 14   10 7 times 10 are how many 70
3 7 times 3 are how many 21   11 8 times 1 are how many 8
4 7 times 4 are how many 27   12 8 times 2 are how many 16
5 7 times 5 are how many 35   13 8 times 3 are how many 24
6 7 times 6 are how many 42   14 8 times 4 are how many 31
7 7 times 7 are how many 49   15 8 times 5 are how many 40
8 7 times 8 are how many 56   16 8 times 6 are how many 48

The 1834 US treaty with Siam may have encouraged some teachers to educate their students about Asian nations. In her diary, Boston student Martha Anne Kuhn drew this imagined view of Siam with a palm tree, a house on stilts above a waterway, and a man in a top hat. Siam House, *April 22, 1836. Courtesy of the Bostonian Society*

But another reason may have prompted class tours from other schools. Afong Moy was the antipode, the very opposite, of what Americans idealized as a "republican" woman. With her bound feet, perceived backwardness, and encumbrances of her culture, she was what American women *should not be* in a democracy. The *Boston Traveler* noted: "Afong Moy walks on an elevated platform, in order that her little feet may be seen to advantage."[31] She therefore was a teachable object lesson in the oppression that women experienced in Asian cultures. Students would see that the lack of female education in China could bring about what they perceived as a decadent culture.[32] This could also be seen as an unconsciously defensive response to American (and Western) women's own lack of authority and a classic case of projection and displacement. Seeing in their own culture the deficiencies women experienced, "republicans" were all the more reactive to another culture's shortcomings.[33]

Some Boston newspaper reviewers were dismissive and harsh in their appraisal of Afong Moy. Unfortunately, the manager paired her presentation with Jonathan Harrington, a magician and ventriloquist. Mr. Harrington, a hometown fellow whose father was a well-known and well-liked master builder in the city, received much of the attention—and affection. A review in the *Boston Morning Post* noted that "Harrington's part of the performance is good, but he has got into poor company [Afong Moy] and it would be as much to his credit to travel with a stuffed skin of a kitten with two heads."[34] A much later, admiring article on Harrington published a full-length lithographic image of him and noted that "as might be inferred from the portrait Mr. Harrington appears physically to be a perfect man."[35] The article outlined his amazing skill as a public performer and the "vigor, vivacity and vitality" that characterized his presentations. In the eyes of Bostonians, Afong Moy was far from the perfect woman. The *Boston Evening Transcript* presented the "Chinese Lady's portrait" as "A homely Indian *squaw*, with her feet cut off and her ancles [*sic*] stuck into a couple of turnips, would be as well worth looking at."[36]

The *Transcript* elaborated by noting that "our Indian squaws [referring to Afong Moy and a Cleopatra figure modelled on a Potawatomi Indian] are becoming classic property" with skin of "half-baked brick and smoked salmon."[37] Afong Moy's persona, conjoined with the image of an Indian "squaw," placed her in the same racial category as that of the aggrieved

American Indian. Like Afong Moy, American Indians were the subject of public presentations on the 1830s stage. After the defeat of Black Hawk and his fellow Sauk warriors by American troops in 1832, Andrew Jackson required them to go on public tour as prisoners of war.[38] They traveled to a number of cities, including Boston, Philadelphia, New York, Albany, Buffalo, and Detroit. Displayed on stage as an exoticized trophy of war, Black Hawk, like Afong Moy, was commoditized and infantilized, and his person was constructed by newspaper editors and stage managers. Because his celebrity tour diminished his honor and warrior status, Black Hawk, unlike Afong Moy, voiced his strong displeasure and resistance in English and to the press.

The "squaw" as "classic property" referred to the recent popularization of a dramatic play featuring Pocahontas. George Washington Parke Custis's production *Pocahontas or the Settlers of Virginia* debuted in Philadelphia in 1830 and was well received, with numerous performances.[39] In Custis's dramatic rendition, the Indian maiden left her "pagan" culture and became Christian, though the biracial marriage to John Rolfe was omitted. The negative association of Afong Moy with the Pocahontas "squaw" belies the generally positive public response to the latter. Most Americans attributed the saving of the Virginia colony to her support and act of courage. Custis's script gave her all the qualities of a virtuous, and Christian, nineteenth-century woman. In the North, Afong Moy did not benefit from Americans' generally positive and virtuous associations with "squaw Pocahontas"; rather, she was linked with her as a member of an inferior race.

Perhaps in an attempt to ameliorate the generally negative Boston press and find an engaging way to present Afong Moy, Hannington tried one more approach near the end of her time in Boston. On July 31 he announced "For the accommodation of ladies, Miss Afong Moy will hold a levee at her room tomorrow afternoon at 3 o'clock."[40] Like the special performances for school audiences, the levee had not been offered in any city that Afong Moy had previously visited.

As a social occasion, the levee originated with French monarchs who entertained selected guests in the morning soon after rising from bed. It was intended as an intimate gathering allowing visitors special access to the sovereign leader in his private chambers. With revisions conforming to a democracy, this type of event made its way to America. First ladies Martha Washington and Abigail Adams held evening levees where the general public might, if dressed in appropriate attire, converse with them. Dolley Madison continued the practice but called them "drawing rooms." Levees therefore had an association with notables, royalty, or others in high places. The managers positioned Afong Moy as a select public figure whom ladies would have the honor to address in her private room. Levees were not activities that entailed a fee and since no address was given in the notice, this had to have been an invited event. It is quite possible that these small gatherings also accommodated Afong Moy's recent attempts at learning English. According to a Boston newspaper account, the manager's wife, Catherine Hannington, who traveled with her, "commenced teaching her the language."[41]

By the end of July, Afong Moy shared the Boston limelight, though not the same stage, with Bahad Marchael, the Eastern Magician; Maelzell's mechanical diorama of the "Burning of Moscow"; and a flea circus that promoted "Learned and Industrious Fleas."[42] It was time to move on. Afong Moy and her retinue left Boston for Salem, Massachusetts.

On August 12, she was installed in what the newspapers listed as Salem's Concert Hall, but the event was probably held in Samuel McIntire's Hamilton Hall, which was built in 1805 and housed a ballroom on the second floor with space to accommodate a large gathering. Salem's East Indian Marine Hall, which held many Asian objects collected by the town's China trade merchants, was located several blocks away. No newspaper article mentioned the association between the "Chineseness" of Afong Moy and the Chinese objects housed in the museum down the street. No one noted that the life-size clay sculptures of Chinese men that inhabited the museum now had a compatriot in a live Chinese woman. When an East Indian "Parsee" with a calico headdress walked the Salem streets, the newspapers recorded his presence. When, for the first time, a Chinese woman walked those same streets, the town was silent. It may have been the matter of Afong Moy's perceived stature. The East Indian was in Salem on business with money and trade to offer. Her activity was not financially beneficial to the townspeople and therefore of less consequence, not worthy of note. This might not have been the case had Benjamin and Augusta Obear accompanied her to Salem. As residents of the area, their association with Afong Moy's journey to America would have been newsworthy.

In Boston, Afong Moy shared the stage with a ventriloquist and magician, but in Salem the additional attraction on the ticket was Johann Nepomuk Maelzel's automata. A German, Maelzel had traveled through American cities since 1826 presenting a variety of his machines.[43] Audiences of all ages were captivated by his mechanical devices that operated without noticeable human intervention. These artful devices appealed to most theatergoers, but Americans knew they entailed a certain amount of trickery. Distinguishing between the actual and the deception raised an element of concern. It was precisely this concern that had earlier demanded an accurate recording of Afong Moy's bound feet by physicians in Philadelphia and Charleston. Yet, neither in Salem nor in any other New England city was there a public challenge as to the veracity of Afong Moy's foot size; nor was she asked to unbind her naked feet in private or in public. Were New Englanders more aware of the effects of unbinding? Was there a greater sense of decorum here? We do not know.

Afong Moy and Maelzel appealed to the same audience: a white middle class comprised of men, women, and children. For an entrance fee of twenty-five cents the public had the opportunity to view both attractions. The early nineteenth-century audience brought to these performances some insights and perspectives that today we might overlook. Possibly they perceived a relationship between the sleight-of-hand automaton activity and the presentation of Afong Moy. Many of those attending would have been familiar with the popular and recently published *The Girl's Own Book* by Lydia Maria Child and its companion, *The Boy's Own Book* by William Clarke. These encyclopedias of games, pastimes, songs, and activities provided suggestions for acceptable recreation for children and young teens.

Both books gave seven to eight pages of text on automata. In Child's book the topic unfolded through a conversation between a young girl and her aunt. The girl commented on her desire to see the mechanical figures the aunt had witnessed in Boston. The aunt affirmed that all the automatons were "done so naturally, that it really seemed as if the little creatures were alive."[44] Another game of deception that both authors included was "Chinese Shadow." Child noted "that children are generally extremely fond of this play."[45] Coming from a Chinese folk tradition of puppets made of translucent parchment manipulated behind a lantern-illumined screen, Westerners heightened the theater's level of optical illusion with oil lamps.[46] For them, Afong Moy represented the Chinese shadow figure, silent, illumined on stage with lanterns, presenting her amazing tiny feet, while Maelzel featured his mechanically manipulated Musical Lady and automaton rope dancers.

Noticeably missing in the Boston and Salem newspaper announcements was any mention of Chinese objects on the stage—there is no record of Chinese paintings, furniture, or fancy goods. In both places Afong Moy was paired with other attractions to create an additional draw. One might assume that after a year's worth of publicity, Boston and Salem audiences had tired of her exoticism and the allure of Chinese objects. In fact, another issue may have challenged Afong Moy's manager. Certain areas of New England, particularly Boston and Salem, were more familiar with Chinese goods. Caroline Howard King, in her reminiscences of early nineteenth-century Salem life, noted that "in almost every house were quaint tokens of the East."[47] She reported that a Salem girl visiting out of town was surprised to find a table absent of blue and white Canton or Nankin ware, so familiar was it in her town.[48] Using Afong Moy to promote or display Chinese objects in cities where such goods were common was not profitable. Instead, Afong Moy, as the first Chinese woman known to visit America, herself became the focal point.

The most outspoken and cogent explanation of what Afong Moy could impart to American audiences came from the newspaper reports of her time in Providence, Rhode Island. Without the distractions of competing programs, her presentation appeared to be focused on the cultural contributions she might convey to her viewers. No moral reformers judged, no drama critics satirized, and no physicians measured her feet. The *Republican Herald* said the visit would provide "a better opportunity than we had ever had before been favored with, of learning something of the manners and customs connected with female life and fashions in the 'Celestial Empire.' She present[s] to us a living specimen of that but which a small portion of our countrymen have any actual knowledge, and which is so different from anything with which they have been acquainted."[49] Here was a straightforward appreciation and recognition that citizens could learn from, rather than judge, a woman who came from a foreign culture.

Her presentation as "a specimen" took place at the Providence Museum. The term "museum" was an elastic word in this period, and a museum could serve as theater as well as reception hall. But true to its present-day function, the museum in Providence featured objects along with Afong Moy herself. Unlike the Boston and Salem locations, lanterns, paintings, costumes, and "curiosities" were advertised as part of the program. All provided "a correct and imposing scene of Eastern magnificence . . . the

Lady of the conductor of the Exhibition [Catherine Hannington] will show the ladies some of her [Afong Moy's] dresses and render any information required."[50]

For the first time, press reports recorded a public that expressed true interest in the life of a Chinese woman. Yet the one person who could convey this information with authority and knowledge was missing. On stage, Atung (or Acung) had previously provided explanatory background on Afong Moy. After the Boston presentations, his name was dropped from all the announcements. This coincided with the Boston commentary that Afong Moy was learning English from the manager's wife. Presumably she would now have less need for an interpreter.

Until Boston, the productions focused on Afong Moy, with additional activities such as writing in Chinese script, and inscribing visitors' names in Chinese on their proffered cards performed by Atung. Now, shared billings with other acts meant there was less opportunity for Atung's portion of the presentation. Up to this point, the presentation on Chinese life and manners would have been relatively accurate and authentic. After Atung's departure, however, Catherine and Henry Hannington assumed this interpretative role, and it is doubtful as to how much "correct" information they could impart on the history of China or on Chinese customs or dress. In addition to the program's loss was the absence of Atung's presence on the road. He was the only person who might have understood Afong Moy's needs, to whom she could confide, and, importantly, could speak her language. He was the last person who knew her from her first venture in America. His absence must have been distressing for the young Chinese woman.

The language lessons had some effect. Afong Moy publicly spoke her first very few recorded words in English in Providence. The reporter for the *Republican Herald* commented that the women in the audience seem:

to pity this young creature for the deformity of her feet, effected in conformity to the fashion of her country; probably because it deprives her of the pleasures of dancing and gadding. She pities them because their feet are, to use her own language "too big—no good"; and we could not help smiling to hear young misses compassioning her case, while they, with waists of about the circumference of mud wasps, could scarcely bend or speak, for stays and corsets. Fashion—what a tyrant —our own customs are always the best.[51]

Fashionable gowns of the mid-1830s accentuated a slim "wasp" waist held tightly by corsets. Some made comparisons between Afong Moy's restrained feet and American women's constrained waists. La Belle Assemblée, *February 1836, National Museum of American History, Division of Home and Community Life, Smithsonian Institution*

This back-and-forth commentary on Chinese and Western women's fashion and dress echoed similar arguments from an article published in New England newspapers forty-five years earlier. The extensive article, purportedly written by Thaliska Toluda, a Chinese lady of Guangzhou, to an unnamed woman in Philadelphia, defended the custom of foot binding on the grounds that it was much less harmful than the Western woman's use of stays. After receiving a gift of dresses with stays from Enoch Willet, an American ship captain, the writer stated: "How is it possible that a lady's waist can ever be accommodated to them, when it is impossible to make them fit the waist of a child of two years old? I would suppose that so tight a ligature drawn across the bowels and breast, would not fail of producing cholics, asthmas and consumptions among your ladies."[52]

To conclude, she requested that the Philadelphia lady, and those in her company, discontinue their rant about the small shoes that she had sent earlier through Captain Barry.[53] "I hope, after this, you will cease to banter me about the small shoes I sent you . . . They do not impose half the restraint upon our bodies, that your stays do upon yours. These shoes never impair our health, nor does the change they produce in the size of our feet, offend the eye, by exhibiting disproportion in the shape of our bodies."[54] Though the 1835 reporter had no agenda or intention to change American women's fashion with his commentary on Afong Moy, the 1790 correspondent did. Using the alias of a Chinese lady, the commentator struck at the common practice of women's lacing and staying as an unhealthful practice by comparing it to foot binding, which most Americans considered the most extreme, unreasonable, and hurtful fashion. According to the author, Chinese foot binding was no less deleterious to the health of womankind than the more intrusive Western fashion of corseting.[55] Neither commentary changed American women's desire to dress fashionably, either in 1790 or in 1835.

From the beginning of September until the end of November 1835, Afong Moy moved from town to town, zigzagging from Providence, Rhode Island, to Worcester, Massachusetts, then on to Hartford and New Haven, Connecticut, down to Newark, New Jersey, up to Concord, New Hampshire, and finally to Albany, New York. Her travel now had less pattern and less reasonable a route than previously. Possibly the demands to make money accelerated.

One other aspect may have altered the pace and the program. Two new performers accompanied her at each of the above venues. Monsieur and Madame Canderbeeck now were part of Hannington's presentations, and probably he was their manager as well. Little is known of this couple, who performed before American audiences from 1829 to 1857. They arrived in Boston in May 1829 with their name slightly muddled on the passenger list. Canderbeech "Monsieur Joh[n]," with his presumed wife "(Mad[ame]," were both listed as musicians.[56] In the first recorded announcement of their work, in Troy, New York, they were introduced as well-known artists from Brussels, Belgium, who had earlier performed in France and Germany. "Monsieur Canderbeech" played the violin. Though he was apparently an accomplished performer with a wide repertoire, his fame rested on simulation. The Philadelphia *National Gazette* supposed that his violin at one moment sounded like a flute, then an English bugle, a Scottish bagpipe, an organ, and finally human—like an old woman, "a monk," the Father Capuchin, and the Mother Abbess. They called it the "ventriloquism of the fiddle."[57] Madame Canderbeeck played the harp and was a vocalist.

Like Afong Moy, the Canderbeecks were similarly displaced persons, though by their own volition. In the 1820s, Belgium was under the control of the Netherlands, with a Belgian Catholic majority ruled by Dutch Protestants, which made for an explosive and uncomfortable environment. At this time, Belgium's rich reserves of coal fueled the Industrial Revolution on the European continent. This, too, reshuffled Belgian lives. In the eighteenth century, Belgian musicians such as the Canderbeecks found employment with the court or the church. By the early nineteenth century, with their country and Europe in general experiencing great change, musicians lost their patrons and their livelihoods. To survive, they performed concerts in large theaters or in the parlors of the wealthy. With few opportunities for employment, the Canderbeecks went abroad to make a living.

Their first collaboration with Afong Moy took place at Zorrester Bonney's Central Hotel in Worcester, Massachusetts, on September 8 billed as a "Novel Examination of Combined Attractions."[58] The advertisement confirmed that the concert of vocal and instrumental music would be divided in two parts, between which the Chinese lady would appear. Though Afong Moy had previously shared the stage with other attractions, this was the first time her performance was linked, in theme, to another. It was music that provided the connection to the Canderbeecks. Now Afong Moy would address the audience in English and sing a Chinese song, as well as showcase Chinese paintings, lanterns, and curiosities. In New Haven, the event was billed as a "Grand Concert" with Afong Moy's contribution of "Chinese Song" in bold and pronounced type. In Hartford, the Grand Concert featuring the three performers took place within Afong Moy's "Chinese Apartment" on the Union Hall stage.

No one at the time commented on Afong Moy's ability as a singer. But the fact that she could sing provides insight into her Chinese experience. Confucius highly valued music, considering it one of the elements that brought people together in an orderly Chinese society. According to the *Record of Music*, which later codified Confucius thought and documented the canons of official Chinese music, there was music, and there was sound. Sound could be discordant and unregulated. Vernacular music fit that category.

Later in Chinese history, women were unable to participate in the ritual of the court ceremonies where proper music was performed, and therefore they were excluded from knowledge of acceptable music. Women performed vernacular music, the music of the people, which was banned from the court. "Female music," *nuyue*, was performed either exclusively for women—perhaps as wedding songs or funeral laments—or, less respectably, for the enjoyment of a mixed audience.[59] Women such as maids, courtesans, entertainers, or prostitutes, who sang vernacular music solely before men, had a low social standing. Their performances were not viewed as musical events but as social activities. It is possible, however, that Afong Moy brought to America one of the first renditions of *muyu*, a folk song tradition prevalent in the Guangdong province from the seventeenth to the mid-twentieth century.[60] *Muyu* songs are narratives that derive from folk tales and legends, incorporating themes of romance, history, religion, and ethical behavior. Whichever form, Afong Moy's songs were of the vernacular genre, and as historians defined it, "accessible" or "low" music. Without knowing her background, it is unclear whether she learned this music as a performer before men, from the confines of her home, or from an acquired folk heritage tradition.

Though there is no record of Afong Moy playing the Chinese
flute (dizi), many young Chinese women in the early nineteenth century engaged in folk music. *A young Chinese lady
playing a flute, c. 1830, unknown artist. A. J. Hardy, Hong Kong*

Because we are familiar with Western and classical music, we can imagine
the Canderbeecks' performance. Monsieur Canderbeeck was said to play in
the style of Paganini; his wife sang arias in German, French, and English.
The songs Afong Moy presented would be difficult to reconstruct. Samuel
Wells Williams, who was familiar with the sounds of the Chinese language
as the author of the *Tonic Dictionary of the Chinese Language in the Canton
Dialect*, wrote: "No description can convey a true idea of Chinese vocal
music, and few persons are able to imitate it when they have heard it."[61] He
noted that all singing, whether male or female, was in falsetto, eliciting a
sound "somewhere between a squeal and a scream," yet often of a soft and
somewhat mournful character. One American newspaper said Afong Moy's
songs had a "peculiar cadence."[62]

Since Afong Moy's song was in Chinese, and Atung was no longer there to translate, no one in the audience would know the words. Yet some lyrics from music of the Chinese countryside have been documented. In the late eighteenth century, the Englishman John Barrow, traveling from Beijing to Guangzhou on a diplomatic mission, recorded the lyrics of the music he encountered on the way. Since he was fluent in Chinese and served as a translator for the English at the Chinese court, we can assume some accuracy of the words and his interpretation. According to his account, the most popular "vernacular" song in the entire country was "Moh Li Hua," or "The Jasmine Flower." The song related the joy of receiving the flower, the happiness it conveyed when worn, and the fear that others would envy the wearer.[63] This might have been one of the pieces Afong Moy included in her repertoire. The subject matter fit the topic, "recollections of home," that newspapers reported as the focus of her presentations.[64]

What common bonds did the Canderbeecks and Afong Moy share? All these performers were migrants who depended on managers and presenters for their subsistence and direction. The language barrier between Afong Moy and the Canderbeecks made their relationship all the more challenging; however, their common foreignness and close quarters were factors that encouraged camaraderie.

The Canderbeecks and Afong Moy arrived together in Albany, New York, in November 1835. They had spent the fall presenting on the same stage, but this would be their last joint performance for several years. In contrast to the other venues, where the newspapers placed the Canderbeecks on an equal, if not elevated, billing, in Albany Afong Moy was the featured attraction: there was a more complete telling of her story and a refocus on Chinese objects for sale.

The Albany Museum where Afong Moy and the Canderbeecks met the public was built as a museum and theater in 1830 on the corner of Broadway and State Streets.[65] The 1848 watercolor of State Street by artist John Wilson clearly depicted the imposing four-story building with a pillared curved façade. Five large murals illustrating the arts hung between the pillars; the word "Museum" stood large at the building's rooftop on a slightly raised dome. It was here that major attractions and exhibits were held. It remains one of the few identifiable venues where Afong Moy presented.

The American flag flies above the Albany Museum on State Street in New York where Afong Moy and the Canderbeecks performed in the fall of 1835. *View of State Street, Albany, 1848, watercolor by John Wilson. Albany Institute of History & Art, x1940.600.23*

Tyrone Power traveled across America in 1833–1835, and described the city of Albany at the time Afong Moy visited as slightly exotic. As the capital of New York, there was an expectation of stateliness. The city spread out across the top of a steep hill overlooking the Hudson River, with the principal street proceeding from the bottom of the hill up to the State House and terminating in a public square. The museum sat on a corner of State Street several blocks east of the state capitol. Power said of the city, "Nearly all the more important public offices have lofty and well-proportioned domes; and these being uniformly covered with tin or other bright metal, impart a gay and picturesque effect . . . the city, viewed from a little distance, with all these cupolas and towering domes reflected in the setting sun, assumes quite an Oriental appearance."[66] The "oriental" imagery he referred to was likely that of onion-shaped domes, rather than Chinese architecture, yet the sense of the place was arresting.

The interior of the museum's lecture room more truly fit what the citizens of Albany might have considered "oriental." The *Albany Argus* announced: "Her Chinese ladyship has arrived, and is nightly receiving crowds of visitors at the Museum, the Lecture Room of which has been fitted up in the richest oriental style, with beautiful carpet, satin damask drapery, lanterns, national emblems, paintings etc."[67] At her most recent presentations in New England, Afong Moy might have been seen as a commodity or production, as part of the stage scenery. In Albany, the distance between the audience and performer contracted. There were numerous mentions of her beginning proficiency in English and her extended conversations with the public.[68] Earlier newspapers accounts had never presented her as hostile, but they did depict her as reserved and somewhat aloof. Those in Albany described her as good humored, affable, and pleasing. A greater competency in English gave her confidence to bridge the divide between the audience and herself.

Described in Albany newspapers as "a bona fide Chinese female," she was dressed in a silk brocade outfit (probably similar in form to that in the lithograph) trimmed with gold and silver. A "Chinese head-dress, richly ornamented with jewelry . . . both novel and beautiful in the peculiar style of her country" constituted a recent addition to her ensemble.[69] In the earlier lithographic view (by Charles Risso and William Browne) of Afong Moy seated on a dais she wore only a small hairpin to secure her tresses. This could not be interpreted as a headdress. In the intervening time since the lithographic image had been created, a diadem of sorts was added to Afong Moy's costume.

The typical use of such elaborate headgear in China was worn at one's wedding, but there is no evidence that Afong Moy had married. Appropriating the decorative and extravagant hair accessory, though she remained unmarried, would have been unrecognized in America, where no one knew Chinese customs. The newspaper's description corresponds to the Chinese villager's nineteenth-century wedding hair adornment: "an ornate headdress made of gilded silver inlaid with kingfisher feathers and embellished with pearls."[70] Small dyed puffballs of fabric attached to the comb or headdress were also popular hair dressings in Afong Moy's homeland in southern Guangdong province. Whether she brought these accessories with her in anticipation of marriage, as elegant attire, or in some manner acquired them in the intervening time is unclear.

If, as the Albany paper averred, large crowds flocked to her stagings, her presence provided an opportunity to change audience perceptions and the way they lived their lives. The transmission of Chinese cultural ways gave middle-class people a chance, as an Albany paper observed, "to peep . . . into the customs of other countries, and gather . . . valuable information from the truths of nature."[71] In Albany, as in other cities that she visited, merchants sold related "oriental" commodities. Albany and New York merchant D. Griffin heavily advertised "Oriental hair" and "Oriental hair dyes" in the fall of 1835.[72] The notice encouraged women to change their gray hair, or hair of any color, to a "beautiful black," or to purchase puffs on combs, perhaps like the puffs Afong Moy wore in her hair.

Afong Moy's hairstyle became so prevalent that it was identified as such in the popular *Godey's Lady's Book*. In the magazine's novelette *Althea Vernon; or, The Embroidered Handkerchief*, the beautiful heroine of the story learned a great deal from the stylish, but kind, heiress Miss De Vincy. Althea admired the "dark, glossy hair of Miss De Vincy, simply fastened at the back of her head with a . . . tortoise-shell comb, and parted on a high, and expanded forehead."[73] Later in the story, Althea Vernon was encouraged to copy the look "with hair stroked back from my forehead, knotted at the top of my head, I shall look like Afong Moy."[74] The fashion instructor commented that "to young people, it is the most becoming style."[75] Numerous fashion plates of the period depicted this look, copying Afong Moy's hairstyle as seen in the lithograph or depicted at her presentations.

Afong Moy won the sympathy of Albany patrons when two city papers published lead stories on her life. Far from complete and considerably inaccurate, the accounts included the intention for her travel: "The laudable motive that has induced her to travel . . . should entitle her to the good wishes of all—it has been for the sole benefit of her parents. Adversity often overtakes the Chinese as well as the people of our own country, blighting the fair prospects of earlier years, and the fortune of a parent is insufficient to support his family and tiny footed daughter; this is an instance. To place the parent beyond the reach of want, Afong has been the first to visit the western world."[76] The expression of sympathetic identification with Afong Moy's plight reflects the imaginative leap into the experience of another. Adam Smith's theory of moral sentiment aptly applied to the *Albany Argus* newspaper's response: "As we have no immediate experience of what other men feel, we can form no idea of the manner in which they are affected, but by conceiving what we ourselves should feel in a like situation."[77]

The commentary established Afong Moy's travel as a benefit to her parents without considering the moneymaking motives of the American merchants. Neither Captain Obear nor the Carnes cousins are identified as the conduits for her extensive travel. The writer attributed to Afong Moy the altruistic motive to support her parents. Remittances, monies sent home to support family, were in fact an accepted Chinese traditional practice and filial duty, though generally performed by male rather than female relatives.[78] Afong Moy had little agency or power to decide what monies were sent home or the amount that had been provided to them in advance. The article whitewashed a contentious issue: that of a young girl displayed for money and hawking goods, by framing her activity in the guise of family support. To make it more palatable, the writer conflated her Chinese experience with one a young American might experience.

Another Albany newspaper article did acknowledge Afong Moy's association with Captain Obear: "Afong Moy was brought to this country by Captain Obear, of the ship Washington, under the care of his lady, and a heavy guarantee to return her in two years to her parents, who are handsomely remunerated for her temporary absence, and is at present under the care of the lady of the conductor of the exhibition."[79] Visitors were assured that neither Captain Obear, nor the manager, nor others involved in Afong Moy's travel to America misused or took advantage of her presence without generous compensation. To place this activity on the up and up, the writer twice referred to women who cared for her along the way, Augusta Obear, who escorted her from Guangzhou to the United States, and the current chaperone Mrs. Hannington (though unnamed in the newspaper), the wife of the manager.

This solicitude confirmed that Afong Moy was a respectable young lady who had been watched over and safeguarded. Such information was necessary once it was stated that her parents had sent her adrift to earn their keep. The specific time limit of her journey signaled a sympathetic understanding of her longing for home, but it was also a sales pitch to encourage visitors to see her and the Chinese objects while they could. To underscore this, the very next sentence of the article announced that books of Chinese paintings and rice paper "brought to the country by Afong Moy" were now available for sale.[80] Afong Moy had no part in bringing goods from China, but the association with her made them all the more exotic. Once again, Afong Moy was both the advertisement and the sales agent for the goods.

While Afong Moy was busy in Albany promoting the Chinese goods that the Carneses had imported on the ship Washington, all was not well in New York City. The Carneses had capitalized on their third China trade venture with the Washington, and in the intervening time had invested in two additional undertakings. After the Washington returned, they joined with partners to send out the vessel Romulus to China in late 1834. In the spring of 1835, Benjamin Obear captained the Mary Ballard on his fourth trip to China, and the Carneses' and partners' fifth China trade venture.

With the return of the *Romulus* in late 1835, the cargoes hit a glutted market. According to Walter Barrett's account in his *Old Merchants of New York City* the "business was overdone."[81] As Barrett explained, some objects brought huge profits but others barely covered their purchase cost in Guangzhou once freight costs were included. That, combined with the duty on the objects, consumed all the profits. As a result, he wrote, "it was decided by these firms to close up, and to abandon the China trade. Their losses were heavy."[82] The entire operation of the Carneses' China trade business collapsed, smothered under the volume of its own imported goods.

It is possible that over time the Carneses might have recouped their losses and attempted another China trade venture; however, in December 1835 their business suffered a further calamity. On the night of December 16 a fire

HANINGTON'S DIORAMIC REPRESENTATION OF THE
GREAT FIRE in NEW YORK Dec. 16 & 17, 1835.
Now exhibiting with other moving dioramic scenes, at the AMERICAN MUSEUM every evening.

Henry Hannington, Afong Moy's manager, re-created the horror of the "Great Fire in New York" in a dioramic representation. The Hannington brothers exhibited the diorama at the American Museum in 1836. *H. Sewell, Museum of the City of New York, 29.100.2087*

started in a warehouse on Merchant Street, the center of New York City's business district. With fierce winds and temperatures below zero, hydrants, fire hoses, and pumps froze. Because the East River was partially frozen, obtaining water there was difficult. By morning more than seventeen square blocks had burned, consuming 674 buildings, including the Merchants' Exchange Building, a number of warehouses, and nearly all of the city's insurance company buildings. Americans had never seen a blaze of this size with so much destruction. Merchants lost their warehouses, and with insurance companies burned and bankrupt, there was little recourse for recovery. The Carneses' warehouses and business was on William Street at the center of the fire; New Yorker Philip Hone specifically recorded in his diary that all of William Street had been consumed. Whatever unsold Chinese goods from the *Romulus* and *Mary Ballard* remained in their warehouses were now gone. The Carneses later listed themselves in the New York City directories as importers, but there is no record of their involvement with the China trade after 1836.

The Carneses' financial reversal and misfortune had an effect on Afong Moy's fate as a reluctant sojourner. According to the Albany newspaper accounts, she had a two-year time commitment to those who brought her, and ten months remained. The fire and its repercussions cemented Afong Moy's transition from a spokesperson for the firm's goods to that of its chief commodity. Though Chinese objects would still have a place in her upcoming presentations, they were now secondary. The Carneses, through auction houses and commission merchants, had sold and shipped some of their imported objects to numerous American towns and cities well before the fire. These would still be available in the cities she later visited. However, much of the focus would now shift to the exotic exceptionality of Afong Moy's person—her race, her bound feet, and her story.

8

Travel to Cuba and up the Mississippi River

AFTER AFONG MOY'S NEW ENGLAND tour, Henry Hannington ambitiously sought new venues to present the Chinese Lady—some as far away as Cuba. Afong Moy's trips to Havana, Cuba, and up the Mississippi River in late 1835 and 1836 with Henry Hannington were likely the most strenuous travel she had yet experienced. She and her company moved swiftly from town to town, covering more than a thousand miles. During this time, she encountered new cultures—Spanish, Indian, Creole, and French—straining her capacities to cope with new languages and ways. The last leg of this American tour was a slow slide into a repetitive and grinding schedule of performances and stagings. That she survived this ordeal is a testament to her stamina.

Decades before Afong Moy arrived in America in 1834, merchants on the Atlantic rim—in Boston, Baltimore, Charleston, and other seaport cities—engaged in the Caribbean and South American trade. From the late seventeenth century onward, the Spanish, Dutch, French, and English jockeyed for position in this far southern complex of islands and coastal ports. These global powers developed intersecting routes of trade to include the Spanish American and West Indian route—the European, West Indian, and Canadian route—and the northeast American, West Indian, and Canadian route.[1] Members of the Carnes family engaged in the latter circuit of trade.

Boston merchant Lewis Carnes, father of China trader Nathaniel, centered his commercial interests on the Dutch settlement of Demerara, in what is now Guyana, on the northern coast of South America. His activity involved the transport and sale of sugar and cotton, the principal staples of the trade. Despite the distance, Carnes apparently traveled back and forth, keeping a shop in Boston.[2] In 1799, Lewis Carnes died in Demerara, and his wife, Martha Greene Carnes, died there thirteen years later. Their oldest son, Nathaniel Greene Carnes, spent portions of his early life in South America since a branch of his mother's family had a five-hundred-acre cotton plantation in Demerara. This early introduction to transglobal trade in South America, as well as his experience as a supercargo on his uncle's vessel to China in 1811, prepared Nathaniel Carnes for his later international trading ventures in China, the Caribbean, and South America. He, and his cousin Francis, living in Europe, became masters of global commerce.

To some extent, early nineteenth-century American China traders also participated in the South American and Caribbean trade. Advertisements in Boston papers in the late 1820s presented the suitability of imported Chinese fireworks for re-export to the Spanish market. In an 1828 letter to John Forbes, Thomas Handasyd Perkins suggested that "if you go to South America but of this you know best [th]at any India crackers will do."[3] In the 1830s, Thomas Russell wrote to John Sword about the marketability of Chinese goods to South America and the Caribbean: "Fire crackers have been consumed in very large quantities on the coast (of South America). There have been but few imported for a long time, and I should think the large stock on hand was nearly consumed and the article might now be recommended."[4] Later, in July 1835, Philadelphia merchant Henry Pratt McKean wrote to his fellow trader Benjamin Etting in Guangzhou regarding the importation of Chinese shawls for the Havana market. McKean's contacts in Havana had just provided him with specific information on the desirability of certain patterns and colors for the "Spaniards'" shawls. Nathaniel Carnes already had this intelligence.[5]

Walter Barrett, in his book *The Old Merchants of New York City*, identified only one Chinese object that the Carneses transshipped to South America (and probably the Caribbean), but surely there were many more. He wrote: "The shawls imported by the Carnes concern were never equaled, and the South American markets were supplied from New York for ten years after with the most costly crimson, scarlet, white, cream-colored and pink shawls."[6] In having some knowledge of this market and with family contacts across the region, Nathaniel Carnes likely provided a variety of Chinese goods to the Caribbean and South American markets. These objects, stocked by merchants in Havana, awaited the visit of Afong Moy and Henry Hannington.

Lewis Carnes would have given little thought to the Caribbean/Cuban market in the eighteenth century, when the island of Cuba served only as a place to replenish ships' supplies between Spain and its Spanish American colonies. But by the 1830s, Cuba's place in the mercantile world had changed, and the Carneses and Hannington were astute to consider it a potentially profitable venture.

Cuba's rise came when Saint-Domingue (Haiti), one of the world's major producers of sugar, ceased growing cane after the 1791 slave rebellion and revolution. As the world's demand for sugar increased and Cuban sugar plantations modernized, the island's sugar production escalated. There were other political issues, both internal and international, that affected Cuba's growth, but the rise and profitability of sugar and coffee plantations had the largest impact.[7] Plantation owners, as well as local merchants and suppliers who serviced them, greatly increased in wealth.[8]

Planters, merchants, and those who previously had few resources—small shopkeepers, artisans, apprentices, and free blacks—now had money and could purchase consumer goods. The Spanish imperial metropolis was unable to meet this consumer demand, but with free trade, the United States could provide much of what was desired. In 1828, 1,057 foreign merchant vessels—a large number American—unloaded their goods in Havana; in 1837, the number more than doubled to 2,524.[9]

In the 1830s, Havana was no longer a colonial outpost; rather, it had a vitality that came from people with money to spend. The theater flourished. Carriages festooned in silver and gold brought women and men adorned in fashionable dress to evening costume balls and dances. The diary of Bostonian Mary Gardner Lowell, who visited Cuba in 1831–1832, described Havana's cosmopolitan atmosphere. Arriving two years before Afong Moy, she provides insight on what Afong Moy would find when she landed on this Caribbean island in late 1835.

Afong Moy boarded the brig *Caspar Hauser* in New York City, bound for Havana, on December 8, 1835, eight days before the great fire broke out. The *New York Evening Post* listed the twenty-two passengers, including "Afong Moy, the Chinese Lady, . . . Mr. Canderbeek and lady, . . . and Mr. Hannington and lady."[10]

Mary Gardner Lowell made a similar trip from Boston to Havana in December 1831. The voyage by sailing vessel took twenty-two days. Because her party had faced high seas and rough weather, Lowell's description of the Havana harbor sounded euphoric: "never shall I forget the astonishment & delight experienced at the scene which burst upon my view. Every thing buildings, trees, boats, men, costumes, were unlike any I had before seen: the whole had the effect of magic."[11] Twenty years later, Joseph Dimock, another American diarist, found Cuba equally arresting: "It is impossible to describe how completely everything differs from what we see in the States. The climate, the people, manners and customs, the foliage, fruit, flowers, vegetables . . . each and all present such a striking contrast to what a Yankee sees at home. . . .The scenery of the island is decidedly oriental, and reminds one of the many descriptions we have all read of the Eastern world."[12] Because Afong Moy had already experienced such marked contrasts between her life in China and that of America, Havana may not have appeared so remarkably different—and it may possibly have seemed familiar in climate and vegetation to her homeland.

To leave the Havana harbor, Afong Moy and her party employed a volanta, an unusual sort of Cuban carriage, a large square box slung low on huge wheels that were set far apart. Lowell found it so amusing that she drew a quick sketch of it in her diary. Joseph Dimock, too, recorded it as a strange apparatus and described that the "driver is mounted on the horse that draws the volante or one by its side and leading the horse in the bars."[13] In the volanta they drove into a city with a population of 130,000, past the Governor's Square and gardens filled with roses and flowering shrubs.[14] Their destination was a guest house, the Leon de Oro (Golden Lion) on the Plaza San Francisco.[15] The plaza, in a mixed residential and commercial area, faced the harbor in the heart of the city.

The guest house served Americans and other foreigners and was comparable in style to the one where Lowell stayed in 1832.[16] According to Lowell's description, these guest houses all had entrances that led into a courtyard surrounded by a two-story building; all the rooms faced the interior courtyard. This layout would have been similar to the structures Afong Moy knew in Guangzhou. The sleeping arrangements in Cuba, too, may have been familiar to Afong Moy. Lowell described the beds as impermanent: "The Spaniards make nothing of sleeping. I have taken the greatest fancy to their cots which are very light & taken away at a minute's warning. In the most magnificent houses you find no beds more costly than these, they are made with holes into which light wooden posts may be inserted to support the mosquito nets & are unusually unprovided even with matresses [sic]."[17] Similarly, most southern Chinese slept on mats that were rolled up and stored during the day.

We have no record of Afong Moy's response to Havana or the environment she found there, but we do have the Cubans' response to her. One local newspaper remarked that Afong Moy was "sweet and pleasant in manner."[18] The Havana paper *El Noticioso y lycero de la Habana* carried the by now familiar woodblock print image of Afong Moy seated on a dais below an elaborately festooned canopy. The English words "The Chinese Lady" on the platform base indicated that the manager carried the standard wood-block engraving with him to be delivered to local newspapers wherever she appeared in public. "La Dama China," inscribed below in the caption, pro-vided translation for the local population. The image was 3 1/4 inches high, larger than in any American newspaper, and significantly bigger than any other notice *El Noticioso* printed in 1836. Afong Moy's presence in Havana was a sensation.

Though the Canderbeecks accompanied her to Havana, they did not ac-company her on stage.[19] She received visitors in a room "richly appointed in the style of her country" at the guest house, Leon de Oro.[20] There, visitors absorbed the exotic surroundings and objects as Afong Moy spoke and sang in Chinese "to convey an idea of the simplicity in the customs of these re-mote peoples," and provided a glimpse of her small feet.[21] Here, Cubans equated simplicity with a distant and foreign culture. In America, she was beginning to communicate in English, but neither Henry nor Catherine Hannington spoke Spanish, and surely there were then no Chinese in Cuba who spoke Spanish.[22] Without a common language, her presentation was without explanation of Chinese customs, traditions, objects, or dress. This would be the first occasion when there was no explication of her past; Atung had conveyed this information for almost a year, after which Catherine Hannington presided, and then Afong Moy, in halting English, provided the context.

Unlike most American notices of her presence, the Havana paper placed a stronger emphasis on her womanhood and the exceptional aspects of her travel as a young woman. They averred that she was the "first woman of the Empire of China to travel beyond its borders and the only one to have come to the West [literally, the "western side of the Universe"].[23] Like the Albany papers, they focused on who brought her, the time frame her family had agreed on for her stay, and the protection afforded by the manager's wife. In addition, the papers went to some length to assure the public that this activity was one of decorum, aboveboard, and proper.

The concern was well founded. As Mary Gardner Lowell discovered, the life of women in Havana was considerably different than that of women in America. Lowell traveled in Cuba with her husband, but she was surprised to find that the rules of respectability precluded her from moving around the city without him. Spanish women screened their faces from public view, rarely were seen on the streets during the day, and traveled only with male relatives. It was for this reason that Afong Moy met visitors in a room of her guest house, and only in the evenings between 7:00 and 9:00 p.m. Such strictures on female interaction with men suited Afong Moy, for they were similar to her experience in Guangzhou. Catherine Hannington and Madame Canderbeeck, like Bostonian Mary Gardner Lowell, who chafed against this restriction, would have felt constrained and cloistered.

Newspaper notices of Afong Moy's presentation did not specify the objects that visitors might see in her salon. However, Lowell's descriptions indicate that Chinese import articles, like those Afong Moy might have pointed out in her salon, were present in Cuba. Lowell explained a Spanish woman's dress: "I will describe Mrs. Collector's [the wife of the Spanish deputy collector] as it is a pretty fair specimen of that worn by ladies on ordinary occasions. A thin . . . muslin with short sleeves . . . a wrought handkerchief on the neck & an embroidered one also in the hand. A watch [sic], long gold earrings, large comb curved in points . . . wrought stockings & a blue canton crepe shawl worked in colors, sufficiently large to be worn as a veil."[24]

Earlier in the nineteenth century a Salem China trade merchant instructed his supercargo on buying Chinese fabrics to "make up some cases of the large plaids and other figures of High and bright colors by themselves for the Havana market."[25] The Carneses, with their pulse on the market, surely would have found a ready market in Havana for their colorful Canton crepe shawls, which Walter Barrett had stated were intended for a South American venue (in Barrett's definition this included the Caribbean). Though their first vessel with Chinese goods did not reach America until May 1832, possibly transshipment of such shawls to Havana occurred soon afterward. The Carneses' pocket handkerchiefs too would have been appreciated in Cuba. Lowell remarked that the Spanish ladies viewed the pocket handkerchief as "indispensable," and they purchased them in great numbers and in a variety of fabrics.

Lowell also recounted the extensive use of fans, employed for both practical and flirtatious purposes. The women waved them at gentlemen when they passed in their carriages and applied them when attending balls, to stir the air. Lowell speculated that their movement conveyed a language that she could not understand. The vast numbers of these fans indicated a demand that the Carneses might have supplied. Straw matting, too, was an article that Lowell noticed in Cuba. Because of the climate, wool carpets were heavy and did not hold up well. When visiting a home in Havana, Lowell remarked that the floors were covered in straw carpet, "the only carpet . . . I have seen in Havana."[26] This, too, was an article of trade that the Carneses could ably deliver, though unfortunately, we have no record of such shipments.

Although Afong Moy presented an exotic view of her country, and was an unusual sensation in Cuba, the opportunity to share her culture was limited by language and gender. The tone of the newspaper articles suggests that Cubans were respectful of her difference, possibly more so than most Americans were. They may have accepted her more graciously because their culture encouraged such decorum. Whatever Afong Moy's desires might have been to remain, Hannington arranged for their departure to Florida in mid-February.

She arrived there "as suddenly & unexpectedly as if she had fallen from the clouds," read the headline in the *Pensacola Gazette* in March 1836.[27] While they were in Havana, Hannington probably had little news of events that had occurred in Florida since their departure from New York in early December. Had he known, he might have chosen a different destination. On December 23, 1835, a band of Seminole Indians attacked US Army soldiers under the command of Major Francis Dade as they marched toward Fort King, near present-day Ocala, some four hundred miles from Pensacola.[28] Only one of the 110 soldiers survived the massacre. Such action enraged Americans, and particularly the Indian fighter in the White House, President Andrew Jackson. In March 1836, Jackson responded.

The tension in this region between Indians and Americans was not new. During the War of 1812, the British recruited and armed the Seminoles and the Creeks to fight the American forces. After the war, Americans in the southeast became concerned that the Indians and fugitive slaves, operating out of an abandoned British fort in Spanish west Florida, might rally their enslaved peoples to revolt. Seizing on the death of some American sailors by the fort's garrison, in 1818 General Jackson, who was still stationed in the area after the Battle of New Orleans, marched into Spanish territory, burned the Indian town of Tallahassee, destroyed other major Seminole villages, and took the fort. Several months later, claiming the Spanish were arming the Indians, Jackson stormed Pensacola. The Spanish retreated, giving up the city to the American general. The action nearly upended the ongoing negotiations with Spain over the purchase of Florida. Eventually Spain gave up its claims to West Florida and ceded the eastern region, thereby establishing Florida as a US territory in 1821. These activities, along with other skirmishes, constituted the First Seminole War.

With the formation of the Florida Territory, the United States pressed the Seminole and other Indian nations to leave their homelands and relocate to the western Indian Territory to make way for white settlers.[29] Under duress, several Seminole chiefs signed an 1832 treaty agreeing to removal. But as they were pressed to leave in 1835, the Seminoles refused. President Jackson countered by demanding that they leave or be taken off the land by force. The December 1835 massacre was the Seminoles' reaction to this forced removal. The Second Seminole War began in March 1836 as General Winfield Scott took command in Florida and began the removal process. It was in this charged atmosphere that Afong Moy entered Pensacola.

On Monday, March 14, a large crowd gathered to view what Afong Moy had not displayed since the previous May in Charleston: one of her feet was uncovered and presented naked. The contrast between her reception and treatment in Havana and that in Pensacola was marked. Not only did crowds gawk, but the *Pensacola Gazette*'s editorial unpleasantly mocked the event. It commented: "We could not avoid thinking what an infallible preventative of corns, the Chinese ladies have fallen upon. In this . . . part of God's creation (the United States) the men (and the ladies too . . .) wear their shoes just tight enough to produce corns . . . but wanting the courage and fortitude of our friend Afong, they stop short half way."[30] The tone was similar to that in the editorials in Boston, but in Pensacola they did not equate Afong Moy with an Indian squaw as they had in Boston; had they done so, she might have been subject to removal.

From the newspapers, we know that she sang (though no mention was made of the Canderbeecks accompanying her), walked before the crowds, and spoke some English, but "*not exactly* as if it were her mother tongue."[31] Neither commodities, clothing, nor Chinese customs made the papers here. Who she was as a Chinese exotic "object," where she had been—Havana—and where she was going—Mobile—seemed the more engaging information to the newspapers, and possibly to her audience.

Afong Moy doubtless comprehended little of the political activities related to Indian removal, but she could see the process carried out as she journeyed with her party further west. The actor Tyrone Power followed a similar path through Alabama and Louisiana in 1835. Traveling by stagecoach outside Mobile, he stopped for breakfast at a tavern. The innkeeper complained about the Indians nearby, who she claimed stole their stock of poultry. Commiserating, Power acknowledged: "I congratulated her upon the late arrangements of Government, which afforded her the prospect of speedily being rid of these neighbors." Having little incentive as the removal process began, the Indians had not planted corn and therefore, as the inn-keeper observed, "Many . . . of these wretched people were at this time suffering from extreme want, and thousands were fast hastening to the like condition, when, unless aided by Government, they must steal or starve."[32] Power commented that planters and settlers were "clearing the cane-break with a rapidity unprecedented even in this country: the Indian reserves are all coming into cultivation as fast as they are vacated."[33] Such misery and displacement could not go unnoticed. It is possible that Afong Moy had seen such dislocation in her own land as a result of the recent years of famine and want in south China. It may also have been the reason for her displacement to this foreign country. As Afong Moy and her company moved on to Mobile, Alabama, she would have encountered the devastation of Indian removal.

Though Afong Moy's stay in Mobile was a brief three days, the presentation appeared to be more sedate than the one in Pensacola, without the naked foot-revealing episode. The *Mobile Daily Register* provided information to the public about her previous life, even though all of it rehashed the same turgid and inaccurate boilerplate—her age cited as sixteen and her feet encased in iron shoes—as repeated from newspaper articles in other cities. Situated in Murray's Large Room in the Alabama Hotel, Afong Moy presented in "a splendid Chinese Saloon." The one-dollar admission fee was the highest that Hannington (or Obear) had yet charged for her viewing. In other cities, tickets cost twenty-five or fifty cents, half price for children. Here children, as well as servants, were charged fifty cents. This, too, was the only place where servants, as a group, were specified in the price list. It is probable that "servant" was a euphemism for slave.

Mobile was a busy and prosperous port on a large bay, opening into the Gulf of Mexico at the mouth of the Alabama River. Money flowed into the port from planters who had newly established the cotton plantations situated up the river. These may have been the very clientele to whom Hannington charged such an excessive admission fee. The port, too, served as the route along which the Seminole were removed by steamboat from Florida to New Orleans, and the Muscogee Creek Indians down the Alabama River. The steamship *South Alabama* transported "removed" Indians along both water routes. It was also the vessel that carried Afong Moy and her company to New Orleans.[34]

It is unclear whether Afong Moy shared the vessel with Indians in the process of removal, but a Mr. Brunette, one of the passengers on board the *South Alabama*, quite possibly was an Indian agent who accompanied them.[35] When removal began in 1836, thousands of Indians, as well as free black Seminole, were sent by steamboat to New Orleans. There they were housed in US Army tents as they awaited shipment up the Mississippi River, and on to Fort Gibson and the west.[36] Sharing the vessel with disgruntled, discouraged, and displaced Indians would have been a disturbing experience for most passengers, but for one who looked somewhat similar to the displaced, it may have been frightening.[37]

The New-Orleans Commercial Bulletin gave the first notice of Afong Moy's travel by steamboat.[38] If she had not experienced this way of travel before, the news about the explosion of the steamboat *Ben Franklin* at the Mobile wharf on March 13, just a few days before she arrived, would not have comforted her. Though steamboat explosions made news quite regularly, this one was exceptionally well covered because it occurred so close to the city and so many people were killed or wounded. The *Mobile Journal* graphically reported: "Scarcely had she disengaged herself from the wharf, when the explosion, took place, producing a concussion which seemed to shake the whole city to its foundations. The entire population of Mobile . . . was drawn to the spot with astonishment and horror. This fine boat . . . was now a shattered wreck, while numbers of her passengers and crew were lying on the decks, either motionless and mutilated corpses, or agonized sufferers panting and struggling in the grasp of death. Many others had been hurled overboard. Many perished in the turbid waters before any human succor could reach them."[39] The *Ben Franklin* disaster, which left fifteen people dead and eleven badly wounded, shook Congress into action. Though the Franklin Institute in Philadelphia had already appointed a committee to look into the causes of exploding steamboat boilers, Congress now insisted on a presentation by the end of March 1836. New laws governing steamboat boiler inspections, maintenance, and licensing went into effect in 1838, but in the meantime, traveling by steamboat was a gamble.[40]

Though the *South Alabama* traveled in open water, which, without confronting floating logs, made the trip less harrowing than on a river, it still was a very different experience from vessels powered by the wind. Mary Gardner Lowell, who traveled to New Orleans on a steamboat, admitted that the heat, noise, and jarring motion of the engine located beneath the cabin made it difficult to sleep. With or without sleep, her companions,

Hannington and his wife, and thirty-one other passengers arrived in New Orleans in about two days' time.[41]

Afong Moy was entering one of America's most unusual cities, with a distinctive terrain and demographic. There were some comparisons to her native city of Guangzhou: both were situated on the delta of a large river which served as a pathway to the interior, and both were on nearly the same latitude with similar, southern climates. Because of their locations, New Orleans and Guangzhou were entrepôts, attracting foreign trade.

New Orleans was a complex mix of cultures. An early French settlement in the late seventeenth and early eighteenth centuries, it then was ceded to Spain in 1763. Returned to France, it was purchased by the United States from Napoleon as part of the Louisiana Purchase in 1803. Soon thereafter, in 1809, more than nine thousand French refugees, whites with their enslaved peoples as well as free people of color, fled to New Orleans from the black-led revolution on the island of Saint-Domingue. Until the 1830s, Creoles and those of African descent outnumbered white settlers. In the 1830s, with an influx of Irish and German immigrants, the city of almost fifty thousand was a nearly even mix of Caucasians and people of color.

The city's history was reflected in its layout. The French pianist Henri Herz, arriving in New Orleans for performances in the 1840s, described it best when he wrote that "in reality there are only two quarters: The English or American, and the French. They are, to all intents and purposes, two cities in one, two cities perfectly distinct from each other in every respect, from physical appearance to spirit of the inhabitants. New Orleans is perhaps the only city in the world which possesses this dual aspect in appearance and population. The only city also having two mother tongues."[42] As a Frenchman, Herz found New Orleans a vital and engaging place despite the presence of slavery.

The Englishwoman Harriet Martineau had also visited New Orleans, just one year earlier than Afong Moy. She too noticed a sharply divided city, remarking that, even at mixed gatherings, the division between the French and the Americans was uncomfortably visible. The French complained that Americans were unwilling to accommodate their language and the Americans mocked the ribald lifestyle of the French. Unlike Herz, Martineau reacted more strongly to the presence of slavery in this city than in any other place she had visited in the South. Slavery came closer to home and was curiously more stressful when Martineau was waited on by a blue-eyed, light-haired girl of white complexion whom her mistress wished to sell in retribution for her presumptuous behavior.[43] The fact that someone who looked so white, so like herself, and yet was enslaved rattled Martineau. Upon leaving the city after eleven days, she wrote: "New Orleans . . . while it affords an instructive study, and yields some enjoyment to a stranger, it is the last place in which men are gathered together where one who prizes his humanity would wish to live."[44]

It might not be surprising that in New Orleans, a place of contradictions, confusions, and multiple identities, Afong Moy's persona would be presented two different ways. A full-length, and large, broadside announced Afong Moy's presence in the city.[45] The upper half of the broadside carried the stock woodblock print of Afong Moy in her regal costuming and elaborate setting often seen in newspapers around the country. The lower portion of the broadside presented the rarely printed New York view of Afong Moy in the simple costume of trousers and surcoat top. In the Charles Risso and William Browne illustration, Afong Moy sat on her dais distantly removed in the background, while the standing Afong Moy familiarly confronted the viewer in the foreground. In the salon picture Afong Moy might have passed as royalty with her full-length robed ensemble. In the New York image, she was unquestionably the "other," a woman in clothing completely foreign to an American populace but possibly more appealing to a New Orleans audience.

The standing representation of Afong Moy used in the bottom section of the New Orleans broadside closely resembled depictions of lower- to middle-class Chinese women employed in the making of silk. The delineation above is one of nobility. No one in New Orleans would know that Afong Moy had significantly fallen in stature from the daughter of a mandarin as presented in the portrayal at the top to the lowly silk worker in the bottom view.

On the broadside, Hannington incorporated the presentation's earlier focus on Chinese objects such as the lanterns and Chinese paintings seen at the top with the more recent attention to Afong Moy, the exotic person of "astonishing little feet," on the bottom half of the poster. At the very bottom, the public learns for the first time that Afong Moy will return to China, embarking for Canton on the *Mary Ballard* just arrived from China.[46] This was an encouragement to see the Chinese "spectacle" before she left the United States.

There was some confusion about where people who desired to attend Afong Moy's "debut" in New Orleans would find her. The broadside announced the "unprecedented attraction" at the North American Hotel on Bienville and Levee Streets. However, newspaper announcements proffered that Mr. Scott, the New Orleans actor and theater promoter, had engaged her at the

FOR ONE WEEK ONLY,
(Owing to other engagements.)

Unprecedented Attraction,

In the large HALL of the

NORTH AMERICAN HOTEL,
Corner of Bienville and Levee streets,

Commencing Monday, March 28, and to close, positively, on Saturday, April 2d.

Exhibition to commence each evening at 8 o'clock

Tickets ONE DOLLAR, children half price.

THE CHINESE LADY,
AFONG MOY,

Lately exhibited in Mobile, Providence, Boston, Salem, Philadelphia, Baltimore, Washington, Richmond, Norfolk, Charleston, New York and New Haven, will have the honor of appearing before the Company in a splendid

CHINESE  SALOON,

fitted up with   rich Canton

Satin Dam-   ask Chinese

Paintings,   Lanterns,

and Cu-   riosities.

AFONG MOY is a native of Canton city, about sixteen years of age, mild and engaging in her manners; addresses the visitors in English and Chinese, and occasionally WALKS BEFORE THE COMPANY, so as to afford an opportunity of observing her

ASTONISHING LITTLE FEET!

For which the Chinese Ladies are so remarkable. Afong's feet is FOUR INCHES and an eighth in length, being about the size of an infant's of one year old. She will be richly dressed in

The CHINESE Costume.

And in order to give the audience an idea of the Language and Cadence of her country, she will sing

A CHINESE SONG.

AFONG MOY is at present under the care of the Lady of the conductor of the exhibition, and is making rapid progress in acquiring the English language. Various Chinese curiosities will be shown and explained to the Company, and every pains taken to satisfy the curious, as to the manners and customs of these singular people

She was brought to this country by Captain Obear, of the ship Washington, under a heavy guarantee to return her to her parents in two years and is now on her way to New York for that purpose, to embark for Canton in the 'Mary Ballard' just arrived from China. The conductor of the exhibition, consequently, can remain but a very short time in each city going up the river, by the way of Pittsburg, and confidently hopes, the same liberal patronage shown in other cities, will not be withheld in this, after travelling so many thousand miles to solicit the favor.

☞ A small quantity of beautiful Chinese Paintings, on rice paper, for sale.

In New Orleans, Hannington passed out these broadsides or placed them in shop windows to draw a crowd. This well-preserved broadside provided the same information as other advertisements, with the exception of Afong Moy's age; here Hannington notes that she is about sixteen years old. *For One Week Only, broadside, March 28, 1835. Courtesy American Antiquarian Society*

When Afong Moy arrived in New Orleans in 1835, the American Theatre, also called the Camp Street Theatre, had the finest amenities of any hall in which she had exhibited. Its large gas-lit auditorium probably astonished her. *New Orleans Directory for 1842. Courtesy New Orleans City Archives Main Branch*

AMERICAN THEATRE.

American Theatre on Camp Street.[47] The confusion stemmed from the increasingly polarized relationships between the Creoles and the Americans, of which Hannington, when publishing his broadside, was ignorant. The North American Hotel on Bienville and Levee (now Decatur Street) was in the Vieux Carré, the Old French Quarter. The American Theatre on Camp Street was in the American, Faubourg Sainte Marie area. In early 1835, it might not have mattered where Afong Moy presented in New Orleans. But by 1836 tensions had escalated, and now it was an issue of concern between the American and French theater promoters and their audiences.

Much of the divisiveness centered on the issues of enfranchisement. In 1835, New Orleanian John Gibson established a nativist organization to counter the Louisiana governor's appointment of non-native and naturalized French citizens to government positions.[48] In the 1830s, nativists in many eastern cities of the United States responded to the flood of immigrants by advocating for tighter immigration and enfranchisement laws. They sought to preserve American institutions and conventions and were alarmed at the possible influence of immigrant cultures and religions (principally Catholicism) on American life. With a French culture and a strongly Catholic base, nativism views, fanned by John Gibson, quickly took hold in New Orleans.

One of the notable New Orleans citizens who early rallied behind the nativist cause was the founder and owner of the American Theatre, James H. Caldwell. In 1824, Caldwell opened the venue (also known as the Camp Street Theatre), as the first English-speaking hall in New Orleans. The one-thousand-person auditorium, situated in the American district, was the first building in New Orleans, and the first American theater, fitted with gaslighting.[49] The competition crushed the French Théâtre d'Orléans, a bastion of Creole culture.

In January 1836, Caldwell and other proponents of xenophobia established *The True American*, a nativist newspaper, and published a pamphlet giving voice to the New Orleans nativist writer and organizer, John Gibson. The content and tone indicated the often-hostile environment in which a foreigner like Afong Moy, and later Chinese sojourners, existed. Gibson wrote:

> The foreigners who come among us yearly, by thousands, will long keep down the genuine spirit which would make us truly a nation. Thus it is that instead of being Americans, a great portion of the nation are Irishmen, Englishmen, Frenchmen, German etc. who instead of having every feeling centered in this country, have at least half of their hearts on the other side of the Atlantic [or Pacific], and who are habituated to customs derived entirely from foreign countries.[50]

Given the rhetoric, it might seem paradoxical that Afong Moy was welcomed into a theater owned by a nativist. That nativists did not recognize this foreigner as a threat to American culture indicated how they viewed this performance and the unlikely potential it had to destabilize American thought.[51] Her presentation was a curiosity, not an advocacy for early multiculturalism, or for acceptance of the Chinese in America.[52] The words "curious" or "curiosities" were employed numerous times in both the broadside and the newspaper advertisements. Because this was a "national" tour originated by Americans, American New Orleanians claimed this as their event, to be performed in the American quarter.

Though Afong Moy initially presented in the American quarter, the French populace still expressed an interest in her. The New Orleans *L'Abeille* (*Bee*), whose articles strongly countered those in the nativist newspaper *The True American*, ran an article on "La Dame Chinoise." Hannington also extended their New Orleans stay until April 6, as the *Bee* stated, "at the request of several families, who were unable to attend the Exhibition last week on account of its being Lent."[53] Hannington accommodated the French Catholics' religious holiday and held the program at the North American Hotel in the French quarter.

It is possible that the French appreciated the aspects of her Chinese culture even more than those in the American quarter. Mary Gardner Lowell, who had visited the previous April, found the French theater one of the more captivating aspects of New Orleans. Although she applauded the high quality of the plays, it was the French women in attendance who interested her most. And it was not their dresses, which she rated as "unbecoming," but their hair that drew her attention: "The ladies I saw at the theatre were all with their heads dressed á la Chinois."[54] The French ladies wore the hairstyle portrayed on the 1836 Afong Moy broadside: hair parted in the middle, pulled flat against the temples, and drawn into a knot at the top of the head. One might imagine Afong Moy looking out on an audience of women all mirroring her Chinese hairstyle. We will never know whether this reciprocity of fashion annoyed, delighted, or surprised her.

As the refrain in each newspaper announcement broadcast, Afong Moy would leave New Orleans to "return(s) by the river to Pittsburg, touching at nearly all the large cities on the route."[55] Once again she experienced life on board a steamboat. Unlike the Mobile–New Orleans steamboat trip, which was in the open waters of the Gulf of Mexico, the trip up the Mississippi was fraught with the dangers of river travel. Harriet Martineau recounted that, as she stepped aboard her steamboat in New Orleans, a helpful acquaintance inquired whether she had been provided with a life preserver. "I concluded he was in joke; but he declared himself perfectly serious, adding that we should probably find ourselves the only cabin passengers unprovided with this means of safety."[56] As a foreigner Martineau quickly learned that the Mississippi River's dangers were unique as a result of quick changes in the channel of the river, fierce downpours and squalls, and most significantly the "snags, planters, and sawyers [trunks of trees brought down from above by the current, and fixed in the mud under water] which may at any moment pierce the hull of the vessel."[57] Whether with life preserver or not, Afong Moy embarked on the Mississippi steamboat for several months of river travel.

The New Orleans papers announced that Natchez was Afong Moy's first stop on the river. After two days on the river, her party arrived in late April. Unlike the flat swampy land of New Orleans, the city of Natchez sat high on the bluffs above the Mississippi. The majestic homes of the planters looked down on the "under-the-hill" Natchez of saloons and gambling halls hugging the riverbank. The rowdy and bawdy environment below contrasted with the refined culture above. Wealth came from the cotton plantations situated in the surrounding countryside.

To reach the city above, Afong Moy and her party took a carriage up the steep and precipitous hill. Once there, she faced a grassy promenade stretching across the range of the bluffs affording an excellent view of the Mississippi River beneath. Behind the promenade stood the homes of some of America's wealthiest citizens, who might welcome the culture that theater activity would bring.

In his published journal, Tyrone Power reported extensively on his performances in Natchez in 1835. His description of the theater confirmed that of the northerner Jonathan Holt Ingraham, who also provided an account of the city in 1835.[58] Both found the theater situated in an odd area half a mile out of town, adjacent to an old cemetery with crumbling, dismantled tombstones nearby—not an encouraging atmosphere for cultural exchange. Though it was built by the Scottish immigrant architect Andrew Brown in 1826, neither commentator praised the theater's appearance. Ingraham described it as "a large, commodious building, constructed of brick, with arched entrances and perfectly plain exterior. Its interior, however is well arranged, convenient, and handsomely painted and decorated."[59]

The theater's seating capacity of about seven or eight hundred accommodated those from the town as well as planters coming from the surrounding countryside. Unlike New Orleans, where free blacks were not permitted to attend Henri Herz's piano concert, the Natchez theater was open to free blacks and the enslaved if they could afford the fifty-cent ticket and were willing to sit in the gallery. William Johnson, a free black barber in Natchez, frequently went to the theater in the 1830s, noting the cost in his ledger and recording what he saw in his diary.[60]

Power found an appreciative Natchez audience: "the men occupying the pit: whilst in the boxes were several groups of pretty and well-dressed women. The demeanor of these border gallants was as orderly as could be desired: and their enjoyment, if one might judge from the heartiness of their laughter, exceeding."[61] Apparently, the audience's reception of Power was atypical. Ingraham indicated that the citizens of Natchez were not an enthusiastic "play-going" group, while Johnson expressed annoyance at the lack of decorous behavior. Newspaper accounts of Natchez audiences claimed them as ill-mannered—talking loudly, catcalling, hooting, and shuffling about.[62] Around the time that Afong Moy presented at the theater, Johnson became so annoyed with the conduct of the theatergoers that he recorded in his ledger: "To the last time I ever goes to this Theatre $.50."[63]

The *Natchez Gazette* provided little information on Afong Moy's reception in the city. Calling her the "tiney [sic] footed stranger from the distant land of pagodas," it asserted that Mr. Scott had arranged for her appearance at the theater on a Friday evening.[64] Presumably the reference to the pagodas assisted the residents of Natchez in associating Afong Moy with the Chinese images they had seen on their dinner plates—Canton or Nanking ware— most typically with a large pagoda at its center. This signaled that she was indeed a stranger from the distant land of the plates' origins. The only other connection that Natchez might have to the word "China" were the china trees or the "pride of China" that many visitors remarked on. Ingraham described the tree at length: its rich green foliage, fragrant lilac-like flowers, its yellow berries in autumn, and its rapid growth. Known to us as the Chinaberry tree, a French botanist brought it to the American South as an ornamental from Asia in the early 1830s. By 1836, it had quickly spread to the Southwest, where it grew profusely. Pagodas and the Chinaberry tree carried positive, though relatively vague, associations with China. Yet Hannington relied on these associations to pull in an audience. What meaning that audience took home with them about Afong Moy, China, or the Chinese is lost to history.

After leaving Natchez, Hannington, his wife, Catherine, and Afong Moy surely stopped at several larger cities along the Mississippi River, although there is no record of their activity at these locations. Mary Gardner Lowell's account of her steamboat travel the year before suggests Afong Moy's route in 1836. Lowell's Mississippi River stops included Vicksburg, Mississippi, then Memphis, Tennessee, and a small town in Missouri. Soon their steamboat met the Ohio River in Illinois. Leaving the Mississippi for the Ohio, the Lowells' vessel went on to Louisville, Kentucky, and from there to Cincinnati, Ohio, the same route taken by Afong Moy. It is here that, once again, Afong Moy's presence was discussed in the newspapers.

In his September 1836 diary, Virginia lawyer James Davidson expressed the sentiments of many who passed through Cincinnati: "With the city of Cincinnati I am much pleased. But I do not admire its people."[65] Davidson's response to the people, whom he labeled bigoted, may have been a reaction to the events that had taken place in the previous months. As Ohio was a free state bordering the South, African Americans sought refuge in nearby Cincinnati, where they competed for jobs previously held by whites. In April 1836, angered by this situation and by the Anti-Slavery Society's propaganda, white mobs turned on the black community, burned their homes, and attacked and killed several blacks. The rioting continued until the governor declared martial law just a few weeks before Afong Moy's May arrival.

The very conditions that promoted such friction—close proximity to southern states—attracted abolitionists who targeted slaveholders across the Ohio River in Kentucky. Cincinnati's Lane Theological Seminary, presided over by Rev. Lyman Beecher, provided a countervailing influence on the intolerant behavior. Beecher's daughter, the novelist Harriet Beecher Stowe, lived in the family home in Cincinnati. Articles that she and her brother Henry wrote for the local paper rebuked the offensive attack on the black community. It was here, amid the contention, that Stowe formed her abolitionist views and collected materials for her novel *Uncle Tom's Cabin*. There is no evidence that Stowe, who at the time was four months pregnant with twins, saw Afong Moy in the Cincinnati theater. She may have been indisposed or too involved in writing for the local papers to attend. However,

The Philadelphia artist John Sartain completed this
portrait of William B. Tappan around 1836, the
year Tappan published his poem on Afong Moy.
*Courtesy of the Pennsylvania Academy of the Fine
Arts, Philadelphia. Bequest of Dr. Paul J. Sartain*

another like-minded person, the Rev. William B. Tappan, did. Like Stowe,
he was a writer, and rather than secreting his views regarding Afong Moy in
a diary, he published them in a poem.

The Massachusetts-born Tappan came to Cincinnati in 1833 to serve the
American Sunday School Union. A non-denominational Christian organization founded in 1824, the Union encouraged the formation of Sunday
schools in deprived or needy locations, particularly in the West and South.
The institution also published and distributed books to Sunday schools in
churches across the nation. With an interest in religious education, writing,
and publishing, Tappan found his calling in developing the western region
of the Sunday School Union headquartered in Cincinnati. Rev. Tappan
moved within the Beecher family's circle, for his first cousin Arthur Tappan
helped establish the Lane Seminary and was the co-founder and president
of the American Anti-Slavery Society.[66]

Rev. Tappan began writing early in his life, issuing his first book of poems
in 1819 and eventually publishing more than a dozen volumes.[67] His work
focused on religious topics and issues of social concern. The poem entitled
"To the Chinese Lady—Miss Afong Moy" was included in a book simply
titled *Poems of William B. Tappan,* published in Boston and Philadelphia
in late 1836.[68] Composed of ten stanzas written in the present tense, and
written from the perspective of a viewer at the Cincinnati event, it was
sympathetic and patronizing. Tappan "marveled" at her unusual visage, her
accent, her exotic strangeness, her feet, and the "oriental boudoir" in which
she was presented. He describes Afong Moy's attitude as proud, rather than
submissive, and as someone who came from a heritage of an ancient past.
Donning that mantle of distinctiveness may have shielded her from discrim-
inatory and derogatory responses in places like Cincinnati.

After situating Afong Moy in the Cincinnati theater in the first five stanzas, Tappan then moved to the larger issues of race and religious salvation. Tappan, as a monogenist, believed that all races were of the same origin. Recognizing that "God of one blood made the kindreds of the earth"—a principle espoused by abolitionists—Tappan decried his country's recent "prejudices" that condemned the Chinese people to an ignorance of God. Presuming that they had been walled in (with an allusion to the Great Wall of China) by superstition, missionaries had freed them to see the "sparkles of the light." Tappan, in his ignorance of the size and complexity of China, ended his poem with the expectation "that China quickly shall be one in Christ, the living Head."[69]

Tappan used both the principles and the language of the abolitionists in the poem; however, he expanded on the concept of enslavement. He considered the Chinese to be enslaved to heathen orthodoxy that had bound them in ignorance to superstitious beliefs.[70] The words were not unlike those of abolitionist William Lloyd Garrison when he implored the South to change its ways after John Brown's hanging: "one God to be worshipped, one Savior to be revered, one policy to be carried out—freedom everywhere to all the people without regard to complexion or race. Oh that the South [and here one might substitute China] may be wise before it is too late, and give heed to the word of the Lord! But whether she will hear or forbear, let us renew our pledges to the cause of bleeding humanity."[71] Tappan's poem defined the cause as freeing Chinese nonbelievers from their doom. Afong Moy's presence represented an opportunity to reform a "heathen," remove her from enslavement, and, through her, bring light to a country ignorant of God. It was only through Christian (specifically Protestant) intercession that the "heathen" Chinese would be saved.[72]

The poem "Books for China" that followed "The Chinese Lady" in the same volume documented Tappan's intent:

To China!—'tis but lately we should chide
The fancy that durst stretch so bold a ken.
Yet knowledge must increase, and God has made
A highway into Sinim. To her need
Shall Sunday-schools be given;—in the shade
Of her great wall, her sons will sit, and read
The winning page, whose precepts lead above;
And they will love the truths *our* children love.[73]

Tappan's missionary zeal extended well beyond the South and the West to the Far East, where he hoped his Sunday school books would open the way for Christian knowledge. In the poem "The Chinese Lady," the personage of Afong Moy was the pretext, the entrée, into Tappan's larger evangelical mission. It is unclear whether he, like Margaret Prior in New York City, proselytized Afong Moy while she was in Cincinnati.

After several days churning up the Ohio River, Afong Moy's steamboat approached Pittsburgh. According to Mary Gardner Lowell's 1835 account, passengers could see the effects of the city well before the city itself became visible. Great clouds of dense smoke rose from the many forges nearby. Proceeding down the river, she described: "On the right bank the mountains rise precipitously and have a very extraordinary appearance with their coal mines and little black hovels and forges. Here and there you see a rail road which brings the coal directly from the mine into the furnace."[74] Lowell found the location of the town, at the confluence of the Allegheny and Monongahela Rivers, impressive, but smoke obscured its beauty. This possibly was the first industrial site Afong Moy had seen. She had not previously visited a New England mill town, nor is it probable she could have viewed the kilns of Jingdezhen, the largest porcelain-making town in China's interior. Pittsburgh provided her a close view of what a manufacturing town offered.

Afong Moy presented in the Musical Fund Theatre, located at the base of a steep bluff called Grant's Hill. Built in 1834, the theater accommodated about one thousand people. Tyrone Power, who had preceded Afong Moy at nearly every location along the Mississippi and Ohio Rivers a year earlier, again provided an excellent description of the theater. He was impressed with its interior, its appointments, and the conveniences of the facility and nominated it a model for other theater buildings. Yet the industrial nature of the city penetrated even here, for he remarked that "the ornamental parts of the interior were already disfigured by the smoke which fills the atmosphere day and night."[75]

According to newspaper accounts, Afong Moy's presentations or "levees" were well attended.[76] The announcement of the Pittsburgh event was similar to many others. Here, too, she displayed some Chinese objects. But now, at the end of her tour, the newspapers announced that only small quantities of Chinese rice paper paintings were available for sale. They warned of her imminent leave-taking for China on the vessel *Mary Ballard*, with the two-year "heavy guarantee to return her to her parents" the stated reason for her swift departure from Pittsburgh.[77]

First, however, she had to find her way out of the Pittsburgh theater after the evening events. Even the able-bodied Power struggled to find his way; "how the people made their way home again I do not know," he wrote, "even the short distance I had to explore on the line of the principal street, I found beset with perils: loose pavement, scaffold-poles, rubbish, and building materials of all kinds blocked up the *trottoir* . . . for light here was none, natural or artificial."[78] A night walk on bound feet in a smoky jungle, as well as the heavy atmosphere of coal dust, surely was one of the less enjoyable experiences of Afong Moy's extensive American travels.

There are no further newspaper advertisements for her presence beyond Pittsburgh. Afong Moy's extensive half-year travel covering more than a thousand miles was coming to an end. The physical rigor of such a journey on bound feet, the frequent, and often large assemblies, the frustrations of the language barrier, and the lack of a Chinese compatriot required enormous stamina. Men, and some women, had traveled a similar route, but very few faced the triple exigencies of racial difference, disability, and gender.

No additional venues claimed her time along this route, and therefore to return east, Afong Moy would take the stage coach. At this point in her trip, Mary Gardner Lowell and seven others had piled into what she called an "Extra"— a Concord coach that could seat six, nine, or twelve people. Afong Moy and her group traveled similarly through the Allegheny Mountains, stopping at taverns along the route. Both parties—the Lowells and Hannington's group—traveled in late spring and therefore saw what Lowell described as numerous "large, covered Pennsylvania wagons loaded with the goods and chattels of emigrants."[79] These were willing immigrants who, unlike Afong Moy, came, as they related to Lowell, not for themselves but for the benefit of their children. They had high expectations for their prospects in the west, which in some measure they could control. Afong Moy, moving in the opposite direction, had but limited influence on the course of her future.

PART IV

FINALE

9

Off Stage

IN THE SPRING OF 1836, numerous American newspapers reported Afong Moy's imminent return to China. The first article appeared in New Orleans in early April, noting that she would embark for Guangzhou on the vessel *Mary Ballard*, which had just arrived in the New York port from China. The press reports followed Afong Moy along her Mississippi River journey, and the refrain helped her manager, Henry Hannington, build an audience as visitors were reminded that this was the last opportunity to view the Chinese lady. Though she probably could not read the reports, the message must have been apparent to Afong Moy. Perhaps Hannington or his wife, Catherine, discussed it with her openly, or the message filtered into her consciousness from the attitudes and comments of others.

In actuality, Afong Moy's journey to China may have been delayed by a year. First promised a return to China after a year's stay, she should have departed on the *Mary Ballard* with Captain Obear in April 1835. That she remained in America indicated that the Carneses and Captain Obear received an offer from her new manager, Henry Hannington, to extend her stay another year to increase their returns on the financial investment they had made in her voyage.

The *Mary Ballard*'s April 1835 journey to Guangzhou without Afong Moy on board has been well documented. Caroline Hyde Butler, wife of the *Ballard*'s supercargo, wrote extensive letters to her husband, Edward, to the Carneses' New York address, as Edward traveled to China. Caroline Butler referenced the presence of Augusta Obear, Captain Obear's wife, on board the vessel. From her letters, it seems the Butler and Obear relationship was a close one. In May, Caroline Butler wrote her husband: "I console my-self very much by reflecting upon the excellent captain and officers you have, and also that Mrs. Obear accompanies you—with her you can talk of us all when the Capt is on duty, and should you be sick (which may Heaven forbid) she will render you all the little attentions and kindness which women know how to bestow SO much more than men."[1] Butler never mentioned why Augusta Obear took this voyage with Butler's hus-band and Captain Obear. It is possible that Augusta Obear was to serve as Afong Moy's chaperone, as she had done when she accompanied Afong Moy to America the year before. Last-minute financial arrangements may have changed Afong Moy's planned trip, but not Augusta Obear's.

Through her letters, Butler shared a sense of Augusta Obear's character, the only insight we have on Augusta Obear's personality. Caroline Butler wrote that Obear was a religiously inclined woman, and supposing it to be a Sunday, Obear would be "as grave as fudge" while reading "the good book."[2] In another letter, Butler imagined the Obears and her husband playing whist. She anticipated that Augusta Obear would say, "no cheating." Butler admonished her husband not to do so, and using "sing-song" Chinese phrases, she addressed Obear: "I hope Mrs. Obear you will savee too much for their old custom—make them a cum show of a box on the ear and I will chin you."[3] This use of the Chinese pidgin language meant that both were familiar with the phrasing, and used it as a mocking reference to cheating, which some Westerners claimed was an aspect of the Chinese character. Applying the sounds of Chinese pidgin indicated a belittling and conde-scending attitude toward the Chinese, and perhaps even toward Afong Moy, that both may have shared.[4] None of Caroline Butler's letters mention Afong Moy or the fact that she was not on board, though surely her situation was familiar to both women. That omission might have been an oversight, or more likely a lack of interest in or concern for the life of someone whom they considered to be of little importance in their experience.

Since Afong Moy had literally missed the boat in April 1835, she might now anticipate the *Mary Ballard*'s return trip to China in the fall of 1836 or spring of 1837. The May and June 1836 New York newspapers stated: "Chinese Lady Afong Moy . . . is on the point of returning in the 'Mary Ballard' to Canton," and "Chinese Lady Afong Moy has been re-engaged for this week, and must positively leave on Saturday, June 11th, as she sails shortly for Canton," and another stated that Afong Moy will be on her way to the Celestial Empire.[5] However, there is no evidence that the *Mary Ballard* made a return trip to China under Captain Obear or any other master as the newspapers stated. Instead, the vessel, under Captain M. H. Parkinson, traveled to Havana and New Orleans in the late 1830s and early 1840s.[6] Afong Moy never set her bound feet on that vessel.

There were many last moments, many biddings of farewell to her numerous friends, and many "now or never" opportunities to view her for the final time. Despite the trumpeting of her return, in July 1836 she was still providing audiences at the Peale Museum with information, now in English, on "Various Chinese curiosities . . . shown and explained to the company . . . and gratifying . . . the curious, as to the manners and customs of these singular people."[7]

Toward the end of August, Henry Hannington gathered all his attractions into one extravagant event at Niblo's Garden. This may have been Afong Moy's first exposure to the fashionable theater complex built by William Niblo in 1828. Its expansive grounds accommodated Hannington's elaborate undertaking. The proceedings included a Grand Concert featuring the "eminent talent" of vocal performers "Howard, Dempster, Cunnington, Scott," and Afong Moy. This was followed by magicians and another round of an elaborately costumed Afong Moy bidding farewell. Next came a display of fireworks and finally Hannington's "splendidly decorated . . . transparent fairy palace." The latter was an illuminated series of paintings joined with special effects in what was considered Hannington's particular style.[8] Here for the first time Hannington married the diorama events for which he was known with the presentation of Afong Moy. It is unclear what part she played in this visualization. Perhaps she wandered before the fairy palace costumed as an oriental "other." Her exotic identity was a commodity, and Henry Hannington made use of all his assets in this extravaganza.[9]

Advertisements stated that this particular event was for Hannington's "Benefit," meaning that all proceeds gathered that evening, minus the cost of the house expenses, would be solely his. It was understood that all the performers would offer their services to assist the named beneficiary. Such "benefits" were common even for managers and often occurred at the end of a season to secure funds to carry on into the fall and winter. There is no record of the evening's "take," but it was probably successful, for Hannington's juxtaposition of Afong Moy and his dioramic skill seen at Niblo's Garden was repeated and, for a period, breathed life into his enterprises.

In the fall of 1836, another opportunity arose that could have provided for Afong Moy's chaperoned return to China. The friendship between the Obears and the Butlers might now work to her benefit. Caroline Butler had raised four children mostly on her own because of her husband's absence as a supercargo, and her health had gradually weakened. By early 1836, her condition, defined as consumption, now called tuberculosis, had become severe, and doctors prescribed a sea voyage as a possible cure. Her husband was leaving again for China as a supercargo in the fall of 1836, which provided the occasion for Caroline Butler's health cure. Leaving their children with relatives, she departed with her husband for China on the vessel *Roman* in October. Here, Caroline Butler's trip provided the appropriate time and circumstance for Afong Moy's return to her home country, with the possibility of an accompanying female chaperone. While away, Butler kept a diary recounting her activities aboard ship and in China. She included no mention of Afong Moy but did describe her responses to both the Chinese women she saw and the Europeans she met on Macao. Yet once again, Afong Moy's opportunity to leave the United States slipped away, or was ignored.

For the rest of the fall and into the winter of 1836 most notices of the Chinese lady's appearances were paired with Hannington's dioramas or moving panoramas at the City Saloon in New York City. These panorama presentations consisted of numerous canvas paintings sewn together and moved by means of a mechanical cranking system. The action occurred as the large paintings were conveyed before a large window, wound from one roller to the other. The panorama took the audience to far-off locations closing the distance between the local and the international scene.[10] In one September 1836 presentation Hannington sent his visitors across the ocean to Switzerland where a reviewer recounts: "The Scenery abounds with the romantic and picturesque, for which the country is so justly celebrated. The rowing and sailing of boats; the shepherds attending his flocks, and other animated objects cannot fail to gratify the curious."[11]

It is unclear exactly how Hannington incorporated Afong Moy into these presentations, for the advertisements just state that she "will appear . . . in conjunction with the Dioramas [panoramas] at the City Saloon. She will be richly attired in her native costume and sing a Chinese Song."[12] Perhaps on these occasions Hannington staged his "Chinese Scene," which was described in a Boston paper some years later as unrivaled and "in which the most striking characteristics of that wonderful people are exhibited."[13] Since we have no record of what these scenic panoramic views of China were, we can only surmise that they were similar to those seen on Chinese rice paper watercolors that Hannington sold at Afong Moy's venues and thus were readily accessible to him. Unlike earlier presentations, where objects and static stage sets stood in for her Chinese environment, now audiences were transported by this visual legerdemain into an exotic domain inhabited by

Afong Moy. She enlivened the panorama by walking before it as a living tableau. The accuracy and authenticity of the Chinese scenes were of little concern to Hannington or the audience.

The continual postponement of Afong Moy's departure mattered little to the public, who were daily promised one last look before losing the opportunity forever because "it will . . . be a long time before a Chinese Lady again visits this country, to astonish the curiosity by an exhibition of her personal charms."[14] However, this constant delay of her return to China must have been wearing on Afong Moy, who never knew, and could not control, the date of her departure. After so many postponements, erroneous public notices, and vessels leaving for China without her, the reality surely became clear—she was not leaving. All the announcements were ploys to heighten public interest.[15]

In the early months of 1837, there were few references to Afong Moy in the press. George Odell's annals of the early nineteenth-century New York theater list only one notice of her appearance in April 1837. In that month, Henry Hannington and his brother William extended their operation from the City Saloon in New York City to a second venue, the Brooklyn Institute, on Fulton and Cranberry Streets. The site was near Fulton Ferry landing, the notable location where Fulton established his steamboat ferry in 1814 to take Manhattanites to Brooklyn. By 1837 Brooklyn was expanding rapidly as a "suburban" location—near enough to commute to work in the city, and yet live outside the urban environment. Boldly, the Hannington brothers reached out to a new clientele in this recently populated area of Brooklyn Heights.

They opened their venue that April with a concert that included the Canderbeecks, W. Bassford on the pianoforte, Afong Moy, and the Hanningtons' Hydro-Oxygen Microscope, a device that magnified and projected droplets of water and small objects.[16] This may have been the first time the Canderbeecks and Afong Moy had shared the stage since their Albany presentation in the fall of 1835. For nearly a month the Hanningtons managed this entertainment. But by early May it was no longer financially sustainable, and they closed the show. Odell quoted an unidentified Brooklyn paper: "Every exertion and expense having been lavishly bestowed without the least encouragement having been given, they can only attribute the hitherto thin attendance to the pressure of the times."[17]

The pressure of the times would greatly affect Afong Moy's experience in America and would determine how she spent her next eight years. Little did Americans anticipate how greatly the upcoming economic crisis would change their lives. In early February of that year, New York City diarist and merchant Philip Hone remarked on the issues that prefigured the financial disaster to come. He recorded a riot that erupted when a New York City mob ransacked and destroyed barrels of flour in merchants' warehouses to protest the cost of bread. Wondering how this action could make bread cheaper, Hone included in his diary the full text of the placards pasted up on the street corners: "Bread, Meat, Rent, Fuel—Their Prices Must Come Down. The Voice of the People Shall be Heard, and Will Prevail. The People will meet . . . to inquire into the cause of the present unexampled distress, and devise a suitable remedy."[18] Though Hone found their remedy misdirected, he pondered what would become of the "laboring classes" as he wandered the Fulton market that week noting it had the "appearance of famine."[19] By March, Hone's businesses began to fail, and he saw crisis "near at hand, if it has not already arrived."[20]

The crisis fully arrived in May. Banks closed, merchants defaulted, and most business transactions evaporated. Hone moaned, "Where will it all end?—In ruin, revolution, perhaps civil war."[21] There were numerous causes for the Panic of 1837. The expansion of credit, extensive land speculation, and a wave of defaulted bank notes—paper money people used because they were unable to obtain silver or gold coin—undermined the economy. Hone blamed Andrew Jackson for much of the turmoil, believing that his refusal to re-charter the Second Bank of the United States was a grave error. Previously the bank had provided some control over state and private bank notes. When its charter expired and was not renewed, state banks became lax in their practices and many defaulted. This situation was compounded when Jackson demanded in his "Specie Circular" that all payments for public land be made in hard cash, a commodity few had.

The Panic of 1837 was one of the most severe economic depressions the nation had experienced. If the defaults had just undermined the fortunes of the speculators and bank directors—those who had principally perpetrated the problem—then it would have been poetic justice. Unfortunately, it also eviscerated the savings of the middle and laboring classes, the farmers, mechanics, and artisans.[22] Among the working classes severe unemployment continued into the early 1840s.[23] Few of these people could afford extra pennies for entertainment.

Yet in late May 1837, either blind to the impending crisis or merely bold and daring, Henry Hannington and his brother opened another exotic, illusionary diorama in Manhattan. This one—the African Glen— "producing the illusion of a grove and shady walks, with the opposite one of wild scenery and savage beasts" could not appropriately incorporate Afong Moy even with some cinematic stretching.[24] According to the frank assessment by the *Commercial Advertiser*, the Hanningtons invited influential and distinguished citizens, the mayors of New York City and Brooklyn, and other dignitaries to "swell the throng of visitors" because most could not afford to attend. The reporter hoped that the Hanningtons' "spirited manner" would pull them through. However, in late September the newspapers posted the results. They reported that the Hanningtons had retired, turning over the operation of the African Glen site with all their painted canvases to an Englishman.[25] The Hanningtons had made a spirited effort to keep their businesses afloat, but entertainment was something few could afford, and most could do without.

When Henry Hannington and his brother finally shuttered their entertainment businesses, Henry could no longer support Afong Moy. But what of those who had initially brought her to America? They, too, had responsibility for her well-being. In 1837, Francis Carnes was still in Paris. A year later his daughter Emmeline married in New York and perhaps he attended the ceremony. If so, there is no record of his assistance to Afong Moy. In June 1837, Nathaniel Carnes, Francis's cousin and business partner, learned that he had lost a case in court. His property in Poughkeepsie, New York, had burned to the ground the previous year, but the court ruled in June that his insurance policy on the property was invalid. He lost the $7,000 premium and the houses.[26] By 1838, things got worse; with a decree order from the court, his New York City parcel of land and storehouse were sold at public auction.[27] Possibly Nathaniel went bankrupt.

During this period there is no record of Captain Obear or his wife Augusta and not until 1842 did Captain Obear resurface in New York City as a merchant.[28] In 1849, while taking a water cure in Brattleboro, Vermont, he fell off his horse and died from his injuries. All those who might have cared for Afong Moy, and earlier had most likely pledged their support, deserted her during these severe economic times.

To make matters worse, Afong Moy's opportunities to return to China were decreasing as China's diplomatic ties with foreign governments deteriorated during the late 1830s. Much of this animosity stemmed from the trade in opium. The Manchus banned the smoking and importing of opium in 1729, and the East India Company (EIC) forbade carrying opium on its ships in 1733. Yet, the trade on private English trading vessels flourished by the 1830s, with rampant bribery and clandestine smuggling operations accepted by both foreigners and Chinese mandarins.

Americans found that selling opium provided them a ready source of cash. Once they established a cheaper supply of opium in Turkey, most American China trade companies engaged in its sale. By the end of the 1830s, the opium trade carried greater value than any other world commodity.[29] Since the Chinese paid for the drug in silver currency, the drain on their specie reserves became critical. Unlike the early trade, when inflow of specie greatly outweighed outflow, the reverse was now the case. This crisis, together with an unpleasant confrontation that erupted when the Chinese attempted to hang an opium user in front of the foreigners' factories in 1838, as well as the abominable effects of opium on the Chinese populace, pressed the emperor into action. After many edicts and remonstrances, the Chinese emperor gave foreign merchants his last warning against their illegal dealing in opium at the end of 1838.

The American press covered the clash between American merchants and the Chinese authorities with great regularity in the late 1830s. In April 1838, the *U.S. Gazette* wrote: "For some time past, the Chinese authorities have been annoying the foreign residents at Canton with edicts, commanding them to leave the country."[30] The paper referenced a late 1837 letter from the hong merchants that asked all foreigners to return home or go to the Portuguese colony of Macao. According to the newspapers' information, the Chinese merchants begged that the foreigners obey without delay. However, the American papers made little mention of why the foreigners were no longer welcome in China. At this tense time, no American merchant would negotiate the return of a Chinese woman who had illegally left her country.[31] That admission came later in 1838 when the Cleveland *Daily Herald and Gazette* reported that "no vessel can be induced to take the responsibility of handling her [Afong Moy] in China."[32]

In the 1830s, those like Afong Moy, devoid of financial support and left adrift, had only a few options in America. Most of the state and community policies responding to the needs of the poor had been adopted from English law. In England, the Elizabethan Poor Law of 1601 assigned the dispensing of poor relief funds through the local parishes and delineated the office responsible as the Overseer of the Poor. In most American states a similar system applied; local townships or precincts, rather than parishes, took responsibility for their poor.[33]

In England and then the United States, the poor were generally categorized into three groups. Those unable to work through no fault of their own, as a result of a disability or advanced age, were deemed the deserving poor. Those termed "vagrants" were capable of work but chose a wandering lifestyle. Those who labored but were still unable to make ends meet were characterized as the working poor. Public sympathy lay with the first and the last group. In most of the American colonies, and later the states, local funds were provided to assist them. However, nearly all communities were unwilling to support the transient, the disorderly, the frivolous, or those who had no known ties to the municipality. With all her travels, Afong Moy had no community. Her itinerant life afforded no place of refuge.

The record of her life—and her life itself—might have ended with the dismal economic tragedy of the 1837 Panic had it not been for several citizens of Monmouth, New Jersey. In March 1838, the *Monmouth Inquirer* published an account based on the investigative work of several people who located Afong Moy in the far reaches of Monmouth County. Perhaps they had been alerted to her presence or recognized the Chinese woman as highly unusual in this rural area of New Jersey.[34] The detailed article reminded its readers that, the year before, the Chinese lady called Afong Moy, last seen in New York, had created great excitement with the public who had "an anxiety to see her." Reporters assumed that her absence indicated that she had finally returned to China.

However, in late February 1838 the correspondents "conversed with several persons, who were induced to go to the place of her residence, from an anxious and commendable desire to ascertain, if possible, how she became thus situated."[35] There they found her living with a widow and her family in "one of the most retired and secluded spots in the country." In discussions with the interviewers, Afong Moy confirmed that she had been brought to this country by a ship captain with the promise of a one-year stay. After her agent "could no longer attract the attention of the public, she was brought to this county, and placed under the direction of a widow woman of very indigent circumstances who . . . is wholly unable to administer to the comforts, and every day wants of her guest."[36]

The paper then turned its investigation to her unnamed agent. The reporter, relaying the questions of the inquirers, wondered why the agent selected such an obscure and secluded place. The citizens averred to the reporter that the circumstances of this situation were disturbing and incongruous and put the blame on the agent, commenting that he "certainly owes it to himself, and to the country . . . to offer [sic] explanation."[37] The article closed with the recognition that Afong Moy deserved the "special attention of the humane and benevolent of our community."

The March 1838 article in the *Monmouth Inquirer* was picked up by numerous newspapers on the East Coast and unleashed a barrage of criticism against those who had abandoned Afong Moy. Although only a relatively small percentage of citizens had actually seen her, a larger number had read about her in the newspapers or seen her image circulated in the press. That the reaction was so widespread and expressed such outrage may be the result of several factors. Many Americans viewed Afong Moy, though by Chinese considerations now a woman, as a relatively young unmarried girl, needful of protection. Despite the manner in which she arrived, or her position as a brand and promoter of Chinese goods, Afong Moy was still perceived as the country's guest of extraordinary uniqueness. Once the supposed inappropriate treatment was uncovered, her neglect reflected poorly on this "republican" nation and its citizens. Though living a life as an advertisement for goods or an object of exotic interest should have been equally unacceptable to the public, that was not perceived as abuse. But being harbored in a poorhouse or boarded out as an indigent was indeed an indignity. The public's efforts to determine the individuals culpable for her state of affairs were as complicated then as they are today.

According to the earliest newspaper account of her in 1838, Afong Moy was placed in a Monmouth County poorhouse. The *Newark Daily Advertiser* explained: "the profits [for her manager] began to decrease and she was finally shamelessly abandoned in Monmouth county in this state, in a helpless situation. She was provided for by the authorities of that county in their poor-house—where she remained . . . when a company of persons redeemed her, by defraying the expenses of her maintenance."[38] Monmouth County, New Jersey, situated in the central part of the state, east of Trenton and south of Newark, lies about fifty miles from New York City. Why was Afong Moy found in a location relatively far from her last presentation in New York City, and how was she admitted into a poorhouse in a county and state unrelated to her previous base of operation?

The poor typically found refuge in the community to which they belonged. Since Afong Moy had no association with any community in the United States, someone else associated with her must have resided in the area, enabling her to qualify for assistance. Her situation in New Jersey was most certainly attributable to her association with Henry Hannington. Though his business activities centered in New York City, Hannington's family lived in Monmouth County; census records list a Henry Hannington with wife and children of appropriate names and ages by 1850.[39]

One might assume that the women who had been closest to Afong Moy would come to her aid. For nearly four years Afong Moy had been associated with Henry and Catherine Hannington. Her chaperonage had transferred from Augusta Obear to Catherine Hannington as the "mistress of the conductor." During this time Catherine accompanied Afong Moy on a thousand-mile-plus journey, presumably attended to her needs, often joined her on stage, and taught her English. As with Augusta Obear on board ship, Catherine lived in close proximity to Afong Moy in rented rooms and ship cabins on their voyages. Despite this physical propinquity, cultural differences may have been a gulf too wide for either Augusta or Catherine to bridge. Neither appeared to place any interest in Afong Moy beyond that of an economic venture their husbands had engineered. In 1838, Henry Hannington's retirement from life as an impresario and salesman ended any possibility of employing Afong Moy for economic gain. Her presence was a drain on household expenses. In addition, the Hanningtons had children, and there was little time to attend to a woman who had bound feet and was largely unable to contribute to household chores. However, her somewhat disabled condition may have given Henry Hannington the poorhouse option. Her bound feet, seen as a disability, made everyday work nearly impossible and qualified her for the poor-house. Since he, and by extension Afong Moy, who moved with him, was a resident of Monmouth County, Hannington could legitimately put forward an application to support a person with a disability who was only peripherally part of his household.

The freeholders of Monmouth County initiated the construction of a poorhouse or almshouse in 1801. At that time they purchased seven hundred acres from William Parker in Shrewsbury for $4,000 and began the con-struction of the building.[40] It was to this site that Afong Moy was brought in 1838. Though she had experienced the rigors of cross-country travel, dubious accommodations, and the trials of facing gawking crowds, the poorhouse would have been a challenging environment. The records of nineteenth-century residents in New Jersey poorhouses indicate that some were insane and nearly all were in some way disabled. A case report in the *Journal of Nervous and Mental Diseases* described the background of two residents in this nineteenth-century Monmouth poorhouse: "A feeble-minded man had by his defective sister an epileptic daughter with criminal instincts; then by this daughter he had four children. . . . The mother and eldest daughter, when not in the county jail, or in the Monmouth County Almshouse live in a cellar in town."[41] In addition to living with such compatriots, Afong Moy suffered further humiliation. After admittance, each resident was required to prominently wear a badge of poverty: a letter "P" worn on the right sleeve of one's clothing.[42]

Neither family unit nor affinity protected Afong Moy from the vagaries of economic upheaval in America. She had been torn from the traditional kinship system in China, where family units were the bedrock of society. Within this tightly woven society, individuals, as parts of a family unit, were generally protected from the sort of social and economic perils Afong Moy experienced in America.[43] Had she remained in China, Afong Moy would have married and entered into her in-law's household, finding some measure of sustenance and security within the kinship structure.

How long she remained in the poorhouse is unclear, but by April 1838, some Monmouth County citizens found her in a rural county household in the vicinity of Freehold. In New Jersey, paupers could be either accommodated in the poorhouse or cared for in the homes of county residents. In a process called "boarding out," New Jersey hosts were reimbursed for the cost of their charges' keep by the County Overseers of the Poor or by others who might help defray expenses. In some cases, this was a short-term arrangement, but in other situations boarding a pauper might be a long-term commitment.[44]

Whether he was flushed out by the county citizens or he took it on himself to respond to accusations from an anonymous correspondent, in late April 1838 Caleb E. Taylor came forward in the newspapers to confirm that he was the person who had charge of the "Chinese girl Afong Moy."[45] Yet, he indignantly refuted the newspaper claims that he had abandoned her. Instead his letters to the editors vociferously affirmed his innocence:

> I allude to the scandalous charge made against me . . . asserting that I had deserted the Chinese lady, Miss Afong Moy, at this place [he gives his address as Monmouth County, New Jersey]. The assertion is not only an unprincipled and malicious *lie*, but is totally unfounded. I have been deeply injured—I fear irreparably so—if an honest man, an American citizen, a member of this free confederacy, is to have his character vilely traduced. . . . The reign of injustice is at hand! Though poor in this world's goods, I feel that I am an American citizen—that I am a freeman—and as such, I dare the author of this vile fabrication . . . to discover himself to me.[46]

Taylor, or a member of his family, likely took in Afong Moy out of economic necessity. He came from a long line of Quakers whose distant ancestors arrived in New Jersey in the 1670s.[47] Taylor's mother was a Wright (also a Quaker) whose family had holdings in Upper Freehold Township in Monmouth County. At least one Wright farm of three hundred acres, Merino Hill, existed in Upper Freehold, and perhaps the Taylor-Wright family owned smaller farms in the area of Freehold.[48] Afong Moy was possibly boarded out on one of these rather remote farms owned by the Taylor-Wright family. Though the financial relationships between the Taylor and Wright families are not clear, it is likely they shared some of the same business activities. With the economic downturn in 1837, the business ventures of Samuel Wright, Taylor's uncle, collapsed.[49] The ripple effect of these failures may have required the extended family to earn income by taking in boarders from the poorhouse.

Taylor, fiercely expressing his rights as an American citizen, provided little information regarding Afong Moy but, rather, defended his character as a freeman. His response could be read as irritation that Americans cared more about Afong Moy's rights than of his own as a "member of this free confederacy." The *New-York Commercial Advertiser* noted: "Mr. Taylor seems to be very indignant at the charge and declares he shall prosecute the author. . . . He does not give any information, however, as to the merits of the case, or the present condition and prospects of the little-footed lady."[50] It is also possible to interpret Taylor's lengthy rebuttal as his defense as a Quaker. A crucial aspect of the faith is that all members act with integrity and forthrightness in their personal and professional lives.[51] Though Quakers did not have a religious creed, they were bound to keep promises and deal honorably in all their activities. The accusation of abandoning Afong Moy challenged Taylor's standing as a Quaker. If his wayward behavior and action were substantiated, he could be disowned from membership in the Society of Friends. Taylor's

Newspapers across the nation published the ongoing saga of the abandoned Afong Moy. Though many printed Caleb Taylor's rebuttal, editors insisted on the "full right" of the "stranger Chinese." *Cincinnati Daily Gazette, April 25, 1838*

AFONG MOY.

We published, recently, a notice that this Chinese female was given up to neglect and want by those who brought her to this country. The individual implicated has published a fierce and furious denial, and thus demands its republication:

"P. S. Editors throughout the Union, in whose papers the slander above alluded to has been published, would but subserve the cause of justice by giving the above an insertion, and thus right an injured man.   CALEB E. TAYLOR."

We would rather be sure that full "right" has been done to the stranger Chinese.

emphatic and righteous reply was perhaps an attempt to protect his place in the Society.

The *Monmouth Inquirer* became the center for news on the abandoned Afong Moy, which it disseminated around the country. In April the paper received yet another letter from a person who offered information on Afong Moy's situation. This message attempted to mollify citizens concerned about her fate. It stated: "I observe a paragraph in your paper . . . relative to a Chinese woman now living near you, and I address you in order to correct an erroneous impression now existing in your neighborhood relative to her. She was put to board in your vicinity with a person who promised to treat her kindly, and supply all her wants until an opportunity occurs of sending her home. The money for her board is regularly paid in this City. And in a pecuniary point of view, she has no need of the attention of the humane and benevolent of your community."[52] The informer expressed his willingness to provide more information if "curious" people found this explanation wanting. The letter was signed by a Mr. J. Brown, 458 Broadway.

The *Inquirer*, responding to his letter on behalf of the public, was not buying the explanation. The editor averred that the public now had no animosity toward the persons boarding Afong Moy. Citizens found that the family cared for Afong Moy as best they could within the means provided them. However, according to the paper, the public refused to accept the clarification from Brown: "it is to those who have her in charge—those who were instrumental in bringing her to this country, that we, and the 'curious people' not only of this county, but elsewhere, raise our voices in condemnation."[53] The article claimed that Afong Moy had been misled about the ready availability of a vessel to return her to China and had waited in vain for such an opportunity. The paper threatened that if activity in this regard did not occur "speedily," it would pursue the case and expose names.

The paper intimated it knew the culpable persons. A Mr. J. Brown had not previously been associated with Afong Moy, and although New York newspapers of the period listed a J. Brown living in New York, near Broadway in fact, he had no obvious connection to the Chinese lady. However, those at 458 Broadway did. In February 1838, Hanington & Company advertised the sale of transparent and ornamental window blinds and its services as decorative painters at their 458 Broadway store.[54] No longer in the business of selling Chinese goods or associated with panoramic entertainments, the Hannington (also spelled Hanington) brothers had fallen back on their original trade of making window blinds. J. Brown was either a pseudonym for Henry, or an associate serving as the intermediary for the manager's dealings with the Chinese lady.

Perhaps through "Brown," Henry Hannington, whom the national newspapers called the "inhuman guardian," eventually contributed $2.50 each week to the family who boarded her.[55] This sum is somewhat comparable to fees paid those who kept paupers as recorded in other New Jersey county poorhouse records of the period. A Mr. Garret Persan was paid $4 a month to keep each pauper at the Paterson, New Jersey, poorhouse in 1840.[56] Hannington paid less than the $13.50 that a Mr. Huggison received to board a pauper per month in 1840 in Paterson, New Jersey, but more than the $8.68 per month that a Mr. Andrew Lynch received for the same service.[57] Though care for numbers of persons at the Paterson poorhouse was less costly per person because of economy of scale compared to caring for one, it is unclear from the records the reasons for variance between what Huggison and Lynch received for the care of one pauper in the same month. It is possible that, as they did for Afong Moy, others contributed to, or shared, the cost of the boarding out with the county. And Afong Moy's care was unlike that of any other "pauper" that Monmouth County had experienced. As the investigating citizens reported to the *Monmouth Inquirer* newsperson, her clothing was exceptional: "Her dresses are of rich and costly nature, principally of silk, and glorious [*sic*] construction."[58] Care for this sort of clothing, for her bound feet, and for other differences related to her culture required persons of sensitivity and contributed to additional costs.

It is unclear whether the general public ever knew who was to blame for Afong Moy's abandonment. Without giving a name, but probably referring to Henry Hannington, the Cleveland *Daily Herald* fingered "a tradesman in New York who made a shew[(*sic*] of her through the United States."[59] Another paper reported a "strong feeling of condemnation was excited in the public mind, towards her agent."[60] For those who had followed Afong Moy's travels, it would have been possible to deduce the responsible party. Yet Hannington tried to remain anonymous.

His concern likely stemmed from the public's accusations and actions against managers of displayed persons that had occurred in New York City several years earlier. In the 1820s, a sealer, Captain Hadlock, displayed three "Esquimaux"—a man, a woman, and her ten-month-old son—he had taken from the Davis Straits.[61] They were presented to New Yorkers in sealskins with a canoe, a sledge, and a team of huskies. When their circumstances were broadcast to the community after the Inuit man was interviewed and responded in English, and after the child died, Hadlock was arraigned and thrown into prison on charges of kidnapping. Though he was eventually released, it was a lesson to those who similarly displayed people from foreign lands.

Probably Hannington was also aware of a more recent event in 1832–1833, when Captain Morrell displayed his "Cannibals" from the South Seas. One of the South Sea Islanders escaped in New York City, was recaptured after wandering the city for a week, and was required to go back on display at the Peale Museum. A letter to the city newspapers soon after expressed disquiet regarding the South Sea Islanders' situation. It appeared that they, too, were being held against their will and without sufficient support. The letter ended with an oblique warning: "the case of the Esquimaux, many years ago, was a painful one to every benevolent mind."[62] Though Morrell did not end up in prison, this episode did not endear him to the public. Hannington, as a businessman who in addition to his panoramic endeavors also sold window blinds and other decorative objects in New York, did not wish to damage his reputation with his customers. Unlike Captains Hadlock and Morrell, he was unable to sail away from his problems.

Afong Moy's internment in New Jersey brought forward issues not publicly addressed when she traveled the country with the Obears and then the Hanningtons from 1834 to 1837. Then, few questioned her rights, her background, or her position as a single, young woman far from her homeland. Here, for the first time, she met and spoke with American citizens without the intervention or presence of her handlers.

Afong Moy's story, as told to the Monmouth County citizens, was similar to what had been previously recorded in the 1834 and 1835 newspapers. She confirmed her travel to America with Captain Obear and asserted, as before, the influential status of her father in China. However, this time in her own words, she mentioned Obear's promise to return her to her "native place in the course of one year." Apparently Afong Moy knew of the agreement, but she lacked the power to enforce it. As to her living conditions, the concerned citizens stated: "She appears to be much dissatisfied with her present situation and mode of living—her personal treatment [sic] we strongly suspect, is not of the most pleasant kind."[63] Though not a true interview, it was the closest she had come to a statement of her personal reaction to her situation.

Newspapers around the country, from Louisiana to New Hampshire, ran articles criticizing those who had abandoned her and encouraging the responsible parties to return her to China. But it is doubtful that Afong Moy ever knew of the public outcry on her behalf. Did the citizens' efforts make a difference in Afong Moy's experience? By shining a light on her distress and discomfort, it is possible that Hannington was forced to add his dollars to those of Monmouth County in support of her boarding out. This might have eased her place as a boarder in the household. The larger issue of Afong Moy's return to China, though stated emphatically by the Monmouth newspaper reporters as one of the conditions for keeping Hannington's name out of the papers, did not occur. She remained in Monmouth, New Jersey, for eight more years.

IO

The Final Act

IN 1845, THE AMERICAN MISSIONARY Samuel Wells Williams returned from a twelve-year sojourn in China and noticed a difference in the way the public viewed China. When Williams left home in 1833 Americans had imagined China as an exotic, enchanting, and distant country of fine silks, pagodas, arched bridges, and willow trees.[1] They envisioned an enigmatic emperor governing an ancient land ordered by millennia-old rules and laws. The many imported Chinese goods were still for the upper class—fine porcelains and other luxury goods. In the intervening time, China's standing in the public's consciousness had suffered a severe decline. Williams inserted this oft-repeated poem in the preface of his two-volume 1848 work on China to indicate the disparaging and derisive attitudes then directed toward the Chinese:

> Mandarins with yellow buttons, handing you conserves of snails;
> Smart young men about Canton in Nankeen tights and peacocks' tails.
> With many rare and dreadful dainties, kitten cutlets, puppy pies;
> Birds nest soup which (so convenient) every bush around supplies.[2]

In his compendium on the Chinese empire and its people, Williams hoped to "divest the Chinese people and civilization of that peculiar and almost undefinable impression of ridicule which is so generally given them; . . . In short, almost every lineament of China and her inhabitants, has been the object of a laugh or the subject of a pun."[3]

While Afong Moy languished in a New Jersey poorhouse in the 1840s, this subtle but pervasive attitude crept into the American discourse on China. The impact of the First Opium War and the resulting consequences for China were one source of the disenchantment. The war was the outgrowth of confrontations between the United Kingdom and the Qing dynasty in Guangzhou of the late 1830s, which centered principally on the opium trade. Smoking opium was not a widespread practice in China until the late eighteenth century; therefore, the swift rise in its use, with a negative effect on China's trade balance with the West, caught Chinese officials by surprise.[4] The enormous profits garnered not just by the British and American companies that sold the drug in China but also by complicit Chinese officials and drug traffickers made the trade difficult to regulate. Foreign traders were emboldened to expand their reach after Hugh Hamilton Lindsay, the East India Company's secretary in Guangzhou, found, during his exploratory trip along the China coast in 1832, that the Chinese themselves had distributed the drug near the coast, and that the defenses of these coastal cities were weak.[5] By the late 1830s, no longer was the commerce in Guangzhou as successful as that of opium trading; no longer were the hong merchants in complete control. Opium was the precipitator of, but not the only reason for, the war. Tensions between the cultures of the East and the West, as manifested in dissimilar business practices and different conceptions of world order, came to a head.

In March 1839, Lin Zexu, an imperial commissioner with orders from the emperor, arrived in Guangzhou to conclusively handle the opium problem. Lin requested the delivery of twenty thousand chests of opium from the foreign traders, primarily British. Handing over the chests, the British assumed that they would receive payment. Upon compliance, their opium was destroyed without remuneration. The conflict escalated with a harsh military response by the British that overwhelmed the Chinese. In 1842 they were forced to sign the British Treaty of Nanjing that resulted in the opening of four additional Chinese ports to foreign traders. It also secured the small island of Hong Kong as an English colony.[6] The United States followed with a treaty of its own. It contained nearly the same stipulations as the British treaty but with several important additions. Americans would be punished and tried only by the US Consul, tariffs would be fixed, Americans could study Chinese, and they might buy land in the treaty ports to erect churches and hospitals.

Foreigners now became aware of China's weak military force and the realities of Chinese life beyond the small slice of land in Guangzhou to which they had formerly been restricted. No longer was the information about this land filtered through the Chinese, who had previously collected artifacts and specimens for foreigners' wondering eyes. Westerners quickly took advantage of the increased access and communicated their findings to a curious and now less credulous world. It is unlikely that Afong Moy knew of the great changes that had taken place in the distant world of her birth. But in an indirect way, these activities in China would later lead to a renewed Western interest in her.

To capitalize on the West's curiosity concerning China, a group of British investors in Hong Kong conceived the bold and outrageous notion of sailing a traditional Chinese junk to London to inform English people about the Chinese and, in the process, make money from the display of the vessel. This effort could never have taken place in Guangzhou, where the purchasing, equipping, and staffing of a Chinese ship by Europeans would have been illegal.[7]

The Chinese junk *Keying* left Hong Kong with a European and Chinese crew in December 1846. London was the destination, but London was not where they ended up. Chinese junks sailed effectively in the coastal waters of the South China Sea when a knowledgeable Chinese crew controlled their maneuvers. It was not so with the *Keying*. The English captain, Charles Kellett, and his English officers shared command with Chinese captain So Yin Sang Hsi. Captain So was tasked with maintaining order with the Chinese crew, while Kellett preserved his role as the captain in charge. Unaccustomed to the rigors and complications of sailing a junk, and with a diverse and often confused Chinese crew, Kellett struggled to keep discipline and make headway. By May 1847, the *Keying*'s slow progress and low provisions required a quick revision in destination. Instead of London, the junk would sail for America. Meeting up with an American brig, Kellett was advised to head for the port of New York. Americans in New York had their first look at a Chinese junk in July 1847.

The New York papers probably exaggerated the *Keying*'s visitor numbers, listing them at four thousand a day. Modern computations, however, estimate that about 980 people a day viewed the Chinese junk.[8] Regardless of the numbers, the interest in things Chinese was a showman's incentive to revitalize the presence of Afong Moy. Washington, DC's *Daily Union* ran this report from New York: "The 'junk' having excited

Small boats (far left) ferry visitors to a Chinese junk, the *Keying*. In late July 1847, Philip Hone toured the *Keying* (center, left) which was moored off the southern tip of Manhattan. *The Bay and Harbor of New York (showing the anchored Keying), c. 1855, Samuel B. Waugh. Museum of the City of New York, gift of Mrs. Robert M. Littlejohn*

our city into a Chinese fever, all China is about to be exhibited. The walls, pumps, and fences, where placards and play-bills 'most do congregate,' have been, for some days, informing our population that the only Chinese woman who came over in the 'junk,' is 'on exhibition at Niblo's.' She has drawn pretty well, 'considering' that no female came passenger in that nondescript."[9] A further notice in the *New York Daily Tribune* identified the Chinese lady.

> We are in possession of authentic information obtained by special mesmeric telegraph . . . that the lady is of a respectable yellow-celestial family. . . . She was brought to this western wilderness . . . about ten years ago, by Captain Obear, and at that time passed by the name of Miss Afong Moy and travelled through the country. . . . Thereupon, Miss A. withdrew to the sacredness of private life in the rural retreats of Monmouth county, New Jersey, where she has remained, . . . until the arrival of Captain Kellett's famous junk revived the taste for Chinese curiosities.[10]

After an absence of eight years, Afong Moy reappeared. Yet her comeback was treated somewhat farcically in the press; one reporter wrote that "contemporaries have been airing their wit in relation to a lady claiming to be Chinese. . . . The burden of the joke with these jocular gentlemen is a doubt as to whether the person in question was really raised under the skies of the Celestial Empire."[11] As the returning missionary Samuel Wells Williams noticed in 1845, the skeptical and satirical tone regarding the Chinese was prevalent. Though this attitude reflected a lessening of respect for China and its exoticism, it also was linked to the humbug-like manner of her promotion and to her audacious promoter. From all indications, the person who instigated her revival was the renowned showman Phineas Taylor (P. T.) Barnum.

His approach to the Chinese lady would be very different from that of her previous managers. Afong Moy's persona had first been shaped by the Carneses and Captain Obear. For them she served to promote and stimulate interest in the middle-class wares they brought from China. For a period of time this promotion continued even under Henry Hannington until the connection to the sale of goods lessened and finally dropped away. At that point, Afong Moy's role as the knowledgeable presenter of all things Chinese became more pronounced and she herself became the oriental commodity. Though she was not scholarly or profound, through her interpreter Afong Moy addressed the dissimilarities of life in China—her bound feet, her clothing, her language, and her customs—from that in America. With her singularity as the only Chinese woman or person many Americans had seen, Afong Moy's public role had been defined and secure. But with the economic upheaval of the Panic of 1837, Hannington's public evaporated, and Afong Moy's presence was no longer in demand.

The 1847 arrival of the *Keying* with Chinese sailors, a Chinese captain, and a small collection of Chinese historical artifacts reawakened interest in Afong Moy, but the methods of publicity now corresponded with Barnum's customary ploys: the plethora of advertising—placards, theatrical bills, and notices—across the city; the specious narrative of Afong Moy's arrival on the *Keying*; and the "mesmeric telegraph" that communicated her background. Yet inexplicably, for the first year or more of their association, Barnum was not identified as her manager.

Barnum had moved to New York City in the fall of 1834, at nearly the same time Afong Moy arrived from China. In his home state of Connecticut, he tried farming, trading, editing, and lottery managing, but New York's bustle matched Barnum's energy, and here he found his calling as a showman. As Afong Moy began her tours along the Eastern Seaboard in 1835, Barnum arranged his first exhibition in New York. This initial effort was perhaps the most controversial of his career and in some aspects a performance not dissimilar from that of Afong Moy's. He purchased the exhibition rights, if not the ownership, of Joice Heth, a presumed 161-year-old African American enslaved woman whom Barnum exhibited as the nurse of young George Washington. Like Afong Moy, Heth had no say in this exhibition arrangement; similarly, her identity was reconstructed to fit the needs of her manager. In an even more odious encounter than the unbinding of Afong Moy's feet by American physicians, after Heth's death Barnum provided her body to surgeons for a semi-public postmortem to identify her age. The irregularities and the callousness of the Heth episode shadowed Barnum the rest of his life.

Though Afong Moy's direct association with Barnum came later, an aspect of the Heth exhibition initiated a personal connection that would influence her life. In his autobiography, Barnum recalled efforts to develop the "Aunt Joice" exhibition. He approached William Niblo, owner of the entertainment facility, to share the cost of her presentation in 1835. Barnum found Niblo's an attractive site:

> the grand walk through the middle of the garden was illuminated on each side by chaste and pretty transparencies. . . . These transparencies were then new in the city of New-York, and were very attractive. They were gotten up by W. J. and H. Hannington, who have since become so celebrated for glass-staining and decorative painting. Mr. H. Hannington prepared me several transparencies . . . which I had placed upon a hollow frame and lighted from the inside. It was painted in colors with white letters, and read—Joice Heth 161 Years Old.[12]

With such admiration of Hannington's work, Barnum continued his association with the sign painter, who later served as signatory on a Barnum project.[13] It is logical that Hannington, who wished to be released from the cost of Afong Moy's care, conveyed her whereabouts to Barnum.[14]

After Heth's death in 1836, Barnum organized and traveled with two roadshows, though there is no record that his path crossed with that of Afong Moy. Barnum's return to New York in 1838 coincided with Afong Moy's withdrawal to the "sacredness of private life" in rural New Jersey. The showman's desire for some stability, additional income, and a measure of respectability encouraged his foray into museum management. In 1841, Barnum purchased Scudder's American Museum, where Afong Moy had presented in the 1830s. At the American Museum, he perfected the art of fakery, imposture, and exaggeration and willingly broadcast his techniques and discoveries. He welcomed visitors to peer behind the veil, accept the guile, and revel in the complications his performances presented.[15]

Barnum found a compatriot in these exploits in the person of Moses Kimball, owner and manager of the Boston Museum. Together they established and shared a stable of exhibits that rotated between the two cities. This was advantageous, for when the audience in New York had been saturated and the exhibition no longer popular, it then went on to Boston; it was also helpful when publicity in one location soured or was controversial. The two entrepreneurs shared the income, as Barnum wrote to Kimball about the exhibition of Charles Stratton—better known as General Tom Thumb—in Boston: "The proposition is this: 1st. You charge your usual price for daytime. 2d. (You to charge) 37½ cts. For evening. 3d. The General to exhibit Saturday evenings. . . . We share the gross receipts for evening performances and to share the gross receipts for daytime whenever those receipts are less than $120—but whenever they are more than that, we have all over $60."[16] Later in the year, Barnum likely applied this same complicated calculus when sharing the revenue from Afong Moy's presentations for Kimball in Boston.[17]

During July and August 1847, Barnum presented Afong Moy at Niblo's. He marketed her as the "only Chinese Lady that ever left the walls of Canton."[18] The junk Keying's presence provided a large quantity of publicity material for Barnum to work with. Its aura was so impressive that some thought Barnum had masterminded the whole affair.[19] Initially the papers informed the public that Chinese ladies had been aboard (as Barnum had probably encouraged), possibly because one of the seamen noted that the junk rode the waves so easily that even a woman on board would not get seasick. When they determined that Afong Moy had not accompanied the junk, the press, surely encouraged by Barnum, promoted a romantic liaison between a Keying Chinese passenger named Xi Sheng (Hesing or Kesing) and Afong Moy. The press announced: "It is rumored in the highest circles that a certain auspicious event is now on the tapis between Mr. Mandarin Kesing, of the Chinese junk, and Miss Afong Moy, the celebrated Chinese lady, for some time a resident of the United States."[20]

PORTRAIT OF HESING.

希生廣東老爺

Depicted in an embroidered robe as an eminent personage
on the Chinese junk, the *Keying*, Xi Sheng was a well-suited
prospect for P. T. Barnum's matchmaking plans for Afong
Moy. A Description of the Royal Chinese Junk, "Keying,"
London: J. Such, 1848. Gutenberg-e

In the 1840s, as Afong Moy returned to meet the public, she was no longer
the young girl who stirred attention because of her youth and vulnerability.
Now in her late twenties, she was of marriageable age, which provided new
fodder for her manager and for the press. Yet the expectation of marrying
within her race narrowed the possibilities. Xi Sheng's arrival on the *Keying*

provided an appropriate opportunity for matchmaking. His superior rank well suited Barnum's positioning of Afong Moy as a Chinese lady of esteem. The topic also provided an opening to evaluate Chinese views on marriage and the traditional relationship between husband and wife.

In mid-July, many of the East Coast papers picked up an article on the *Keying* in the *New York Tribune*. One of the *Tribune* editors, undoubtedly city editor Charles A. Dana, well known for his ironic commentary, visited the junk, chatted with Captain Kellett, and interviewed Xi Sheng.[21] Dana, himself an avid collector of Chinese porcelain, wryly observed: "the dinner, though served on board the junk, was not composed of Chinese dishes, not a single rat or joint of a young puppy being on the table."[22] He reported: "Hesing is a man of some intelligence, and communicated to us a variety of information relating to Chinese manners and customs. He told us that he was the husband of three wives and said 'no man catchee more, costee too muchee dollar.' On inquiring what course he pursued on occasion of too lively domestic difficulties among these partners of his affection, he replied with perfect gravity, 'horse whippee.'" When Xi Sheng then queried Dana on American marriage practices, the editor assured him that in America "no can catchee more than one wife."[23] Like Harriet Low in 1830 and Caroline Butler in 1835, Dana infantilizes Xi Sheng—even after noting his intelligence—by quoting his remarks in pidgin.[24]

Several weeks later the *Tribune* ran another story, presumably also by Dana. He engaged Xi Sheng as he walked in Castle Garden, a place of public entertainment at the tip of Manhattan.[25] Xi Sheng remarked "that ladies in this country were 'too muchee plenty,' and 'too muchee talkee, talkee!'"[26] The editor commented: "He evidently holds the barbarous opinion that they should only speak when spoken to by their lawful lords and masters."[27]

This ironic and critical tone toward the Chinese treatment of women was reminiscent of the attitude expressed in an 1841 book entitled *The Porcelain Tower; or Nine Stories of China* by the English author Thomas Henry Sealy, known for his amusing and caustic literary approach, and illustrated by the master caricaturist John Leech.[28] It was probably the sarcastic nature of this book that incensed the missionary Samuel Wells Williams. Sealy's volume was well reviewed in American periodicals such as *Graham's Lady and Gentleman's Magazine* and the *Magnolia; or Southern Monthly*. Dana, as a literary man, would have seen and probably read the book.

Sealy's stated intent was to give those in the West some knowledge of the Chinese as they went to war (the Opium War) with these "excellent and well-bred" people. His preface averred that he compiled his stories about the "real China" from original sources; however, the reader would quickly catch the fallacy with Sealy's tongue-in-cheek play on the word "parties," as he wrote that he would inform all parties "and, particularly, small Tea-Parties" on Chinese life.[29] Of the nine stories in the book, seven focus in a mocking way on Chinese women's experiences in courtship and marriage. Yet Sealy had never been to China, and he knew nothing of the ways of Chinese life; nothing of filial piety or of the three sacred bonds (*san-kang*) that obligated obedience to parents, subordination of wife to husband, and allegiance of subject to sovereign.

In the first story, Sealy presented the Chinese philosopher Poo-Poo who, against propriety, insisted that his daughter So-Sli choose her marriage partner rather than wed one of the mandarins, Hang-Yu or Yu-be-Hung. Against all odds, So-Sli outwitted all her suitors, and eventually even her husband, but she was strangled to death for her audacity. Tou-Keen, the smart and beautiful daughter of a physician, became the empress, but she overreached and drowned in a bathtub. To-To, in the story "Fashions in Feet," illumined the beginnings of foot binding when, as the wife of an emperor, she strayed too far and her large feet were mercilessly chopped off. "Marriage in a Mask" featured the libertine wooer of women Ou-Rang-Ou-Tang; the "Feast of Lanterns" chronicled the adventures of the young and audacious woman Hey-Ho.

From Sealy's roster of farcical Chinese ladies, American reporters identified Afong Moy as the model for the cunning and shrewd character So Sli, and she was thus described in the August 1847 *Commercial Advertiser*.[30] Though not specifically referenced, the analogy was a commentary on the press's mention of her potential marriage with the "mandarin" Xi Sheng, and how she might outwit him. Wildly exaggerated, using puns, sarcasm, and wit, the stories placed Chinese society and the Chinese treatment of women beyond the pale of Western respectability and reason. Now, Afong Moy indirectly represented all that the West found curious and reprehensible in Chinese customs, lifestyle, and the treatment of women.

As the innuendo regarding Afong Moy and Xi Sheng swirled through the press, other activities surrounding the display of the *Keying* took a turn for the worse in late August. Twenty-six Chinese crew members on the junk claimed they had not been paid. When they pressed their case, Captain Kellett, or one of the officers, had the seven ringleaders arrested on charges of assault; apparently, the rest backed down. The newspaper headlines broadcast the event: "Riot on Board the Junk," "Difficulty at the Chinese Junk," and "A Chinese Junketing." Some of the papers claimed that the difficulty arose when the crew became disruptive after "they had smoked opium so freely . . . that the riotous spirit obtained ascendency."[31] However, opium does not provoke agitated behavior; rather, it makes one somnolent. The press assumed the sailors' anger was fueled by drugs rather than by a rightful cause. The reportage that followed would become the standard: a disdainful and derisive attitude toward the Chinese. Initially Barnum must have been delighted in the additional press that the *Keying* occasioned in August. All the discussion might drive additional interest in the Chinese lady he was displaying.

The seven Chinese crewmen's case against Captain Kellett and his investors in the *Keying* went forward in the New York Court of Special Sessions at the beginning of September 1847. They were represented pro bono by W. Daniel Lord, a leading New York lawyer who had previously expressed concern for seamen.[32] To strengthen his case and to provide translation for the seamen, Lord secured the help of Samuel Wells Williams, the missionary who had voiced his annoyance with American attitudes toward the Chinese. Williams had ample reason to object to Kellett: he suspected him of an earlier involvement in the opium trade; Kellett was British; and Williams detected a condescending tone toward his Chinese crew.

Probably to the surprise of many, the court ruled the seven men not guilty. Lord successfully defended the men against assault and clarified their desire to seek payment for back wages and then to be returned to China. In complete antithesis of what might have been expected, the magistrate allowed the Chinese crew to bring suit against the ship and therefore against Captain Kellett, the ship's representative. Kellett lost the case; the twenty-six Chinese crewmen were housed in the New York's Sailor's Home at the ship's expense, and all were paid back wages and repatriated to Hong Kong that fall. The entire affair illustrated the complication of managing an interracial crew and the inchoate nature of this culturally diverse ship. Kellett bore the brunt of the blame, for this was partly his scheme and he was in command. Yet his attitudes and maritime ways were typical of most sailors of his time.

By that fall, with the *Keying* and its crew in the midst of legal difficulties, and little to be gained by associating with the now negative Chinese-junk publicity, Barnum arranged for Afong Moy's departure to Boston. Captain Kellett, concerned about his reputation and the loss of more crew members, would soon be following her to the same city. However, expediting a beleaguered Chinese junk took a much greater effort and a longer lead time than sending Afong Moy to Boston.

Afong Moy had last appeared in Boston with her manager Henry Hannington in October 1835. Barnum and the Boston manager Moses Kimball hoped Bostonians might have forgotten her previous visit and that now, recast with the junk *Keying*, she would offer new insights attractive to audiences. Kimball must have had high expectations. He booked the Tremont Temple rather than his newly built Boston Museum for her presentation.[33] The Temple, owned by the Baptist church, contained a large auditorium that seated 2,500 people, whereas Kimball's Boston Museum hall seated only 1,200.

The Tremont Temple building, constructed as a theater in 1827, had an unusual history and purpose. It was founded by Timothy Gilbert and fellow Baptist abolitionists when they were expelled from the Charles Street Baptist Church for inviting black friends to share their pews. Purchasing the Tremont Theatre in 1839, they established a free Baptist church within the building where the poor, black or white, might worship without charge for the use of a pew. As the first integrated church in America, its membership strongly supported the abolition movement.

Though used as a church, its auditorium was frequently available for nonreligious purposes. In a history of Tremont Temple in 1898, the Rev. George Lorimer recalled what had been conveyed to him regarding the church history: "The hall was to be let for any serious discussion touching matters of public interest . . . as the congregation was relatively small, and the building not very much used during the week for church purposes, the public did not think of it as a church, or associate with it pre-eminently the religious idea, but considered it as a great hall, where during the week, entertainments were given, debates were held, where truth and error with singular impartiality were allowed to propound their theories."[34] Afong Moy presented in a hall that was noted for its performers and lecturers, including orator Daniel Webster, writer Charles Dickens, actress Fanny Kemble, and P. T. Barnum himself.

Advertised in the *Boston Daily Atlas* as an "Extraordinary Exhibition," this performance differed from that in New York. Because the *Keying* had not yet arrived in Boston, a model of the junk had to suffice. Perhaps the "Chinese Man of War Junk" model she presented at the first 1834 museum exhibition in New York was still available as a prop. Afong Moy could provide little information regarding the *Keying*, though it is likely she had seen the vessel in New York. Compensating for this paucity, Barnum and Kimball played upon an aspect that had greatly attracted the public visiting the junk in New York. Numerous newspaper articles focused on the Chinese seamen's worship of "idols" that they had installed, and Captain Kellett had often highlighted, on tours of the junk. The *New York Herald* reported: "In this saloon, we . . . saw the guilded image of 'Josh,' a Chinese idol, in the form of a woman . . . and another idol called 'Sea Josh,' or 'Sinhow,' as well as we could understand the term."[35]

What the *Herald* reporter and the public actually saw was the "idol" Tianhou, or the Empress of Heaven; "Sinhow" was as close a transliteration in English as could be expected. The worship of Tianhou originated in southern China around 960 CE. The religious daughter of a simple, pious, fishing family, Tianhou began performing miracles in her teen years. Magic charms allowed her spirit to travel apart from her body and enabled her to save those in peril, particularly those on the high seas.[36] Dying young and unmarried, she rose to heaven aided by the Jade Emperor. As one assisted by charms, Tianhou shared the Daoist tradition; as one birthed with the help of Guanyin, the Buddhist goddess of mercy, she was part of the Buddhist faith; and in her pious filial conduct, she partook of Confucian practice. The tripartite assimilation of these elements made, and continues to make, her cult popular with many Chinese.

The widespread influence of Tianhou's cult has been attributed to her adoption by fisherfolk, and later seamen, who carried her statue on the bows of their vessels along the South China coast and across the ocean. The gilded wood statue often clad in a flowing robe, as on the *Keying*, was magnificently embroidered to indicate her imperial rank. The sailors burned incense before her on the deck throughout the voyage to establish good luck.[37]

The advertisement of Kimball's "Extraordinary Exhibition" noted that Afong Moy was in her "magnificent WORSHIPPING ROBE of the pure gold Embroidery which is of immense value."[38] In the Tremont Temple, Afong Moy was presented as Tianhou, the deity who had guided the Chinese seamen to New York and whose "guilded" sculpture sat in prominence on board the junk. Perhaps pointing to the spot where the figure of Tianhou resided on the vessel, she relayed "many other interesting peculiarities . . . to the company."[39] We can wonder whether Afong Moy turned to the deity Tianhou to find comfort in this distant place. In her impersonation, she perhaps found gratification.

It was appropriate that, in 1847, Afong Moy presented the Chinese deity in Tremont Temple where, as Rev. Lorimer averred, "truth and error with singular impartiality were allowed to propound their theories." Her performance and explanation of a Chinese belief were significant: she was the first Chinese person, a woman no less, to speak in the Temple. The next time the

Chinese would serve as a subject of interest in Tremont Temple was in July 1870. Then, the striking shoemakers' union, the Secret Order of St. Crispin, held an assembly objecting to their replacement with Chinese workers by a North Adams shoe manufacturer. Claiming they wished to avoid being "reduced to the Chinese standard of rice and rats," they rallied workers to their cause in the temple.[40] Yet true to the church's tenet, twenty-two years after that the temple provided the same hall to Chinese-American activist Wong Chin Foo to explain his new organization: the Chinese Equal Rights League. And the well-known pastor of Tremont Temple Baptist Church, Rev. George C. Lorimer, was in attendance to support Wong.[41]

Afong Moy's stay in Boston was brief. By the end of September, she had moved on to Troy, New York, presenting at the recently opened city museum. Peale's Troy Museum was not unlike Barnum's American Museum, though in miniature. At its opening a journalist gushed: "No one can traverse these elegant rooms . . . and through the medium of old-time relics hold communication with past ages, without coming away, if not better, at least a wiser person."[42]

As in the past, Afong Moy had joined other performers on stage, but for the first time, the newspapers noted that a Chinese gentleman, Eu Tong, accompanied her.[43] His presence is a mystery. His name was never mentioned in newspapers or Barnum accounts again. Possibly this was a connection made in Boston, or improbably, he was a seaman from the *Keying* junk.[44]

Not until the early spring of 1848, at Washington Hall in Newark, New Jersey, did Afong Moy reappear in public. For the first time, Barnum joined her with his leading stage attraction, General Tom Thumb. It was not unlike Barnum to test such a performance in a second-tier location such as Newark to ascertain whether the performers worked well together. The *Newark Daily Advertiser* welcomed Afong Moy back to New Jersey with this notice: "It appears . . . that an old experiment in the way of exhibitions has been revived: The Chinese girl, Afong Moy, now exhibiting at Washington Hall, is the same we understand, who was brought to this country in 1835."[45] The advertising copy for Tom Thumb stated: "He is truly, as the bills say, a perfect man in miniature—only 35 inches in height and weighs only 38 lbs. Yet he is 20 years of age."[46] In fact, Tom Thumb was only ten.

The two performers' lives could not have been more different. In 1842, P. T. Barnum "found" Charles Stratton in his home state of Connecticut at four years of age. The child had stopped growing when he was six months old, though his limbs were well proportioned and his intellect was keen. That same year, Barnum presented Charles Stratton, now dubbed General

Tom Thumb, at the American Museum as an eleven-year-old "dwarf." At first Barnum had the child strike poses of historical figures, but when he noticed that Thumb had a comedic skill, he launched him into more sophisticated theatrical parts. Soon Thumb was a huge attraction.

Six months after Thumb's first performance at the American Museum in 1843, the New York diarist Philip Hone brought his daughter Margaret to see "the greatest little mortal who has ever been exhibited; a handsome well-formed boy, eleven years of age, who is twenty-five inches in height and weighs fifteen pounds. Gen. Tom Thumb (as they call him) is a handsome, well-formed, and well-proportioned little gentleman."[47] Astutely, Thumb's handler pointed out the ex-mayor seated in the audience; the young boy strode up to him, introduced himself, and welcomed him to the museum.

Philip Hone's assessment of Tom Thumb corresponded to the way he had evaluated Afong Moy when encountering her nine years before in New York. As with Afong Moy, he repeated in his diary the erroneous age and details of Thumb's birth provided by the management. Likewise, he judged Thumb's intelligence, but, unlike Afong Moy, Hone found him "with no deficiency of intellect, as a phrenologist would certainly infer from his perfectly shaped head."[48] In contrast, he had described Afong Moy as having "a large Head, small features and a countenance devoid of expression . . . from want of Education . . . she is deficient in ideas."[49] Hone's interest in phrenology is evident here, but so too is his bias regarding gender and race.

In January 1844, six months after Hone saw Thumb, Barnum's six-year-old celebrity sailed for England. While there he entertained Queen Victoria and the Duke of Wellington, charming them with his wit. In one of his letters home Barnum provided an account of their reception at Buckingham Palace: "The General (Tom Thumb) advanced with a firm step, and he came within hailing distance, made a very graceful bow and exclaimed, 'Good evening, *Ladies and Gentlemen.*' The queen then took him by the hand, led him about the gallery and asked him many questions, the answers to which kept her and all assembled in an uninterrupted strain of laughter."[50]

Thumb's successful experience in England and France from 1844 to 1847 perhaps emboldened Barnum to consider a similar opportunity for Afong Moy. Throughout 1847, newspapers announced that audiences might want to rush to see her "prior to her departure for Europe."[51] Though this notice was published many times, no doubt to heighten visitor interest or suggest the importance of her presence, Barnum never sent Afong Moy to Europe. Possibly the loss of his American Museum manager "Parson" Hitchcock, who suffered a mental breakdown while Barnum was abroad with Stratton, deterred Barnum from arranging an international tour for Afong Moy.

When he returned, Barnum was so overwhelmed by his museum obligations that he complained to Kimball that he was doing the work of ten men and unable to undertake additional activities.

Barnum must have been satisfied with the public's response to Afong Moy and Tom Thumb's joint presentation in Newark. In late April, he scheduled them together again at his American Museum, at Broadway and Ann Street. The five-story building gaudily covered with signs and banners hawked the attractions within and drew thousands of daily visitors. The announcement located their performance in the museum, likely in the small, and rather cramped, "Lecture Room" that seated several hundred people.[52] Barnum's use of the term indicated his appeal to those who found theaters vice-ridden and morally suspect, whereas lecture halls were upstanding places of learning. This label bowed to the same sensibilities to which Afong Moy's managers responded to in the 1830s, when she was often staged in lyceums and athenaeums rather than theaters.

VIEW OF THE AMERICAN MUSEUM, BROADWAY, NEW YORK.

An 1853 engraving of the American Museum demonstrates the museum's popularity: men and women congregate at the entrance while others lean over the balconies above. Visitors from around the nation flocked to see P. T. Barnum's wonders within. *Gleason's Pictorial Drawing Room Companion, Library of Congress, LC-USZ62-2640*

Their presentations, according to newspaper accounts, and surely puffed up by Barnum, drew such crowds that they had to extend their engagement. The "two astonishing natural curiosities," said the *New York Herald*—one nearing thirty years old and the other merely ten—must have been an entertaining sight. George Odell, in the *Annals of the New York Stage*, quoted an undocumented source that, at this April 1848 event, Afong Moy ate with her chopsticks, "which render[s] the exhibition highly interesting to the lovers of curiosity."[53] One might imagine a routine where Tom Thumb attempted to do the same, with comical results.

Afong Moy and Tom Thumb presented on the same stage together for several years under Barnum's management. That their partnership served Barnum and found popularity among audiences is evident in the seven-page pamphlet that Barnum produced to promote them together. The pamphlet was entitled *Affong Moy Nanchoy, the only Chinese Lady Ever Exhibited in the United States of America. Also, A Brief Sketch of Major General Tom Thumb, The Smallest Man Living; His Birth, Parentage, &c.*[54] It is not clear why Barnum gave Afong Moy the new last name Nanchoy. It is possible she married; more likely Barnum sought new audiences by changing her name and providing a slightly different narrative.

During his lifetime, Barnum produced quantities of similar promotional materials. These advertising brochures can be seen as vehicles to develop a particular audience, and to encourage certain visitor attitudes. Today they provide insight on the prejudices, beliefs, hopes, and desires that patrons carried with them into his exhibition venue.[55]

In the pamphlet, the explanation of Afong Moy and her life came first and was the more extensive write-up. The copy focused on the particular aspects that made Afong Moy, the "product," an attraction. Most significant was the rare opportunity to intimately view the only Chinese woman in America. Second was her nature as an "opposite," as John Kearsley Mitchell had presented her in his 1835 poem. The pamphlet remarked on her "habits, every-day occupations and pursuits of a being so opposite to all the received notions of every other civilized nation on the face of the earth."[56]

In the Afong Moy section of the pamphlet Barnum appealed to an audience of ladies. Through promotions and programs Barnum welcomed women into the museum. His invitations variously appealed to the traditional, genteel, parlor-dwelling ladies or to the unescorted, single women who would feel safe in a moral atmosphere of learning. The copy in this pamphlet catered to the former, who were defined as "ladies of discernment." It listed embroidery, singing, and ornamental arts as Afong Moy's occupations

PAMPHLET DESCRIPTIVE

OF

AFFONG MOY NANCHOY,

THE ONLY

CHINESE LADY

EVER EXHIBITED IN THE UNITED STATES OF AMERICA.

ALSO,

A BRIEF SKETCH OF

MAJOR GENERAL TOM THUMB,

THE SMALLEST MAN LIVING;

HIS BIRTH,

PARENTAGE, &c.

NEW-YORK:
PRINTED BY J. BOOTH, CORNER OF ANN AND NASSAU STREETS,
ENTRANCE 109 NASSAU.

1849.

In comparison to P. T. Barnum's 1843 *Feejee Mermaid* pamphlet, whose cover carried images and flash, the 1849 Affong Moy Nanchoy and Tom Thumb pamphlet frontispiece was sedate, informative, and visually understated. *Courtesy American Antiquarian Society* and suggested that "ladies, if they please to be good humoured and kind, may extract a fund of pleasant information from Afong."[57] Then, as if in an aside, the pamphlet cautioned that in coming, these ladies best leave their colored domestics at home, for Afong Moy's sensibility, as a Chinese lady of rank, would be offended.[58] Here Barnum not only laid racism at Afong Moy's feet but also indicated what sort of lady would want to associate with a woman of Chinese "nobility."[59]

All of Barnum's major spectacles were provided with spurious origin stories: Joice Heth had supposedly served as George Washington's nurse; Zobeide Luti, one of the Circassian girls, was rescued from a Turkish harem; the Feejee Mermaid was caught by a fisherman in South America. Afong Moy's origin story was equally preposterous. Barnum's pamphlet claimed that her appetite for fancy goods, finery, and gold had induced her to escape China with her "advisors" for the riches of America.[60] According to the account, the potential for wealth, as well as a desire for fame in America, meant more to her than family, religion, or country. In this explanation, the volition to leave China came from Afong Moy herself, rather than from the American merchants. In this way, it absolved Americans from any wrong-doing; at the same time, it curiously belied the Western contention that Chinese women had little agency or strength of will; the contradiction seemed invisible to either the writer or, likely, the reader.

The pamphlet portrayed Afong Moy as vain, conceited, prideful, and shallow. It noted that she "reads little or nothing, as a very limited degree of education is bestowed on women in China, a few accomplishments making up the sum total of their intellectual training."[61] This was not unlike the narrative presented in the *Keying*'s 1847 public brochure, which stated that the Chinese people were said to be "false and faithless, trifling and shame-less."[62] In this unflattering depiction, and unlike the figure of Tom Thumb, whom visitors admired, Barnum presented a woman whom people might wish to disparage to reassure themselves of the West's superiority. As in pre-vious newspaper accounts and in Mitchell's poem, the intent was to provide a contrast between the limited and backward nature of Chinese women and the advanced position and sensibilities of American women. Barnum rein-forced his visitors' preconceived notions of China, the Chinese, and Chinese women, rather than enlightening them with accurate accounts.

The pamphlet did raise questions and provided readers some informa-tion about Afong Moy's religious views that visitors, presumably Christian, would find of interest. The writer recognized this curiosity: "Many have been the inquiries relative to her religious sentiments."[63] Not surprisingly, given the harassment she had received from moral reformers thirteen years earlier, the writer found her reticent to divulge her beliefs. But without any substantiation the pamphleteer opined that "she worships the rising Sun and Moon, is certain."[64]

In order not to discourage visitors who might be troubled by Afong Moy's "heathen" ways, the writer, possibly Barnum, provided a bridge to Christianity. In a rambling section defining those things that Afong Moy found appealing in America, he remarked that she was pleased to find that Americans followed the Chinese precept of Shoo (Shu), or "Do unto others as thou would'st they should do unto thee." The pamphleteer, surely not aware of the Chinese context of this belief, peculiarly interpreted the concept: "In order to render this remark of Afong perfectly intelligible, it must be mentioned, that by the unalterable edict of the reigning emperor . . . no Chinaman can venture, without permission, beyond the limits of his native country—without the loss of all his property."[65] Presumably the writer meant that if the emperor would not wish this law imposed on himself, likewise he should not impose it on his people. This had little to do with the Chinese concept of Shu, and the interpretation made little sense.

In fact, the precept of Shu stemmed from writings in the *Analects* compiled by Confucius's disciples based on his words and actions. Roughly translated, it stated: "What you do not want done to yourself, do not do to others."[66] The Confucian teachings of reciprocity meant that one would appropriately serve one's father in order that one's son serve one; or that one serve one's brother as one would hope one's younger brother would in turn care for one. This reciprocity in the family extended broadly into the Chinese civic world and, if correctly applied, ensured that the nation was well governed. Therefore, this rule was a doctrinal rather than a moral law as Christians understood it. Perhaps after reading the pamphlet, visitors might question Afong Moy on the concept of "Shoo." Yet neither the Chinese nor the Christian precept of reciprocity was fulfilled in Afong Moy's life; both cultures largely excluded her from reasonable care.

Afong Moy's section of the pamphlet ended by promoting the opportunities of learning: "a personal visit to this remarkable lady will inform the enquirer on many subjects with which it may naturally be supposed he cannot be well acquainted."[67] The pamphleteer also encouraged visitors to pose questions of any nature to "the gentleman, or guardian, who is in attendance as her interpreter." As a man of information, and "extremely communicative," he could provide an even fuller understanding of her Chinese experience. Unfortunately, the interpreter's name was withheld.

Possibly this was Eu Tong, the same Chinese gentleman who accompanied her to Troy, New York, in the fall of 1847.

Presumably because most visitors were better acquainted with Tom Thumb's history, his portion of the pamphlet was brief. The writer stated his admirable qualities: his politeness, humor, conversational wit, and taste. The text listed his capabilities as a "Statuist," posing as one of the twenty heroes and demigods from Greece and Rome, and also as a small person taking on the large personas of Frederick the Great and Napoleon. The portrayal of Tom Thumb's theatrical character as a man of the West—heroic, majestic, royal, and admirable—contrasted with the portrayal of Afong Moy as the woman of the East—shallow, vain, and untutored.

What linked the two was their authenticity. Unlike the Feejee Mermaid or the Circassian girls, Afong Moy and Stratton were what they were purported to be. Stratton was small; Afong Moy was Chinese and had bound feet. Barnum deluded the public about the details of their past, their age, and their motivations, but not about who they were as spectacles. As different as Afong Moy and Charles Stratton were from each other, they both appealed to an audience who found them real.

Barnum's two attractions periodically presented together for nearly two years. In late 1849, Barnum, with Charles Stratton's father, established a touring circus, the Great Asiatic Caravan, Museum, and Menagerie. Though the title might suggest Afong Moy's participation as an "Asiatic," she did not appear on the roster as a performer, though Tom Thumb accompanied the caravan. Instead, her prominence as a featured Barnum spectacle began to wane. In later 1849 and into 1850, promoted as Affong Moy Nanchoy, she shared the stage in Baltimore, Washington, DC, and Philadelphia with Signor Canto, the Wonderful Man Monkey, and the fifteen-year-old 430-pound Ohio Mammoth Girl. By the end of May 1850, Afong Moy's name had almost entirely disappeared from the newspapers.

Barnum purposefully eliminated Afong Moy from all his publicity. According to the master promoter, a new Chinese lady had arrived in New York on April 9 from Guangzhou, "en route for London," on the vessel *Ianthe*. Barnum's technique of supplanting one performer by bringing in a competing act was not without precedent. In 1848, he even applied this technique to his most favored and most lucrative performer, Tom Thumb. Drumming up competition, he brought forward Tom Thumb's replacement, "Major Littlefinger," at the American Museum.[68] The public did not respond well, reminding Barnum that there was only one Tom Thumb. Unfortunately, Afong Moy did not have the same devoted followers who might question or contest the veracity of her replacement. Since Barnum did this more than once, he must have found that undermining and supplanting one of his exhibition personages to give credibility to another were effective publicity ploys.

Like the Afong Moy of sixteen years earlier, Barnum's new Chinese lady, Pwan-Ye-Koo, was young and had small bound feet. Barnum claimed that the seventeen-year-old Chinese lady was accompanied on the *Ianthe* by her twenty-three-year-old maidservant, Lum-Akum; a professor of music, Mr. Soo-Chune, thirty-two, with his children Miss Amoon, age seven, and Master Mun-Chung, age five; and their eighteen-year-old interpreter, Mr. Aleet-Mong. The identification of this group—"The Living Chinese"— came from Nathaniel Currier's 1850 colored lithograph commissioned by Barnum as part of his "Gallery of Wonders" series.[69]

The vessel *Ianthe* did arrive in New York from Guangzhou in April 1850, but no passenger list exists to confirm the presence of Chinese people onboard. Barnum billed them as a family who had arrived in New York together. At a later venue, visitors overheard the Chinese lady speak in a "low Yankee slang."[70] Pwan-Ye-Koo may actually have been born in New York City, the offspring of a Chinese father and a Caucasian mother.[71] Such a possibility was alluded to in newspapers: one reporter remarked that: "he (Barnum) is exhibiting several Chinese of the 'upper ten,' as he calls them, who are said to have arrived here a week or two since, but probably have been living for some time past in some obscure part of the city, and brought out for the occasion."[72] Barnum's family group had been knit together from various other programs and quite possibly none of them had ever set foot on the *Ianthe*.

Barnum distinguished Pwan-Ye-Koo from Afong Moy by alluding to the young girl's aristocratic Chinese origin, her position as a "lady," and her upcoming marriage to a high Chinese official. Pwan-Ye-Koo was described as the "only Chinese Lady out of China—a genuine lady and no mistake."[73] In the *Annals of the New York Stage*, George Odell echoed that description: "the first lady of distinction that has ever left her Lotus Leaf home, and been seen by outside barbarians."[74] Barnum's puff in the papers refuted all he had alleged about Afong Moy the previous year and even until May 1850. Pwan-Ye-Koo's fictitious origin story put Afong Moy in the shade, insinuating that Americans were, for the first time, meeting a genuine Chinese lady, not a commoner from China. It would appear that Barnum worked at cross purposes. As late as May 1850 he also promoted Afong Moy as "a Chinese Lady—a veritable Celestial—the first female that ever visited this country."[75]

However, he assumed that the public cared little about the actual truth, nor would they challenge the discrepancies. If they did, he embraced the debate, encouraged the talk, and welcomed the confusion that might draw ticket sales. Yet at times this approach had unintended consequences; what the public presumed to be fake was actually real. Afong Moy fit that category.

Because Barnum's American Museum was under renovation, the new Chinese lady and her attendants performed in Barnum's new Chinese Museum at 539 Broadway. To advertise the new museum, he mounted a large pagoda on a cart with bells jingling at the four corners and dragged it through the New York streets. The museum's contents had been loaned from Peters's Chinese Museum in Boston, and the Chinese group "presided over his temple of curiosities." It was promoted as a place of substance as well as spectacle with displays lauded as good, useful, and curious. The terms used encouraged those who wished to learn as well as the fashionable who wanted to be in the know.

In July 1850, the new Chinese lady and her attendants presented in Boston at Armory Hall. The studio of daguerreotypist Lorenzo Chase was nearby, and there he captured Pwan-Ye-Koo's visage. It was the first photograph of what was assumed to be a native-born Chinese woman. The image portrayed a young girl looking toward the photographer with an insipid demeanor. Newspaper reporters wrote of her "charming vivacity" and Barnum spoke of her bright eyes and light-hearted smile. None of that animation transferred through the camera's lens. Her clothes looked too large for her small frame and she appeared unsettled within them.[76] One wonders how Afong Moy might have presented herself had Chase photographed her in his studio when she visited Boston in 1847.[77]

Soon after the Chinese troupe's presentation in Boston, Barnum readied its members for a trip to England, as he had foreshadowed in the newspaper promotions when they "arrived" on the *Ianthe* in April 1850. Since his prior notion of sending Afong Moy to Europe in 1847, Barnum had probably mulled over the possibility of dispatching one or more Chinese people abroad. Once Barnum had procured the Chinese family, the possibility of their performance at the 1851 London Great Exhibition galvanized him into action. Soon they left for England. There the American papers recorded: "The exhibitions are so numerous that, like the attractions of the Crystal Palace, it is difficult to decide which way to turn. For instance, 'the chief lion of the day' is the 'small-footed Chinese lady,' (sent over by the indefatigable Barnum) whose feet are only two and a half inches in length, and who expressed her sense of extreme gratification afforded her 'in being

P. T. Barnum's description of Pwan-Ye-Koo as an aristocratic and vivacious Chinese lady contrasted with photographer Lorenzo G. Chase's portrait of this solemn girl, taken in 1850. *Courtesy of the Peabody Museum of Archaeology and Ethnology, Harvard University PM# 35-5-10/53055*

the only Chinese female happily blessed with golden-water-lilies, permitted to leave the Chinese Empire upon the great event of the Exposition.' "[78] In 1852, all the American papers carried the news that Barnum's Chinese lady had sung before Her Majesty. Surely Barnum's earlier triumph with Tom Thumb at the English court paved the way for Pwan-Ye-Koo.[79]

Barnum's exhibitions went both ways: from America to England, and from Europe to America. In September 1850 Barnum brought the renowned Swedish singer Jenny Lind to the United States. His preoccupation with her reception, and the costly effort her tour required, totally eclipsed all his other enterprises, including his dealings with Afong Moy. Not only could Jenny Lind sing, which Afong Moy was less able to do, she also epitomized the ideal Western woman. In advance of her arrival Barnum placed a notice in the New York papers announcing the ratification of his contract with the singer. In contrast to Barnum's pretext for Afong Moy's American visit—for her to seek a fortune—foreigner Jenny Lind came because of her "great anxiety to visit America. She speaks of this country and its institutions in the highest terms of rapture and praise; and, as money is by no means the greatest inducement that can be laid before her, has determined to visit us."[80] In the extensive article, which he signed, Barnum defined the characteristics that Americans valued in a woman. Her vocal ability was uncontested, yet what he emphasized was her charity, simplicity, and goodness. He pointed out that much of her concert fees went to charity, for she considered her voice a "gift from heaven, for the melioration of affliction and distress."[81] Such hyperbole differed greatly from the negative qualities of pride and vanity that were assigned to Afong Moy.

Barnum's Jenny Lind concerts were huge successes and great moneymakers, not only because of her voice but because of the "female" values that she embodied, Barnum promoted, and Americans applauded. The brief pairing of Tom Thumb and Jenny Lind—Thumb "following in the wake of Jenny Lind everywhere"—illustrated how differently Barnum presented these two foreign women with his other successful performer. In New Orleans "The General" knelt before Lind, kissed her hand, and offered compliments. Then he magnanimously presented her with his small jeweled watch as a token of his esteem.[82] This scene was in stark contrast with Afong Moy's presentations with Tom Thumb, when Barnum highlighted the dissimilarities between them.

Afong Moy, as the opposite, briefly surfaced once more in Cleveland, Ohio.[83] There, on February 21, 1851, she presented in the city's Empire Hall, relating the peculiarities, habits, and customs of the "flowery land of tea, small feet, and exaggerated tails (tales)—the Celestial Empire."[84] Bell ringers accompanied her. They were most likely the troupe of bell ringers whom Barnum had discovered in Lancashire, England, while on his grand tour with Tom Thumb in 1844. As he had done for so many other performers, Barnum insisted that their origin story be revised; they were transformed from English to Swiss bell ringers and outfitted with Swiss costumes and fake accents.[85] The two Barnum acts were in Cleveland for a great celebration. All the leading state and city officials gathered that day to inaugurate the Cleveland-Columbus-Cincinnati railroad. It is unknown whether Afong Moy joined the 425 passengers who took the grand excursion to Columbus.

During her seventeen years as a sojourner in America, Afong Moy witnessed the technological and commercial growth of the country. Her early travels by stagecoach and sailing vessel gave way to journeys by steamboat and train. The small towns of Ohio she visited in 1836 had become bustling centers of commerce by 1851. The muted concerns regarding slavery that Afong Moy experienced in the Ohio of the 1830s became more stridently anti-slavery. Nonetheless, life principally remained the same for Afong Moy. With changes in managers, her role was redefined, yet, to the last, her small feet and her cultural differences defined her. Afong Moy's effect on Americans can be measured through commentaries, poems, objects, and diary accounts. Americans' influence on Afong Moy remains unknowable.

Epilogue

AFONG MOY'S LIFE ENDED AS it began, shrouded in the inconclusive and the indefinite. A search for "Afong Moy" in nineteenth-century US census records, as well as possible variations of her name, yields nothing. Newspaper announcements of theatrical events through the 1850s and 1860s do not mention her. P. T. Barnum's records, letters, and account books do not list her presence after 1850. Yet in mid-nineteenth-century America, the life of an Asian, and of a woman—even when that woman lived an extraordinary life—was destined to obscurity; therefore, her absence is not surprising.

The process of addressing the possible outcomes of her life is not dissimilar from addressing her beginnings. Applying the theory of parsimony offers some assurances. That theory, which generally applies to biological principles, is that the simplest of contending explanations is most likely the correct solution. For example, the biological application of the theory helps in the understanding of the evolution of species. If there were three birds, A, B, and C, and A and B had feathers, but C did not, it is likely that A and B were linked in some way.

Applying this principle to historical issues is unusual but possibly useful. The most logical explanation for Afong Moy's fate is that she returned to the places she knew. New York City and New Jersey present the simplest explanation. If she returned to New York City, she was likely absorbed into the Chinese community. Numbers of Chinese lived in the Third, Fourth, and Fifth Wards of New York in the late 1850s. There she may have married within the community, taking a new name and losing her identity as Afong Moy (which was not her real name in any case).

A Chinese community had not yet been firmly established in New Jersey. Finding a compatible and sympathetic environment of Chinese in that locale is unlikely. In desperation, she may have returned to the Monmouth County poorhouse or to those who had previously boarded her in the county. Surely it was not a particularly desirable place, yet it had provided her an established and consistent environment for eight years—the longest time she remained in any one place in America. But Afong Moy, or any variation of her name, does not appear in extant New Jersey poorhouse records.[1] Admittedly, the lists are incomplete and therefore unreliable sources.

Nor does it appear that P. T. Barnum provided support for Afong Moy. Little is known concerning the outcomes of most of Barnum's presenters and "curiosities"—Charles Stratton (Tom Thumb) was the exception. However, the Kunhardt family's research on Barnum's performers found a disturbing account related to the well-known "Aztec Children." According to Barnum's origin story, Maximo and Bartola represented a lost race from Central America. Said to have come from El Salvador, they may have been children afflicted by microcephaly. They performed with Barnum at the American Museum and with his circus off and on between the late 1850s and early 1880s. General Henry S. Taylor, head of the US Army's supplies and transportation services, later confirmed that he had located the "Aztec Children" in an Ohio insane asylum from which they had been plucked a number of years previously.[2] Without alternatives, a number of Barnum's performers, like the "Aztec Children" and Afong Moy, probably returned to those peoples or institutions that had previously cared for them.

It does not seem likely that Afong Moy returned to China. In her first period of travel with Captain Obear and Henry Hannington in the 1830s, it was assumed that she would return to her homeland. Her one comment while in the poorhouse indicated that she had expected to make a quick return to China after a year's stay in America. Newspapers and reports recorded her imminent departure on vessels that left without listing her on board. Initially, she may have been coerced to remain. As time passed, her return to a China hostile to Western powers during the Opium War made her something of a hostage in the United States. No ship captain would risk his vessel, reputation, and cargo to return a Chinese woman whose leave-taking may have been illegal. By the late 1840s, Afong Moy's options had narrowed. Barnum had no incentive to assist in her return to China; those initially responsible for her arrival had died or departed the scene. In addition, she recognized that, after the passage of seventeen years apart from family, few might recognize or support her. Possibly they would reject her as suspiciously foreign, unchaste, and wayward. She likely resigned herself to a life in America without hope of seeing her native land again.

This paucity of records regarding Afong Moy—her beginnings, her travels, and her end—disheartened my efforts. Jill Lepore, considering her biographical work on Jane Franklin Mecom, remarked: "In writing this book I have had to stare down a truism: the lives of the obscure make good fiction but bad history."[3] What historical conclusions can be ascertained from the tiny fragments of commentary stitched together regarding a life that few in her time considered worthy of remark? How might a woman who never wrote a word, and whose brief statements were filtered through others, help us learn how Americans perceived and experienced China in the early and mid-nineteenth century?

Much of this history we see by reflection and refraction. As a reflective foil, Afong Moy, and the objects she promoted, provided the antipode to which Americans responded. She was the medium through which an often-distorted view of China emerged. Some of these distortions about the Chinese would later materialize with the passage of the 1882 Chinese Exclusion Act. Still, as a real being, and not an imaginary one, her substantiality placed China squarely before Americans' gaze. With the wide range of her travels and the extent of her publicity, the "Chinese Lady" and, by extension, the ways of her country were observed and scrutinized by thousands. As the public occasionally commented, her presence offered a concrete representation of the Chinese that had previously resided only in fabrics, wallpapers, or porcelains.

In many places throughout America today, Asian faces are common, but this is a comparatively recent development. In 1829, before Afong Moy's arrival, Chang and Eng Bunker were brought to the United States from Siam. They were a sensation as the first Asians exhibited in the United States, and more so as conjoined twins (called the Siamese Twins). Because there were so few Asians in the country, one newspaper even speculated that they would be likely suitors for Afong Moy.[4] With the gold rush in 1849, some southern Chinese made the difficult journey across the ocean to the California gold mines with hopes of securing their financial futures, and then returning home. Many faced discrimination and harsh reprisals in the mining fields.

Most of these sojourners were men, though some Chinese women braved the trip, or were coerced into coming. Ah Toy came willingly, reportedly on her own, from Hong Kong to San Francisco in 1849. Upon arrival, she found there were few women in the West and much demand for companionship, which she supplied as she plied her trade as a well-known courtesan. Most significantly, she successfully defended herself numerous times in California courtrooms. In 1872 Polly Bemis (Lalu Nathoy) arrived in California from northern China as a slave to a Chinese man but was freed in Idaho, where she married a white boardinghouse owner and miner. These, and a small number of other Chinese women, such as Pwan-Ye-Koo, were relatively exceptional in nineteenth-century America.

Forty-eight years after Afong Moy's time on the American stage, the plight of Chinese in America got much worse. The Chinese Exclusion Act of 1882 banned all but a few select Chinese from entering the country. They were the only immigrant group ever explicitly denied admittance. Moreover, it forbade courts from granting US citizenship to Chinese who were already in the country. Afong Moy and the Chinese community she may have identified with lived their lives as permanent aliens, excluded from US citizenship. The law was not repealed until 1943, and even then, the quota allowed only 105 Chinese people entrance per year.

The 1965 Immigration and Nationality Act (the Hart-Celler Act) opened the United States to Asian immigrants. The act eliminated the restrictive national origins system, instead instituting quotas and preferences and encouraging the reunification of families. The act resulted in a large migration of those from Asia, Mexico, and Latin America. Of approximately 18 million peoples admitted to the United States from 1971 to 2002, about 7.3 million were Asian. Over time, that influx has changed American culture.[5] This can be seen in the growth and acceptance of Chinese restaurants and other Asian cuisines, in forms of exercise such as tai chi and the martial arts, in the respect accorded Asian spiritual traditions, and in the appreciation of Asian aesthetics and art forms.

Beyond Afong Moy as a person, the goods she promoted and displayed in the 1830s—rice paper images, fans, lanterns, baskets that Americans purchased—remained long after she left the stage. This sales effort represented the first mass marketing of Chinese articles in America, the golden chain of global commerce that bound Americans to objects from China. By the end of the 1840s, it is estimated that, in urban areas on the East Coast, nearly 10 percent of all household goods in middle-class homes were made in China.[6] Many of these articles were indigenous to China and inexpensive, the sort probably used or known by Afong Moy when she resided in Guangzhou.

Chinese goods continued to flow into American homes throughout the nineteenth century. However, with the opening of Japan in 1854, objects imported from both countries often were broadly categorized as "oriental." In fact, this term covered all things non-occidental—Turkish carpets and towels, Japanese screens, and blue-and-white Chinese porcelains. The character Rose in Louisa May Alcott's 1876 book *Rose in Bloom* describes in detail her room full of "oriental" objects that transported the young woman into a hybridized "Arabian Nights" environment that Afong Moy would not have recognized.[7] The later nineteenth-century consumption of objects specifically because of their "oriental" nature was quite different from consumers' acquisition of Chinese goods earlier in the century, which were desired principally for their inexpensive attractiveness. Most middle-class consumers cared less about their origin and more about their cost and usefulness.

With the passage of time, practicality, politics, and economy trumped everything else. President Nixon's historic trip to China in 1971 set the stage for an unprecedented period of diplomatic and commercial engagement with the Middle Kingdom that continues to the present. By the end of the twentieth century, and into the beginning of the twenty-first, "Made in China" objects comprised more than 13 percent of all articles on a Walmart shelf.[8] Using a method similar to the one the Carneses had experimented with in the 1830s, sample goods are conceived and designed in the West, then mass produced by cheap Chinese labor, and shipped for Western consumption. These include inexpensive plastic bowls, colorful plastic cocktail glasses, flashlights, fashion beads, clothes, small toys, and assembled electronics, often from US-made parts.

In 2012, the United States imported about $35 billion worth of goods from China compared to about $9 billion dollars of US goods exported to China.[9] Though there has been a negative reaction to Chinese-made products—goods that displaced those made by American workers—many of these items were so cheap that Americans found them hard to pass up. While inexpensive, like the objects of the early nineteenth-century China trade, nearly all these twenty-first-century objects are prototypically Western in type, design, and style. Today Americans and Chinese cultures mostly share these forms. Fifteen hours by air instead of a three-to-four-month interval on a vast ocean has blurred some cultural differences.

With all these changes over time, Afong Moy might still recognize the places where she lived and visited nearly two hundred years ago. In the winding back alleys of Guangzhou, she would find some of the same food products and medicines she consumed in the 1830s. Should she return to the far corners of Monmouth County, New Jersey, she would find parts of it still rural and somewhat forbidding. The Charleston, South Carolina, long room, similar to the place where she displayed her unbound feet, is still open, accessed by a side alley on a cobblestone and brick street. In

Havana, Cuba, the Plaza de San Francisco, with its Leon De Oro fountain, remains much as Afong Moy would have remembered it when she boarded on the square in 1835. In these few places, the "Chinese Lady" could slip back in time. Possibly some clue to her later life will resurface in one of those places.[10]

NOTES

Introduction

1. *Maryland Journal and Baltimore Daily Advertiser*, August 12, 1785.
2. Dael Norwood, "Mr. Jefferson's Mandarin, Or, a Controversial Promotion," *The Readex Report*, November 2013, http://www.readex.com/readex-report/mr-jefferson%E2%80%99s-mandarin-or-controversial-promotion; Frances Ruley Karttunen, *The Other Islanders: People Who Pulled Nantucket's Oars* (New Bedford, MA: Spinner, 2005), 146; John Kuo Wei Tchen, *New York before Chinatown: Orientalism and the Shaping of American Culture, 1776–1882* (Baltimore: Johns Hopkins University Press, 1999), 41–42. All three authors note Punqua Winchong's presence in America.
3. Tchen, *New York before Chinatown*, xxi.
4. Dane A. Morrison, *True Yankees: The South Seas and the Discovery of American Identity* (Baltimore: Johns Hopkins University Press, 2014). Morrison provides an insightful study of five Americans: Samuel Shaw, Amasa Delano, Edmund Fanning, Harriet Low, and Robert Bennet Forbes, as they navigate the meaning of their country's values in contrast to the "other" they find in the South Seas.
5. Stanley Lebergott, "Wage Trends, 1800–1900," in *Trends in the American Economy in the Nineteenth Century* (A Report of the National Bureau of Economic Research) (Princeton, NJ: Princeton University Press), 478.
6. Edward Said, *Orientalism* (New York: Vintage, 1979), 202–3.
7. Josephine Lee, *Performing Asian American: Race and Ethnicity on the Contemporary Stage* (Philadelphia: Temple University Press, 1997), 7.

Chapter 1

1. It was later determined that Richard Lawrence's assassination attempt had no political motive. He was found innocent by reason of insanity.

2. Harriet Martineau, *Retrospect of Western Travel*, ed. Daniel Feller (Armonk, NY: M.E. Sharpe, 2000), 58. Originally published in 1838.

3. *Essex Gazette*, November 22, 1834. It is unclear what Van Buren meant by "her cast."

4. *Globe* (Washington, DC), March 12, 1835.

5. Jonathan Spence, *The Question of Hu* (New York: Vintage Books, 1988). In *The Question of Hu*, Jonathan Spence recounts the Chinese man's discomfiture when he had an audience with the papal nuncio Massei in Paris in 1722. Hu tried to rearrange the chairs in an honorific configuration. Afong Moy indicated the same sense of discomfort when she visited President Andrew Jackson in Washington, DC.

6. James G. Barber, *Old Hickory: A Life Sketch of Andrew Jackson* (Washington, DC: National Portrait Gallery, Smithsonian Institution; Nashville: Tennessee State Museum in association with the University of Washington Press, Seattle, Washington, 1990), 16.

7. Martineau, *Retrospect of Western Travel*, 53.

8. Barber, *Old Hickory*, 94. Durand complained about "having to dance attendance on great men."

9. Ibid.

10. Jackson's Indian removal policy forced the Cherokees from Georgia, Tennessee, Texas, Alabama, and North Carolina to present-day Oklahoma and resulted in the "Trail of Tears."

11. Barber, *Old Hickory*, 22. "The Jackson administration . . . signed the first treaty with an Asian nation in 1833, when Siam agreed to American trade on the basis of a most favored nation, a principle that became the basis of other treaties with South America and other Near Eastern countries." Roberts died in Macao in 1836 before he could embark on his second trip to secure a treaty with Japan.

12. *Globe* (Washington, DC), issue 233, col. E, March 12, 1835.

13. With Anson Burlingame's Mission to the United States in 1868, two high-ranking Chinese envoys, Zhi and Sun, met President Andrew Johnson.

14. Republic of China's ambassador, Alfred Sao-ke Sze, served from 1935 to 1936.

15. I am indebted to Doug Sinclair, Augusta Obear's great, great nephew, for his thorough investigation of Samuel Haskell's life and the documents he uncovered.

16. Caroline Howard King, *When I Lived in Salem* (Brattleboro, VT: Stephen Day Press), 1937, 28.

17. Doug Steward, "Salem Sets Sail," *Smithsonian Magazine* (June 2004), 92–99. Daniel Finamore, curator at the Peabody Essex Museum, has noted that "they considered them to be physical embodiments of knowledge about the world—pieces of information."

18. King, *When I Lived in Salem*, 29.

19. Nancy Ellen Davis, "The American China Trade, 1784–1844: Products for the Middle Class" (PhD diss., George Washington University, 1987), 79.

20. See John Kuo Wei Tchen, *New York before Chinatown: Orientalism and the Shaping of American Culture, 1776–1882* (Baltimore: Johns Hopkins University Press, 1999), for a detailed study of the New York port and its impact on the China Trade.

21. *Essex Institute Historical Collections* (1905) 41, 162; Katharine P. Loring, *Ober Family Genealogy* (Beverly, MA: Beverly Historical Society, 1941); "Register of Ships, transcribed from the Lloyd's Register of British and Foreign Shipping," Niles Register, 1830, as provided by Gilbert Provost, http://www.reach.net/-scoo11198/ShipsN.htm.

22. John Carnes Jr. owned a store first on Boston's State Street in 1782 and by 1784 a shop at the corner of Court and 54 Cornhill Streets, Boston. State Street information as noted in *The Independent Ledger and the American Advertiser* (Boston, Massachusetts), vol. 5, no. 232 October 14, 1782, 3. Court and Cornhill Street information as noted in *The Independent Ledger and the American Advertiser* (Boston, Massachusetts) 7, no. 358 (November 22, 1784): 3, and the *Boston Price Current and Marine Intelligencer* 3, no. 38 (January 15, 1798): 3. John's brother Lewis also had a shop at 60 Cornhill Street in 1794 as noted in *Columbian Centinel* (Boston, Massachusetts) 21, no. 38 (July 19, 1794): 4.

23. Thomas R. Hughes, *American Ancestry: Giving the Name and Descent in the Male Line of Americans Whose Ancestors Settled in the United States Previous to the Declaration of Independence, AD 1776* (Albany, NY: Joel Munsell's Sons, 1887), 11:134.

24. *Boston City Directory*, 1822. The business was listed at 3 Lindall Street, Boston.

25. The Carnes Family *Bible*, Olana New York State Historic Site. The genealogy in the front pages of the Bible listed Francis's second child Emmeline as born in Paris in 1819. Francis's daughter Isabel married the artist Fredric Church in 1860 and moved to his home on the Hudson River in New York State.

26. Davis, "American China Trade," 53.

27. Ibid.

28. Walter Barrett, *A Second Series of* The Old Merchants of New York, *Being a Continuation of the Work* (New York: Worthington Co., 1864), 40.

29. Thomas Fletcher to William & L. Brown, April 14, 1831; Thomas Fletcher to W. H. Aspinwall, December 13, 1831; Thomas Fletcher to W. B. Gardiner, February 4, 1831; Thomas Fletcher Papers, 1815–1867, Joseph Downs Collection of Manuscripts and Printed Ephemera, # 75.10.1, Winterthur Library. In the year 1831 Thomas Fletcher's letters record that the firm paid F. and N. G. Carnes $4,138 for fancy goods. These are not the complete records; therefore, the amount could be higher.

30. Fancy goods include smaller sorts of fine objects such as ladies work boxes, japanned tea trays, hair combs, gloves, reticules (purses), perfume, handkerchiefs, china, and china figures.

31. Donald L. Fennimore and Ann K. Wagner, *Silversmiths to the Nation: Thomas Fletcher and Sidney Gardiner, 1808–1842* (Woodbridge, Suffolk, UK: Antique Collectors' Club, 2007), 51.

32. Ship Manifest Records, Manuscript M 1066 Row # 3, National Archives and Records Administration. Though this record stated the vessel *Howard* at two hundred tons, the information accompanying the watercolor image of the vessel at the Peabody Essex Museum states it at 290 tons.

33. Barrett, *Old Merchants of New York*, 40. Information on Chinese objects that the Carneses imported came from numerous sources including Barrett's notations, copious newspaper advertisements, The Mills Brothers auction catalog for the ship *Washington*, and the *Mary Ballard* manifest. The cargo manifests for the Carneses other vessels have been lost.

34. Ibid., 41.

35. Ibid., 42.

36. Ibid., 43–44.

37. Marquis de Lafayette to Francis Carnes, October 31,1827, OL.1982.1037.34, Carnes Family Scrapbook, Olana New York State Historic Site; Marquis de Lafayette to Francis Carnes, April 24, 1834, OL.1982.1037.39, Carnes Family Scrapbook, Olana New York State Historic Site.

38. Invitations to the Carnes family, 1829, 1832, 1834, Carnes Family Scrapbook, Olana New York State Historic Site.

39. The "V" trade is my own designation of the transshipment of goods from one country to a second for replication and then shipment to a third for final sale.

40. Barrett, *Old Merchants of New York*, 40, 43, 44.

41. *Canton Register, Shipping Intelligence*, December 31, 1831.

42. William C. Hunter, *"Fan Kwei" at Canton before Treaty Days* (London: Kegan Paul, Trench, 1882), 2, 3.

Chapter 2

1. Passenger Manifest List for the Ship "*Washington*," October 18, 1834, National Archives and Records Administration, Washington, DC; Passenger Lists of Vessels Arriving New York 1820–97, M237, roll #25, October 13, 1834–March 25, 1835. Augusta Obear's name is listed on the vessel *Washington*'s October 1834 manifest.

2. I have not located papers in China or America that confirm this agreement regarding Afong Moy, yet the arrangement surely had been planned previous to the Obears' arrival in Guangzhou. It is not clear who conceived of the plan.

3. *New York Daily Advertiser*, November 22, 1834. An advertisement for the sale of the *Washington* soon after its return from China listed the registration information for the ship noting its age, tonnage, and capacity.

4. Joan Druett, *Hen Frigates: Wives of Merchant Captains under Sail* (New York: Simon & Schuster, 1998), 50.

5. Ibid., 40.
6. Ibid., 46.
7. Harriet Low Hillard, *My Mother's Journal: A Young Lady's Diary of Five Years Spent in Manila, Macao, and the Cape of Good Hope from 1829–1834*, ed. Katharine Hillard (Boston: George H. Ellis, 1900), 237.
8. Druett, *Hen Frigates*, 58.
9. Hillard, *My Mother's Journal*, 240.
10. Anjer no longer exists. It was destroyed by a volcano in 1883. Other voyagers note stopping at Batavia (now Jakarta) on the other side of the Strait of Sunda; however, most spoke disparagingly of it.
11. Hillard, *My Mother's Journal*, 36.
12. Most Chinese interpreters had little knowledge of foreign languages, but their services were required by Chinese law.
13. "The hong" is a Chinese term for a foreign commercial establishment. The twelve or thirteen Chinese merchants in Guangzhou who were permitted by the Chinese government to engage in this foreign trade were called hong merchants. The hong was also the place where foreign merchants lived, did their business, and sometimes warehoused their goods.
14. *Canton Register*, February 2, 1831.
15. Hillard, *My Mother's Journal*, 75.
16. Ibid., 78.
17. Ibid., 79.
18. Ibid., 80.
19. *Canton Register*, February 16, 1832.
20. *Canton Register*, March 8, 1832.
21. John King Fairbank, *The United States and China*, 4th ed. (Cambridge, MA: Harvard University Press, 1983), 95.
22. With careful reading of all the Guangzhou English-language papers and annuals of trade during this time period, no Chinese or foreigner commented on Augusta Obear's entry into the city. The New York City papers note that the *Washington* arrived in Guangzhou on February 18, 1834.
23. *Beverly Citizen*, February 28, 1891.
24. My research at the Guangdong Provincial Archives, Guangzhou, China, as well as a separate investigation by another researcher with extensive Chinese-language ability, did not uncover a record of Afong Moy, or any Chinese woman, departing with the Obears on the ship *Washington*. The Archives have no custom records before 1861. No mention has been found in any of the Guangzhou foreign newspapers regarding Afong Moy's leave-taking. It is presumed that Augusta Obear's presence would have been required by the authorities and the family to take Afong Moy into Captain Obear's custody. Without such precautions, her removal would have been considered kidnapping.
25. The name was probably assigned based on a phonetic transliteration of her Chinese informal name. In pinyan her name is "Mei A Fang."
26. Charles Toogood Downing, *The Fan-qui in China, in 1836–37* (London: Henry Colburn, 1838), 1:246.

27. *New-York Commercial Advertiser*, October 28, 1834.

28. *New York Sun*, October 18, 1834.

29. Gerry Mackie, "Ending Footbinding and Infibulation: A Convention Account," *American Sociological Review* 61, no. 6 (1996): 999–1017, 1001.

30. Dorothy Ko, *Cinderella's Sisters: A Revisionist History of Footbinding* (Los Angeles: University of California Press, 2005), 3.

31. Ibid., 131.

32. *Chinese Repository*, vol. 3, no. 12, April 1835.

33. Ko, *Cinderella's Sisters*, 131.

34. Louisa Lim, "Painful Memories for China's Footbinding Survivors," NPR Online, Morning Edition, March 19, 2007, www.npr.org/templates/story/story.php?storyId=8966942.

35. Hillard, *My Mother's Journal*, 32.

36. Ibid., 177.

37. Robert Bennet Forbes, *Letters from China: The Canton-Boston Correspondence of Robert Bennet Forbes, 1838–1840* (Mystic, CT: Mystic Seaport Museum, 1996), 72.

38. William Wood, *Sketches of China, with Illustrations from Original Drawings* (Philadelphia: Carey & Lea, 1830), 135, 137.

39. Hillard, *My Mother's Journal*, 232.

40. *Chinese Repository*, April 1835.

41. Hillard, *My Mother's Journal*, 145. Hillard mentions wet nurses and Chinese female servants in her journal when she repeats what she hears from an English woman: "Mrs. Macrondray . . . says there is an order issued to take away all Chinese women servants from the foreigners. As they are generally wet-nurses, this is a very cruel thing." It is presumed that George Chinnery's portrait is of the Charles Marjoribanks family. Marjoribanks was the president of the Select Company of the East India Company in Guangzhou. However, it is possible that it was of the Christopher Fearon Family whose home Chinnery frequented in Macao.

42. Mae Ngai, *The Lucky Ones: One Family and the Extraordinary Invention of Chinese America* (New York: Houghton Mifflin Harcourt, 2010). The *mui tsai* in America are more generally associated with the later nineteenth-century Chinese female's experience in California. They were brought as servants but more than occasionally ended up in prostitution. Mae Ngai provides an explanation of their experiences in California.

43. Caroline Hyde Butler Laing, *A Family Heritage—Letters and Journals of 1804–1892*, ed. Edith Nevill Smythe (East Orange, NJ: Abbey Printers, 1957), 56.

44. Wood, *Sketches of China*, 134–35.

45. Downing, *Fan-qui in China*, 84.

46. Ibid., 83.

47. John Kearsley Mitchell, "Diary of a Trip to China, 1817–19," September, 1817, MS 2/0241/ 03 Box 3, S. Weir Mitchell Collection, Historical Medical Library, College of Physicians of Philadelphia.

48. Downing, *Fan-qui in China*, 243.

49. Wood, *Sketches of China*, 59.

50. John Kearsley Mitchell to Matilda, February 20, 1821, MS 2/0241/03 Box 3, S. Weir Mitchell Collection, Historical Medical Library, College of Physicians of Philadelphia.

51. Susan Mann, *Precious Records: Women in China's Long Eighteenth Century* (Stanford, CA: Stanford University Press, 1997), 43.

52. Robert B. Marks, *Tigers, Rice, Silk, and Silt: The Environment and Economy in Late Imperial South China* (Cambridge: Cambridge University Press, 1998), 196.

53. *Chinese Repository*, August 1833.

54. *Chinese Repository*, May 1833.

55. *Canton Register*, July 8, 1834.

56. My research in the Guangdong Provincial Archives uncovered an 1834 Chinese treasury account of monies provided the Chinese by foreigners. The note read: "A report in funds taken for the poor (?) for flood relief in 1834."

57. *Baltimore Patriot,* October 21, 1834.

58. *Albany Evening Journal*, November 13, 1835.

59. *New York Herald*, June 14, 1836.

60. Forbes, *Letters from China*, 210.

61. Paul A. Van Dyke, "Operational Efficiencies and the Decline of the Chinese Junk Trade in the 18th and 19th Centuries: The Connection," in *Shipping and Economic Growth 1350–1850*, ed. Richard W. Unger (Boston: Brill, 2011), 240.

62. John Rogers Haddad, *The Romance of China: Excursions to China in U.S. Culture, 1776–1876* (New York: Columbia University Press, 2008).

63. Hillard, *My Mother's Journal*, 320.

64. Ibid., 268.

65. Ibid., 300.

66. Forbes, *Letters from China*, 213.

67. Ibid., 252.

68. Ibid., 79–83.

69. *Baltimore Patriot*, September 25, 1834. The newspaper noted the vessel *Washington*'s location as Mawbay. This is most certainly the current location of Mowbray, South Africa which is very near Cape Town. Many American vessels stopped at, or near, Cape Town to take on provisions.

70. Hillard, *My Mother's Journal*, 247.

71. *Canton Register*, November 1, 1831.

72. Harriet Martineau, *Retrospect of Western Travel*, ed. Daniel Feller (Armonk, NY: M.E. Sharpe, 2000), 4. Originally published in 1838.

73. Ibid., 6.

Chapter 3

1. Philip Hone, *Manuscript Diary of Philip Hone 1826–1845*, November 12, 1834, 60–61; Hone MS, vol. 9, New-York Historical Society Museum and Library, Manuscript Division.

2. Ibid., 60.
3. John R. Haddad, "Imagined Journeys to Distant Cathay: Constructing China with Ceramics, 1780–1920," *Winterthur Portfolio* 41, no. 1 (Spring 2007): 53–80. Haddad notes that Americans carried idealized Chinese scenes in their heads based on the chinaware they so frequently used.
4. Hone, *Manuscript Diary*, 60.
5. *New-York Commercial Advertiser*, November 15, 1834, 2.
6. Selected Papers of Elizabeth Cady Stanton and Susan B. Anthony, *Their Place inside the Body-Politic, 1887 to 1895*, ed. Ann D. Gordon (New Brunswick, NJ: Rutgers University Press, 2009), 5:725; Elizabeth Cady Stanton, "Speech to the Reunion of the Pioneers and Friends of Woman's Progress," November 12, 1895, as recorded in the *Woman's Tribune*, December 28, 1895.
7. *Community Church News* (Stow, Ohio), March 29, 1935.
8. Hone, *Manuscript Diary*, 60.
9. *New-York Commercial Advertiser*, November 15, 1834, 2.
10. Ibid.
11. *New-York Spectator*, November 17, 1834, 3.
12. Hone, *Manuscript Diary*, 61.
13. *New-Hampshire Gazette*, November 18, 1834, 2.
14. Ibid.
15. Hone, *Manuscript Diary*, 61.
16. New York City newspaper accounts note that she was available for public viewing in Captain Obear's salon from 10:00 a.m. to 2:00 p.m. and again from 5:00 p.m. to 9:00 p.m.
17. Ronald Takaki, *Iron Cages: Race and Culture in 19th-Century America* (New York: Oxford University Press, 1990), 40
18. *New-Hampshire Gazette*, November 22, 1834.
19. *New-Hampshire Gazette*, November 18, 1834; *Farmer's Gazette*, October 31, 1834.
20. Valery Garrett, *Chinese Dress from the Qing Dynasty to the Present* (Rutland, VT: Tuttle, 2007), 98.
21. John Kearsley Mitchell to Matilda, February 20, 1821.
22. Garrett, *Chinese Dress*, 106.
23. Mary Kinsman Munroe, "The Daily Life of Mrs. Nathaniel Kinsman in Macao, China, Excerpts from Letters of 1845," *Essex Institute Historical Collections* 87 (1951): 126.
24. *Farmers Gazette*, October 31, 1834.
25. In China, blue symbolized immortality.
26. Charles Toogood Downing, *The Fan-qui in China, in 1836–37* (London: Henry Colburn, 1838), 1:305.
27. Shelagh Vainker, *Chinese Silk: A Cultural History* (London: British Museum Press, 2004), 176.
28. Paul A. Van Dyke, *The Canton Trade: Life and Enterprise on the China Coast, 1700–1845* (Hong Kong: Hong Kong University Press, 2005), 95–96.

29. The comparison of Afong Moy to Napoleon's Empress was noted in the *Farmers Gazette*, October 31, 1834.

30. Ibid.

31. For Chinese hairpinning traditions see Susan Mann, *Precious Records: Women in China's Long Eighteenth Century* (Stanford, CA: Stanford University Press, 1997), 59; for issues of opening the face, see Garrett, *Chinese Dress*, 103.

32. Osmond Tiffany Jr., *The Canton Chinese or the American's Sojourn in the Celestial Empire* (Boston: James Munroe, 1849), 50.

33. *Family Matters: Portraits from the Qing Court*, exhibition at the Arthur M. Sackler Gallery, Smithsonian Institution, June–January, 2011–12.

34. *Farmers Gazette*, October 31, 1834.

35. Munroe, "Daily Life of Mrs. Nathaniel Kinsman," 126.

36. *Northampton Whig* (Easton, Pennsylvania), November 19, 1834.

37. Tiffany, *Canton Chinese*, 69.

38. Herbert Schiffer, Peter Schiffer, and Nancy Schiffer, *Chinese Export Porcelain* (Exton, PA: Schiffer, 1975), 240. This book illustrates two rose medallion Chinese export vases of a similar shape and size.

39. Carl L. Crossman, *The Decorative Arts of the China Trade* (Woodbridge, Suffolk, UK: Antiques Collectors' Club, 1991), 256.

40. Tiffany, *Canton Chinese*, 84.

41. Downing, *Fan-qui in China*, 168.

42. Ibid., 167.

43. Tiffany, *Canton Chinese*, 106.

44. Ibid.

45. Nathan Dunn to Hannah Risley, April 13, 1824, MS 1163, Box 6, folder 1, Dunn-Osborn-Battey Family Papers, 1744–1927, Quaker and Special Collections, Haverford College.

46. Downing, *Fan-qui in China*, 2:133.

47. Ibid., 209.

48. *Daily National Intelligencer* (Washington, DC), issue 6799, col. C, November 25, 1834.

49. *Globe* (Washington, DC), issue 221, col. D, February 26, 1835.

50. David Johnson, "Communication, Class, and Consciousness in Late Imperial China," in *Popular Culture in Late Imperial China*, ed. David Johnson, Andrew J. Nathan, and Evelyn S. Rawski (Berkeley: University of California Press, 1985), 34–72.

51. Rachel Tamar Van, "Free Trade and Family Values, Kinship Networks and the Culture of Early American Capitalism" (PhD diss., Columbia University, 2011), 257.

52. Munroe, "Daily Life of Mrs. Nathaniel Kinsman," 79.

53. Ibid., 31. The Kinsman family identified John Alley as Malay, but it is possible that he was of Chinese descent. The family owned several daguerreotypes of him as a young man, and another in later life.

54. Charles A. Maxfield, "The Formation and Early History of the American Board of Commissioners for Foreign Missions," from "The 'Reflex

Influence' of Missions: The Domestic Operations of the American Board of Commissioners for Foreign Missions, 1810–1850" (PhD diss., Union Theological Seminary, Richmond, Virginia, 1995), http://maxfieldbooks.com/abcfm.html.

55. John Andrews, "Educating the Heathen: The Foreign Mission School Controversy and American Ideals," *Journal of American Studies* 12, no. 3 (1978): 331–42.

56. In 2010 the Cornwall Historical Society in Cornwall, Connecticut, presented an exhibition on the Mission School entitled *Visions and Contradictions: The Foreign Mission School.* The Chinese Friendship Album was displayed in the exhibition.

57. Though newspapers at the time noted that Atung was seventeen and recently arrived from Canton, they could have been misinformed.

58. Malacca (in the state of Malaysia) was in the southern area of the Malay Peninsula, not far from the Strait of Malacca. It was ceded to the British by the Dutch in 1824.

59. This school later became the Anglo-Chinese College in Malacca where many Americans studied Chinese.

60. Achik to William Lockhart, November 23, 1840, The Lockhart Correspondence, transcripts by Alan P. Hughes, 1995, British Library, University of London, School of Oriental and African Studies, Archives, Manuscripts, and Rare Book Division.

Chapter 4

1. See John Kuo Wei Tchen, *New York before Chinatown: Orientalism and the Shaping of American Culture, 1776–1882* (Baltimore: Johns Hopkins University Press, 1999), for an in-depth discussion of the development of New York City and the role of the port culture as it affected the Chinese.

2. Robert Greenhalgh Albion, *The Rise of the New York Port, 1815–1860* (Boston: Northeastern University Press, 1984), 91.

3. Ibid., 279.

4. Walter Barrett was the pseudonym of Joseph Alfred Scoville.

5. *Catalogue of Canton Fans, Grass Cloths, and Fancy Goods* (Mills, Brothers & Co. Auction Catalogue) (New York: Snowden, June 5, 1832). Reprinted from the original for the Childs Gallery Inc., Boston, Massachusetts, September 1968.

6. William T. McCoun and Charles Edwards, *Reports of Chancery Cases Decided in the First Circuit of the State of New York* (Albany, NY: Gould, Banks & Co., 1837), 2:652.

7. See Richard Lyman Bushman, *The Refinement of America: Persons, Houses, and Cities* (New York: Vintage, 1992), the authoritative book on the practices of gentility. Margaret Bayard Smith, *What Is Gentility? A Moral Tale* (Washington, DC: Pishey Thompson, 1828), provides a period view of gentility.

8. Howard P. Chudacoff, *Children at Play* (New York: New York University Press, 2007), 39.

9. Jerry Slocum, "Tangram: The World's First Puzzle Craze," in *Play It Again: Asian Games and Pastimes* (New York: E. & J. Frankel, Ltd., 2004), 46.

10. Ibid., 50.

11. Wei Zhang and Peter Rasmussen, *Chinese Puzzles: Games for the Hands and Mind* (San Francisco: Chinese Culture Center of San Francisco, 2008), 28.

12. Osmond Tiffany Jr., *The Canton Chinese or the American's Sojourn in the Celestial Empire* (Boston: James Munroe, 1849), 93.

13. "Invoice of merchandise shipped by Edward Butler on board the Barque *Mary Ballard*," Butler Family Correspondence, MS 242, folder 20 and 21, Mortimer Rare Book Room, Smith College Libraries.

14. Tiffany, *Canton Chinese*, 76.

15. Samuel Wells Williams, *The Middle Kingdom* (New York: Charles Scribner's Sons, 1904), 2:59.

16. Rosemary Mahoney, introduction to *Twice-Told Tales*, by Nathaniel Hawthorne (New York: Random House, 2001), 93.

17. Michael Sullivan, *The Arts of China* (Berkeley: University of California Press, 1979), 85.

18. *Boston Daily Advertiser*, February 8, 1832.

19. Thomas H. Perkins to John Bennett Forbes, May 3, 1828, Forbes Family Papers, MS N-49.70, Massachusetts Historical Society.

20. Invoice of Merchandise, *Mary Ballard*, Butler Family Correspondence, MS 242, folder 20 and 21, Mortimer Rare Book Room, Smith College Libraries, Smith College.

21. These numbers include those on the vessel *Howard* as noted in the 1832 auction catalogue and those on the invoice of merchandise on the ship *Mary Ballard*.

22. Invoice of Merchandise, *Mary Ballard*, Butler Family Correspondence.

23. *The Papers of Thomas Jefferson* (Princeton, NJ: Princeton University Press, 1950), 2:306. Notation from "A Bill to Prevent Gaming," part of series of bills proposed in a comprehensive effort led by Jefferson to revise the laws of Virginia.

24. James A. Bear Jr. and Lucia C. Stanton, eds., *Jefferson's Memorandum Books: Accounts, with Legal Records and Miscellany, 1767–1826* (Princeton, NJ: Princeton University Press, 1997), 206, 212, 252, 259.

25. Tiffany, *Canton Chinese*, 53.

26. Philip Hone, *The Diary of Philip Hone 1828–1851*, ed. Alan Nevins (New York: Dodd, Mead, 1936), 1:268.

27. Hone, *Diary of Philip Hone*, 2:548.

28. *Niles Register*, July 5, 1834.

29. Hone, *Diary of Philip Hone*, 1:268.

30. Mary Sword to John Sword, March 24, 1848, Coll. 1878, Sword Family Papers, Historical Society of Pennsylvania.

31. G. W. Mortimer, *A Manual of Pyrotechny* (London: Simpkin and R. Marshall, 1824), 47.
32. *Catalogue and Price List of Fireworks* (London: Marston and Wells, 1890), 59.
33. Ibid., 61.
34. Ibid.
35. John Robert Morrisson, *A Chinese Commercial Guide, consisting of a collection of details respecting foreign trade in China* (Canton, China: Printed at the Albion Press, 1834), 159.
36. Hone, *Diary of Philip Hone*, 1:295.
37. *Godey's Lady's Book*, July 1830, 274.
38. Verity Wilson, "Studio and Soiree: Chinese Textiles in Europe and America 1850 to the Present," in *Unpacking Culture: Art and Commodity in Colonial and Postcolonial Worlds*, ed. Ruth B. Phillips and Christopher B. Steiner (Berkeley: University of California Press, 1999), 240.
39. Susannah Worth, "Embroidered China Crepe Shawls: 1816-1863," *Dress* 12, no. 1 (1986): 43–54. See also the entry on "China Shawls": Jessica Schwartz, *Clothing and Fashion: American Fashion from Head to Toe*, ed. José Blanco and Mary D. Doering (Santa Barbara, CA: ABC-CLIO, 2016), 2:70–71.
40. John Lauris Blake, *The Parlor Book or Family Encyclopedia* (New York: John L. Piper, 1835), 224.
41. Tiffany, *Canton Chinese*, 79.
42. Walter Barrett, *A Second Series of* The Old Merchants of New York, *Being a Continuation of the Work* (New York: Worthington Co., 1864), 44.
43. John Sword to Mary Parry, December 19, 1835, Coll. 1878, Sword Family Papers, Historical Society of Pennsylvania.
44. Henry Pratt McKean to Benjamin Etting, Esq., July 8, 1835, Coll. 405, Thomas McKean Papers, Historical Society of Pennsylvania. My thanks to Doris Bowman for bringing this to my attention.
45. Ibid.
46. William Bell's Letterbook, Box 4, Constable-Pierrepont Papers, New York Public Library New York. The cost appears to be that paid in Guangzhou, China.
47. Tiffany, *Canton Chinese*, 46–47.
48. Lenore Gershuny, *Fanfare* (Washington, DC: Smithsonian Institution Press, 1984), 1.
49. Harriet Martineau, *Retrospect of Western Travel*, ed. Daniel Feller (Armonk, NY: M.E. Sharpe, 2000), 90. Originally published in 1838.
50. June Sprigg, *The Gift of Inspiration: Art of the Shakers, 1830–1880* (New York: Hirsch Adler Gallery, 1979), 21.
51. Blake, *Parlor Book*, 338.
52. John Neville Trons, "Export Fans of the South China Coast," *Arts Asia*, January–February 1982, 127.
53. Tiffany, *Canton Chinese*, 77.

54. Merchant Tyshing: Walter Muir Whitehill, "Remarks on the Canton Trade and the Manner of Transacting Business," *Essex Institute Historical Collections* 73, no. 4 (1937): 306. Merchant Linching: Jean Gordon Lee, *Philadelphians and the China Trade, 1784–1844* (Philadelphia: Philadelphia Museum of Art, 1984), 162. Luechun: Christina H. Nelson, *Directly from China: Export Goods for the American Market, 1784–1930* (Salem, MA: Peabody Museum of Salem, 1985), 5.

55. Morrison, *Chinese Commercial Guide*, 136.

56. John Sword to Mary Parry, December 19, 1835, Sword Family Papers.

57. Tiffany, *Canton Chinese*, 77.

58. William Bell's Letterbook, Constable-Pierrepont Papers.

59. Captain John Suter Papers, 1804–48, MS. N-49.50, Box 2, Massachusetts Historical Society.

60. Invoice of Merchandise, *Mary Ballard,* Butler Family Papers.

61. Kathy Peiss, *Hope in a Jar: The Making of America's Beauty Culture* (New York: Metropolitan Books, 1998), 19.

62. Barrett, *Old Merchants of New York*, 43.

63. Howard Higson, "The Historical Legacy of the China Rose," Quarry Hill Botanical Garden, Glen Allen, California, http://wwwquarryhillbg.org, accessed June 25, 2015.

64. Mary Gay Humphreys, *The Woman's Book* (New York: Charles Scribner's Sons, 1894), 1:155.

65. Eleanor McD. Thompson, *Trade Catalogues at the Winterthur Museum, Part II* (Bethesda, MD: University Publications of America, 1991). See entry for Cutter & Hurd, New York, New York Catalogue, 1836, R152C99.

66. *Boston Mercantile Journal,* November 29, 1834, 3.

67. *Cassell's Domestic Dictionary: An Encyclopedia for the Household* (New York: Cassell Petter, Galpin, 1878), 231.

68. Barbara G. Carson, *Ambitious Appetites: Dining, Behavior, and Patterns of Consumption in Federal Washington* (Washington, DC: American Institute of Architects Press, 1990), 104.

69. Williams, *Middle Kingdom*, 2:802.

70. Thomas H. Perkins to Robert Forbes, 1828, Forbes Family Papers, Massachusetts Historical Society.

71. Thompson, *Trade Catalogues*. See entry: "Longworth's American Almanac, New-York Register and City Directory," New York, 1839.

72. Valery Garrett, *Chinese Dress from the Qing Dynasty to the Present* (Rutland, VT: Tuttle, 2007), 92.

73. *Boston Daily Advertiser*, May 4, 1826.

74. *Cassell's Domestic Dictionary*, 1127.

75. Jean Breton de la Martinère, *China: Its Costume, Arts, Manufactures* (London: Printed for J.J. Stockdale: 1813), 35.

76. Blake, *Parlor Book*, 182.

77. Ibid.

78. *Catalogue of Canton Fans, Grass Cloths, and Fancy Goods* (Mills Brothers & Co. Auction Catalogue), 1832.

79. *Godey's Lady's Book*, July 1831, 52.

80. *Cassell's Domestic Dictionary*, 855.

81. Williams, *Middle Kingdom*, 1:599.

Chapter 5

1. Philip Hone, *The Diary of Philip Hone 1828–1851*, ed. Alan Nevins (New York: Dodd, Mead, 1936), 1:121. Many questioned Astor's wisdom in establishing a hotel so far uptown, but time proved them wrong. Astor House, also known as the Park Hotel, was a financial success.

2. Ibid., 1:127–28.

3. *New-York Commercial Advertiser*, November 15, 1834.

4. Hone, *Diary of Philip Hone*, 1:234.

5. John Rogers Haddad, *The Romance of China: Excursions to China in U.S. Culture, 1776–1876* (New York: Columbia University Press, 2008), 8. Haddad provides an excellent overview of the making of these watercolors.

6. Walter Barrett, *A Second Series of* The Old Merchants of New York, *Being a Continuation of the Work* (New York: Worthington Co., 1864), 44.

7. Jan Stuart and Evelyn S. Rawski, *Worshipping the Ancestors: Chinese Commemorative Portraits* (Washington, DC: Freer Gallery of Art and the Arthur M. Sackler Galleries, Smithsonian Institution, in association with Stanford University Press, 2001), 37, 49. The work provides a thorough analysis of both ancestor worship and portraiture's place within it.

8. As noted ibid., in 1760 the Qing emperor requested that the court artists paint full-length standing portraits of worthy officials which were not memorial images. This may be the origin of these images.

9. Barrett, *Old Merchants of New York*, 43.

10. Charles Toogood Downing, *The Fan-qui in China, in 1836–37* (London: Henry Colburn, 1838), 1:62–63.

11. Osmond Tiffany Jr., *The Canton Chinese or the American's Sojourn in the Celestial Empire* (Boston: James Munroe, 1849), 81.

12. Hone, *Diary of Philip Hone*, 1:291.

13. Edgar de N. Mayhew and Minor Myers Jr., *A Documentary History of American Interiors from the Colonial Era to 1915* (New York: Charles Scribner's Sons, 1980), 104. The book includes an illustration of Richard Rush's library with his portable desk, 1836–42.

14. Herman Melville, *Moby-Dick; or, The Whale* (New York: Harpers & Brothers, 1851), 322.

15. William Vipond Pooley, *Settlement of Illinois, 1830–1850*, History Series (Madison: University of Wisconsin, 1908; repr.), 1:373.

16. *Aurora General Advertiser* (Philadelphia), December 1792.

17. Thomas H. Perkins to Robert Forbes (no day noted), 1822, Forbes Family Papers.

18. William R. Quynn, ed., *The Diary of Jacob Engelbrecht, 1818–1878* (Frederick, MD: Historical Society of Fredrick County, Inc., 2001), 168. Engelbrecht, born in 1797 as the son of a Hessian Revolutionary War soldier who became an American citizen, recorded his life and the activities in Frederick, Maryland, in his diary until his death in 1878. In 1824, Engelbrecht was twenty-seven, and perhaps was trying to kick the habit while wooing Elizabeth Ramsburg, whom he married in 1825.

19. Ibid.

20. E. N. Anderson, *The Food of China* (New Haven, CT: Yale University Press, 1988), 140.

21. Samuel Wells Williams, *The Middle Kingdom* (New York: Charles Scribner's Sons, 1904), 2:394

22. Barbara S. Mouffe, "Preface," in *Hawthorne's Lost Notebook, 1835–1841: Facsimile from the Pierpont Morgan Library* (University Park: Pennsylvania State University Press, 1978), 7, 8.

23. Hone, *Diary of Philip Hone*, 2:728.

24. William Milburn, Esq., *Oriental Commerce* (London: Black, Parry and Co., 1813), 545.

25. John Lauris Blake, *The Parlor Book or Family Encyclopedia* (New York: John L. Piper, 1835), 774.

26. Elisha Tibbits to John Latimer, 1825, Box 6, John Latimer Papers, Library of Congress Manuscript Division, Washington, DC.

27. It is unclear what the black whangee canes cost for they were listed on the Mills Brothers auction catalogue without a price.

28. Captain John Suter Papers, 1820–30 Account Book.

29. Harriet Low Hillard, *My Mother's Journal: A Young Lady's Diary of Five Years Spent in Manila, Macao, and the Cape of Good Hope from 1829–1834*, ed. Katharine Hillard (Boston: George H. Ellis, 1900), 32.

30. Hone, *Diary of Philip Hone*, 1:185. Hone uses the exchange medium of shillings and pence, but earlier in the passage he mentioned the purchase of a ton of hay for thirty dollars using the dollar exchange medium.

31. Anderson, *Food of China*, 80.

32. Eric Jay Dolin, *When America First Met China* (New York: Liveright, 2012), 53.

33. Nicholas B. Wainwright, ed., *A Philadelphia Perspective: The Diary of Sidney George Fisher Covering the Years 1834–1871* (Philadelphia: Historical Society of Pennsylvania, 1967), 33, 47.

34. The light coming in from the window in the lithograph indicates an earlier time of day. The incongruity may have been to provide accent light on the objects in the room.

35. *Cupid at a Rout at Cincinnati* by Auguste Hervieu, pen, ink, and watercolor, 1830 (Cincinnati Art Museum) depicts three American women seated for a repast with their handkerchiefs/napkins held in their laps in a similar fashion.

36. Though one might expect the Carneses to import quantities of ceramic ware, very little was listed in their manifests and accounts. They may have assumed that by this time most Americans owned sufficient quantities of Chinese canton ware with little incentive to purchase more and perhaps it was not cost-effective.

37. Waverly Root, ed., *Herbs and Spices* (New York: Alfred Van der Marck Editions, 1985), 124.

38. Barrett, *Old Merchants of New York*, 40.

39. Milburn, *Oriental Commerce*, 502.

40. Nancy Ellen Davis, "The American China Trade, 1784–1844: Products for the Middle Class" (PhD diss., George Washington University, 1987), 150.

41. Hezekiah Pierrepont, Notes on the China Trade, 1796, Constable-Pierrepont Papers, 1762–1911, New York Public Library, Manuscript Division.

42. Edward H. Schafer, "Food During the T'ang," in *Food in Chinese Culture*, ed. K. C. Chang (New Haven, CT: Yale University Press, 1977), 111.

43. Valerie M. Garrett, *Heaven Is High, the Emperor Far Away: Merchants and Mandarins in Old Canton* (New York: Oxford University Press, 2002), 119.

44. Bernard Mergen, *Play and Playthings: A Reference Guide* (Westport, CT: Greenwood Press, 1982), 25.

45. Barrett, *Old Merchants of New York*, 43.

46. J. P. Brissot de Warville, *New Travels in the United States of America, 1788*, trans. Mara Soceanic Vamos and David Echevearic (Cambridge, MA: Belknap Press of Harvard University, 1964), 254.

47. Rodris Roth, *Floor Coverings in 18th Century America* (United States National Museum Bulletin # 250, Museum of History and Technology, Paper 59) (Washington, DC: Smithsonian Press, 1967), 27.

48. Elizabeth Latimer to John Latimer, June 1, 1833, John Latimer Papers, Library of Congress Manuscript Division, Washington, DC.

49. Tiffany, *Canton Chinese*, 77.

50. It is not clear what measurements were used in these descriptions.

51. Newspapers noted that matting came in colored, white, brown, red and blue checked, white, blue, and red checked, red, blue, straw-colored, black and green, red checked, checked red and black, yellow and white, white and fancy checked, and red and white.

52. Davis, "American China Trade," 53. Philadelphia ship manifests record 1,202 rolls (each roll contained 25 blinds), 512 bundles, 73 boxes, and 51 packs of blinds from 1784 to 1844. The greatest number came into the Philadelphia port in the 1830s and they were more heavily advertised at this time.

53. Elisabeth Donaghy Garrett, *At Home: The American Family, 1750–1870* (New York: Harry N. Abrams, 1990), 264. An illustration in Garrett's book shows a trade card for Ball and Price's Plain and Fancy Blind Factory, New York City *c.* 1835.

54. Tiffany, *Canton Chinese*, 21.

55. Harriet Martineau, *Retrospect of Western Travel*, ed. Daniel Feller (Armonk, NY: M.E. Sharpe, 2000), 2:123. It is possible that the blinds Martineau saw in New Orleans were exterior blinds.

56. Frances Trollope, *Domestic Manners of the Americans* (1832; repr., Donald Smalley, ed., New York: Alfred A. Knopf, 1949), 37.

57. The silk blinds in the *Howard*'s hold measured variously 4' x 4'; 6' x 4'; 6¼' x 3½'; 6½' x 3½'.

58. William Bell's Letterbook, Constable-Pierrepont Papers. The cost of blinds was noted in Bell's Letterbook. Philip Chadwick Foster Smith, *The Empress of China* (Philadelphia: Philadelphia Maritime Museum, 1984), noted on page 264 that Lunqua of Hog Lane was the principal supplier of bamboo blinds in Guangzhou.

59. Mary Sword to John Sword, June 26,1848, Sword Family Papers, Historical Society of Pennsylvania.

60. George Henry Mason, *The Costume of China* (London: W. Miller, 1800), plate 49.

61. Sarah Sword to John D. Sword, August 14, 1845, Sword Family Papers.

62. Valery M. Garrett, *Traditional Chinese Clothing* (New York: Oxford University Press, 1991), 71.

63. Tiffany, *Canton Chinese*, 77.

64. Garrett, *Traditional Chinese Clothing*, 71.

65. It is possible that Afong Moy's press was inaccurate. Her handlers may have presented Afong Moy as more genteel than she was by representing her as an embroiderer.

66. *Virginia Free Press* (Charlestown, West Virginia), issue 39, col. F, November 20, 1834.

67. Susan Mann, *Precious Records: Women in China's Long Eighteenth Century* (Stanford, CA: Stanford University Press, 1997), 103, 161. Mann includes an illustration of the Chinese painting *Weary from Embroidering*.

68. Ibid., 14.

69. Ibid., 159.

70. Laurel Thatcher Ulrich, *The Age of Homespun: Objects and Stories in the Creation of an American Myth* (New York: Vintage Books, 2001), 148.

71. Ibid.

72. David Jaffee, *A New Nation of Goods: The Material Culture of Early America* (Philadelphia: University of Pennsylvania Press, 2010), 70. According to Jaffee four hundred female seminaries were established between 1790 and 1830 and more women than men attended academies during these years.

73. Barrett, *Old Merchants of New York*, 42.

74. Lydia Maria Child, *The American Frugal Housewife* (Boston: Carter, Hendee, 1833), 24, 25, 29.

75. *Cassell's Domestic Dictionary: An Encyclopedia for the Household* (New York: Cassell Petter, Galpiny, 1878), 986.

76. Ibid.

77. John Furman, *The India Trader's Directory in Purchasing the Drugs and Spices of Asia and the East Indies* (New York: John Furman, 1800), 155.

78. Barrett, *Old Merchants of New York*, 42.

79. Furman, *India Trader's Directory*, 155.

80. Hezekiah Pierrepont Papers, Constable-Pierrepont Papers.

81. Williams, *Middle Kingdom*, 1:365. Williams noted that Chinese officials confidently assumed that the world so depended on tea and rhubarb that foreign merchants would purchase these commodities at any price and therefore the Chinese could impose heavy restrictions and high levies.

82. T. Bradley and R. Batty, *The Medical and Physical Journal* (London: Richard Phillips, 1808), 19:459.

83. Henry A. Crosby Forbes, *Shopping in China: The Artisan Community at Canton, 1825–1830* (Washington, DC: International Exhibitions Foundation, 1979). The exhibition catalog provides an image of a Drugs and Dyeing Shop where cinnabar, vermillion, and white lead are sold. In the back of the shop it appears that a worker is grinding materials perhaps for paint. Another watercolor is labeled "A Doctors Shop" which sold medicines. The image of the shop is more closely aligned to Downing's description than the Drugs and Dyeing shop. Here a mortar and pestle lie on the counter, a slicing instrument sits on the back shelf, and jars and boxes hold the medicines.

84. Downing, *Fan-qui in China*, 3:145.

85. Ibid., 3:144.

86. *Minutes of the Medical Society of the County of New York*, vol. 1, May 1833.

87. Barrett, *Old Merchants of New York*, 40–41.

88. *New York Spectator*, col. A, November 17, 1834.

89. *Baltimore Patriot*, October 21, 1834, 2.

90. Edward V. Gulick, *Peter Parker and the Opening of China* (Cambridge, MA: Harvard University Press, 1973), 12.

91. Ibid., 57. Presumably the women were attended by relatives. This indicates that Chinese women were not apprehended in the foreign factory area if they had good reason to be there. Afong Moy, like the women who were treated by Dr. Parker, came into the foreign factory because Chinese permission had been granted.

92. Williams, *Middle Kingdom*, 1:125.

93. Ibid., 1:127.

94. Ibid., 1:126.

95. Sue Fawn Chung, *In Pursuit of Gold: Chinese American Miners and Merchants in the American West* (Chicago: University of Illinois Press, 2011), 110. The author notes that *the Golden Mirror of Medicine* first published in 1742 was a respected self-help medical manual that Chinese immigrants brought to America. Marta Hanson, "The Golden Mirror in the Imperial Court of the Qianlong Emperor, 1739–1742," *Early Science and Medicine* 8, no. 2 (2003): 111–47. Hanson noted that the publication reached a broad public audience in China.

96. Western subjects such as the Madonna and child, or forms intended for Western applications such as chestnut dishes and plant holders, required the Chinese to modify their designs. Oliver Impey, *Chinoiserie: The Impact of Oriental Styles on Western Art and Decoration* (London: Oxford University Press, 1977), illustrates this.

Chapter 6

1. Robert Ernst, *Immigrant Life in New York City, 1825–1863* (Syracuse, NY: Syracuse University Press, 1994), 187. The majority of immigrants were British or Irish.

2. Private journal of a Princeton University student, August 6, 1834–November 30, 1836, September 21, 1836, Post Medieval Manuscript Bound vol. 108, Special Collections, Bryn Mawr College Library.

3. John Kearsley Mitchell to Matilda Mitchell, January 27, 1835, S. Weir Mitchell Collection, College of Physicians Library, Philadelphia, Pennsylvania.

4. Harriet Martineau, *Retrospect of Western Travel*, ed. Daniel Feller (Armonk, NY: M.E. Sharpe, 2000), 7.

5. Henri Herz, *My Travels in America*, trans. Henry Bertram Hill (Madison: State Historical Society of Wisconsin for the Department of History, University of Wisconsin, 1963), 17.

6. http://factsanddetails.com/china/cat14/sub93/item1129.html, accessed July, 2015.

7. *New York Star*, October 21, 1834.

8. *New-York Daily Advertiser*, November 7, 1834.

9. *New-Hampshire Patriot*, November 24, 1834.

10. The information at the bottom of the page noted the existence of several rooms.

11. "Catalogue of Chinese Curiosities," Mss Col. 2993, Samuel J. Tilden Papers, New York Public Library. I earlier knew of the catalogue's existence from a newspaper notice (*Eastern Argus* (Portland, Maine), December 1, 1834) which claimed that Chinese coins listed in the salon catalogue were stolen from Afong Moy's salon. They were later returned. Samuel J. Tilden was twenty and a student at either Yale University or New York University when Afong Moy arrived in 1834. There is no record of his visit to Afong Moy's salon; however, with the inclusion of the catalogue in his papers, it is likely he attended. Tilden later became governor of New York State and a democratic presidential candidate in 1876.

12. "Album of Silk Production," 1849, Col. 111, box 1, folder 1, Joseph Downs Collection of Manuscripts and Printed Ephemera, Winterthur Library.

13. Shillaber was in Guangzhou when Captain Obear arrived there in early 1834. There was confusion as to Caroline's relationship to John Shillaber. The newspaper *American,* August 17, 1833, noted that Caroline, Shillaber's youngest daughter, was married to Thomas Colledge in Macao in March 1833. However, in her correspondence home, Harriet Low stated how pleased

she was that Caroline, as Shillaber's sister and Low's classmate in Salem, had arrived in Macau. In letters to Andrew Jackson in 1834, Shillaber outlined possible China policies and anticipated his appointment to the consular position in Guangzhou. He may not have known that Edward Livingston had left his post in May 1833. David Gedalecia's two articles, "Letters from the Middle Kingdom, the Origins of America's China Policy," *Prologue* 34, no. 4 (Winter 2002), https://www.archives.gov/publication/prologue/2000/winter/gedalecia, define Shillaber's efforts to influence Jackson's China policy.

14. Thomas Colledge established the first hospital in China, known as Colledge's Ophthalmic Hospital, to treat Chinese patients with eye afflictions.

15. It is also possible that the hong merchants assisted either Obear or Shillaber in these efforts.

16. The dating of the objects falls within the correct dynastic reigns.

17. There is no record of what later happened to the catalogue objects.

18. *Baltimore Patriot*, November 11, 1834.

19. *Nashville Whig*, December 12, 1834.

20. *New-York Commercial Advertiser*, November 15, 1834.

21. *Boston Mercantile Journal*, November 29, 1834.

22. *New-York Mirror*, December 6, 1834.

23. *New-York Spectator*, November 17, 1834.

24. *Nashville Banner*, December 12, 1834.

25. *New York Journal of Commerce*, January 16, 1835.

26. Samuel Breck Diary, 1833–35, Coll. 1887, series 1, vol. 6, Historical Society of Pennsylvania.

27. *American Sentinel*, February 18, 1835.

28. Washington Hall is no longer standing in Philadelphia. It has been replaced by townhouses.

29. *American Sentinel* (Philadelphia), January 22, 1835.

30. Robert E. Schofield, "Charles Willson Peale and His Philadelphia Museum, 1784–1827," *American Studies* 30, no. 2 (Fall 1989): 21.

31. Ibid.

32. *American Sentinel* (Philadelphia), February 18, 1835.

33. As reported in the *Globe* (Washington, DC), February 26, 1835.

34. Ibid.

35. *Atkinson's Saturday Evening Post*, February 14, 1835.

36. See Joseph Andrew Orser, *The Lives of Chang and Eng: Siam's Twins in Nineteenth-Century America* (Chapel Hill: University of North Carolina Press, 2014), 23. Chang and Eng Bunker, the Chinese-Thai twins joined at the sternum, toured America and abroad from 1829 to the 1860s. During that time, they were frequently examined in private by well-known American doctors. Often this was done before a performance to heighten public interest. This practice may have been the precedent set for Afong Moy.

37. "Manners and Customs in the East," *Parley's Magazine for Children and Youth* (January 1, 1835), 73.

38. Dorothy Ko, *Cinderella's Sisters: A Revisionist History of Footbinding* (Los Angeles: University of California Press, 2005), 41.

39. John Kearsley Mitchell to Matilda Henry, Canton, China, February, 1821, MS 2/0241/03/ Box 3, S. Weir Mitchell Collection, College of Physicians Library, Philadelphia, Pennsylvania.

40. Ko, *Cinderella's Sisters*, 41.

41. Ibid., 42. Ko quoted Youning Li and Zhang Yufa, eds., *Jindai Zhongguo nüquan yundonng shiliano* (Documents on the feminist movement in modern China, 1842-1911) (Taipei: Zhuanji wenxue chubanshe, 1975), 508.

42. *Atkinson's Saturday Evening Post*, February 14, 1835, 3.

43. For information on Samuel Morton, his skull collecting, and the development of his theory on race, see Ann Fabian, *The Skull Collectors: Race, Science, and America's Unburied Dead* (Chicago: University of Chicago Press, 2010). For information on Samuel Morton and issues of religion and race, see William Stanton, *The Leopard's Spots: Scientific Attitudes toward Race in America, 1815–59* (Chicago: University of Chicago Press, 1960). James Fairhead, *The Captain and the "Cannibal"* : An Epic Story of Exploration, Kidnapping, and the Broadway Stage (New Haven, CT: Yale University Press, 2015) provides a succinct discussion of race as it relates to peoples brought to America.

44. Samuel Morton, *Crania Americana* (Philadelphia: J. Dobson, 1839), 45.

45. The quote is included in the text in Nicholas B. Wainwright, "The Age of Nicholas Biddle, 1825–1841," in *Philadelphia: A 300 Year History*, ed. Russell F. Weigley (New York: W.W. Norton, 1982), 275.

46. *National Gazette and Literary Register*, January 22, 1835.

47. *Philadelphia Inquirer*, January 31, 1835.

48. John Kearsley Mitchell to Matilda Henry, February 21, 1821.

49. John Kearsley Mitchell, "To Afong Moy," in *Indecision: A Tale of the Far West and Other Poems* (Philadelphia: E. L. Carey & A. Hart, 1837), 145–46.

50. Ibid., 144.

51. It is unclear whether Mitchell was a believer in the polygenic theory, but as a well-known Philadelphia doctor he surely knew Morton.

52. Mitchell, "To Afong Moy," 147.

53. John Kearsley Mitchell to Matilda Henry, February 21, 1821.

54. Ibid.

55. Mitchell, "To Afong Moy," 150.

56. Edgar A. Poe, "J.K. Mitchell Autography," in "A Chapter on Autography," *Graham's Magazine* 19, no. 6 (December 1841): 277.

57. Dwight Rembert Thomas, "Poe in Philadelphia 1834–1844: A Documentary Record" (PhD diss., University of Pennsylvania, 1978), 852–54.

58. James Silk Buckingham, "Review of Indecision: A Tale of the Far West and Other Poems," *The Athenaeum* (August 10, 1839): 615.

59. Samuel Breck Diary, February 15, 1835, 167. Samuel Breck had a tangential relationship to the China trade through his wife Jean Ross. Ross's father, John, was an active and successful East Indies merchant. After his death,

Ross's debts came due to hong merchant Consequa. The hong merchant brought charges against Ross's son-in-law, Samuel Breck, to recover the debt. It is unclear how this activity affected his response to China and Afong Moy. See entry on John Ross in Jean Gordon Lee, *Philadelphians and the China Trade, 1784–1844* (Philadelphia: Philadelphia Museum of Art, 1984), 61.

60. Ibid.

61. See Robert G. Lee, *Orientals: Asian Americans in Popular Culture* (Philadelphia: Temple University Press, 1999), 3. Lee notes that those foreigners who signaled their presence as a temporary visitor were often seen as desirable and acceptable as guests rather than as a threat.

62. Samuel Breck, *Passages from the Note-books*, "The Other Side," July 22, 1835, Coll. 1887, series 3, 275–76, Samuel Breck Papers, Historical Society of Pennsylvania.

63. "Communication. For the National Intelligencer. Our City," *Daily National Intelligencer* (Washington, DC), issue 6907, April 1, 1835.

64. Ibid.

65. Ibid.

66. *Congressional Globe*, 23rd Cong., 2nd Sess., (February 20, 1835), 2:274.

67. Ibid.

68. Ibid.

69. Born without arms, Martha Ann Honeywell cut silhouettes with her toes and mouth and exhibited that talent to public audiences around the country. In 1835 she lodged at a Mr. Gary's boardinghouse in Washington, DC. Laurel Daen, who completed a dissertation at the College of William and Mary on itinerant artists and performers with physical disabilities, shared this information with me.

70. Barbara G. Carson, *Ambitious Appetites: Dining, Behavior, and Patterns of Consumption in Federal Washington* (Washington, DC: American Institute of Architects Press, 1990), 138.

71. Ibid., 143.

72. Haynes McMullen, *American Libraries before 1876* (Westport, CT: Greenwood Press, 2000).

73. *Globe* (Washington, DC), March 12, 1835.

74. *National Intelligencer* (Washington, DC), February 27, 1835.

75. Roberts died in Macao in 1836 before completing the mission.

76. *Globe* (Washington, DC), March 12, 1835.

77. Ibid.

78. Ibid.

79. Sally Lambert to Elizabeth Galt, Williamsburg, May 25, 1835, (I) MSS 78G13, Item 17, Galt Family Papers, Special Collection Research Center, Earl Gregg Swem Library, College of William and Mary. The assumption that Eliza Lambert visited Afong Moy in Washington is based on the fact that the Afong Moy trips after Washington in 1835 did not appear to include Richmond. She went from Washington to Baltimore, and then on to Charleston by boat. She then left Charleston by boat for Baltimore. The

date of the letter indicates that the Afong Moy visit occurred sometime before May 1835. Washington would have been the nearest venue and likely Lambert saw her here.

80. There is no way to know whether this was Atung's answer. Since this information about Afong Moy had been previously published in the papers, Eliza Lambert (via Sally) may have repeated it from newspaper accounts.

81. Sally Lambert to Elizabeth Galt, Williamsburg, May 25, 1835.

82. Charles Augustus Murray, *Travels in North America during the Years 1834, 1835 and 1836* (New York: Harper & Brothers, 1839), 143.

83. Her leave-taking was noted in the Washington *Globe*, March 12, 1835.

84. Tyrone Power, *Impressions of America during the Years 1833, 1834, 1835* (Philadelphia: Carey, Lea & Blanchard, 1836, repr. New York: Benjamin Blom, 1971), 203.

85. Most travelers on the Pike stopped at Spurrier's Tavern. One might assume Afong Moy tarried there. The tavern burned down in late 1835.

86. *Baltimore Gazette and Daily Advertiser*, March 14, 1835.

87. Nancy Davis, *The Baltimore Album Quilt Tradition* (Tokyo, Japan: Kokusai Art, 1999), 19.

88. "My Album," *Ladies Repository* 3, no. 10 (October 1843): 301.

89. Martineau, *Retrospect of Western Travel*, 53.

90. *Baltimore Gazette and Daily Advertiser*, April 4, 1835, 2.

91. *Atkinson's Saturday Evening Post* of March 28, 1835, reported that the work was to be "printed simultaneously in the Celestial empire and Philadelphia—none of the chapters are to be suppressed."

92. Frances Trollope, *Domestic Manners of the Americans* (1832; repr., Donald Smalley, ed., New York: Alfred A. Knopf, 1949), 124.

93. Frances Anne Butler, *Journal of a Residence in America* (Paris, France: A. & W. Galignani, 1835), 232.

94. Shirley Hune, *Teaching Asian American Women's History* (Washington, DC: American Historical Association, 1997). Her work has enlarged our understanding of Asian American women's roles and dispelled some stereotypical assessments.

95. Frances Trollope's Cincinnati bazaar failed financially soon after Trollope left the city.

96. Mitchell, "To Afong Moy," 147.

97. John Gordon and his wife lived on Fayette Street in Baltimore.

98. John Gordon Diary, March 1835, MS 398, Gordon-Blackford Papers, Manuscript Department, H. Furlong Baldwin Library, Maryland Historical Society. *Maryland Historical Society Magazine* 49 (1954): 196–213, provided a transcription of the Gordon diary. This is fortunate because the manuscript has degraded since then and little of the wording is now visible.

99. Chapman founded the Medical Institute of Philadelphia and was the first president of the American Medical Association. Surely he would have been one of those selected to inspect Afong Moy's feet. Possibly he was out of town at the time the inspection took place.

100. Margaret S. Gibson to John Gibson, March 26, 1835, MS 1294, the Grundy-Gibson Papers, H. Furlong Baldwin Library, Maryland Historical Society. Margaret queried her brother John: "Did you observe the Chinese pictures around the room?" implying that he too had visited Afong Moy's salon, but not in Maryland.

101. Baltimore was the site of several balloon ascensions. The painter Nicolino Calyo recorded a Baltimore balloon ascension from Fairmount Park, Baltimore in 1834, giving us some idea of what Afong Moy would have seen in 1835.

102. William R. Quynn, ed., *The Diary of Jacob Engelbrecht, 1818–1878* (Frederick, MD: Historical Society of Frederick County, 2001), 478.

103. Commodore David Geisinger from Frederick Maryland was earlier the commanding officer of the *USS Peacock* which carried Edmund Roberts to Siam in 1833 to negotiate the first US treaty with Asia.

104. Quynn, *Diary of Jacob Engelbrecht*, 692–93.

105. *The Lutheran Observer and Weekly Religious and Literary Visitor* (Baltimore, Maryland), March 13, 1835.

106. Ibid. The exact quote in the *Lutheran Observer*: "He speaks the English language (which he learned at one of the factories in Canton)." Perhaps Atung informed the reporters of this fact in Baltimore. His schooling had not been previously mentioned in any other newspaper article.

107. Martineau, *Retrospect of Western Travel*, 85–86.

108. *Charleston Courier*, April 20, 1835.

109. In 1830, Charleston was the sixth-largest city in the United States.

110. Maurie Dee McInnis, "The Politics of Taste: Classicism in Charleston, South Carolina, 1815–1840" (PhD diss., Yale University, 1996). McInnis's study was helpful in understanding the social milieu of Charleston.

111. Martineau, *Retrospect of Western Travel*, 94.

112. The Cherokee rose or rosa laevigata was brought from China to England in the eighteenth century. Most likely English settlers introduced the rose to America where it is still found in old Southern gardens.

113. Gwynne Stephens Taylor, "The West Indian Islands—How Close Were They?," *Journal of Early Southern Decorative Arts* 2 (November 1972): 32. The recent French immigrants joined the much earlier eighteenth-century Protestant French Huguenots who settled in Charleston after the revocation of the Edict of Nantes.

114. *Charleston Courier*, April 20, 1835, 3.

115. Medical Society of South Carolina Minutes, 1834–58, 49. Lowcountry Digital Library (South Carolina), http://lcdl.library.cofc.edu/lcd/catalog/lcdl:42987#!prettyPhoto.

116. *Charleston Courier*, May 2, 1835.

117. Ibid.

118. Ibid.

119. Samuel Henry Dickson, *Remarks on Certain Topics Connected with the General Subject of Slavery* (Charleston: Observer Office Press, 1845).

120. Dickson, *Remarks*, 3.
121. See commentary on Samuel Henry Dickson's response to a monogenist in William Stanton, *The Leopard's Spots: Scientific Attitudes toward Race in America, 1815–1859* (Chicago: University of Chicago Press, 1960), 74.
122. Nathaniel Cheairs Hughes, *Yale's Confederates: A Biographical Dictionary* (Knoxville: University of Tennessee Press, 2008), 57, https://books.google.com/books.
123. "Tried in Charleston, May Term, 1835, James Thompson and wife of Murray vs. Dr. J. W. Schmidt," *Report of Law Cases Determined in the Court of Appeals*, vol. 1, Term 1836, https://catalog.hathitrust.org/Record/007699836.
124. See Michael Tadman's commentary in Michael Tadman, "The Interregional Slave Trade in the History and Myth-Making of the U.S. South," in *The Chattel Principle: Internal Slave Trades in the Americas*, ed. Walter Johnson (New Haven, CT: Yale University Press, 2004), 134–35. The City Council's statement and proceedings quoted by Tadman were printed in the *Charleston Daily Courier*, January 10, 1856.
125. The Charleston slave broadside noting a public sale by Richard Clagett on March 5, 1833. Though the broadside was for sale on eBay, it has been digitized and is available as part of the Digital Collection at the University Libraries of South Carolina.

Chapter 7

1. *Lowell Patriot*, August 21, 1835.
2. Edward Butler, the supercargo on the *Mary Ballard*, directed his wife to send all his letters through the Carneses while in Guangzhou, indicating that the voyage was underwritten by them.
3. *The Evening Post* (New York), April 8, 1835.
4. Augusta Obear's obituary makes reference to her many sailing trips with her husband, as well as her residence in France in the early part of her marriage. It is unlikely that Obear accompanied Afong Moy as a chaperone without the presence of her husband.
5. Henri Herz, *My Travels in America*, trans. Henry Bertram Hill (Madison: State Historical Society of Wisconsin, 1963), 29.
6. The name is alternatively spelled Hanington.
7. For a thorough explanation of the history of the panorama and diorama see Erkki Huhtamo, *Illusions in Motion: Media Archaeology of the Moving Panorama and Related Spectacles* (Cambridge, MA: MIT Press, 2013).
8. John Scudder died in 1821.
9. On the American Museum, New York City, see Gerald Bordman and Thomas Hischak, eds., *The Oxford Companion to American Theatre* (New York: Oxford University Press, 2004), 25.
10. John Robert McDowall soon left New York City for a trip and therefore this would have been the only period of time he was present in New York City to see Afong Moy at the museum.

11. Margaret Prior and Sarah R. Ingraham, *Walks of Usefulness, Or, Reminiscences of Mrs. Margaret Prior* (New York: American Female Moral Reform Society, 1851), 80–81.

12. Lisa Shaver, "'No Cross, No Crown': An Ethos of Presence in Margaret Prior's 'Walks of Usefulness,'" *College English* 75, no. 1 (September 2012), 61.

13. Philip Hone, *The Diary of Philip Hone 1828–1851*, ed. Alan Nevins (New York: Dodd, Mead, 1936), 1:45.

14. Phebe McDowall, *Memoir and Select Remains of the late John Robert McDowall* (New York: Leavitt & Lord & Co., 1838), 254.

15. Marilyn Wood Hill, *Their Sisters' Keepers: Prostitution in New York City, 1830–1870* (Berkeley: University of California Press, 1993), 35.

16. See Page Putnam Miller, *A Claim to New Roles* (Lanham, MD: Scarecrow Press, 1985), 20, on the development of female missionary efforts within the Presbyterian Church of the 1830s. According to Miller, the female interdenominational missionary effort was not successful.

17. Ibid.

18. These numbers were recorded in the 1839 report as noted in Shaver, "No Cross, No Crown," 64.

19. Prior and Ingraham, *Walks of Usefulness*, 82.

20. Ibid.

21. Kaori Abe, *Chinese Middlemen in Hong Kong's Colonial Economy, 1830–1890* (New York: Routledge, 2018), 18.

22. This is the Chinese merchant Punqua Winchong as noted in the introduction.

23. Abel Bowen, *Picture of Boston: The Citizen's and Strangers Guide* (Boston: Lilly Wait & Co., 1837), 90, https://archive.org/details/bowenspictureofb1833bowen.

24. This is according to the account by the Grimké sisters' biographer Gerda Lerner, *The Grimké Sisters from South Carolina: Pioneers in Women's Rights and Abolition* (Chapel Hill: University of North Carolina Press, 2009).

25. *Boston Morning Post*, August 6, 1835, 3.

26. See Stephanie Kermes, "To Make Them Fit Wives for Well Educated Men: 19th Century Education of Boston Girls," for the Boston Historical Society, New England Women's Club Fellowship, 2004, online paper. As well as Carl F. Kaestle, *Pillars of the Republic Common Schools and American Society, 1780–1860* (New York: Hill and Wang, 1983).

27. See Benjamin Rush, "Thoughts upon Female Education, Accommodated to the Present State of Society, Manners, and Government," delivered in 1787 at the Young Ladies' Academy of Philadelphia, in Frederick Rudolph, ed., *Essays on Education in the Early Republic* (Cambridge, MA: Harvard University Press, 1965), 27–40.

28. See Mary Beth Norton, *Liberty's Daughters: The Revolutionary Experience of American Women, 1750–1800* (Ithaca, NY: Cornell University Press, 1996).

29. *Boston Traveler*, July 17, 1835.

30. The interest in Siam (now Thailand), and Asia more generally, may have stemmed from Andrew Jackson's recent treaty with Siam and his interest in extending that treaty with Japan as noted in chapter 6.

31. *Boston Traveler*, July 17, 1835, 3.

32. Tellingly, the article directly beneath Afong Moy's descriptive portrait in the *Boston Traveler* lauded the accomplishments of Miss Harriet H. L. Story who had just completed her examinations in the Albany Female Seminary and received Honors of the Institution and a Diploma of the First Degree for her "academical studies." Though the contrast was possibly unintentional, it yet illustrates the perceived difference between the Chinese woman and an American woman who was nearly her same age.

33. See Jean-Christophe Agnew, *Worlds Apart: The Market and the Theatre in Anglo-American Thought, 1550–1750* (Cambridge: Cambridge University Press, 1986). Regarding David Leverenz's view that: "Puritans saw themselves in what they hated" in David Leverenz, *Language of Puritan Feeling: An Exploration in Literature, Physiology, and Social History* (New Brunswick, NJ: Rutgers University Press, 1980), 24.

34. *Boston Morning Post*, July 31, 1835, 2.

35. *Gleason's Pictorial Drawing Room Companion*, May 15, 1852, 320.

36. *Boston Evening Transcript*, July 31, 1835, 2. The *Transcript* reported the *Boston Morning Post*'s commentary.

37. Ibid.

38. Ostensibly the tour was to impress the Indians with the might of the United States. The interpretation of Black Hawk's tour in Rosemarie K. Bank, *The Theatre Culture in America, 1825–1860* (New York: Cambridge University Press, 1997), is that of a staging of defeat and humiliation.

39. Laura Mielke, *Moving Encounters: Sympathy and the Indian Question in Antebellum Literature* (Amherst: University of Massachusetts Press, 2008), 238. Mielke notes that the drama was reenacted twelve times.

40. *Boston Traveler*, Boston, Massachusetts, July 31, 1835.

41. *Boston Traveler*, July 17, 1835, 3.

42. A broadside handbill that was submitted to the Boston City Council as part of an application for a permit to hold the flea circus on Washington Street in the Joy Building defines the many activities the fleas will engage in. *City Council Proceedings 1822–2000*, Item 1835-0039-C2 (Collection # 0100.001), City of Boston Archives. The public's appetite for ridiculous display is noted in the *New Hampshire Sentinel*, July 30, 1835: "Boston at this time has peculiar attractions. Mr. Maelzell burns Moscow in an improved style. The Eastern Magician, Bahad Marchael astonishes crowded audiences by raising and laying ghosts. . . . The Chinese Lady, Afong Moy, has arrived there from the South—and last, as well as *least*, there is an exhibition of trained *fleas*, that draw carriages, ride on *flea*-back, and fight with the broad-sword! Either of these wonderful exhibitions would set a whole village like ours in commotion."

43. When Maelzel died, John Kearsley Mitchell, the Philadelphia physician who wrote the poem "To Afong Moy," purchased his automaton chess player. See James W. Cook, *The Arts of Deception: Playing with Fraud in the Age of Barnum* (Cambridge, MA: Harvard University Press, 2001), 30.

44. Mrs. L. Maria Child, *The Girl's Own Book* (Boston: Carter, Hendee, and Babcock, 1834), 198.

45. Ibid., 60.

46. Fan-Pen Li Chen, *Chinese Shadow Theatre: History, Popular Religion, and Women Warriors* (Montreal, Quebec, Canada: McGill-Queen's University Press, 2007).

47. Caroline Howard King, *When I Lived in Salem* (Brattleboro, VT: Stephen Day Press), 1937, 31.

48. Ibid., 22.

49. *Republican Herald* (Providence, Rhode Island), September 2, 1835.

50. *Providence Journal* (Providence, Rhode Island), August 31, 1835.

51. *Republican Herald* (Providence, Rhode Island), September 2, 1835.

52. "Letter from a Chinese Lady to Mrs. ——— of Philadelphia," *Salem Gazette*, December 21, 1790. The letter was also published in New Hampshire and Hartford, Connecticut, papers in 1790.

53. The Captain Barry would have likely been Captain John Barry who was an officer in the Continental Army and considered the father of the American Navy. After the Revolutionary War Barry entered the China trade as Captain of the vessel *Asia* that left Philadelphia for Guangzhou in 1787 and returned in 1789.

54. "Letter from a Chinese Lady," *Salem Gazette*.

55. Though difficult to prove, it is possible that Benjamin Rush anonymously wrote this editorial for wide distribution in east coast newspapers. His focus on women's education extended to his concern regarding women's health.

56. *Passenger Lists of Vessels Arriving at Boston, Massachusetts, 1820–1891*, Boston, Massachusetts, National Archives and Records Administration, Micro publication, M277, rolls 1–36.

57. *Philadelphia National Gazette*, April 3, 1830.

58. *Worcester Spy Newspaper* September 8, 1835. Nathaniel Paine, *Random Recollections of Worcester, Massachusetts, 1839–1843* (Worcester, MA: F. Rice, 1885), 38, https://archive.org/details/randomrecollectioopain, provided information regarding Z. Bonney's establishment and the accommodations for traveling exhibitions. Paine noted that it was "customary for the smaller shows to have their headquarters at one of the taverns, and give exhibitions either in some room or in a tent in the yard outside" (p. 38). In 1838 the Siamese twins presented at the Central Hotel and in 1843 the Hotel exhibited fifteen buffalo captured from the Rocky Mountains. During the night, the herd got loose and the city folks of Worcester conducted their first buffalo hunt to retrieve them.

59. See Joseph S. C. Lam, "The Presence and Absence of Female Musicians and Music in China," in *Women and Confucian Cultures in Premodern China,*

Korea, and Japan, ed. Dorothy Ko, JaHyun Kim Haboush, and Joan R. Piggott (Berkeley: University of California Press, 2003).

60. Su Zheng, *Claiming Diaspora: Music, Transnationism, and Cultural Politics in Asian/Chinese America* (New York: Oxford University Press, 2010), 135, 347–48.

61. Samuel Wells Williams, *The Middle Kingdom* (New York: Charles Scribner's Sons, 1904), 2:96.

62. *Albany Argus*, November 12, 1835.

63. John Barrow, *Travels in China . . . Subsequent Journey through the Country from Pekin to Canton* (London: T. Cadell & W. Davies, in the Strand, 1804), 193, 314–16.

64. *Albany Argus*, November 13, 1835.

65. Albany architect Marcus T. Reynolds, who was sensitive to historical accuracy. designed the late nineteenth–early twentieth-century bank building after the earlier 1830 museum building on the site. See Diana Waite, ed., *Downtown Albany: Crossroads of Commerce and Transportation* (Albany, NY: Mount Ida Press Partnership, 1993).

66. Tyrone Power, *Impressions of America during the Years 1833, 1834, 1835* (Philadelphia: Carey, Lea & Blanchard, 1836 repr., New York: Benjamin Blom, 1971).

67. *Albany Argus*, November 11, 1835.

68. It is possible that Herman Melville was in the audience, for he was in Albany at that time. Melville's great uncle Captain John D'Wolf traveled to China and traded at Guangzhou. Melville spent time in his presence, and included him as a character in *Redburn*. Melville's brother, Thomas, also captained a China Trade vessel. See Donna Ferrantello, *Moby-Dick and Peace* (Marietta, GA: Open Sky Press, 2000).

69. *Albany Evening Journal*, November 11, 1835.

70. Valery M. Garrett, *Traditional Chinese Clothing* (New York: Oxford University Press, 1991), 39; Valery Garrett, *Chinese Dress from the Qing Dynasty to the Present* (Rutland, VT: Tuttle, 2007). Kingfisher feathers were used as inlay on decorative objects. Guangzhou was the center for the manufacture of kingfisher jewelry.

71. *Albany Argus*, November 16, 1835.

72. *Albany Evening Journal*, November 10, 1835. The black hair dye was sold for seventy-five cents a box.

73. "Althea Vernon: Or the Embroidered Handkerchief," a Novelette by Miss Leslie, *Godey's Lady's Book* (April–May 1838), vol. 16–17, 105.

74. Ibid., 173.

75. Ibid.

76. *Albany Argus*, November 13, 1835. The *Albany Argus* noted that they took this as an extract from a *New-York Times* article on Afong Moy.

77. Adam Smith, *The Theory of Moral Sentiments* (London: A Millar, 1759), 9.

78. Madeline Y. Hsu, *Dreaming of Gold, Dreaming of Home: Transnationalism and Migration between the United States and South China, 1882–1943*

(Stanford, CA: Stanford University Press, 2000), 112. Hsu quotes Sandra Wong's informant about his obligatory remittances: "They are my family, don't you think I should help them out? That's my mother and father, you know, they're not friends. I've always sent them money. It is a way to pay respect to your ancestors."

79. *Albany Evening Journal*, November 13, 1835.
80. Ibid.
81. Walter Barrett, *A Second Series of* The Old Merchants of New York, *Being a Continuation of the Work* (New York: Worthington Co., 1864), 44.
82. Ibid., 45.

Chapter 8

1. Caroline Frank, *Objectifying China, Imagining America: Chinese Commodities in Early America* (Chicago: University of Chicago Press, 2011), 110.
2. Lewis Carnes as a Boston and Demerara merchant and shopkeeper: John Haven Dexter, ed., *The 1789 Boston City Directory* (Boston: New England Historic Genealogical Society, 1989); *American Ancestry: Giving the Name and Descent in the Male Line of Americans Whose Ancestors Settled in the United States Previous to the Declaration of Independence*, vol. 11 (Albany, NY: Joel Munsell's Sons, 1898); *Boston Patriot*, November 6, 1813; Nathaniel Dearborn, *Boston Notions: Being an Authentic and Concise Account of That Village from 1630–1847* (Boston: N. Dearborn, 1848); *Ancestry.com* accessed October 12 and 19, 2011; *Boston City Directories*, 1791, 1796–1810.
3. Thomas H. Perkins to John Forbes, 1828, Forbes Family Papers, Massachusetts Historical Society.
4. Thomas Russell to John Sword, April 22, 1837, Sword Family Papers, Historical Society of Pennsylvania.
5. Henry Pratt McKean to Benjamin Etting, Esq., July 8, 1835, Coll. 405, Thomas McKean Papers, Historical Society of Pennsylvania.
6. Walter Barrett, *A Second Series of* The Old Merchants of New York, *Being a Continuation of the Work* (New York: Worthington Co., 1864), 44.
7. This enormous increase in sugar production required a great increase in the number of enslaved peoples to work the plantations. The trade in slaves was immensely lucrative.
8. The following works provided insight on the rise of Cuba in the early nineteenth century: Louis A. Perez Jr., ed., *Impressions of Cuba in the Nineteenth Century: The Travel Diary of Joseph J. Dimock* (Wilmington, DE: Scholarly Resources, 1998); Clifford L. Staten, *The History of Cuba* (Westport, CT: Greenwood, 2003); Franklin W. Knight, "Origins of Wealth and the Sugar Revolution in Cuba, 1750–1850," *Hispanic American Historical Review* 57, no. 2 (1977): 231–53; Louis A. Perez Jr., ed., *Slaves, Sugar, and Colonial Society: Travel Accounts of Cuba, 1801–1899,* (Wilmington, DE: Scholarly Resources, 1992).
9. Knight, "Origins of Wealth and the Sugar Revolution," 246.

10. *New York Evening Post*, December 8, 1835, 3. Once again, the Canderbeecks' name was misspelled on the *Caspar Hauser* passenger list. Here they were listed as Canderbeek; on the 1829 passenger list as Canderbeech.

11. Karen Robert, ed., *New Year in Cuba: Mary Gardner Lowell's Travel Diary, 1831–1832* (Boston: Massachusetts Historical Society and Northeastern University Press, 2003), 38.

12. Perez, *Impressions of Cuba in the Nineteenth Century*, 85–86.

13. Ibid, 5. Lowell found the volante so unusual that she drew a picture of it in her diary.

14. Robert, *New Year in Cuba*, 39. Lowell described her entrance into the city.

15. Havana newspapers defined the location and name of Afong Moy's residence. A public fountain named "Leon" had just been built in the center of the square; her residence was named after the fountain which still exists in the center of the square.

16. The Lowells stayed at Mrs. Howard's guest house while in Havana. Lowell does not provide the name of this guest house or the location, but she indicated that at this time most Americans resided at Howard's guest house.

17. Robert, *New Year in Cuba*, 60.

18. *El Noticioso y lucero de la Habana*, January 30, 1836. My thanks to Thomas Garcia for assisting me in the translations.

19. There was no notice of the Canderbeecks' performances in the *El Noticioso* newspaper. I was unable to locate other early Cuban newspapers to confirm their presence or performances in Cuba.

20. *El Noticioso y lucero de la Habana*, January 30, 1836.

21. Ibid.

22. In twelve to fifteen years this would change as large numbers of Chinese laborers were brought from southern China to work the Cuban sugar fields. Afong Moy's presence would not then have been so graciously and ceremoniously received. Chinese male workers were not highly regarded and were not well treated by the Cubans.

23. *El Noticioso*, January 30, 1836.

24. Robert, *New Year in Cuba*, 64–65.

25. Carl L. Crossman, *The Decorative Arts of the China Trade* (Woodbridge, Suffolk, UK: Antiques Collectors' Club, 1991), 381. Crossman quotes a notation from Pickering Dodge of Salem to supercargo Benjamin Shreve as found in the Benjamin Shreve Papers at the Peabody Essex Museum.

26. Robert, *New Year in Cuba*, 49.

27. *Pensacola Gazette*, March 19, 1836.

28. Though Ocala is four hundred miles from Pensacola, the reverberations from the attack rattled the populace as far away as the Carolinas where the event was covered extensively in newspaper accounts.

29. The Indian Removal Act passed by Congress in 1830 intended to deploy many Native Americans to land west of the Mississippi River. Thousands were removed.

30. *Pensacola Gazette* (Pensacola, Florida), March 19, 1836.

31. Ibid.

32. Tyrone Power, *Impressions of America during the Years 1833, 1834, 1835* (Philadelphia: Carey, Lea & Blanchard, 1836 repr. New York: Benjamin Blom, 1971), 143–44.

33. Ibid., 212.

34. Several sources state that the steamboat *South Alabama* was used for Indian removal. See *Van Buren Site Report*, University of Arkansas at Little Rock, Sequoyah National Research Center, n.d., and Shirley Boteler Mock, *Dreaming with the Ancestors: Black Seminole Women in Texas and Mexico* (Norman: University of Oklahoma Press, 2010).

35. A Jean Brunette was on the list of names in the "Disbursement to Indians" letter sent to the Secretary of War on February 18, 1835. The list defined names of people charged with disbursement of funds, goods, or money to the Indians.

36. Mock, *Dreaming with the Ancestors*, 44.

37. Though the passenger list only notes thirty-four passengers, we know that the vessel could accommodate at least 249 passengers based on Indian removal accounts from the *South Alabama*. Possibly not all the passengers were listed.

38. *New-Orleans Commercial Bulletin*, March 28, 1836. It is possible that in late 1835 Afong Moy traveled from New York to Albany by steamboat but no mention has been found of this travel in newspapers accounts or documents.

39. *Mobile Journal*, March 14, 1836.

40. William M. Evan and Mark Manion, *Minding the Machines: Preventing Technological Disasters* (Upper Saddle River, NJ: Prentice Hall, 2002), 177. Evan and Manion note that the 1838 laws had little teeth and not until 1852, with even more stringent laws, that lives lost by steamboat travel were reduced. The statistics they provide from another source (Louis C. Hunter, *Steamboats on the Western Rivers* [Cambridge, MA: Harvard University Press, 1949], 178–80) note that between 1830 and 1840 there were 104 steamboat accidents resulting in the deaths of 1,018 people.

41. *New-Orleans Commercial Bulletin*, March 28, 1836, listed the vessel's arrival and names of the passengers. The Canderbeecks were not included in the passenger list.

42. Henri Herz, *My Travels in America*, trans. Henry Bertram Hill (Madison: State Historical Society of Wisconsin for the Department of History, University of Wisconsin, 1963), 83.

43. Enslaved light-skinned females called "fancy girls" were often marketed for sex exploitation in New Orleans.

44. Harriet Martineau, *Retrospect of Western Travel*, ed. Daniel Feller (Armonk, NY: M.E. Sharpe, 2000), 116. Originally published in 1838.

45. "Afong Moy, For One Week Only," broadside, BDSDS, 1842, Record ID 207260, American Antiquarian Society.

46. Ibid.

47. *Mississippi Free Trader*, April 22, 1836; *New-Orleans Commercial Bulletin*, April 9, 1836.

48. Edward L. Miller, *New Orleans and the Texas Revolution* (College Station: Texas A&M University Press, 2004), 10.

49. Don B. Wilmeth with Tice L. Miller, eds., *Cambridge Guide to American Theatre* (New York: Cambridge University Press, 1996), 42.

50. Miller, *New Orleans and the Texas Revolution*, 12.

51. For a discussion of nativism, see Geoffrey S. Smith, "Nativism," *Encyclopedia of the New American Nation*, http://www.americanforeignrelations.com/E-N/Nativism.html; John Higham, *Strangers in the Land: Patterns of American Nativism* (New Brunswick, NJ: Rutgers University Press, 1963); Dale T. Knobel, *America for the Americans: The Nativist Movement in the U.S.* (New York: Macmillan), 1996.

52. The Chinese did not come to Louisiana until after the Civil War to assume the work in sugar and cotton plantations previously done by the enslaved.

53. *New Orleans Bee*, April 5, 1836.

54. Robert, *New Year in Cuba*, 131.

55. *New Orleans Bee*, April 1, 1836.

56. Martineau, *Retrospect of Western Travel*, 117.

57. Ibid., 118.

58. Joseph Holt Ingraham, *The South-West by a Yankee* (New York: Harper & Brothers, 1835).

59. Ibid., 41.

60. Edwin Adams Davis and William Ransom Hogan, eds., *The Barber of Natchez* (Baton Rouge: Louisiana State University Press, 1992).

61. Power, *Impressions of America*, 191.

62. Davis and Hogan, *Barber of Natchez*, 191.

63. Ibid., 190.

64. James M. Scott was an actor but also a manager and booking agent for the Vicksburg Theater and, for a shorter period of time, the Natchez theater. During the April 1836 season, he competed with the presence of a circus which William Johnson mentioned in his diary. Afong Moy was Scott's sophisticated answer to that competition. See William Bryan Gates, "The Theatre in Natchez," *Journal of Mississippi History* 3, (April 1941): 71–97; Joseph Miller Free, "The Ante-Bellum Theatre of the Old Natchez Region," *Journal of Mississippi History* 5 (January 1943): 14–27.

65. Herbert A. Kellar, "A Journey through the South in 1836: Diary of James D. Davidson," *Journal of Southern History* 1, no. 3 (August 1935): 350. Davidson remarked that it appeared to him that the people "look like a selfish, reserved, bigoted people. And such I am told is their character." Mary Gardner Lowell wrote in her diary (Robert, *New Year in Cuba*, 148) that: "We were delighted with the appearance of the city, as we approached, the fine clean streets and thriving aspect of all about us." She was not as critical of the people she met there, but called some "stupid."

66. Brothers Arthur (1786–1865) and Lewis (1788–1873) Tappan from Northampton, Massachusetts, and William Bingham Tappan (1794–1849) from Beverly, Massachusetts, were grandsons of Rev. Benjamin Tappan (1720–1790) of Newbury, Massachusetts. Arthur and Lewis established a successful dry goods wholesale and retail business in New York City. They used their extensive wealth to fund social programs including the Magdalen Society, the Lane Seminary, newspapers and organizations that supported abolition, and the American Missionary Association. Lewis founded the *National Era*, which in 1852 published Harriet Beecher Stowe's *Uncle Tom's Cabin*. See Bertram Wyatt-Brown, *Lewis Tappan and the Evangelical War against Slavery* (Cleveland, Ohio: Case Western Reserve University Press, 1969).

67. William B. Tappan's other works include *New England and Other Poems* (1819), *Poems* (1822), *Lyrics* (1822), *Poetry of the Heart* (1845), *Sacred and Miscellaneous Poems* (1848), *Poetry of Life* (1848), *The Sunday School and Other Poems* (1848), *Late and Early Poems* (1849), and *Sacred Poems* (1849).

68. William B. Tappan, *The Poems of William B. Tappan* (Philadelphia: Henry Perkins, 1836), 203.

69. Ibid., 204.

70. There is no direct evidence that William Tappan was an abolitionist, but considering his association with his two cousins who were strong abolitionists, and the nature of his writings, it would appear that he was of the same mind.

71. William Lloyd Garrison's 1859 speech in Boston printed in William Jennings Bryan, ed., *The World's Famous Orations* (New York: Funk and Wagnalls, 1906).

72. Kathryn Gin Lum, *Damned Nation: Hell in America from the Revolution to Reconstruction* (New York: Oxford University Press, 2014), 65.

73. Tappan, *Poems of William B. Tappan*, 206.

74. Robert, *New Year in Cuba*, 160.

75. Power, *Impressions of America*, 311.

76. Scott C. Martin, *Killing Time: Leisure and Culture in Southwestern Pennsylvania, 1800–1850* (Pittsburgh: University of Pittsburgh Press, 1995), 53. On attendance, Power also commented that the house was full.

77. *Pittsburgh Gazette*, May 20, 1836.

78. Power, *Impressions of America*, 312.

79. Robert, *New Year in Cuba*, 164.

Chapter 9

1. Caroline Butler to Edward Butler, May 8, 1835, Butler-Laing Family Papers, MS 94, Box 1, Folder 1-4, New-York Historical Society Museum and Library.

2. Caroline Butler to Edward Butler, April 19, 1835.

3. Caroline Butler to Edward Butler, April 25, 1835.

4. Caroline also recorded in the May 8, 1835, letter that she had attended a ladies' fair whose object was to raise monies for missionary work. She noted: "the

object of which was to educate another missionary for the heathen to eat up." Later, she noted that they were successful and "collected about $140— too much for a cannibal stew." This indicated the prevalent attitude about who were heathen—the Chinese—and those who were not Christian. Probably the commentary in this case referred not to the Chinese but to the "cannibal" Dako from New Guinea whom Captain Benjamin Morrell had enslaved and displayed in New York and elsewhere. See James Fairhead, *The Captain and "the Cannibal": An Epic Story of Exploration, Kidnapping, and the Broadway Stage* (New Haven, CT: Yale University Press, 2015).

5. *Public Ledger*, May 31, 1836, 3; *Public Ledger*, June 10, 1836, 3; *Herald* (New York), June 14, 1836.

6. *New York Shipping and Commercial List*, 1841, and *Index to the Executive Documents of the 27th Congress*, 1842, 183.

7. *New York Times*, July 9, 1836.

8. Erkki Huhtamo, *Illusions in Motion: Media Archaeology of the Moving Panorama and Related Spectacles* (Cambridge, MA: MIT Press, 2013), 157.

9. The event was described in the *New York Evening Post*, August 25, 1836. Henry Yu, *Thinking Orientals: Migration, Contact, and Exoticism in Modern America* (New York: Oxford University Press, 2001), 160.

10. Huhtamo, *Illusions in Motion*, 5.

11. *Newark Daily Advertiser*, September 15, 1836.

12. *New York Herald*, November 25, 1836.

13. *Boston Traveler*, September 22, 1840.

14. Cited in the *New York Herald*, October 25, 1836.

15. Even as her career with Henry Hannington began to fade, Afong Moy had such wide name recognition that a Virginia horse breeder named his filly after her. *American Turf Register and Sporting Magazine*, January 1836, 240.

16. According to Joseph Shackell, the Hydro-Oxygen Microscope magnified a drop of water 500,000 times so one could see objects such as flies and fleas with great clarity. Joseph Shackell, *The Olio or Museum of Entertainment* (London: Joseph Shackell, 1833), 11:105, https://archive.org/stream/olioormuseument07unkngoog/olioormuseument07unkngoog_djvu.txt.

17. George C. D. Odell, *Annals of the New York Stage* (1834–43; repr. New York: AMS Press, 1970), 4:186.

18. Philip Hone, *The Diary of Philip Hone 1828–1851*, ed. Alan Nevins (New York: Dodd, Mead, 1936), 1:241. .

19. Ibid., 243.

20. Ibid., 248.

21. Ibid., 255.

22. Edward Pessen, *Jacksonian America: Society, Personality, and Politics* (Homewood, IL: Dorsey Press, 1969), 152.

23. Pessen, *Jacksonian America*, 49. Pessen estimated that perhaps one-third of the working class were jobless in this period.

24. *Evening Post* (New York), May 27, 1837.

25. *Evening Post* (New York), September 22, 1837. It is unclear whether Henry Hannington fully retired from all entertainment activities (he and his brother advertise their window blind business at this point), but there are no newspaper notices of his dioramas or his other entertainment activities in New York for several years.

26. *Spectator* (New York), June 15, 1837. The paper mistakenly identified Nathaniel Carnes as Nicholas Carnes, but later in the article he is called N. G. Carnes, which was Nathaniel's business name. Later records note that Nathaniel had business connections in Poughkeepsie.

27. *Evening Post*, July 17, 1838.

28. The New York City Directories list Benjamin Obear as a New York City merchant from 1842 to 1849. After his death in 1849, his widow Augusta is listed in the 1850 United States federal census as living with her sister Mary Ann Ellingwood in Beverly, Massachusetts. In 1855 she contributed funds to the public library in Beverly. In 1880 the United States federal census noted that she was "keeping house" in Beverly and that the minister Jabez Newton Emery and his wife lived with her. She died in 1891 and was buried in the Central Cemetery in Beverly.

29. James R. Gibson, *Otter Skins, Boston Ships, and China Goods: The Maritime Fur Trade of the Northwest Coast, 1785–1841* (Seattle: University of Washington Press, 1992), 104.

30. *U.S. Gazette* (Philadelphia), April 4, 1838.

31. It was illegal for Chinese citizens to leave the country; doing so jeopardized their return.

32. *Daily Herald and Gazette* (Cleveland, Ohio), May 21, 1838.

33. John A. Grigg, "Ye relief of ye poor of sd towne": Poverty and Localism in Eighteenth-Century New Jersey," *New Jersey History* 125, no. 2 (2010): 23.

34. *Monmouth Inquirer*, March 21, 1838.

35. Ibid.

36. Ibid.

37. Ibid.

38. *Newark Daily Advertiser*, April 7, 1838.

39. The 1850 US Federal Census Records for Monmouth County, New Jersey, list a Henry Hannington, age fifty-two (born about 1798), a wife named Cam, age thirty-five, a child Celia, age fifteen, a son Charles, age eleven, and twins Isabel and Marry, age six. The 1855 New York State Census in the New York State Archives, Albany, New York list Harry Hannington, age fifty (born about 1805), a wife named Cath, forty-one years, a child Celia, nineteen years, and a son Charles, age twelve. Perhaps the twins died, as they are not listed. Such differences in details of census records are not unusual. Though three other Hannington family members are listed in the 1855 census, they may be the illegitimate children of Hannington's sister, who is listed as twenty-six years and resided with the family.

40. My thanks to George Joyson, research assistant, and Gary D. Saretzky, archivist in the Monmouth County Archives; to Randall Gabrielan, Monmouth

County historian; to Gail Hunton, the county's historic preservation specialist, and John Fabinano, at the Monmouth County Historical Commission, for sharing their research on the Monmouth County Almshouse.

41. Charles Benedict Davenport and David F. Weeks, "A First Study of Inheritance in Epilepsy," *Journal of Nervous and Mental Diseases* 38, no. 11 (1911): 646.

42. Monmouth County poorhouse inmates were required to wear these badges until the rule was abolished in 1874. This was not unusual. Baltimore County Almshouse inmates were often similarly required to wear a crimson badge with B.P. (for Baltimore Poorhouse) on their clothing. Baltimore information from: Seth Rockman, *Scraping By: Wage Labor, Slavery, and Survival in Early Baltimore* (Baltimore: Johns Hopkins University Press, 2009), 200. Monmouth information from Monmouth County Archives History, *Overseers of the Poor, 1754–1911*, Record Group COUNT10200, History.

43. John King Fairbank, *The United States and China*, 4th ed. (Cambridge, MA: Harvard University Press, 1983), 25.

44. Grigg, "Ye Relief of ye poor of sd towne," 32.

45. *Charleston Courier*, April 27, 1838. A May 10, 1838, *Monmouth Inquirer* article said of Caleb E. Taylor: "no person, to our knowledge . . . of that name, lives in this county." This is the only refutation of Taylor's connection to Afong Moy that was found. Taylor sends his rebuttal notices to the Monmouth County newspapers which points to his presence in the New Jersey area.

46. *United States Gazette*, April 12, 1838.

47. The language that Caleb E. Taylor used to address his uncle indicated that he was a member of the Society of Friends. In a letter to his uncle, Samuel Gardiner Wright, Taylor used "thy and thee"—a Quaker designation. The New Jersey Wright family was also Quaker. Samuel G. Wright's father, Caleb, was involved in anti-slavery activity as a member of the Society of Friends. Taylor family members are buried in the Quaker Freehold Cemetery. The first Quaker meeting in New Jersey took place in 1664 in what later became Freehold Township.

48. Wright Family Papers, Historical Notes, Accession 1665, Manuscript and Archives Department, Hagley Museum and Library. The papers define the family relationship between the Taylors and the Wrights. Caleb E. Taylor was Samuel Gardiner Wright's nephew. A letter from Caleb to his uncle in 1843 asked for letters of introduction to Samuel Wright's friends in the West in preparation for Caleb's planned trip to Illinois.

49. Ibid.

50. *New-York Commercial Advertiser*, April 24, 1838.

51. Raymond P. Miller, "What Is a Quaker," in *Religions in America: Ferment and Faith in an Age of Crisis*, ed. Leo Rosten (New York: Simon and Schuster, 1975), 222.

52. *Monmouth Inquirer*, April 12, 1838.

53. Ibid.

54. *Evening Post* (New York), February 17, 1838. The advertisement reads in full: "Hanington & Company. Transparent and Ornamental Window Blinds and Decorative Painters, 458 Broadway, Corner of Grand Street. Signs of every description painted with taste, economy and dispatch. Orders forwarded to any part of the Union."
55. *New York Spectator*, April 12, 1838.
56. William Nelson, ed., *Records of the Township of Paterson, New Jersey, 1831–1851* (Paterson, NJ: Evening News Job Printing, 1895), 89.
57. Ibid., 83, 84.
58. *Monmouth Inquirer*, March 21, 1838.
59. *Daily Herald and Gazette* (Cleveland, Ohio), May 21, 1838.
60. *Monmouth Inquirer*, May 10, 1838.
61. Fairhead, *The Captain and "the Cannibal,"* 85. Fairhead provides a detailed description of the Esquimaux plight.
62. Ibid., 85.
63. *Monmouth Inquirer*, March 21, 1838.

Chapter 10

1. John R. Haddad, "China of the American Imagination: The Influence of Trade on US Portrayals of China, 1820 to 1850," in *Narratives of Free Trade: The Commercial Cultures of Early US-China Relations*, ed. Kendall Johnson (Hong Kong: Hong Kong University Press, 2012), 81.
2. Samuel Wells Williams, *The Middle Kingdom* (New York: Charles Scribner's Sons, 1904), 2:14–15.
3. Ibid.
4. John King Fairbank, *Trade and Diplomacy on the China Coast* (Cambridge, MA: Harvard University Press, 1964), 63.
5. Ibid., 66.
6. The deep-water harbor sixty-four nautical miles from Guangzhou is near the estuary of the Pearl River and the South China Sea.
7. Stephen Davies, *East Sails West: The Voyage of the Keying, 1846–1855* (Hong Kong: Hong Kong University Press, 2014), 124–25. Davies provides a thorough recounting of the *Keying*'s voyage.
8. Ibid., 124–25.
9. *Daily Union* (Washington, DC), August 11, 1847, 3.
10. Ibid.
11. "The Chinese Lady," *New York Tribune*, August 10, 1847.
12. P. T. Barnum, *The Life of P.T. Barnum: Written by Himself* (1855; repr., Champaign: University of Illinois Press, 2000), 152.
13. Henry Hannington and P. T. Barnum signed an agreement with an unknown person for use of the New York City Castle Garden grounds. Castle Garden Records, 1844, Folder 1, AHMC, New-York Historical Society Museum and Library.

14. As noted earlier Henry Hannington applied his glass-making skills in diverse ways to earn a living. In 1836 he received a silver medal at the American Institute Fair for his transparencies. The *Mechanic's Magazine, and Journal of the Mechanics' Institute* 8 (1836): 306 noted: "Mr Hannington's luminous conceptions are well known to every inhabitant of Gotham." It was a natural progression to the creation of panoramas and dioramas, and then to the broader activity of entertainment and presentation that included Afong Moy. Like Barnum, Hannington's creativity and business acumen spilled over into many different arenas. The application of multiple skills to make a living was not unusual in this time period.

15. Neil Harris, *Humbug: The Art of P.T. Barnum* (Chicago: University of Chicago Press, 1973), 57.

16. A. H. Saxon, ed., *Selected Letters of P.T. Barnum* (New York: Columbia University Press, 1983), 38.

17. It is unclear what Barnum paid Afong Moy. It is estimated that the Chinese lady who Barnum employed in 1850 made about forty dollars a month. John Kuo Wei Tchen, *New York before Chinatown: Orientalism and the Shaping of American Culture, 1776–1882* (Baltimore: Johns Hopkins University Press, 1999), 122.

18. *New York Herald*, July 27, 1847.

19. *Schenectady Cabinet*, July 20, 1847, affirmed in an article: "Barnum has nothing to do with her, [*Keying*] and none of her owners are Americans."

20. *Daily Union* (Washington, DC), September 4, 1847. Xi Sheng's role on the *Keying* has never been clear. Stephen Davies speculated that Xi Sheng might have negotiated the sale of the junk in Guangzhou for Kellett and therefore had a stake in its success. Though he did not participate in the sailing of the vessel, later in London he was incongruously recognized as in command of the Chinese crew. Despite the New York press announcements, it is unclear whether Afong Moy ever met Xi Sheng or any members of the *Keying*'s Chinese crew.

21. Charles A. Dana joined the *New York Tribune* under Horace Greeley in 1847 as the city editor.

22. *Boston Evening Transcript*, July 17, 1847.

23. Ibid.

24. Like Harriet Low and Caroline Butler, Dana applied the racist parody of the Chinese as he used these words.

25. In 1855 Castle Garden became an immigration center.

26. *Rondout Freeman* (Kingston, New York), July 31, 1847. Reprinted from the *New York Times*.

27. Ibid.

28. *Life in China: The Porcelain Tower* was published in London in 1841, and in Philadelphia a year later. Leech was the established caricaturist for the English magazine *Punch* and known for his illustrations in Charles Dickens's *A Christmas Carol*.

29. Thomas Henry Sealy, preface to *Life in China: The Porcelain Tower; or Nine Stories of China* (Philadelphia: Lea and Blanchard, 1842), ix–xii.

30. The *New-York Commercial Advertiser*, August 7, 1847, referred to Afong Moy: "We presume the exhibited lady—So Sli, we would name her daughter of the innocent Chee-Tee-Mee and the sagacious Chee-Tee-Yu—is a *'single person,'* hearing that she is the 'only lady who ever escaped from the walls of Canton.' Her sister, Oi-Mi-Fi, could not scale the enclosure, having her infant Chub-Bee-Cheek in her arms."

31. *New-York Commercial Advertiser*, September 8, 1847.

32. Davies, *East Sails West*, 125–29, provides a careful exegesis of the trial.

33. Moses Kimball built the new Boston Museum on Tremont Street in 1846.

34. Rev. George C. Lorimer, *Tremont Temple Sketch Book: Containing a Brief History of Tremont Temple Church* (Boston: St. Botolph Press, 1896), unpaginated.

35. *New York Herald*, July 12, 1847.

36. Joseph Bosco and Puay-Peng Ho, *Temples of the Empress of Heaven* (Hong Kong: Oxford University Press, 1999). The authors provide a history of the cult and explore the contemporary manifestations of the worship of Tianhou (also known as Mazu) by transnational Chinese today.

37. Bosco and Puay-Peng Ho note that Tianhou's robe is made of yellow silk and richly embroidered with floral motifs.

38. *Boston Daily Atlas* (Boston, Massachusetts), September 7, 1847.

39. Ibid.

40. The phrase was used in the article "Voice of Free Labor" in the *Boston Investigator*, July 6, 1870.

41. Scott D. Seligman, *The First Chinese American: The Remarkable Life of Wong Chin Foo* (Hong Kong: Hong Kong University Press, 2013), 203.

42. Arthur James Weise, *The City of Troy and Its Vicinity* (Troy: Edward Green, 1886), 157, https://archive.org/stream/citytroyanditsvooweisgoog/citytroyanditsvooweisgoog_djvu.txt.

43. *Troy Budget*, September 20, 1847.

44. A thorough review of census records, the *Keying* list of seamen, and newspaper searches has not turned up Eu Tong's name. It is unclear what relationship Afong Moy had with this man, whether as a fellow performer or as a partner. It is possible Eu Tong was one of three Chinese men whom John Peters employed to interpret in his Boston Chinese Museum, which closed in 1847. The other two are named; one is not. Perhaps the unnamed is Eu Tong.

45. *Newark Daily Advertiser*, April 5, 1848. The newspaper is incorrect in its date; Afong Moy arrived in 1834.

46. *Newark Daily Advertiser*, April 4, 1848. Charles Stratton's appearance in Newark, New Jersey, in April 1848—not at the age of twenty but as a ten-year-old—came soon after he returned from another extensive tour through the southern United States; Havana, Cuba; New Orleans; and up the Mississippi River to Cincinnati, Pittsburgh, and then Newark. His trip mirrored Afong

Moy's journey ten years earlier. The Newark performance in April may have been the first time Afong Moy and Stratton met because Stratton spent little time in New York in 1847, the time of Afong Moy's public reentrance. In Newark one might assume they conversed about their similar travels and stage experiences. Sadly, none of these performers' interpersonal experiences are recorded.

47. Philip Hone, *The Diary of Philip Hone 1828–1851*, ed. Alan Nevins (New York: Dodd, Mead, 1936), 2:664.

48. Ibid.

49. Unpublished manuscript of Philip Hone's diary, November 12, 1834, 60–61.

50. James W. Cook, *The Colossal P.T. Barnum Reader: Nothing Else Like It in the Universe* (Chicago: University of Illinois Press, 2005), 66.

51. *New York Herald*, July 27, 1847.

52. In 1850 Barnum considerably renovated the Lecture Room at the American Museum which then could seat nearly three thousand people.

53. George C. D. Odell, *Annals of the New York Stage* (1834–43; repr. New York: AMS Press, 1970), 5:398.

54. "Pamphlet Descriptive of Affong Moy Nanchoy, the Only Chinese Lady; Also, A Brief Sketch of Major General Tom Thumb" (New York: Printed by J. Booth, Corner of Ann and Nausau Streets, 1849), Misc. Pamp, 1849 Pamp. Record ID 372129, courtesy of the American Antiquarian Society.

55. Cook, *Colossal P.T. Barnum Reader*, 103.

56. "Affong Moy Nanchoy," 1.

57. Ibid.

58. See James Cook's introduction in *Colossal P. T. Barnum's Reader*, 6, which notes that Barnum's racial views changed dramatically over his lifetime. In the 1830s and 1840s African Americans' attendance at the American Museum was restricted to certain hours that were publicly advertised. Initially critical of the abolitionist cause, he later supported anti-slavery and ran as a candidate supporting universal manhood suffrage.

59. "Affong Moy Nanchoy," 1: "it may be as well that they do not introduce their domestics if they should happen to be colored, as the pride of her Chinese nobility immediately shows itself on coming in contact with any of the colored race."

60. "Affong Moy Nanchoy," 4: "Her pride of person and passion for finery overcame whatever prejudice, of religion, caste, or early attachment might be supposed to intervene. Affong Moy . . . has no sorrowful reflections of home . . . she is wrapped up in the conceit of her own superiority."

61. Ibid.

62. *"The Chinese Junk "Keying," Being a Full Account of That Vessel, with Extracts from the Journal of Capt. Kellet* (New-York: Printed by Israel Sackett, No. 1 Nassau Street, 1847), 15. AHMC Castle Garden Records, 1844, Folder 1, New-York Historical Society Museum and Library.

63. "Affong Moy Nanchoy," 7.

64. Ibid.

65. Ibid., 5. John R. Peters Jr., *Guide to the Catalogue of the Boston Chinese Museum* (Boston: Eastburn's Press, 1845), used this maxim of Shoo and explained it. Barnum's writer probably picked it up from Peter's catalogue but misapplied it.

66. *Analects of Confucius, 15:23*, trans. A. Charles Muller, accessed April 10, 2016, http://www.acmuller.net/con-dao/analects.html.

67. "Affong Moy Nanchoy," 7.

68. Eric D. Lehman, *Becoming Tom Thumb: Charles Stratton, P.T. Barnum, and the Dawn of American Celebrity* (Middletown, CT: Wesleyan University Press, 2013), 88. Lehman says that: "Barnum 'unkindly' distributed advertisements that proclaimed 'Tom Thumb in the Shade' trying to drum up support for Littlefinger."

69. "The Living Chinese," Nathaniel Currier, 1850, Library of Congress, control number 2002708598.

70. Arthur Bonner, *Alas! What Brought Thee Hither?: The Chinese in New York, 1800–1950* (Cranbury, NJ: Associated University Presses, 1997), 4.

71. An 1855 New York census taker recorded that eleven Chinese seamen and operators of boardinghouses were married to Irish women in New York City. See Tchen, *New York before Chinatown*, 77.

72. *Daily Morning News* (Savannah, Georgia), April 29, 1850, from Correspondence of the *Daily Morning News* (New York).

73. Ibid.

74. Odell, *Annals of the New York Stage*, 5:580.

75. *Daily National Intelligencer* (Washington, DC), May 17, 1850.

76. Pwan-Ye-Koo may have been from China and fully Chinese, yet her photographic image raises some doubt as to her background.

77. Lorenzo Chase's studio was at 257 Washington Street, Boston, from 1846 to 1850. There is no record that he made a daguerreotype of Afong Moy when she visited Boston in 1847. Had she been photographed at that time she would have had the distinction of being the first Chinese woman to be photographed in America.

78. *North American and United States Gazette* (Philadelphia), May 22, 1851.

79. As with most of Barnum's exhibits, nothing is known of the "Living Chinese" after their presentation in England.

80. *New-York Commercial Advertiser*, February 20, 1850.

81. Ibid.

82. *Baltimore Sun*, March 21, 1851.

83. Because Pwan-Ye-Koo was in England at the time, the Chinese Lady must have been Afong Moy.

84. *Plain Dealer* (Cleveland, Ohio), February 21, 1851.

85. Cleveland newspapers note that the Barnum's Swiss Bell Ringers drew crowds in Columbus and Cleveland in late 1850.

Epilogue

1. A review of New York City poorhouse and almshouse records from 1851 to1860 reveals no evidence of Afong Moy or any Chinese names.

2. Philip B. Kunhardt Jr., Philip B. Kunhardt III, and Peter W. Kunhardt, *P.T. Barnum: America's Greatest Showman* (New York: Alfred A. Knopf, 1995), 150.

3. Jill Lepore, *Book of Ages: The Life and Opinions of Jane Franklin* (New York: Alfred A. Knopf, 2013), 269.

4. *The Daily Picayune*, June 9, 1838, jocularly commented: "One of the Siamese twins is shortly to be *united* with Miss Afong Moy, the little Chinese lady. The happy bridegroom has invited his brother to *stand up* with him and act as grooms man."

5. http://www.asian-nation.org/1965-immigration-act.shtml#sthash. DiPIYsRT.dpbs, accessed June 12, 2018.

6. Nancy Ellen Davis, "The American China Trade, 1784–1844: Products for the Middle Class" (PhD diss., George Washington University, 1987), 221.

7. Maria Yoshihara, *Embracing the East: White Women and American Orientalism* (New York: Oxford University Press, 2003). Yoshihara provides an excellent overview of the construction of American orientalism, with several chapters exploring the oriental object in the American home between 1870 and 1940.

8. Ted C. Fishman, *China*Inc.* (New York: Scribner, 2005), 54.

9. US Census Bureau, Foreign Trade Statistics, 2012, https://www.census.gov/ foreign-trade/index.html.

10. Recognizing that my amateur genealogical skills might leave some stones unturned in the quest to define Afong Moy's later life, I consulted a number of professionals in the field. Unfortunately, all their efforts and recommendations were fruitless.

SELECTED BIBLIOGRAPHY

Manuscript Collections and Unpublished Sources

Afong Moy "For One Week Only" broadside. BDSDS, 1842. Record ID 207260. American Antiquarian Society.

Album of Silk Production. 1849. Col. III, box 1, folder 1. Joseph Downs Collection of Manuscripts and Printed Ephemera. Winterthur Library.

Breck, Samuel Papers. Coll. 1887. Historical Society of Pennsylvania.

Butler Family Correspondence. MS 242, folders 20, 21. Mortimer Rare Book Room, Special Collections. Smith College.

Butler-Laing Family Papers. MS 94, Box 1, Folders 1–4. New-York Historical Society.

Captain John Suter Papers. 1804–48. MS N-49.50, Box 2. Massachusetts Historical Society.

Carnes family Bible. Olana New York State Historic Site.

Carnes family scrapbook. Olana New York State Historic Site.

Castle Garden Records. 1844. Folder 1. New-York Historical Society.

Constable-Pierrepont Papers. 1762–1911. New York Public Library. New York.

Dunn-Osborn-Battey Family Papers. 1744–1927. MS 1163, Box 6, folder 1. Quaker and Special Collections. Haverford College.

Fletcher, Thomas Papers. 1815–67. Joseph Downs Collection of Manuscripts and Printed Ephemera. Winterthur Library.

Forbes Family Papers. MS N-49.70. Massachusetts Historical Society.

Galt Family Papers. (I) Mss. 78G13 Item 17. Special Collections Research Center, Earl Gregg Swem Library. College of William and Mary.

Gordon-Blackford Papers, MS 398. Manuscript Department. H. Furlong Baldwin Library. Maryland Historical Society.

Grundy-Gibson Papers. MS 1294. H. Furlong Baldwin Library. Maryland Historical Society.

Guangdong Treasury Accounts. Guangdong Provincial Archives. Guangzhou, China.

Hone, Philip. Manuscript diary. BV Hone, Philip, MS. 1549. New-York Historical Society.

Incoming Ship Manifests to the Port of New York. National Archives and Records Administration. Washington, DC.

Latimer, John, Papers. Manuscript Division, Library of Congress. Washington, DC.

Medical Society of South Carolina Minutes. 1834–58, p. 49. Lowcountry Digital Library, South Carolina. http://lcdl.library.cofc.edu/lcd/catalog/lcdl:42987#!prettyPhoto.

Mitchell, S. Weir Collection. Historical Medical Library, College of Physicians of Philadelphia.

Monmouth County Historical Society Library Archives.

Pamphlet Descriptive of Affong Moy Nanchoy. Record ID 372129. American Antiquarian Society.

Passenger Lists of Vessels Arriving New York 1820–97. National Archives and Records Administration, Washington, DC.

Perkins, Thomas Handasyd Papers. Manuscript Division. Library of Congress, Washington, DC.

Private Journal of a Princeton University Student (No Name). Post Medieval Manuscript Bound Volume, 108. Special Collections. Bryn Mawr College Library.

Sword Family Papers. Coll. 1878. Historical Society of Pennsylvania.

Tilden, Samuel J. Papers. MSS Col. 2993. New York Public Library.

Wright Family Papers. Accession 1665. Manuscript and Archives Department. Hagley Museum and Library.

Newspapers and Periodicals

Albany Argus
Albany Evening Journal
American Sentinel (Philadelphia, Pennsylvania)
Atkinson's Saturday Evening Post (Philadelphia, Pennsylvania)
Baltimore Patriot
Boston Daily Advertiser
Canton Register (Guangzhou, China)
Canton Register, Shipping Intelligence (Guangzhou, China)
Charleston Courier
Chinese Repository (Guangzhou, China)
Daily National Intelligencer (Washington, DC)
Daily Union (Washington, DC)

El Noticioso y lucero de la Habana (Havana, Cuba)

Evening Post (New York)

Gleason's Pictorial Drawing Room Companion (Boston, MA)

Globe (Washington, DC)

Godey's Lady's Book (Philadelphia, Pennsylvania)

L'Abeille de la Nouvelle-Orléans (*New Orleans Bee*)

The Lutheran Observer and Weekly Religious and Literary Visitor (Baltimore, Maryland)

Maryland Journal and Baltimore Daily Advertiser

Monmouth (New Jersey) *Inquirer*

Newark (NJ) *Daily Advertiser*

New-Hampshire Patriot (Concord)

New-Orleans Commercial Bulletin

New-York Commercial Advertiser

New York Herald

New-York Spectator

New York Star

New York Sun

Niles' Weekly Register (Baltimore, MD)

North American and United States Gazette (Philadelphia, Pennsylvania)

Parley's Magazine for Children and Youth (Boston, Massachusetts)

Pensacola Gazette

Pittsburgh Gazette

Plain Dealer (Cleveland, Ohio)

Republican Herald (Providence, Rhode Island)

Published Primary and Secondary Sources

Abe, Kaori. *Chinese Middlemen in Hong Kong's Colonial Economy, 1830–1890.* New York: Routledge, 2018.

Agnew, Jean-Christophe. *Worlds Apart: The Market and the Theater in Anglo-American Thought, 1550–1750.* Cambridge: Cambridge University Press, 1986.

Albion, Robert Greenhalgh. *The Rise of the New York Port, 1815–1860.* Reprint, Boston: Northeastern University Press, 1984.

Anderson, E. N. *The Food of China.* New Haven, CT: Yale University Press, 1988.

Bank, Rosemarie K. *Theatre Culture in America, 1825–1860.* Cambridge: Cambridge University Press, 1997.

Barber, James G. *Old Hickory: A Life Sketch of Andrew Jackson.* Washington, DC: National Portrait Gallery, Smithsonian Institution; Nashville: Tennessee State Museum in association with the University of Washington Press, Seattle, 1990.

Barnum, P. T. *The Life of P.T. Barnum: Written by Himself.* 1855. Reprint, Urbana: University of Illinois Press, 2000.

Barrett, Walter. *A Second Series of* The Old Merchants of New York, *Being a Continuation of the Work.* New York: Carleton, 1864.

Barrow, John. *Travels in China; and a Subsequent Journey from Pekin to Canton.* London: T. Cadell & W. Davies, in the Strand, 1804.

Barth, Gunther Paul. *Bitter Strength: A History of the Chinese in the United States, 1850–1870.* Cambridge, MA: Harvard University Press, 1964.

Bluford, Adams. *E Pluribus Barnum: The Great Showman and the Making of U.S. Popular Culture.* Minneapolis: University of Minnesota Press, 1997.

Bogdan, Robert. *Freak Show: Presenting Human Oddities for Amusement and Profit.* Chicago: University of Chicago Press, 1988.

Bonner, Arthur. *Alas! What Brought Thee Hither?: The Chinese in New York, 1800–1950.* Cranbury, NJ: Associated University Presses, 1997.

Bordman, Gerald, and Thomas Hischak, eds. *The Oxford Companion to American Theatre.* 3rd ed. New York: Oxford University Press, 2004.

Bosco, Joseph, and Puay-Peng Ho. *Temples of the Empress of Heaven.* Hong Kong: Oxford University Press, 1999.

Breton de la Martinère, Jean. *China: Its Costume, Arts, Manufactures Etc.* London: Printed for J.J. Stockdale, 1812.

Butsch, Richard. *The Making of American Audiences: From Stage to Television, 1750–1990.* New York: Cambridge University Press, 2013.

Carson, Barbara G. *Ambitious Appetites: Dining, Behavior, and Patterns of Consumption in Federal Washington.* Washington, DC: American Institute of Architects Press, 1990.

Chan, Sucheng, ed. *Remapping Asian American History.* New York: Altamira Press, 2003.

Chan, Sucheng, and Madeline Y. Hsu, eds. *Chinese Americans and the Politics of Race and Culture.* Philadelphia: Temple University Press, 2008.

Choy, Philip, Lorraine Dong, and Marion K. Horn, eds. *Coming Man: 19th Century American Perceptions of the Chinese.* Seattle: University of Washington Press, 1995.

Chung, Sue Fawn. *In Pursuit of Gold: Chinese American Miners and Merchants in the American West.* Chicago: University of Illinois Press, 2011.

Cook, James W. *The Arts of Deception: Playing with Fraud in the Age of Barnum.* Cambridge, MA: Harvard University Press, 2001.

———, ed. *The Colossal P.T. Barnum Reader: Nothing Else Like It in the Universe.* Urbana: University of Illinois Press, 2005.

Crossley, Pamela Kyle, Helen F. Sui, and Donald Sutton. *Empire at the Margins: Culture, Ethnicity, and Frontier in Early Modern China.* Berkeley: University of California Press, 2006.

Crossman, Carl L. *The Decorative Arts of the China Trade.* Woodbridge, Suffolk, UK: Antiques Collectors' Club, 1991.

Davies, Stephen. *East Sails West: The Voyage of the Keying, 1846–1855.* Hong Kong: Hong Kong University Press, 2014.

Davis, Janet M. *The Circus Age: Culture and Society under the American Big Top.* Chapel Hill: University of North Carolina Press, 2002.

Davis, Nancy Ellen. "The American China Trade, 1784–1844: Products for the Middle Class." PhD diss., George Washington University, 1987.

De Warville, J. P. Brissot. *New Travels in the United States of America, 1788.* Translated by Mara Soceanic Vamos and David Echevearic. Cambridge, MA: Belknap Press of Harvard University Press, 1964.

Dolin, Eric Jay. *Fur, Fortune, and Empire: The Epic History of Fur Trade in America.* New York: W.W. Norton, 2010.

———. *When America First Met China.* New York: Liveright, 2012.

Downing, Charles Toogood. *The Fan-qui in China, in 1836–37.* 2 vols. London: Henry Colburn, 1838.

Downs, Jacques M. *The Golden Ghetto: The American Commercial Community at Canton and the Shaping of American China Policy, 1784–1844.* Introduction by Frederic D. Grant Jr. Hong Kong: Hong Kong University Press, 2014.

Druett, Joan. *Hen Frigates: Wives of Merchant Captains Under Sail.* New York: Simon & Schuster, 1998.

Eckhardt, Celia Morris. *Fanny Wright: Rebel in America.* Cambridge, MA: Harvard University Press, 1984.

Edwards, Holly, ed. *Noble Dreams, Wicked Pleasures: Orientalism in America, 1870–1930.* Princeton, NJ: Princeton University Press, 2000.

Fabian, Ann. *The Skull Collectors: Race, Science, and America's Unburied Dead.* Chicago: University of Chicago Press, 2010.

Fairbank, John King. *Trade and Diplomacy on the China Coast.* Cambridge, MA: Harvard University Press, 1964.

———. *The United States and China.* 4th ed. Cambridge, MA: Harvard University Press, 1983.

Fairhead, James. *The Captain and "the Cannibal": An Epic Story of Exploration, Kidnapping, and the Broadway Stage.* New Haven, CT: Yale University Press, 2015.

Fishman, Ted C. *China*Inc.* New York: Scribner, 2005.

Forbes, Henry A. Crosby. *Shopping in China: The Artisan Community at Canton, 1825–1830.* Washington, DC: International Exhibitions Foundation, 1979.

Forbes, Robert Bennet. *Letters from China: The Canton-Boston Correspondence of Robert Bennet Forbes, 1838–1840.* Mystic, CT: Mystic Seaport Museum, 1996.

Frank, Caroline. *Objectifying China, Imagining America: Chinese Commodities in Early America.* Chicago: University of Chicago Press, 2011.

Garrett, Valery M. *Chinese Dress from the Qing Dynasty to the Present.* Rutland, VT: Tuttle, 2007.

———. *Heaven Is High, the Emperor Far Away: Merchants and Mandarins in Old Canton.* New York: Oxford University Press, 2002.

———. *Traditional Chinese Clothing.* New York: Oxford University Press, 1991.

Gibson, James. *Otter Skins, Boston Ships, and China Goods: The Maritime Fur Trade of the Northwest Coast, 1785–1841.* Seattle: University of Washington Press, 1992.

Gregg, Melissa, and Gregory J. Seigworth, eds. *The Affect Theory Reader.* Durham, NC: Duke University Press, 2010.

Grigg, John A. "Ye relief of ye poor of sd towne": *Poverty and Localism in Eighteenth-Century New Jersey.*" *New Jersey History* 125, no. 2 (2010): 23–35.

Grimsted, David. *Melodrama Unveiled: American Theatre and Culture, 1800–1850*. Chicago: University of Chicago Press, 1986.

Gulick, Edward V. *Peter Parker and the Opening of China*. Cambridge, MA: Harvard University Press, 1973.

Gyory, Andrew. *Closing the Gate: Race, Politics, and the Chinese Exclusion Act*. Chapel Hill: University of North Carolina Press, 1998.

Haddad, John R. "China of the American Imagination: The Influence of Trade on US Portrayals of China, 1820 to 1850." In *Narratives of Free Trade: The Commercial Cultures of Early US-China Relations*, edited by Kendall Johnson, 57–83. Hong Kong: Hong Kong University Press, 2012.

———. "Imagined Journeys to Distant Cathay: Constructing China with Ceramics, 1780–1920." *Winterthur Portfolio* 41, no. 1 (2007): 53–80.

———. *The Romance of China: Excursions to China in U.S. Culture, 1776–1876*. New York: Columbia University Press, 2008.

Harris, Neil. *Cultural Excursions: Marketing Appetites and Cultural Tastes in Modern America*. Chicago: University of Chicago Press, 1990.

———. *Humbug: the Art of P.T. Barnum*. Chicago: University of Chicago Press, 1973.

Hedrick, Joan D. *Harriet Beecher Stowe: A Life*. New York: Oxford University Press, 1994.

Herz, Henri. *My Travels in America*. Translated by Henry Bertram Hill. Madison: State Historical Society of Wisconsin for the Department of History, University of Wisconsin, 1963.

Hill, Marilyn Wood. *Their Sisters' Keepers: Prostitution in New York City, 1830–1870*. Berkeley: University of California Press, 1993.

Hillard, Harriet Low. *My Mother's Journal: A Young Lady's Diary of Five Years Spent in Manila, Macao, and the Cape of Good Hope from 1829–1834*. Edited by Katharine Hillard. Boston: George H. Ellis, 1900.

Hone, Philip. *The Diary of Philip Hone 1828–1851*. 2 vols. Edited by Alan Nevins. New York: Dodd, Mead, 1936.

Hsu, Madeline Y. *Dreaming of Gold, Dreaming of Home: Transnationalism and Migration Between the United States and South China, 1882–1943*. Stanford, CA: Stanford University Press, 2000.

Huang, Yunte. *Inseparable: The Original Siamese Twins and Their Rendezvous with American History*. New York: W.W. Norton, 2018.

Huhtamo, Erkki. *Illusions in Motion: Media Archaeology of the Moving Panorama and Related Spectacles*. Cambridge, MA: MIT Press, 2013.

Hune, Shirley. *Teaching Asian American Women's History*. Washington, DC: American Historical Association, 1997.

Hunter, William C. *The "Fan Kwei" at Canton before Treaty Days, 1825–1844*. London: Kegan Paul, Trench, 1882.

Jackson, Carl T. *The Oriental Religions and American Thought: Nineteenth Century Explorations*. Westport, CT: Greenwood, 1981.

Jaffee, David. *A New Nation of Goods: The Material Culture of America*. Philadelphia: University of Pennsylvania Press, 2010.

James, Joseph, and Daniel Moore. *A System of Exchange with Almost all Parts of the World to which is added The India Trader's Directory in Purchasing the Drugs and Spices of Asia and the East Indies.* New York: John Furman, 1800.

Johnson, David. "Communication, Class, and Consciousness in Late Imperial China." In *Popular Culture in Late Imperial China,* edited by David Johnson, Andrew J. Nathan, and Evelyn S. Rawski, 34–72. Berkeley: University of California Press, 1985.

Johnson, Kendall, ed. *Narratives of Free Trade: The Commercial Cultures of Early US-China Relations.* Hong Kong: Hong Kong University Press, 2012.

Johnston, Patricia, ed. *Seeing High and Low: Representing Social Conflict in American Visual Culture.* Berkeley: University of California Press, 2006.

Johnston, Patricia, and Caroline Frank, eds. *Global Trade and Visual Arts in Federal New England.* Hanover, NH: University Press of New England, 2014.

Kasson, John F. *Rudeness and Civility: Manners in Nineteenth-Century America.* New York: Hall and Wang, 1990.

King, Caroline Howard. *When I Lived in Salem.* Brattleboro, VT: Stephen Day Press, 1937.

Ko, Dorothy. *Cinderella's Sisters: A Revisionist History of Footbinding.* Berkeley: University of California Press, 2005.

Ko, Dorothy, JaHyun Kim Haboursh, and Joan R. Piggot, eds. *Women and Confucian Cultures in Premodern China, Korea, and Japan.* Berkeley: University of California Press, 2003.

Kunhardt, Philip B., Jr., Philip B. Kunhardt III, and Peter W. Kunhardt. *P. T. Barnum: America's Greatest Showman.* New York: Alfred A. Knopf, 1995.

Laing, Caroline Hyde Butler. *A Family Heritage—Letters and Journals of 1804–1892.* Edited by Edith Nevill Smythe. East Orange, NJ: Abbey Printers,1957.

Lam, Joseph S. C. "The Presence and Absence of Female Musicians and Music in China." In *Women and Confucian Cultures in Premodern China, Korea, and Japan,* edited by Dorothy Ko, JaHyun Kim Haboursh, and Joan R. Piggot, 97–120. Berkeley: University of California Press, 2003.

Lee, Erika. *The Making of Asian America: A History.* New York: Simon & Schuster, 2015.

Lee, Jean Gordon. *Philadelphians and the China Trade, 1784–1844.* Philadelphia: Philadelphia Museum of Art, 1984.

Lee, Josephine. *Performing Asian America: Race and Ethnicity on the Contemporary Stage.* Philadelphia: Temple University Press, 1997.

Lee, Josephine, Imogene L. Lim, and Yuko Matsukawa, eds. *Re/collecting Early Asian America: Essays in Cultural History.* Philadelphia: Temple University Press, 2002.

Lee, Lily Xiao Hong, A. D. Stefanowska, and Clara Wing-chung Ho, eds. *Biographical Dictionary of Chinese Women: The Qing Period, 1644–1911.* Armonk, NY: M. E. Sharpe, 1998.

Lee, Robert G. *Orientals: Asian Americans in Popular Culture.* Philadelphia: Temple University Press, 1999.

Lehman, Eric D. *Becoming Tom Thumb: Charles Stratton, P.T. Barnum, and the Dawn of American Celebrity.* Middletown, CT: Wesleyan University Press, 2013.

Lepler, Jessica M. *The Many Panics of 1837: People, Politics, and the Creation of a Transatlantic Financial Crisis*. New York: Cambridge University Press, 2013.

Lepore, Jill. *Book of Ages: The Life and Opinions of Jane Franklin*. New York: Alfred A. Knopf, 2013.

Lewis, Robert M. *From Traveling Show to Vaudeville: Theatrical Spectacle in America, 1830–1910*. Baltimore: Johns Hopkins University Press, 2003.

Levine, Lawrence W. *Highbrow/lowbrow: The Emergence of Cultural Hierarchy in America*. Cambridge, MA: Harvard University Press, 1988.

Lum, Kathryn Gin. *Damned Nation: Hell in America from the Revolution to Reconstruction*. New York: Oxford University Press, 2014.

Mann, Susan. *Precious Records: Women in China's Long Eighteenth Century*. Stanford, CA: Stanford University Press, 1997.

Marks, Robert B. *Tigers, Rice, Silk, and Silt: The Environment and Economy in Late Imperial South China*. Cambridge: Cambridge University Press, 1998.

Martineau, Harriet. *Retrospect of Western Travel*, 1838. Edited by Daniel Feller. Armonk, NY: M.E. Sharpe, 2000.

———. *Society in America*, 1837. Edited and abridged by Seymour Martin Lipset. New Brunswick, NJ: Transaction, 1981.

Mason, George Henry. *The Costume of China*. London: W. Miller, 1800.

Milburn, William, Esq. *Oriental Commerce*. London: Black, Parry, 1813.

Miles, Tiya. *Ties that Bind: The Story of an Afro-Cherokee Family in Slavery and Freedom*. Berkeley: University of California Press, 2005.

Mitchell, John Kearsley. *Indecision: A Tale of the Far West and Other Poems*, "To Afong Moy." Philadelphia: E.L. Carey & A. Hart, 1837.

Moon, Krystyn R. *Yellowface: Creating the Chinese in American Popular Music and Performance, 1850s–1920s*. New Brunswick, NJ: Rutgers University Press, 2005.

Morrison, Dane A. *True Yankees: The South Seas and the Discovery of American Identity*. Baltimore: Johns Hopkins University Press, 2014.

Morrison, John R. *A Chinese Commercial Guide*. Macao, China: S.W. Williams, 1844.

Moy, James S. *Marginal Sights: Staging the Chinese in America*. Iowa City: University of Iowa Press, 1993.

Murray, Charles Augustus. *Travels in North America during the Years 1834, 1835 and 1836*. New York: Harper & Brothers, 1839.

Nelson, Christina. *Directly from China: Export Goods for the American Market, 1784–1930*. Salem, MA: Peabody Essex Museum, 1985.

Ngai, Mae. *The Lucky Ones: One Family and the Extraordinary Invention of Chinese America*. New York: Houghton Mifflin Harcourt, 2010.

Odell, George, C.D. *Annals of the New York Stage*. Vol. 4 (1834–43). Reprint, New York: AMS Press, 1970.

Okihiro, Gary Y. *The Columbia Guide to Asian American History*. New York: Columbia University Press, 2001.

Orser, Joseph Andrew. *The Lives of Chang and Eng: Siam's Twins in Nineteenth-Century America*. Chapel Hill: University of North Carolina Press, 2014.

Peters, John R., Jr. *Guide to the Catalogue of the Boston Chinese Museum*. Boston: Eastburn's Press, 1845.

Pessen, Edward. *Jacksonian America: Society, Personality, and Politics.* Homewood, IL: Dorsey Press, 1969.

Poignant, Roslyn. *Professional Savages: Captive Lives and Western Spectacle.* New Haven, CT: Yale University Press, 2004.

Power, Tyrone. *Impressions of America During the Years 1833, 1834, 1835, 1836.* Reprint, New York: Benjamin Blom, 1971.

Prior, Margaret, and Sarah R. Ingraham. *Walks of Usefulness, Or, Reminiscences of Mrs. Margaret Prior.* New York: American Female Moral Reform Society, 1851.

Qureshi, Sadiah. *Peoples on Parade: Exhibitions, Empire, and Anthropology in Nineteenth-Century Britain.* Chicago: University of Chicago Press, 2011.

Quynn, William R., ed. *The Diary of Jacob Engelbrecht, 1818–1878.* Frederick, MD: Historical Society of Fredrick County, 2001.

Reiss, Benjamin. *The Showman and the Slave: Race, Death, and Memory in Barnum's America.* Cambridge, MA: Harvard University Press, 2001.

Robert, Karen, ed. *New Year in Cuba: Mary Gardner Lowell's Travel Diary, 1831–1832.* Boston: Massachusetts Historical Society and Northeastern University Press, 2003.

Rockman, Seth. *Scraping By: Wage Labor, Slavery, and Survival in Early Baltimore.* Baltimore: Johns Hopkins University Press, 2009.

Said, Edward. *Culture and Imperialism.* New York: Knopf, 1993.

———. *Orientalism.* New York: Vintage, 1979.

Sanchez-Eppler, Karen. "Copying and Conversion: An 1824 Friendship Album 'From a Chinese Youth.'" *American Quarterly* 59, no. 2 (2007): 301–39.

Saxon, A. H., ed. *Selected Letters of P.T. Barnum.* New York: Columbia University Press, 1983.

Sealy, Thomas Henry. *Life in China: The Porcelain Tower; or Nine Stories of China.* Philadelphia: Lea and Blanchard, 1842.

Seligman, Scott D. *The First Chinese American: The Remarkable Life of Wong Chin Foo.* Hong Kong: Hong Kong University Press, 2013.

Siu, Helen F., ed. *Merchants' Daughters: Women, Commerce, and Regional Culture in South China.* Hong Kong: Hong Kong University Press, 2010.

Smith, Philip Chadwick Foster. *The Empress of China.* Philadelphia: Philadelphia Maritime Museum, 1984.

Spence, Jonathan. *The Question of Hu.* New York: Vintage, 1988.

Stanton, William. *The Leopard's Spots: Scientific Attitudes Toward Race in America, 1815–59.* Chicago: University of Chicago Press, 1960.

Takaki, Ronald. *Iron Cages: Race and Culture in 19th-Century America.* New York: Oxford University Press, 1990.

Tappan, William B. *The Poems of William B. Tappan.* Philadelphia: Henry Perkins, 1836.

Tchen, John Kuo Wei. *New York before Chinatown: Orientalism and the Shaping of American Culture, 1776–1882.* Baltimore: Johns Hopkins University Press, 1999.

Tiffany, Osmond, Jr. *The Canton Chinese or the American's Sojourn in the Celestial Empire.* Boston: James Munroe, 1849.

Trollope, Frances. *Domestic Manners of the Americans*. 1832. Edited by Donald Smalley. Reprint, New York: Alfred A. Knopf, 1949.

Tsai, Henry Shih-shan. *The Chinese Experience in America*. Bloomington: Indiana University Press, 1986.

Tweed, Thomas A. *The American Encounter with Buddhism, 1844–1912: Victorian Culture and the Limits of Dissent*. Chapel Hill: University of North Carolina Press, 2000.

Ulrich, Laurel Thatcher. *The Age of Homespun: Objects and Stories in the Creation of an American Myth*. New York: Vintage, 2001.

Van Dyke, Paul A. *The Canton Trade: Life and Enterprise on the China Coast, 1700–1845*. Hong Kong: Hong Kong University Press, 2005.

———. "Operational Efficiencies and the Decline of the Chinese Junk Trade in the 18th and 19th Centuries: The Connection." In *Shipping and Economic Growth 1350–1850*, edited by Richard W. Unger, 223–46. Leiden, The Netherlands: Brill Academic, 2011.

Wagner, David. *The Poorhouse: America's Forgotten Institution*. Lanham, MD: Rowman & Littlefield, 2005.

Williams, Samuel Wells. *The Middle Kingdom*. 2 vols. New York: Charles Scribner's Sons, 1904.

Wilmeth, Don B., and Tice L. Miller, eds. *Cambridge Guide to American Theatre*. Cambridge: Cambridge University Press, 1996.

Wolf, Arthur P., ed. *Religion and Ritual in Chinese Society*. Stanford, CA: Stanford University Press, 1974.

Wood, William. *Sketches of China, with Illustrations from Original Drawings*. Philadelphia: Carey & Lea, 1830.

Wright, Conrad Edick, and Katheryn P Viens, eds. *Entrepreneurs: The Boston Business Community, 1700–1850*. Boston: Northeastern University Press, 1997.

Yao, Esther S. Lee, *Chinese Women: Past and Present*. Mesquite, TX: Ide House, 1983.

Yoshihara, Maria. *Embracing the East: White Women and American Orientalism*. New York: Oxford University Press, 2003.

Yu, Henry. *Thinking Orientals: Migration, Contact, and Exoticism in Modern America*. New York: Oxford University Press, 2001.

Zheng, Su. *Claiming Diaspora: Music, Transnationalism, and Cultural Politics in Asian/Chinese America*. New York: Oxford University Press, 2010.

INDEX

Figures are indicated by an italic *f* following the page number.